Securities Operations

Wiley Finance Series

Securities Operations

A Guide to Trade and Position Management

Michael Simmons

JOHN WILEY & SONS, LTD

Other Wiley Editorial Offices

John Wiley & Sons Inc., 111 River Street, Hoboken, NJ 07030, USA

Jossey-Bass, 989 Market Street, San Francisco, CA 94103-1741, USA

Wiley-VCH Verlag GmbH, Boschstr. 12, D-69469 Weinheim, Germany

John Wiley & Sons Australia Ltd, 33 Park Road, Milton, Queensland 4064, Australia

John Wiley & Sons (Asia) Pte Ltd, 2 Clementi Loop #02-01, Jin Xing Distripark,
Singapore 129809

John Wiley & Sons (Canada) Ltd, 22 Worcester Road, Etobicoke, Ontario M9W 1L1

Wiley also publishes its books in a variety of electronic formats. Some content that
appears in print may not be available in electronic books.

Library of Congress Cataloging-in-Publication Data

Simmons, Michael.
    Securities operations / Michael Simmons.
        p. cm. — (Wiley finance series)
    Includes index.
    ISBN 0–471–49758–4 (alk. paper)
        1. Securities industry. I. Title. II. Series.

HG4521 .S574 2001
332.63´2´068–dc21

                              2001055777

British Library Cataloguing in Publication Data

A catalogue record for this book is available from the British Library

ISBN 978 0471 49758 5 (hbk)

Typeset in 10/12pt Times by Laserwords Private Limited, Chennai, India
Printed and bound in Great Britain by Biddles Ltd, King's Lynn, Norfolk
This book is printed on acid-free paper responsibly manufactured from sustainable forestry,
in which at least two trees are planted for each one used for paper production.

To Allyson, Keir and Freya

Disclaimer

'The Author of Securities Operations, occasionally refers to well-known organisations within the financial community in order to illustrate the context of typical trading scenarios. The scenarios created, and the relationships and transactions referred to, are for illustrative purposes only and have no factual basis.'

Contents

Foreword

A career in securities operations has long required years of apprenticeship training. This less visible, but critical segment of the global capital markets, has been characterized by its own culture, lexicon and ideosyncracies. Securities operations professionals have typically spent years developing an understanding of individual product operations, a variety of systems and processing environments, and a multitude of laws and regulations. For those who are close to this profession, including myself, the challenges and complexities have increased significantly over the past few years.

For all of capital markets, but particularly the securities operations component of the overall process, this past decade has been one of significant change. Capital flows and their associated transaction volumes have increased substantially, particularly cross-border, demanding innovative processing solutions. The financial engineering creativity of the industry has produced a steady stream of new products with their attendant back office demands. The industry has also witnessed a surge of consolidation resulting in the creation of very large financial institutions with unique global operations issues. Many of these consolidated firms also reflect the convergence of banking, capital markets, insurance and related financial services businesses creating a new class of senior operations managers. This consolidation has also affected the infrastructure of securities processing, resulting in the simultaneous increase in trade execution venues with the creation of Alternative Trading Systems and Electronic Communications Networks, as well as the reduction in the overall number of traditional exchanges and depositories. Finally, the ascendancy of internet technologies offers operations managers and analysts opportunities to reconfigure processes in ways not imagined until recently.

For securities operations professionals these changes have raised the bar of competency for success. In addition to the requisite industry experience, the discipline now requires broad analysis and management skills in areas such as overall process architecture, technology deployment, outsourcing, management accounting, standards development and international business. Competency today requires an understanding of both the larger picture of global securities operations as well as one's specific area of interest or responsibility.

Mick Simmons has assisted the profession in gaining this understanding with the publication of this valuable book. He has provided a clearly written text on the securities industry and trading operations that will be useful for both the novice and experienced reader. The book ensures a foundation understanding of the securities trade lifecycle from which the reader can move on to deeper, more specialized topics. He has amplified the text with a number of relevant examples, and demonstrates throughout the book his own practical experience. I believe this book will be an important addition to the industry's reference library.

Bill Irving
Partner, Global Capital Markets
PWC Consulting

Introduction

To many people, the inner workings of the securities industry are regarded as a mystery that only a limited number understand. The degree of complication regarding securities trading or trading related activities can be very high and difficult to comprehend.

That which follows the act of trading, generally termed operational activities, may seem initially to be as mysterious as trading. However, such activities are in reality a series of logical steps, most of which are relevant and comparable to any company trading in any goods.

Whilst training people on the topic of securities operations, it became very apparent that little material exists as a means of gaining an understanding of the essential concepts and the connectivity between the operational activities; the logical result of continued requests for recommended reading is represented within these pages.

This book is aimed at a number of different types of reader:

- those who are new to the securities industry;
- those who have had some involvement with securities operations and who seek a broader understanding;
- those who have worked in specific areas of securities operations and who seek a deeper knowledge of how prior actions affect their role and how their actions affect others subsequently.

The content of the book should be relevant to those who fall into the second and third categories above, whether the reader has gained experience within a securities trading organisation (such as traders, salespeople, trade support personnel, static data personnel, reconciliation staff, compliance officers, credit controllers and accountants) has associations with securities trading organisations (such as securities issuers, custodian organisations and registrars), or supplies services to the securities industry (such as static data vendors, software engineers and management consultants).

This book is written primarily from the perspective of a securities trading organisation (STO); at a very high level, I would define such an organisation as:

- being active in a number of securities markets,
- buying and selling securities for its own account (rather than as an agent acting on behalf of another investor), and
- needing to borrow cash in order to fund its inventory of securities

although the majority of the content of the book is directly relevant to many organisations that operate in a different capacity within the securities industry.

OBJECTIVES AND STRUCTURE OF THE BOOK

The objective of this book is to de-mystify the subject of securities operations by breaking the subject into logical components, explaining the issues relating to each component and at the same time conveying the accumulated effect and the overall picture.

The book is structured into three main areas: the first nine chapters provide an essential foundation regarding securities and the characters within the marketplace; between chapters 10 and 21, the trade lifecycle is described in its component parts, and from chapter 22 position management resulting from trading activity is described.

My intention is to express the general operational processes as typically managed within a securities trading organisation, whilst:

- conveying the necessary internal controls
- highlighting the risks and how to mitigate them
- suggesting ways of maximising opportunity and minimising costs

from an operational standpoint.

As the industry becomes increasingly automated, both within an organisation and between that organisation and the parties with which the organisation must communicate, understanding of the start-to-end operational processes and the underlying reasons for tasks to be performed is likely to diminish.

An observation drawn from my years within the operations areas of different organisations is that the industry needs many more people who understand the bigger picture, can visualise the impact of an operational action and put in place measures that provide benefits to the organisation concerned.

Rather than cover the practices within specific locations around the globe, I have attempted to convey concepts that will be applicable to the majority of locations. The intention is for the reader to apply these concepts in any location, as each of the major points covered within the book is typically practised within each market, but there is every possibility that each market has its own nuances in dealing with a particular point.

I have in general attempted to gradually accumulate the reader's knowledge by describing the various components of a topic, conceptually and by giving examples, and by making forward reference to later topics, and backward reference to earlier topics. My objective has been to enable the reader to gain a complete overview of securities operations, subsequently enabling communication with other people on any and all of the topics covered.

Due to the accumulation effect within the book, the chapters (particularly in the second half of the book) make numerous references to points covered within prior chapters; consequently, it is recommended that the book is read chapter-by-chapter, rather than reading chapters in isolation.

At times, the text may touch on certain topics (e.g. legal and regulatory) to a superficial level, as they are deemed to fall outside of the main focus and coverage of the book.

Words and terms explained within the Glossary of Terms are highlighted in *italics* within the main text.

I have written this book entirely independently and not for or on behalf of my employer; consequently, all views expressed within this book are my own and do not necessarily reflect the views of my employer.

In a number of places within the text Industry Anecdotes, gathered from a variety of sources, are related in order to emphasise the risks involved and the importance of exercising certain trading and operational controls.

Although every effort has been made to remove errors from the text, any that remain belong to me! However, I would welcome the chance to correct any errors or ommissions.

If the reader has any observations on the style or content of the book, I would appreciate being informed of such comments by e-mail to info@mike-simmons.com.

Michael Simmons

Acknowledgements

It would not have been possible to complete this book without the involvement of the following:

Bob Ewart
Colin Baker
Chris Howard
Cristina Baker
David Martin
David Westbrook
Dave Yurasits
Ian Clark
Jeff Cruikshank
John Ryan
Mark Woodgate
Paul Arnup
Paul Barton
Paul Clark
Sanjay Shah
Stuart Wilson
Tim Kent-Phillips

each of whom provided (out of their own time) invaluable guidance from their wealth of professional knowledge, for which I am extremely grateful.

I would also like to thank Sam Whittaker and Monica Twine at the publisher, John Wiley & Sons, for their patience and help in the production of the book.

In particular, I would like to say a special thank you to Elaine Dalgleish and Kevin Croot, whose dedication to the review of the entire book (including numerous iterations of many chapters), from an accuracy, continuity and grammatical perspective, has been paramount in its completion.

Finally I thank my wife Allyson, who not only allowed me to indulge my desire to write the book, but also corrected my grammar.

1
Essential Trading and Settlement Concepts

1.1 INTRODUCTION

For any company in any industry, remaining in control of its goods and cash is fundamental to successful and efficient operation of its business. This involves maintaining up-to-date internal records of trading activity, deliveries and receipts of goods, as well as payments and receipts of cash, thereby enabling the prediction of future stock and cash flows and the reconciliation of internal records with external entities, including goods held in warehouses and cash held at banks.

This chapter highlights similarities and differences between a deal undertaken by an everyday business (for example, a sports goods retailer) and a company within the securities industry. In addition, typical terminology used within the securities industry is highlighted and explained.

1.2 TERMINOLOGY

Figure 1.1 lists the components of two trades; the trade in the upper half is undertaken by a sports goods retailer and the trade in the lower half is executed by a Securities Trading Organisation (STO).

Many of the phrases and terms used within the securities industry can be related to those used in the outside world. It is important to understand the meaning of the components of a trade in order to appreciate their impact following the agreement to trade.

Component	Description
Trade date	The date the parties to the trade agreed to trade; the date of *trade execution*
Operation	The type and direction of the trade, e.g. buy or sell, lend or borrow
Quantity	The number of units of the goods being exchanged
Goods	The specific goods being exchanged
Price	The price of each unit being exchanged
Supplier	The entity with whom the trade has been executed (the deliverer of goods and the receiver of cash)
Delivery date	The agreed intended date of delivery of goods by the supplier and payment of cash by the buyer
Cash due	The cash value of the trade due to be paid to the supplier upon delivery of the goods
Required location of goods	From the buyer's perspective, the desired storage location of the goods
Cash to be paid from	From the buyer's perspective, the specific bank from which payment is to be made

---

SPORTS GOODS RETAILER

Buys 100 Training Shoes (colour blue) at USD 70.00 each from the Sports Supply
Company (SSC) on 15th June for delivery on 25th June - total due to pay USD 7000.00

the following is recorded

Trade Date	Operation	Quantity	Goods	Price	Supplier	Del. Date	Cash Due
15th June	Buy	100	Trainers Blue	USD 70.00	Sports Supply Co.	25th June	USD 7000.00

Required location of trainers: Retailer's Warehouse No. 1, New York	Cash to be paid from: Retailer's account at Bank X, New York

---

SECURITIES TRADING ORGANISATION (STO)

Buys 2000 Sony Corporation shares at Yen 14,100 each from Counterparty X,
London on 15th June for delivery on 25th June - total due to pay Yen 28,200,000

the following is recorded

Trade Date	Operation	Quantity	Securities	Price	Counterparty	Value Date	Cash Due
15th June	Buy	2000	Sony Corp. Shares	Yen 14,100	Counterparty X	25th June	Yen 28,200,000

Required location of securities: STO's *CUSTODIAN*, Cust. E, Tokyo	Cash to be paid from: STO's *CUSTODIAN*, Cust. E, Tokyo

Figure 1.1 Comparison of terms

1.3   DIFFERENCES IN TERMINOLOGY

Of the terms listed above, within the securities industry the following terms differ:

Term	Securities Industry Term
Goods	The goods in which STOs invest are referred to as *securities* or instruments. From this point forward the term securities will be used in this book
Supplier	The party with whom the trade is conducted is known as the *counterparty*, whether buying or selling, lending or borrowing
Delivery date	The agreed intended date of delivery is known as the *value date* or contractual settlement date. From this point forward the term value date will be used in this book

Note: the focus of this book is primarily from the perspective of *securities trading organisations*; the abbreviation STO will be used throughout the book.

1.4   DIFFERENCES IN THE EXCHANGE OF GOODS/SECURITIES AND CASH

If a comparison is made of a local retailer and an STO, a major difference is likely to be found in the 'required location of goods' and 'cash to be paid from' areas.

A local retailer is likely to take direct delivery of goods purchased and then store the goods in a local warehouse, with cash being paid by handing over a cheque to the seller. Under this arrangement, the buyer is able to verify that the goods are those that were purchased, that they are not damaged and that none are missing. Following a sale, delivery of goods by the retailer will also be under the retailer's direct control and receipt of a cheque upon delivery of goods to the buyer can be banked immediately.

By contrast, the securities industry is a global industry; numerous STOs in many of the world's financial centres invest in securities that are normally delivered locally to the security's place of issue. For example, an STO based in Stockholm may choose to invest in a Japanese security. There may be nothing to prevent the Stockholm-based STO taking delivery of the securities in Stockholm, however, from an efficiency and cost perspective STOs typically require delivery to occur in the normal place of issue and delivery of the securities, in this example Tokyo. The alternative is that securities would be delivered from Tokyo to Stockholm, with lengthy delivery timeframes and the costs (e.g. insurance) of such a delivery to be considered, and with the seller likely to demand payment for the securities before the securities leave the seller's possession. If the buyer agrees to this arrangement, he would be taking a risk of being without both securities and cash—an unacceptable risk to most STOs.

In order to minimise this risk and to exchange securities and cash in the most efficient manner for all securities in which they invest, STOs typically utilise local agents to exchange securities and cash on their behalf. Local agents are often referred to as depots/nostros or custodians; the term *custodian* will be used in this book. Securities are held within a custodian securities account (also known as a depot account) and cash is held within a custodian cash account (also known as a nostro account). A large STO may employ the services of numerous custodians located in various financial centres around the globe, each custodian being responsible for exchanging securities and cash as a result of buying and selling by the STO, and for holding the resultant securities and cash in safekeeping on behalf of the STO.

Figure 1.2 illustrates the relationship that an STO typically has with its various custodians, according to the origin of each security.

In summary, a local retailer is likely to have direct control over its:
• goods; checked for completeness and quality at time of receipt, then stored in a warehouse until sold and
• cash; cheque written by the retailer

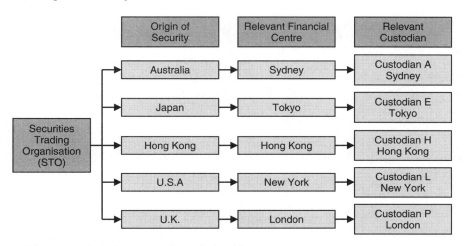

Figure 1.2   Example STO to custodian relationships

whereas STOs typically manage the exchange of securities and cash remotely through custodians, with the assets of the STO being under the trust of (but not owned by) the custodians.

1.5   METHODS OF EXCHANGING SECURITIES AND CASH

The exchange of securities and cash is known as *settlement* within the securities industry. The act of settlement should be viewed as no different from buying or selling goods in one's personal life. For instance, most people are reluctant to pay the purchase cost of a car without taking delivery of the car at the same time. Conversely, most people would not feel happy about handing over a car that they were selling without receiving the buyer's cash at the same time. The risk, applicable to both buyer and seller, is that at one point in time they may be in possession of neither asset, whether goods or cash.

STOs are typically very risk averse and they try to avoid these situations whenever possible. The most efficient and risk-free method of settlement is known as Delivery versus Payment (DvP), whereby simultaneous exchange of securities and cash is effected between buyer and seller (through their custodians), the seller not being required to deliver securities until the buyer pays the cash and the buyer not being required to pay cash until the seller delivers the securities, thereby ensuring that both parties are protected.

The STO and its counterparty typically decide upon the method of settlement at the time of trade execution. In most cases, the method of settlement is assumed to be DvP, unless one of the parties specifically requests the alternative.

The alternative to settling on a DvP basis is to settle on a Free of Payment (FoP) basis, whereby one (or both) parties to the trade will need to arrange delivery of securities or payment of cash prior to taking possession of the other asset. Due to the risks involved, most STOs avoid settling in this manner, whenever possible.

However, the ability to settle trades on a DvP basis in all financial centres around the globe depends upon the historic and current practices of the particular financial centre. For the moment, suffice it to say that it can be a costly mistake to assume settlement occurs on a DvP basis in all financial centres. These points will be explored within later chapters of the book.

1.6   REMAINING IN CONTROL

It is of paramount importance for a company to remain in control of its goods and cash, regardless of the nature of its business. For an STO, this means maintaining within its *books and records* complete and up-to-date records of the following.

Item	Description
Trades	A complete record of all trades executed
Trading positions	The net sum (by quantity) of all trades in each security
Open trades	Trades which have yet to settle and which are outstanding with counterparties
Settled trades	Trades which have settled at the custodian and which are no longer outstanding with the counterparty
Settled positions	The net sum of all settled trades in each security, and in each currency

In order to prove that the STO's records are accurate, each of these items should be reconciled independently with external sources.

Furthermore, an STO's complete picture of an individual security can be reconciled internally by comparing:

- the trading position (also known as the 'ownership' position) with
- the sum of open trades and the settled position (also known as the 'location' position).

The value in performing an ownership versus location comparison is that it is intended to confirm that whatever quantity of goods the STO owns as a result of trading (represented by the trading position) is:

- held within the control of the STO (at the STO's custodian), and/or
- due to be delivered to the STO by counterparties from whom the STO has purchased securities, and/or
- due to be delivered by the STO to counterparties to whom the STO has sold securities

and that its records balance internally.

These concepts are important as they form the basis for good operational management and proper control over assets.

The three example trades listed in Table 1.1 will now be used as the basis to calculate ownership versus location positions at various moments in time within the books and records of an STO. All three trades are in the same security (Sony Corporation shares); there was no trading position prior to the first trade executed on 15th June and the time gap between trade date and value date is deliberate, to make the examples easier to follow.

Table 1.1

Counterparty	Trade date	Value date	Operation	Quantity	Trading position
'X'	15th June	25th June	Buy	2000	+2000
'Y'	1st July	10th July	Buy	6000	+8000
'Z'	15th July	20th July	Sell	5000	+3000

Tables 1.2 to 1.6 show the ownership versus location position of Sony Corporation shares at various points in time, relating to the three trades listed in Table 1.1. Note that the convention used in these tables is:

- within 'ownership'
  - the STO's positive trading position is represented by a '+' sign, and consequently
- within 'location'
  - an open purchase due from a counterparty will be shown as a '−' sign
  - a settled purchase held at the STO's custodian will be shown as a '−' sign
  - an open sale due to a counterparty will be shown as a '+' sign.

Table 1.2 shows the position immediately after the first trade has been executed. It shows that 2000 shares are owned by the STO and that these shares have not yet been delivered to the STO's custodian by the counterparty, as the value date (the intended date of delivery) is in the future.

Up to and including one day prior to value date (i.e. 24th June), the ownership versus location position remains the same as in Table 1.2 due to the fact there were no more

Table 1.2

Sony Corporation shares (as at 15th June)			
Ownership		Location	
STO	+ 2000	– 2000	Counterparty 'X'
	+ 2000	– 2000	

trades executed as at that date, and settlement has not yet occurred for the trade which has been executed.

Assuming that the trade settles on value date (at the custodian), the internal records will need to be updated as in Table 1.3. This shows that 2000 shares are owned by the STO and that these shares have been delivered by the counterparty to the STO's custodian, Custodian E, Tokyo. It also shows that there are no open trades in this security.

Table 1.3

Sony Corporation shares (as at 25th June)			
Ownership		Location	
STO	+ 2000	– 2000	Custodian E, Tokyo
	+ 2000	– 2000	

If the ownership versus location position were now viewed after the second trade was executed on 1st July, it would be as in Table 1.4. This shows that, as a result of the second trade, the ownership position has increased; part of the position is held at the STO's custodian and the remainder is open with the counterparty. (This purchase settled on value date (10th July)).

Table 1.4

Sony Corporation shares (as at 1st July)			
Ownership		Location	
STO	+ 8000	– 2000	Custodian E, Tokyo
		– 6000	Counterparty 'Y'
	+ 8000	– 8000	

Moving ahead to 20th July, Table 1.5 reveals that the ownership position has been reduced due to the sale on 15th July, that 5000 shares have failed to settle on the value date and are still owed to the counterparty and that the securities owed to the counterparty are still held in the STO's Tokyo custodian. The reasons for *settlement failure* will be explored in Chapter 19.

Table 1.5

Sony Corporation shares (as at 20th July)			
Ownership		Location	
STO	+ 3000	− 8000	Custodian E, Tokyo
		+ 5000	Counterparty 'Z'
	+ 3000	**− 3000**	

Viewing the situation on 22nd July, Table 1.6 shows that the sale is still outstanding and will remain so until settlement occurs.

Table 1.6

Sony Corporation shares (as at 22nd July)			
Ownership		Location	
STO	+ 3000	− 8000	Custodian E, Tokyo
		+ 5000	Counterparty 'Z'
	+ 3000	**− 3000**	

In all cases, the ownership position is equal to the sum of the location position. Providing that *double-entry bookkeeping* methods are employed, it should not be possible for the ownership versus location position to become out-of-balance, whether using manual methods or a *books and records* system. Although the focus in the given examples has been on the quantity of securities, the same concepts are applicable to cash.

1.7   RECORDING DETAILS OF INDIVIDUAL TRADES

The accurate recording of every trade executed, inclusive of the components of each trade, enables an STO to track

- in terms of securities:
  - those that are due to be received from counterparties
  - those that are due to be delivered to counterparties
- in terms of cash:
  - that which is due to be paid to counterparties
  - that which is due to be received from counterparties

all of which in turn provides the basis for accurate cash management and minimal banking costs.

1.8   SUMMARY

Failure to maintain up-to-date and accurate records of its trading and settlement activity means that an STO is highly likely to be:

* uncertain of its trading positions
  * affecting the STO's ability to trade with confidence
* uncertain of the trades which are open with counterparties
  * affecting the STO's ability to assess the risk of counterparties failing to settle trades
  * for purchases, affecting the accurate prediction of incoming securities and outgoing cash
  * for sales, affecting the accurate prediction of outgoing securities and incoming cash
* uncertain of the quantity of securities and cash held by custodians
* unable to reconcile the securities and cash it believes it owns based on its internal records with the statements of settled security positions and cash balances provided by its custodians.

If an STO fails to predict incoming and outgoing movements of securities and cash, and/or fails to deliver sold securities to the counterparty on value date and fails to pay cash to counterparties when the seller is able to deliver the securities, the STO will be prone to excessive operational costs with a direct negative impact on overall company profits.

Ultimately, if the business is not controlled adequately, operational costs can become so excessive that the ongoing viability of the organisation will be at risk. These operational risks will be explored at various points throughout this book.

2
The Securities Marketplace

2.1 INTRODUCTION

In any street market, the goods that are sold are manufactured outside of the marketplace and the characters involved are those who visit the marketplace in order to buy goods and those who reside within the marketplace in order to sell those goods.

A direct comparison can be made with the securities marketplace as follows:

- the goods (securities) are originated by organisations (issuers of securities) outside the marketplace;
- investors visit the marketplace in order to buy and sell securities, either directly or via an agent;
- STOs reside within the marketplace in order to sell securities to and buy securities from investors and agents;
- the marketplace provides the infrastructure to allow trading to occur, within a regulated environment.

Figure 2.1 illustrates such relationships.

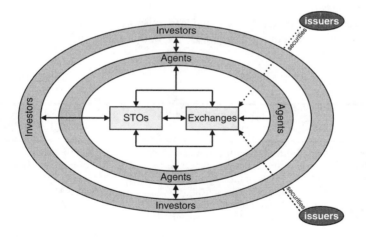

Figure 2.1   The securities marketplace: overview

The various goods, the roles of the

- issuers
- investors
- agents acting on behalf of investors
- STOs
- securities markets and exchanges

and the inter-relationships between them are described within this chapter.

2.2   SECURITIES

Organisations occasionally need to raise cash (or capital) in order to expand their business through, for example, buying new premises, building new factories or acquiring other companies. The options open to such organisations for raising the necessary capital include:

- borrowing cash from banks,
- selling a part of their existing business,
- selling part ownership in the company (issuing shares), and
- borrowing cash from investors (issuing bonds)

with both shares and bonds generically known as *securities*.
    The securities marketplace:

- facilitates the process of bringing new securities to the marketplace, and
- provides a structured and regulated method of buying and selling existing securities for the protection of the investors.

2.2.1   Issuers of Securities

Those who raise capital through the creation and distribution of securities to investors are known as *issuers*. Table 2.1 lists the normal types of issuer with well-known examples of such organisations. It is important to note that only companies or corporations can issue shares, whereas all the issuer types listed can raise capital through the issue of bonds. The differences between equity and bonds, for both issuers and investors, are described below.

Table 2.1

Issuer type	Typical method of raising cash	Example issuers
Companies or corporations	Either by selling shares/equity (representing ownership) to investors, or by selling bonds (representing a borrowing of cash) to investors. Some issuers do both	Colgate-Palmolive (USA) Cheung Kong (Hong Kong) Marks & Spencer (UK) Nestlé SA (Switzerland) Qantas (Australia) SASOL (South Africa) Telebras (Brazil)
Sovereign entities	Selling bonds to investors	Kingdom of Denmark New Zealand
Local governments	Selling bonds to investors	City of Barcelona
Government agencies	Selling bonds to investors	Federal National Mortgage Association
Supranational organisations	Selling bonds to investors	International Bank for Reconstruction & Development (World Bank) Inter-American Development Bank

2.2.2   Common Security Types

The two most common types of security issued by companies are equity (also known as shares, or 'stock' in the USA) and debt (also known as bonds). A brief description of the basic attributes of each follows, and variations of such securities are described in Chapter 7.

Equity

Equity represents ownership in a company; the purchase of shares by an investor gives the investor partial ownership in that company (a 'share' in the company). The issuer effectively dilutes the ownership of the company by spreading ownership across hundreds or thousands of investors, dependent upon the size of the company and the number of shares in issue.

The issue of equity provides the company with 'permanent' cash; in other words when the company sells shares initially there is no intention to repay to shareholders the capital received (however, on an exceptional basis an issuer may decide to buy back shares from shareholders).

If the company performs well, investors will reap the benefit through increases in the market price of the share as well as through greater profit distribution (for example through income [dividend] payments). However, a typical equity issue has no predefined amounts of income which are payable to the shareholders, or predefined points in time when income is payable.

Consequently, from the shareholders' perspective payments of income are neither guaranteed nor predictable (even if a company has paid dividends at regular intervals historically, there is no guarantee that this will be the case in future). If an investor wishes to sell his shareholding, the shares are not normally purchased by the issuer but are sold in the marketplace and ultimately purchased by another investor.

Examples of existing equity issues with the description of the share are given in Table 2.2, illustrating geographical coverage, currency of issue and the face value of a share. The description of the shares will be explained in Chapter 7.

Table 2.2

Issuer	Description of issue
Colgate-Palmolive (USA)	USD 0.01 common stock
Cheung Kong (Holdings) Ltd (Hong Kong)	HKD 0.50 shares
Marks & Spencer plc (UK)	GBP 0.25 ordinary shares
Nestlé SA (Switzerland)	CHF 1.00 shares
Qantas Airways Ltd (Australia)	AUD 1.00 ordinary shares

Debt

A debt issue reflects a borrowing of a specific amount of cash by an issuer (such as a company, government or government agency) in a specified currency; the purchase of bonds by an investor is effectively an 'IOU'—a promise by the issuer to repay the capital to the investor at a future point in time and to make periodic payments of interest to the investor at predefined points in time and (normally) at a predefined rate of interest. Interest on bonds is commonly referred to as *coupon*; this topic is explored in Chapter 6.

From an issuing company's perspective, there is no dilution of ownership in the company as a result of issuing a bond; therefore investors in bond issues are not owners of the company. The issue of debt provides the issuer with a temporary receipt of cash, as it will be repaid at a future point in time (even if the period of the borrowing is as much as 30 years). Outgoing cash payments by the bond issuer are normally predictable throughout the life of the bond issue. The terms of the issue are set at the time of issue, including the date repayment of capital (also known as the maturity date) will be made, as well as the amount and dates for periodic payments of coupon. There are some exceptions to such rules, and these will be highlighted at the appropriate points in the book.

If an investor wishes to sell his bondholding, the bonds are not normally purchased by the issuer but are sold in the marketplace to another investor, as is the case for equities.

Examples of existing bond issues are given in Table 2.3, illustrating geographical coverage, currency of issue, coupon rate and maturity date.

Table 2.3

| | Description of issue | | |
Issuer	Currency	Annual coupon rate	Maturity date
Alliance & Leicester plc	Pounds Sterling (GBP)	5.875%	14th August 2031
China (Peoples Republic of)	Japanese Yen (JPY)	4.65%	11th December 2015
France (Government of)	Euros (EUR)	3.0%	25th July 2009
Inter-American Development Bank	US Dollars (USD)	7.125%	15th March 2023
Mexico (Government of)	Netherlands Guilder (NLG)	5.31%	31st December 2019
New Zealand Government	New Zealand Dollars (NZD)	6.5%	15th April 2013
Saskatchewan (Province of)	Canadian Dollars (CAD)	9.6%	4th February 2022
United Airlines	US Dollars (USD)	8.65%	24th December 2009
Zurcher Kantonalbank	Swiss Francs (CHF)	3.25%	29th July 2005

Equity versus Debt—Similarities and Differences

A comparison of the characteristics of equity and debt would reveal significant differences from the perspective of both issuer and investor:

- equity dilutes ownership in a company whereas debt does not
- equity issuers are not expecting to repay cash received from issuing securities, whereas bond issues are repayable by the issuer on maturity of the bond
- payments of income on equities are not predictable as they are dependent upon profits, whereas bond income is (normally) predictable and obligatory regardless of profits

but with some similarities:

- both are issued to raise capital

- following their launch into the securities marketplace, the market value of both is subject to fluctuation according to the laws of supply and demand
- income is payable on both equity and debt
- when an investor wishes to sell his holding, both equities and debt are sold in the marketplace, not usually repurchased by the issuer.

One Issuer—One or Many Issues

An individual company may have issued equity but have no bonds in issue. Other companies may have both equity and bonds in issue simultaneously, with a single equity issue at the same time as having one or many bond issues.

Governments, government agencies and supranational organisations cannot be owned and therefore cannot issue equity. However, it is entirely feasible that a bond issuer of any type can have many bond issues running concurrently, but differences will be apparent in the features of each issue, usually relating to the:

- currency of issue,
- size of issue (the cash amount borrowed by the issuer),
- rate of coupon payable,
- coupon payment dates, and
- maturity dates.

2.2.3 Security Price Fluctuation

Once a security has been brought to the marketplace the laws of supply and demand come into play; when the demand for goods is high the price of those goods increases and vice versa where the demand is lower. Those who have the foresight to identify profit-making opportunities and are prepared to back their foresight and pay cash to invest may make profit for themselves, but many factors can affect the price of a security.

Equity Price Fluctuation

Equities are usually regarded as being more volatile than bonds; this is because equities have no guaranteed income or repayment upon maturity which can be used as a measure of their value, whereas bonds typically have a known rate of interest throughout their life and a known maturity price and maturity date, all of which can be a measure of their value.

Factors that cause volatility in equities include:

- speculation—for example the suspicion or knowledge that a company is a takeover target is likely to increase the share price of the target company;
- projected profits—company analysts specialising in particular industrial sectors (e.g. textiles) are employed by STOs to project the profits that companies within that industrial sector may make. The results of the analysis are publicised with the STO potentially recommending to investors that a particular share should be bought or sold. A projected decrease in profits for the current trading period versus a previous comparable period is likely to decrease a company's share price prior to the announcement of the actual profits;
- actual profits—when a company announces its results for the latest trading period, this may or may not be in accordance with the projected profits. Where the latter is the case

and the company has announced profits that are, for example, 5% above the projected profits, the share price is likely to increase;

- local and worldwide economic conditions—occasionally in the past, stock market prices in one or many financial centres have been affected by general outlook and trends where, for instance as happened in 1987, share prices which had been at their peak fell dramatically due to a sudden loss of confidence by investors.

In each case, the increase or decrease in the share price reflects the expectation of greater or lesser profits and dividends.

Bond Price Fluctuation

Bond prices tend not to be static, but are generally not subject to dramatic change to the same extent as equities; however, prices are affected for reasons such as:

- *money market* interest rates—because (in most cases) an investor is able to predict the income receivable on a bond, a direct comparison can be made between the return from placing cash on deposit in the money market and income on a bond. When money market interest rates are low, generally speaking demand for bonds will be greater where the coupon rate of bonds is higher and conversely demand for bonds will be lower when money market rates are high;
- falling share prices—the price of bonds tends to increase due to greater investor demand when equity prices decrease and investors sell equity, as bonds are regarded by many as being a 'safe haven' where spectacular growth may not be possible but a predictable income will be earned.

In the case of both equities and bonds, market forces dictate that greater investor demand results in increased prices while lesser demand holds prices down. The available supply of securities also has an impact on prices; the shorter the supply the higher the price. It is these forces that create the opportunity to operate a market.

2.2.4   Securities Markets and Exchanges

The marketplace is generally considered to be the environment within which securities are bought and sold. Central to some marketplaces is the existence of a stock exchange, which acts as the primary meeting point for those wishing to buy and sell securities, while other markets may exist without a stock exchange, with buyers and sellers contacting each other directly. Trades executed over an exchange are generally termed 'on-exchange' or 'exchange-traded', whereas other trades are executed by telephone on an 'OTC' (Over-the-Counter) basis. The evolution of these markets around the globe has involved the introduction of rules and regulations to ensure that an individual market is regarded as a fair and just place to conduct business.

The various markets developed their rules, regulations and methods of operation over many years to suit their local needs, and in some markets national governments imposed rules. This resulted in, for example, strict dividing lines between the activities of the market participants and fixed commission amounts charged to clients for buying and selling securities.

However, in many markets the removal (or reduction) of controls imposed by governments has occurred in the last quarter of the 20th century, in order to promote competition between market participants and resulting in the removal of fixed commission charged to clients. The removal or reduction in controls is known as *deregulation*.

Each securities market has an associated and recognisable place for sellers and buyers to effect settlement of their trading activity, so that trading in a security within a specific market, such as:

- trading HSBC shares on the Stock Exchange of Hong Kong typically means settling the trade at the Central Clearing and Settlement System (CCASS), while
- trading French Government bonds in the Paris Bourse typically means settling at Euroclear France.

Table 2.4 gives examples of financial centres and associated stock exchanges, by country within continent. Note that in some countries, regional exchanges exist.

Table 2.4

Continent	Country	Financial centre	Stock exchange title
Africa	Ghana	Accra	Ghana Stock Exchange
	Kenya	Nairobi	Nairobi Stock Exchange
	South Africa	Johannesburg	Johannesburg Stock Exchange
Americas	Argentina	Buenos Aires	Bolsa de Comercio de Buenos Aires
	Brazil	Sao Paulo	Bolsa de Valores de Sao Paulo
	Canada	Toronto	Toronto Stock Exchange
	Mexico	Mexico City	Bolsa Mexicana de Valores
	USA	New York	New York Stock Exchange
Asia	China	Shenzhen	Shenzhen Stock Exchange
	Hong Kong	Hong Kong	Stock Exchange of Hong Kong
	India	Bombay	Bombay Stock Exchange
	Japan	Tokyo	Tokyo Stock Exchange
	Korea	Seoul	Korea Stock Exchange
	Malaysia	Kuala Lumpur	Kuala Lumpur Stock Exchange
	Singapore	Singapore	Stock Exchange of Singapore
	Thailand	Bangkok	Stock Exchange of Thailand
Australasia	Australia	Sydney	Australian Stock Exchange
	New Zealand	Wellington	New Zealand Stock Exchange
Europe	Austria	Vienna	Wiener Borse AG
	France	Paris	Paris Bourse SBF SA
	Germany	Frankfurt	Deutsche Borse
	Italy	Milan	Borsa Italiana SpA
	Netherlands	Amsterdam	Amsterdamse Beurzen NV (AEX)
	Spain	Madrid	Bolsa de Madrid
	Sweden	Stockholm	OM Stockholmsborsen AB
	Switzerland	Zurich	Swiss Exchange (SWX)
	UK	London	London Stock Exchange (LSE)

The majority of securities have historically been traded only within their domestic exchange, but increasingly, popular securities can be traded over multiple exchanges. From an operational perspective, the exchange/market over which a trade has been executed may well affect the location of settlement. An example of a market which has no associated stock exchange is the *eurobond* market.

2.3   PARTICIPANTS

2.3.1   Introduction

The characters involved historically within securities marketplaces were those who organised a venture and those who decided to participate financially in the hope that their investment would be rewarded at some future point in time. Because of doubt over the outcome, the investment is generally considered a gamble rather than a certainty.

In the past, a house builder may have seen an opportunity to make significant profits if only he could raise sufficient cash to buy the raw materials to build the houses; he would seek to involve others in the venture, offering a proportionate share of the profits according to the amount invested by each of the investors. Profit (or loss) for an individual investor would be realised either when the houses were built and subsequently sold, or if a market existed for the sale and purchase of the investment and the investment were sold.

Any individual or company that decides to invest in the securities marketplace is taking a gamble and risks losing some or all of the cash invested. Conversely, huge profits may be made, but investors have to decide for themselves whether the proposed investment has an acceptable level of risk or not, as risk is specific to an investor's own circumstances.

Those who participate in the securities marketplace include:

- investors
- agents for investors
- STOs
- regulators
- custodians

whose roles (along with the roles of other participants) are described in the following pages.

2.3.2   Investors

In general there are two types of investor, the individual and the institutional investor.

Individual Investors

Most individuals invest in securities for their personal gain, whether their focus is capital growth through an increase in the market value of their investment or regular income through the receipt of dividends on shares or coupon on bonds.

Individual investors visit the marketplace via agents (also known as intermediaries), as listed in Table 2.5, through whom the buying and selling of securities is effected. Note that the proliferation in the number and type of organisations that offer share-dealing services on behalf of individual investors means that the list in Table 2.5 should not be regarded as exhaustive. Furthermore, many of the titles given to those who act as agents for investors differ, but the services they provide to their clients are broadly similar.

To buy or sell securities, an individual usually places with an agent a request (commonly known as an *order*) to buy or sell a specific quantity of a specific security (and may also state a specific price); this is illustrated in Figure 2.2.

Table 2.5

Agent	Description
Clearing bank	A bank that operates standard cash accounts for its clients and which typically offers a share-dealing service
Broker or Stockbroker	A company that specialises in fulfilling requests from its clients, to buy or sell securities
Retail broker	An alternative name for a stockbroker
Internet broker	An organisation whose clients place requests to buy and sell securities via the Internet
Financial adviser	An individual or organisation that gives investment advice to its clients

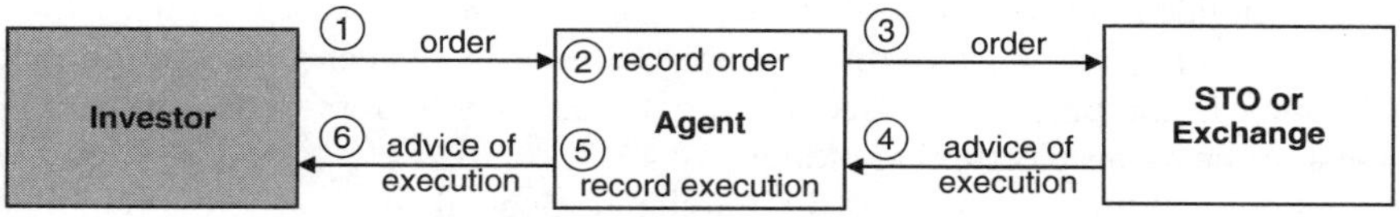

Figure 2.2   The securities marketplace: trading by individual investors

From the investor's perspective, step 1 shows the placement of the order and step 6 shows the receipt of advice of completion or *execution* of that order. An order may not result in a successful execution if the investor states a specific price at which they wish to buy or sell that is too aggressive relevant to the price within the marketplace. Note that all other steps will be described in Sections 2.3.3 and 2.3.4.

An individual may decide to operate one or more securities accounts; these are known as portfolios and may be used, for example, to distinguish between holdings in equities versus debt, or international versus domestic securities, thereby enabling separate assessment of profitability in a way that suits the investor. Similarly for cash accounts, an individual may require an income account to be maintained to reflect receipts of *dividends* on equities and *coupon* on bonds, whilst having a separate capital or investment account over which the cost of purchases is debited and sale proceeds are credited.

Where individuals have a portfolio that is managed by an agent, the agent may offer to operate the portfolio on:

- an advisory basis, where the agent provides advice on investments;
- a discretionary basis, where the individual empowers the agent to make investment decisions;
- an execution only basis, where the agent reacts to orders to buy or sell placed by the individual.

The agent charges the individual according to the type of service provided.

For non-discretionary accounts, the purchase or sale of securities is usually begun by the individual placing an *order* with their agent to buy or sell. Various media exist for the placement of orders including letter, fax, the Internet or over the telephone to a call centre or a portfolio manager. If the order is successful and securities have in fact been bought or sold, the individual is typically charged a commission by the agent through whom the trade has been executed.

Recent additions to the ranks of individuals who trade in securities are 'day traders' who, by use of the Internet, buy and sell a security on the same date, hoping to make an instant profit. It is not unusual for day traders to trade in large quantities of securities to exploit small price changes.

An investor may choose to buy or sell directly in a specific security, such as Sony Corporation shares or US Treasury 6.25% bonds maturing 15th May 2030; however, an investor may choose to invest in a fund of investments which invests in many securities, thereby spreading the risk that an individual security will result in a total loss of the invested cash. These funds (known as 'mutual funds' or 'unit trusts' in different parts of the globe) are described in more depth in the following subsections.

Following purchases of securities, an individual can choose whether to look after their portfolio of securities themselves, or to have their portfolio held and managed by their agent for which a fee may be charged to the individual. Historically, *certificates* representing an individual's ownership of shares or bonds would have been either held by the individual or held in *safe custody* by a broker, bank or investment manager on behalf of the individual. In the present day, securities holdings may be represented by a certificate of ownership, or by an electronic holding.

The method of settlement of sales by individuals depends upon where the individual's certificate of ownership is held (unless it is in electronic form). Where the individual holds the certificate, this will need to be delivered to the agent through whom the sale has been effected, against payment of cash (or credit to the individual's account) on the value date of the trade. If the agent has control of the individual's securities (whether in electronic or certificated form), the agent will usually effect removal of the security from the individual's portfolio automatically.

Institutional Investors

The terms *institutional investor* or institutional client are collective terms used to describe companies (rather than individuals) that visit the securities marketplace and invest in securities. The type of organisation that constitutes an institutional investor varies but includes companies in the capacity of:

- *mutual fund managers* (also known as unit trust managers)
- *pension funds*
- *insurance companies*
- *hedge funds*
- *charities*

and each will be described within this chapter.

As for individual investors, when wishing to buy or sell securities institutional investors place orders with an agent who typically charges a commission when a trade is executed. However, institutional clients may also trade directly with an STO. Both methods are illustrated in Figure 2.3.

Method A is essentially the same as for individual investors, but method B is typically open only to institutional investors. Method A will be described in Section 2.3.3 whilst method B will be described in Section 2.3.4.

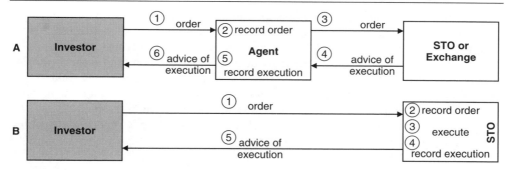

Figure 2.3   The securities marketplace: trading by institutional investors

Mutual Funds. Rather than invest directly in an individual equity or bond, individual investors may opt to invest in a mutual fund.

Mutual funds invest the cash received from numerous individuals into various equities or bonds, or a combination of both, thereby reducing the risk to the investor. Risk is reduced as the investor's cash is effectively spread across investments in numerous securities so that in the event of a dramatic reduction in the price of a single equity security within the fund, the investor is, relatively speaking, cushioned as the value of the overall fund is only affected with respect to the amount invested in that one security. Where there is a regional or global stock market crash, however, the majority of the fund's investments are likely to fall in price and therefore the fund value will fall accordingly.

The mutual fund company usually sets up and operates on an ongoing basis a range of funds; the individual funds are designed to appeal to individual investors' needs and preferences. For instance, a fund management company may operate the following funds:

- Developing Markets Fund
- German Growth Fund
- Organic Industry Fund

enabling investors who seek, for instance, long-term capital growth, regular income, investment in technology or ecology conscious companies or investment in a geographical area to select an appropriate fund in which to invest. Each fund is operated by an investment manager, an individual (or team) who specialises in the past performance and outlook of companies within the sector of business in which the fund is focused. The investment manager's responsibility is to make good investment decisions on behalf of the fund (and therefore on behalf of its individual investors) whilst investing in equities and bonds falling within the fund's scope of operation.

Following execution of a trade to buy or sell securities, mutual funds effect settlement of trades either by utilising the services of a *global custodian* that has a network of sub-custodians in numerous financial centres around the globe, or by having direct relationships with *custodians* in the relevant financial centres. The use of custodians is described later in this chapter.

Pension Funds. The accumulated pension contributions paid by companies on behalf of their employees and by individuals are invested by the pension fund in order to maximise the available funds for distribution to existing and future pensioners.

In a similar way to the method of operation of a mutual fund manager, a pension fund manager normally operates a number of funds from which the beneficiary can select the most appropriate fund into which the pension contributions are invested.

According to the risk profile of the individual fund, the pension fund manager invests in equities and bonds of his choosing. The risk of the total pension fund value being adversely affected whenever there is a significant fall in the market value of a single bond or share is reduced due to the diversity of investments within the fund.

Pension funds may choose to have direct relationships with local custodians or to utilise a global custodian for the settlement of trades.

Insurance Companies. The premiums paid to insurance companies to cover events which may occur are invested in equities and bonds in an attempt to maximise the return on investments relative to the amounts paid out by insurance companies to satisfy claims made by the policyholders.

Insurance companies can often make zero profit on the premiums received from the insured parties relevant to the amounts of cash paid in insurance claims; this is known as underwriting profit or loss. However, overall trading profit can be made by insurance companies by virtue of their securities investment decisions.

In the UK, the Department of Trade and Industry (DTI) sets rules regarding securities investments by insurance companies, including:

- a maximum percentage that may be invested in equities,
- a minimum amount in readily available funds, and
- the balance able to be used for long-term investments

with the intention of ensuring that insurance companies have sufficient funds to pay claims by policyholders.

As for other institutional investors, insurance companies may choose to have direct relationships with local custodians or to utilise a global custodian for the settlement of trades.

Other Institutional Investors. The following institutions are also active in the securities marketplace:

- hedge funds—funds belonging to very wealthy ('high net worth') individuals are invested in securities, typically on a huge scale and using a very diverse range of investment strategies;
- charities—charitable organisations invest the donations received into securities, in order to grow the available funds prior to distribution to good causes.

Summary for All Institutional Investors. Institutional investors have the power to select the agents and STOs with whom they trade; the quantity and size of orders and trades originated by institutional investors forms a significant portion of business transacted across the world's securities markets. They choose to trade with certain STOs on factors such as:

- execution performance—the speed of response to requests to buy and sell securities, and the competitiveness of prices;

- the research information provided—STOs employ analysts who study securities markets, companies and securities and provide forecasts and investment advice to institutional clients;
- operational performance—the speed and accuracy of applying post-trade confirmation of trades to the institutional client within the agreed timeframe (amongst other services). At the time of writing, some STOs are developing client service teams to give maximum focus to the operational service provided to institutional clients.

Institutional clients demand a high quality service from STOs, and if the service provided to the institutional client falls below an acceptable level the institutional client may cease trading with a specific STO and take its business to a competitor.

Some institutional clients place the responsibility for holding securities and for the settlement of purchases and sales in the hands of a *global custodian*; these organisations typically have a network of custodians in the various financial centres around the globe. Under these circumstances, following the execution of a trade the institutional client issues a *settlement instruction* to only one destination, its global custodian, who in turn instructs the appropriate local custodian (according to the security type) to carry out *settlement*.

Other institutional clients may choose to have direct arrangements with custodians located in the normal place of settlement of the security type; for instance, New Zealand equities will be held at the institutional client's Wellington custodian, and the Paris custodian will hold French Government bonds. Following purchases and sales of securities, the institutional client issues a *settlement instruction* direct to the relevant custodian to perform settlement (the exchange of securities and cash) on the institutional client's behalf. Following settlement, the resultant securities and cash positions will be updated by the custodian and reported to the institutional client.

2.3.3   Agents for Investors

There exists in the securities marketplace a type of company that can be categorised as acting in an agency or intermediary capacity, in relation to buying and selling securities on behalf of its clients (not on its own behalf) who may be individuals only, institutions only, or a combination of both. Types of companies operating business in this fashion include those listed within Table 2.5, earlier in this chapter.

Besides providing a trading (or dealing) service to their clients, these companies may also operate as custodians of their clients' securities, for which the client may be charged a fee.

These companies effect the order and execution process differently, according to whether the client (individual or institutional) account operates on a discretionary basis or on an advisory or execution only basis. Where the client account operates on a discretionary basis, the agent is the originator of the order and places the order with the marketplace on the client's behalf. Conversely, where the client account operates on an advisory or execution only basis, the agent carries out requests to trade by receiving orders from its clients and forwarding the order to the marketplace where an STO may execute the order if the terms of the order are reasonable (e.g. the price at which the client wishes to buy is not too low relevant to the current market price).

Figure 2.4 looks at the order and execution process from the agent's perspective, where the client has originated the order.

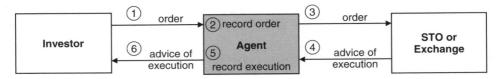

Figure 2.4   The securities marketplace: agents for investors

Step 1: the individual or institutional investor (the agent's client) places an order to buy or sell securities with the agent.

Step 2: the agent records the details of the order.

Step 3: the agent forwards the order to an STO or to the relevant stock exchange that acts on the order and the trade is executed.

Step 4: the trader or exchange sends an advice of execution to the agent.

Step 5: the agent records the details of the trade.

Step 6: the agent issues an advice of execution to the client.

Historically, the method of a client placing orders with an agent has been by letter, fax or telephone. The advent of the World Wide Web has allowed brokers to develop systems enabling individual investors to place orders via the Internet; consequently in many parts of the globe competition between Internet brokers to provide these services to new investors has become intense.

Companies acting as agents are required by law to pass on to their clients the price as executed by the third party within the marketplace; the agent's objective is to make profit by charging *commission* to the client placing the order, for successfully executing the client's order. Agents are not allowed to buy securities at one price and 'mark-up' (increase) the price before selling to the client so as to make profit on the traded price, or to decrease the price when the client is selling.

Prior to the *deregulation* of markets or financial centres, scales of commission were typically fixed by the local stock exchange and agents were not allowed to charge a lower or higher rate of commission to their clients. However, following deregulation over the last 20–30 years where 'free and open' markets have become the norm, agents can decide upon the scales of commission which they charge their clients. An agent may choose, for instance, to charge a lower percentage or scale of commission to institutional investors than to individuals, as the average size of a trade for an institution is normally much larger than for an individual.

Table 2.6 is an example of an agent's scale of commission for individual investors, showing that this agent is prepared to charge a lesser rate of commission where orders are placed over the Internet, reflecting the agent's reduced processing costs due to minimal manual intervention. If the size of the trade is very small, agents usually charge a minimum commission amount.

Competition Between 'Discretionary' Agents

Those agents responsible for operating their clients' accounts on a discretionary basis are responsible for the management of investors' securities in order to maximise the return for the investor. Such companies employ investment managers who are skilled at making

Table 2.6

Gross cash value of trade (GBP)	Commission (GBP)	
	Order via Internet	Order via telephone
0–1000	12.00	20.00
1001–2000	15.00	24.00
2001–4000	24.00	36.00
4001–20,000	36.00	54.00
Over 20,000	50.00	75.00

good investment decisions on behalf of their clients. The investment strategy employed by the agent (for example low, medium or high risk) is dependent upon the client's particular investment objectives, for instance whether the aim is to better the return on a specific stock market index.

Agents conducting business with this focus are under significant pressure to outperform their competitors and to keep costs to a minimum, as the client can quite simply move his portfolio if underperformance has occurred or if costs are too high. Investors utilising the services of discretionary agents may choose to place their securities in the hands of one or more discretionary agents in the hope and expectation that the value of their portfolio will be maximised over a given period and in order to compare performance.

Such agents make profit by charging commission on trades and by charging periodic fees based on the market value of an investor's portfolio of securities.

2.3.4 Securities Trading Organisations

The term *securities trading organisation* is a collective term that describes those who reside within the securities marketplace, namely traders and market makers, who (on their own behalf) sell securities to or buy securities from:

- agents acting on behalf of individuals or institutional investors
- individuals (usually of high net worth) and institutional investors who have opted not to use an agent
- other STOs such as traders and market makers

(and does not refer to those who act as agents or intermediaries between investors and those who reside within the marketplace).

Figure 2.5 illustrates the order and execution process from the STO's perspective, where the STO will communicate:

- with an agent acting on behalf of the investor (situation A);
- directly with the investor (situation B).

Situation A: the STO receives the order from an agent, executes the order, records the detail of the execution and communicates the details of the execution to the agent (who in turn will apply commission to the trade and communicate the details of the execution to the investor). Note that the STO will not normally be made aware of the identity of the investor. The STO's client in this situation is the agent.

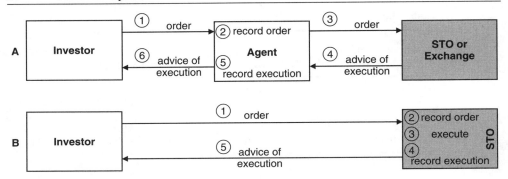

Figure 2.5   The securities marketplace: securities trading organisations

Situation B: the STO receives an order directly from the investor, and following execution and recording of the execution details, communicates the execution details directly to the investor. The STO's client in this situation is the investor.

It is common to find that within the same group of companies providing financial services, one company may exist that is an agent for investors (typically having both individual and institutional investors as clients) and a separate company may exist that is an STO (typically having institutional investors and agents for investors as clients). This structure allows the group of companies to give the necessary focus to its clients, according to the type of client.

Traders

Traders (employed by STOs within the securities marketplace) act in a similar manner to a street market trader, in that their intention is to buy securities at a low price and sell at a higher price in order to generate a profit for the STO.

Traders execute trades with different types of counterparty, including:

- institutional clients
- agents acting on behalf of individuals or institutional clients
- *market makers*
- other STOs.

Unlike an agent who must pass on the price at which a trade has been executed, a trader sells securities at a price that may well be different from the price at which the securities were purchased. Where this is the case, the trader is carrying out securities trading (in the name of the STO) on a *proprietary* basis and is said to have traded 'as principal' or 'on a principal basis', whereas an agent conducts trading 'as agent' or 'on an agency basis'.

For example, a trader may start a given day with a zero trading position (assume there have been no prior trades) in a specific security, say HSBC shares; at 8.00am, he feels that this share looks cheap so decides to buy 10,000 shares at a price of Hong Kong Dollars (HKD) 105.50 per share, from another STO. At 8.20am, an institutional client telephones with an order to buy the same security; a trade is executed and the trader sells 10,000 HSBC shares at a price of HKD 106.75 per share, thereby generating a profit of HKD 1.25 per share, equating to HKD 12,500.00 trading profit. Both the purchase and the sale have been executed by the trader on a 'principal' basis as he was acting on his own behalf and not acting as an agent for an investor (although he traded with an investor).

The capacity in which an STO carries out its trading is of fundamental concern to the regulatory authorities within securities marketplaces around the globe in order to protect investors from exploitation by unscrupulous STOs. Therefore it is extremely important for STOs to record correctly the capacity in which they have in fact executed each trade; a trade executed by a trader with an institutional client on a principal basis but reported by the STO as having been executed on an agency basis may mean that the institutional client has not received a fair market price. A false statement by an STO as to the capacity in which it has traded is therefore deemed against regulations.

It is perfectly normal for STOs to invest for their own account and to maintain positive (also known as 'long') trading positions in hundreds or thousands of different securities at any one point in time. The trading position in some securities may have been acquired one minute ago, last month or even years ago and may be the result of one or many purchases and sales. In many markets around the globe, traders are allowed to sell securities that they do not own, with the intention of buying at a later time and at a lower price in order to generate profit for themselves. This is known as 'short selling' and results in a negative trading position.

Table 2.7 is an example of a trader's trading position showing a current trading position of +23.50 million shares, made up of a number of trades (assume today to be 14th December). Being in a positive securities trading position means that there will be a negative cash position (providing settlement of trades has occurred), but as STOs tend not to have a sufficient store of their own cash that can be used to pay for purchases and positive trading positions, the funds will need to be borrowed. The cost of borrowing cash has a detrimental impact on trading profit, so a vitally important activity is that of borrowing funds at the cheapest rate of interest. This topic is explored in Chapter 23.

Table 2.7

Operation	Quantity	Trade date	Trading position
		6th January	zero
Buy	10,000,000	7th January	+10,000,000
Buy	5,000,000	2nd February	+15,000,000
Sell	13,000,000	21st July	+2,000,000
Buy	40,000,000	16th August	+42,000,000
Sell	6,000,000	14th September	+36,000,000
Sell	12,500,000	29th September	+23,500,000

Unlike arrangements made by some institutional investors regarding the use of global custodians, most STOs hold securities representing their positive trading positions directly with custodians located in the normal place of settlement of the security. Following purchases and sales of securities, the STO issues a *settlement instruction* to its relevant custodian to perform settlement on the STO's behalf. Following settlement, the resultant securities and cash positions will be updated by the custodian and reported to the STO, which will then need to update its internal *books and records* in order to maintain an accurate picture of outstanding trades with *counterparties* and settled securities and cash positions in the outside world, in turn enabling the STO to remain in control of its business.

Market Makers

Market makers act in a similar fashion to traders in that they typically execute trades (in the name of the STO) on a principal basis, hold positive trading positions, may sell short and will need to borrow cash to fund their positive trading positions.

The fundamental difference between traders and market makers is as follows:

- a trader may decide to trade in some securities and not in others, or decide to trade or not to trade according to the price at which a prospective counterparty wishes to trade;
- a market maker publicises the price at which he is prepared to trade specific securities of his choosing (typically via computer screens viewable by potential investors and other STOs). Table 2.8 illustrates the type of information publicised by a market maker in equities, and Table 2.9 correspondingly for bonds.

Table 2.8

Issue	Bid price	Offer price
ABC Corporation shares	USD 12.24	USD 12.28
LMN plc ordinary shares	NZD 31.81	NZD 31.87

Table 2.9

Issue	Bid price	Offer price
Denmark 6.75% bonds 1st May 2020	98.40%	98.50%
World Bank 7.0% bonds 15th March 2015	96.85%	96.90%

Note that:

- the bid price is the price at which the market maker is prepared to buy from, and
- the offer price is the price at which the market maker is prepared to sell to

prospective counterparties. The difference between the bid and offer prices is known as the 'spread'.

The exchange/market for the relevant securities grants the STO the right to be a market maker and requires that the market maker behave according to rules set for market makers. These rules normally include the times each day at which the publication of prices must occur, and the method of publication.

Note that within some STOs there are both traders and market makers, their trading activity often differentiated by the securities in which they trade.

Settlement arrangements are normally the same as for traders, with market makers tending to have direct relationships with local custodians.

2.4 REGULATORS

Regulatory authorities exist within the securities industry in order to ensure that the business undertaken within the securities marketplace is conducted in a proper manner for the protection of investors and those within the marketplace.

The type of activity with which regulators are involved includes:

- assessing the suitability of STOs to conduct their business;
- overseeing the disclosure by *issuers* of meaningful information to enable investors (individual or institutional) to make sound investment decisions;
- monitoring the business undertaken by STOs, investment advisers and fund managers;
- guarding against criminal action such as *insider trading*;
- enforcement of laws, which brings about prosecution of violations of securities laws.

All transactions undertaken by STOs are normally required to be reported to the STO's local regulator within a specified timeframe, either during or at the end of the trade date. The regulator scrutinises the transactions for any trading activity that appears abnormal, such as the buying or selling of securities in a company by a person who has information that is not yet in the public domain.

Table 2.10

Country	Regulatory authority
Australia	Australian Securities and Investments Commission
Canada	Ontario Securities Commission
France	Commission des Operations de Bourse
Hong Kong	Securities & Futures Commission
India	Securities & Exchange Board of India (SEBI)
UK	Financial Services Authority
USA	Securities & Exchange Commission

Table 2.10 lists examples of regulatory authorities in various financial centres around the globe. The topic of reporting trades to regulators is described in Chapter 15.

2.5 CUSTODIANS

With much of today's securities trading by investors, agents and STOs being executed in securities originating overseas, the services offered by custodians are normally used to provide greater efficiency and less risk in relation to trade *settlement* and the holding of securities in *safe custody* on behalf of the owner.

When securities are bought or sold, it is normal for institutional clients, agents for investors and STOs to utilise the services of their specific custodian in the financial centre relating to the traded security.

An STO, for example, is likely to have set up arrangements with numerous custodians in various financial centres around the globe. When buying or selling individual securities, the STO will require the settlement of the transaction to be effected through its appropriate custodian within the relevant financial centre. This is illustrated in Table 2.11. Following execution of a trade, an STO must decide which of its custodians is appropriate in order

Table 2.11

Individual Security	Origin of Security	Relevant Financial Centre	Relevant Custodian
Qantas Shares	Australia	Sydney	Custodian A, Sydney
Japanese Gov't 3.8% bonds 15th April 2018	Japan	Tokyo	Custodian E, Tokyo
HSBC Shares	Hong Kong	Hong Kong	Custodian H, HK
U.S. Treasury 5.0% bonds 1st May 2015	USA	New York	Custodian L, NY
Marks & Spencer Shares	UK	London	Custodian P, London

to carry out the settlement of the trade, then issue a message (commonly known as a *settlement instruction*) to the relevant custodian.

The settlement instruction contains details of the trade, and tells the custodian to deliver or receive securities, and to pay or receive cash on the value date of the trade. The counterparty to the trade (typically an institutional client, agent for investors or another STO) will also need to issue a settlement instruction to its custodian within the relevant financial centre.

Having each received a settlement instruction, the seller's and the buyer's custodians will attempt to match the details. Once a match has been achieved, on value date the securities and cash are exchanged and the resultant increase or decrease in securities and cash is recorded by the STO's custodian against the STO's securities and cash accounts maintained by the custodian. Note that although the intention is to settle trades on value date, *settlement failure* can occur; the reasons for this are explained in Chapter 19.

Table 2.12

Term	Description
Custodian	An organisation that holds securities and (usually) cash on its clients' behalf; and may effect settlement of trades on its clients' behalf
Global custodian	As per custodian above, but has a network of local (or sub-) custodians that hold securities and cash and effect settlement of trades on behalf of the global custodian
Local custodian	A custodian that operates within a specific financial centre
Sub-custodian	A custodian within a global custodian's network of custodians
Central Securities Depository (CSD)	An organisation that holds securities, normally in *book-entry* form; usually the ultimate place of settlement, effected through book-entry transfer.
National Central Securities Depository (NCSD)	A CSD that handles domestic securities of the country in which it is located
International Central Securities Depository (ICSD)	A CSD that handles domestic and international securities. Only two organisations are recognised as ICSDs, namely Clearstream (Luxembourg) and Euroclear (Brussels)
Settlement agent	An organisation that effects the exchange of securities and cash on behalf of its clients; resultant securities and cash balances may or may not be held

Where the custodian holds securities and cash on behalf of the STO, the custodian is responsible for:

- holding the securities in safekeeping on behalf of the account holder,
- holding cash balances in safekeeping on behalf of the account holder,
- reporting of securities and cash positions to the STO, and
- collection of benefits (e.g. income payments) falling due on the securities,

amongst other services.

Various terms are used to describe those involved in the provision of trade settlement and custodial services on behalf of those that execute trades; such terms include those listed in Table 2.12, each of which performs a specific custodian's role. <u>Note: For ease of reference, the term custodian is used throughout this book.</u>

This topic is described fully in Chapter 17.

2.6   OTHER PARTICIPANTS IN THE SECURITIES MARKETPLACE

Besides those already mentioned in this chapter, a number of other individuals and organisations are involved within the securities marketplace, including (but not limited to) those listed in Table 2.13. Each of these participants will be described at the appropriate points within subsequent chapters.

Table 2.13

Participant	Description
Securities data providers	Organisations that provide details of new and existing securities to various industry participants
Registrars	Organisations that record share ownership and changes in share ownership on behalf of the *issuer*
Coupon-paying agents	Organisations that make payments of bond interest on behalf of the issuer
Salespeople	Individuals employed by STOs who are the primary contact between the STO and institutional clients
Trade-matching services	Organisations that provide software to compare sellers' and buyers' trade details
Settlement instruction communication mechanisms	Organisations that provide communications software to link those who trade to those who settle trades

2.7   GLOBALISATION

In the ca. 200 years since the first securities marketplaces originated, new exchanges/ markets have been formed in many parts of the globe. The operating methods of each marketplace have evolved according to local law and the needs of the local participants, and although the aims and objectives of all markets are broadly similar, each market has its own way of operating. This is particularly apparent in the area of trade settlement and specific examples will be highlighted at appropriate points in the following chapters.

However, in the last decade of the 20th century, trading and settlement practices in different marketplaces have become more common, whilst institutional investors have increasingly viewed investment in other countries and in other continents as the norm; investment by individuals has never been easier, whilst participants within securities marketplaces in numerous financial centres around the globe have moved towards closer working relationships.

The relaxation of government controls (commonly known as *deregulation*) within securities marketplaces, and the significant involvement of Information Technology (IT), have played a major role in enabling the securities industry to achieve the expansion to date. This has been noticeable in areas such as:

- the increasing openness and availability of company information, securities prices and analytics which has widened investment opportunities for individual investors;
- the use of the Internet for order placement by individual investors, bringing investing into the home;
- methods of *trade execution* becoming more open and easy to use;
- the move towards *straight-through processing* of trades within the securities industry;
- the international nature of everyday trading (commonly known as *cross-border trading*).

Today, it is perfectly normal for an investor based in any financial centre to trade in equities and bonds where the marketplace for the security is the other side of the globe.

For example, at 3.00pm (EST) an institutional client (a mutual fund manager) based in Boston places an order with his New York-based stockbroker (who will act as the agent for the transaction) to sell 20 million ST (Singapore) shares. By 3.15pm the stockbroker routes the order to his Singapore office, which (overnight New York time) agrees to buy the security at the order price.

The detail of the trade execution is conveyed via the reverse route by which the order was placed and each party to the transaction will need to record the details of their particular trade (or trades):

- the mutual fund manager will need to record a sale to the New York stockbroker, inclusive of commission payable;
- the New York stockbroker will need to record a purchase from the mutual fund manager and a sale to his Singapore office. Note that this pair of trades must be recorded as agency trades where the price of both purchase and sale is identical, but with the institutional client being charged commission. This will result in a zero trading position for the stockbroker;
- the stockbroker's Singapore office will need to record a purchase from the New York office (not the institutional client) at the agreed price. Note that this transaction will create a positive trading position in the specific security and a principal trade will be recorded as it was the decision of the Singapore office to trade at the order price and to increase their trading position. The Singapore office was not acting in an agency capacity.

After this point, the stockbroker's Singapore office may prefer to sell all 20 million ST shares immediately (preferably at a higher price), sell some shares immediately and the remainder at a later date, or retain all 20 million shares over the long term.

Two days later the Singapore office receives an order from its Wellington, New Zealand branch (acting as agent for an asset manager who in turn is acting as agent for a pension fund) to buy 12 million ST shares at a specified price. The Singapore office agrees to execute the trade, reports the execution to its Wellington office and records the details of its sale (on a principal basis) in its internal books and records. The result of these trades is that the Singapore office now has a positive trading position of 8 million shares and has made a profit or loss on the 12 million shares sold.

Confidentiality is paramount and each party will know only the identity of the parties with whom it has traded. Once each party has recorded the trade detail, for each organisation the focus changes to the many operational activities that occur after trade execution, including the settlement of each trade.

2.8 SUMMARY

Globally, the securities industry is vast in terms of those involved, from investing individuals through to large corporations and governments. Although all marketplaces exist for the same basic reasons (as described within this chapter), each has evolved in ways that suit their local environment.

However, regardless of the marketplaces in which trading and settlement are conducted, from an STO's perspective the operational objectives tend not to differ: the STO aims to manage its business in as cost-effective and risk-free a manner as possible, whilst ensuring its clients are given a top quality service.

As the pace of change within the industry increases (described throughout the book and in particular in Chapter 29), so will the challenges of STOs being able to meet their objectives.

3
Bringing Securities to the Marketplace

3.1 INTRODUCTION

An important component to understanding how the securities marketplace works as a whole is to understand how securities are brought to the marketplace, and the impact of this on the various operations undertaken by the STO, for example the *settlement* of transactions. The terms used to describe securities undergoing this process include 'when issued', 'new issues' and 'IPO' (Initial Public Offering).

The majority of trades executed in securities marketplaces around the globe on a daily basis are in securities that have been brought to the marketplace at a prior point in time. Securities that fall into this category are said to be trading in the *secondary market*.

Securities that are in the process of being brought to the marketplace are said to be trading in the *primary market* and usually this activity accounts for a much lower percentage of daily trading volume than that conducted in the secondary market. The following describes the activity within the primary market.

3.2 METHODS OF ISSUING SECURITIES

The process of bringing securities to the marketplace is one that requires specialist skills. An *issuer* (refer to Chapter 2) of securities typically operates in an industry other than the securities industry and consequently does not possess the expertise to manage the process efficiently.

It is therefore common practice for issuers to appoint specialists in the field of issuing securities; these experts typically reside within the corporate finance departments of international investment banks. Their responsibility is to provide their client (the issuer) with the most suitable means of raising cash given the prevailing market conditions, in order to expand their business, often resulting in new issues of *equity* or *debt*. The generic name given to those who advise issuers, distribute the securities to investors and ensure that the issuer receives the necessary cash at the agreed time is *lead manager*. For providing this service and expertise, the lead manager (plus other managers that support the issuance of the security) receives a fee from the issuer.

Various methods exist for issuing securities, dependent upon whether the issue is equity or debt and the historic practices within the financial centre in which the issue is launched. In most cases the issuer will publish a *prospectus* that details:

- the terms of the issue, such as
  - quantity of shares or bonds being issued
  - the issue price
- a description of the company's activities
- the reasons for raising the cash

- the financial history of the company
- the debt or ownership changes the issue will create

and a statement by independent accountants that verifies the data contained within the prospectus (as part of the legal requirement for a company producing a prospectus). Prospectuses provide a means for potential investors to become better informed prior to making an investment decision.

3.2.1   Methods of Issuing Bonds

Two of the methods used for issuing bonds are described below.

Auction

The US Treasury and the Bank of England (for example), on behalf of their respective governments, issue bonds via auction where the securities are sold to the highest bidders.

Syndication

Bonds are often issued by a method known as syndication, where the lead manager forms a consortium, usually with a number of banks or STOs who agree to take a percentage of the issue and work together to promote the distribution of the bond to investors. Such issues are explained in more detail later in this chapter.

3.2.2   Methods of Issuing Equity

The most common methods of issuing equity (also known as a flotation) are described below.

Initial Public Offering/Public Offer for Sale

An equity issue may be offered to potential investors by the issuer placing advertisements in the financial and national press and by the publication of a prospectus. In some markets it is usual for a syndicate of STOs to receive share allotments from the lead manager (on behalf of the issuer) and then to allot some or all of the shares to their clients. Such issues are commonly known as IPOs.

Alternatively, for some issues the public can apply for shares directly to the issuer; this style of issuance is known as a Public Offer for Sale and will be explained in more detail later in this chapter.

Private Placement

Equities can also be issued restrictively by targeting the offer of shares to a select group of institutional investors, such as pension funds and insurance companies; such issues are not offered to the public directly.

Note that a bond issued through the syndication process and an equity issued via public offer for sale will be used to illustrate the securities issue process and the operational implications. This will be achieved by initially outlining the characteristics of the issue type, followed by an example of the typical interaction between the issuer, market participants and investors, to bring the security to the marketplace.

3.3   BOND ISSUES VIA SYNDICATION

In order to focus on the typical steps involved in the issuance of a bond, the example of a bond issued via the syndication process will be used.

3.3.1   Characteristics of a Bond Issued by Syndication

Figure 3.1 highlights the terminology and an example timeline relating to a bond issued by syndication.

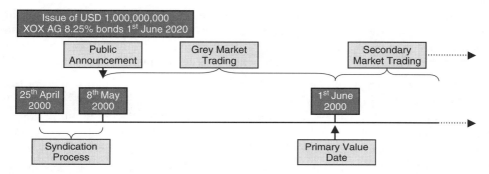

Figure 3.1   Example timeline of a bond issued via the syndication process.

Syndication

The lead manager, operating on behalf of the issuer, invites other STOs to participate in the launch of the new issue; when formed, the group of STOs is known as the syndicate.

Each syndicate member is allotted an agreed quantity of bonds and underwrites (guarantees) to pay the agreed cash value of the allotted bonds, on the *primary value date* (see below). This usually occurs prior to the public announcement date of the issue and its terms. The members of the syndicate are paid a fee for their participation, through being allotted the bonds at a discounted price from the offer price.

The generic term that describes the official distribution of bonds via the syndication process is the *primary market*.

Grey Market

The buying and selling of bonds prior to the primary value date is known as *grey market trading*.

Primary Value Date

From an operational perspective, a key milestone in the issue process is that of the *primary value date* (also known as the closing date), as it is usually at this point that the decision as to whether to proceed with the issue is made. Therefore until this date arrives, there is no guarantee that the bond will be brought to the marketplace, despite the fact that trading in the bond may have occurred.

On the primary value date, a signing ceremony is normally held between the issuer, the lead manager and syndicate members involved in the launch of the new issue; at this time the issuer must finally decide whether to proceed with the issue or not. If the issuer's circumstances have changed or market conditions have become less favourable to issuing bonds, the issuer may decide not to proceed with the issue. The timing of this decision therefore requires that the syndication process and trading conducted prior to the primary value date are all undertaken in anticipation of the bond being issued.

Although a rare occurence, should the issuer decide not to proceed, all trades will be declared null and void as the bond will simply not exist and there are therefore no goods to exchange. For trading conducted prior to the primary value date, to acknowledge the possibility that trades may be cancelled in the event of a decision not to proceed with the issue, *trade confirmations* (refer to 'Gaining Agreement to Trade Detail with the Counterparty' in Chapter 4) issued by STOs to counterparties contain wording relating to the security such as 'if, as and when issued'. Such wording is not contained on trade confirmations relating to securities that have been brought to the marketplace previously.

Where the decision is made to proceed with the issue, on the primary value date:

- the syndicate members will be required to make payment to the lead manager for their portion of the bond issue,
- the lead manager will pay the cash to the issuer, less the fee due to the underwriters
- a document of ownership in the issue will be made available, normally in the form of a global certificate; this is explained later in this chapter and in Chapter 6.

The value date of all trades in the new issue is normally the primary value date. On this date the delivery of securities and payment of cash occurs and STOs need to ensure that all trades executed in the weeks prior to the primary value date do not have an earlier value date, as it is not possible to settle earlier.

An individual STO may participate in the issue by:

1. being a member of the syndicate, thereby receiving an allotment and (possibly) selling some or all the allotment to its institutional clients or to other STOs, and
2. buying and selling in the grey market,

which will require the details of the allotment and subsequent sales (1) and purchases and sales (2) to be recorded within the STO's books and records, and for a number of operational activities to occur, resulting in the settlement of each trade.

Secondary Market Trading

Secondary market trading refers to the trading of securities after the successful launch of the security. Whereas primary market trading may last for a number of weeks at most (until the primary value date is reached), secondary market trading relates to all trading beyond the primary value date, until the bond matures.

3.3.2   Structure of a Bond Issued by Syndication

Figure 3.2 represents the typical characters involved with the process of issuing a bond via the syndication method. The following are fictitious;

- the issuer (XOX AG)
- the bond issue (XOX AG, 8.25% bonds 1st June 2020)
- the lead manager entitled Bond & Equity Issuing (BEI)
- the syndicate member and STO entitled World Securities International, London (WSIL).

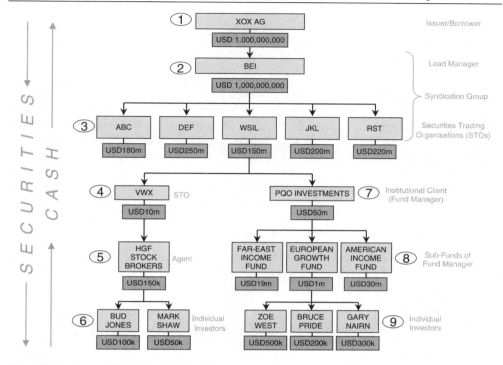

Figure 3.2   Issue of USD 1,000,000,000 XOX AG 8.25% bonds 1st June 2020

The Issue

XOX AG wish to raise USD 1,000,000,000.00 in cash by issuing a bond which will pay a fixed rate of interest (also known as *coupon*) of 8.25% on a fixed date of 1st June every year beginning in 2001 and ending in 2020; the bond will mature on 1st June 2020 at which point the capital sum will be repaid by XOX to the bondholders at that time. The primary value date of the issue is 1st June 2000, therefore the first payment of coupon is due exactly 12 months after the investors have paid for the bonds and XOX has received the cash.

The coupon rate payable is a major factor in issuing a bond; clearly XOX would not wish to issue a bond with a coupon rate which is so low that it attracts few or no investors, neither would XOX want to pay too much interest over the 20-year life of the bond. The issuer will ensure that the rate of interest it pays on the bond is competitive, both from its perspective of borrowing cash and from the potential investor's perspective, who will typically consider all forms of investment (including, for example, the *money market*) prior to actual investment.

The maturity date of the bond is likely to relate to the period over which the issuer requires capital to fund its expansion project (refer to Chapter 2), in this case 20 years.

Note that in Figure 3.2, the amounts stated beneath each character represent the quantity of bonds being exchanged; for example, at the top of the diagram, XOX have effectively sold USD 1,000,000,000.00 bonds to BEI, who in turn sell USD 150 million bonds to WSIL, who sell USD 50 million bonds to PQO Investments, etc.

Certificates representing the bond issue (refer to Chapter 6) are denominated as follows: half of the issue is in USD 5000.00 and the remainder in USD 20,000.00 denominations.

The entire issue will therefore be made up of:

- 100,000 certificates denominated in USD 5000.00 (total USD 500 million) and
- 25,000 certificates of USD 20,000.00 (total USD 500 million)

requiring that purchases and sales of the bond are executed as a minimum and multiples of the smallest denomination, otherwise it would be impossible to deliver the bond from seller to buyer, as it is not possible to split a bond into a quantity that is less than the lowest denomination. These amounts are known as the bond nominal value or face value. At issuance of the bond, usually a global certificate is created and placed with a common depository. Where individual ('definitive') certificates are due to be issued for a particular issue, these are usually issued after a specified 'seasoning' period. When sold, such certificates are delivered to the buyer as per the issued denominations; following issue of the bond, the issuer typically does not have sight of the bond again until *maturity date*. Today, for some types of bonds, certificates are not always printed and issued. These aspects of securities will be explored in Chapter 6.

Bond Face Value and Price

When a bank note with a face value of, for instance, USD 10.00 is first put into circulation it is worth exactly USD 10.00 and it could be said to have a price of 100%. After being put into circulation the note retains its market price and its market value remains at USD 10.00.

By comparison, a bond has a face value of, for instance, USD 5000.00 that is issued at a specified price, commonly 100%, and therefore the cash value is USD 5000.00. After its launch, the face value of the bond remains constant, but the price is subject to fluctuation according to market forces. For example, a purchase of a USD 5000.00 bond with a current market price of 101.50% would require the buyer to pay USD 5075.00, but a current market price of 98.25% would require the buyer to pay USD 4912.50. A bond priced at 100% is said to be trading at par; where the price is above par, bonds are said to be trading at a premium, and where below par, trading at a discount. The price of the XOX bond at launch was 100%.

The Issuer (No. 1 in Figure 3.2)

XOX are described as being the *issuer* of bonds as well as the *borrower* of cash; they will issue USD 1,000,000,000.00 of bonds against receipt of the same amount in cash, less fees due to the underwriters. XOX will require a guarantee from the lead manager that they will receive the cash amount on the primary value date.

The Lead Manager (No. 2)

The issuer appoints BEI as lead manager, who:

- forms a syndicate of STOs,
- guarantees full payment to the issuer on the primary value date, 1st June 2000,
- receives a fee from the issuer.

Wide distribution of the issue is effected through the members of the syndicate agreeing to acquire a portion of the issue.

Securities Trading Organisations/Syndicate Members (No. 3)

Each member of the syndication group guarantees to the lead manager that under any circumstances they will pay for their portion of bonds on the primary value date. At this point and prior to selling, each of the syndicate members has a risk that the market value of their bonds may fall. However, an STO may take the view that this bond issue will be a good investment and consequently choose to invest in all or some of the bonds over the long (years), medium (months) or short (days or weeks) term, or may decide to sell all or some of the bonds immediately.

Figure 3.2 shows that WSIL took an allotment of USD 150 million of bonds from the lead manager and opted to sell USD 10 million to VWX and USD 50 million to PQO Investments. WSIL's unsold quantity of bonds will be held as a trading position pending further sales.

Securities Trading Organisations (Non-syndicate Members) (No. 4)

VWX is an STO that has purchased USD 10 million of bonds from WSIL and who have sold USD 150,000.00 bonds to HGF Stockbrokers. VWX is shown as an example of an STO that is not part of the syndication group but who chose to invest in the XOX bond and then to sell some bonds to another entity.

Agent for Investors (No. 5)

HGF Stockbrokers have purchased the bonds in order to satisfy requests (orders) from their clients to buy the XOX bond. HGF is acting in an agency capacity, meaning that purchases and sales of securities that they effect are executed only on behalf of their clients, not on their own behalf.

Individual Investors (No. 6)

Bud Jones and Mark Shaw have become aware that XOX have issued a bond paying 8.25% coupon and have placed an order with their bank's securities arm, HGF Stockbrokers, resulting in an executed trade. This is an example of individuals investing directly in a specific security, as opposed to indirectly (see below).

Institutional Clients (No. 7)

PQO Investments is a fund manager (also known as a mutual fund or unit trust manager) which invests on behalf of its own range of funds, that in turn invest for their clients, normally individuals. Within the securities marketplace, mutual funds are part of an unofficial group of investors collectively referred to as *institutional investors*. When a mutual fund manager executes trades, it usually does so on behalf of one or many of its underlying funds.

Funds of Institutional Clients (No. 8)

Prior to or following the purchase of securities, it is usual for the mutual fund manager to allocate internally the full quantity of the purchase into smaller allotments for distribution amongst its funds.

Individual Investors (No. 9)

The individual investor chooses to invest in a specific fund managed by a fund manager; it is the fund manager who usually makes the decisions as to the securities in which the fund will invest (within the fund's defined investment parameters). Consequently, the investor normally has no influence over the fund's specific investment decisions. Therefore, when the fund manager decides to buy a security he does so on behalf of the investors in the particular fund, but the investors are typically unaware of the specific securities in which the fund has invested, on a day-to-day basis. This is an example of individuals investing indirectly in a specific security, as opposed to directly (see above).

3.3.3 Settlement

As mentioned in Chapter 1, the STOs' preferred method of exchanging securities and cash is by *DvP*, where neither the seller nor the buyer are at risk as the seller's security will not be delivered unless the buyer is able to pay, and the buyer's cash will not be paid unless the seller is able to deliver the securities.

For each sale and purchase of securities, each of the parties involved will normally require delivery and payment to occur at their (relevant) custodian, according to the type of security. Sellers and buyers will need to swap details of one another's custodians, as the seller's and buyer's custodians will need to verify (through a *settlement instruction* matching process) the details of the intended delivery of securities and payment of cash, prior to settlement occurring.

In the case of the XOX bond issue used in the previous section, the lead manager would ask syndicate members where they wished to take delivery of the bonds. On the primary value date, the bonds will be delivered from the lead manager's custodian to the syndicate member's custodian on a DvP basis. If the syndicate member does not sell the securities, the bonds will remain in the syndicate member's account at the custodian, until they are sold at a later point in time, or until the bonds mature.

Where a syndicate member has sold some or all of the securities it has been allotted, delivery will normally be made from its account at the custodian to the buyer's custodian on a DvP basis. Settlement of sales and purchases will continue in this fashion, until the bonds arrive in the ultimate buyer's custodian account. At any time after the primary value date, that buyer may sell the securities in the secondary market, requiring delivery to the new buyer on a DvP basis.

3.4   EQUITY ISSUES VIA IPO AND PUBLIC OFFER FOR SALE

The majority of new equities are issued by companies, the minority being issued by governments from the sale of state-owned utilities. Different methods exist for issuers to bring equity securities to the marketplace and the investing public, including Initial Public Offerings, Public Offers for Sale and Private Placement (as described earlier in this chapter).

3.4.1   Characteristics of an Initial Public Offering (IPO)

This method, popular in some countries (such as in the US and Canada), is similar to bonds issued via syndication as often:

- a *lead manager* is appointed by the issuer;
- investment banks are invited to *underwrite* a certain percentage of the issue;
- a *syndicate* of underwriters is formed, headed by the lead manager;
- a *prospectus* is published;
- the syndicate members are responsible for distributing shares to investors;
- prior to the primary value date, trading is known as *grey market trading*;
- *secondary market* trading occurs after the initial issuance of the security.

Dependent upon the nature of the issue, institutional investors may be invited (by the syndicate) to invest in the issue and in some cases obtain the majority of shares on offer at the offer price. Individual investors may be able to obtain shares at the offer price via application through their broker.

3.4.2   Characteristics of a Public Offer for Sale

The main characteristic of a Public Offer for Sale is that members of the public may apply for shares directly to the issuer. An issue may be split where a specific proportion of the issue is offered to the public and the remaining portion to institutional investors. In some cases the shares may be offered to overseas investors as well as investors resident in the country of issue.

For the public offer, the share price is normally stated from the outset. For issues with an institutional offer, a minimum price may be set and institutional investors are invited to place bids.

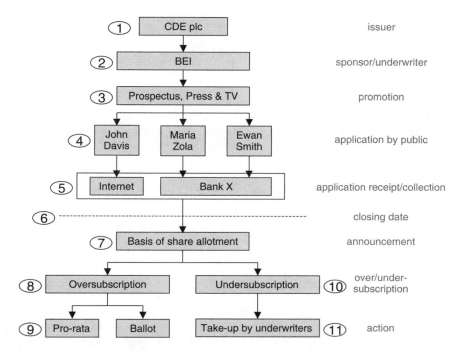

Figure 3.3   Issue of 100,000,000 CDE plc GBP 1.00 Ordinary Shares

Figure 3.3 represents the typical sequence of events relating to a public offer for sale. The following are fictitious; the issuer (CDE plc), the issue (CDE plc GBP 1.00 ordinary shares) and the issuing agent Bond & Equity Issuing (BEI).

The Issue

The owners of CDE plc have decided to undertake a stock market flotation of their company and have met the necessary entry criteria, which includes the soundness and honesty of the directors, the size of the company, a financial statement and the number of shares on offer. The purpose of the flotation is for CDE to raise cash for further investment; CDE wish to raise GBP 50,000,000.00 by the issuance of 100,000,000 GBP 1.00 ordinary shares at a price of GBP 0.50 per share.

Within the title of the shares, the GBP 1.00 is known as the *par value* (or nominal value or face value) and is used in the issuer's internal accounting but has no significance in relation to the market price of the share.

The Issuer (No. 1 in Figure 3.3)

CDE are described as the issuer of shares; as for bond issues, the issuer will require a guarantee from the underwriters that they will receive the amount of cash they wish to raise (less fees due to the underwriters).

The Sponsor/Underwriter (No. 2)

The issuer appoints a sponsor (the equivalent of a lead manager in a bond issued via syndication), normally an investment bank, in order to advise the issuer, promote the issue to prospective investors, and to underwrite the issue.

Promotion (No. 3)

A prospectus is published and is made available to all potential investors, outlining the general terms of the issue and usually containing an application form. In addition, the details of the offer are normally advertised in the national press (incorporating an application form) and for very large issues on the TV.

Application by the Public (No. 4)

For those that wish to apply for the offer, the application form requires the completion of:

- the name and address of the applicant;
- the quantity of shares applied for;
- the application monies payable.

Note that the issuer may stipulate in the terms of the issue the minimum share quantity (and possibly share multiples) that may be applied for. Completed application forms inclusive of application monies must be received by the issuer's appointed agent by a specified deadline.

Application Receipt/Collection (No. 5)

In order to administer the processing of application forms, it is normal practice for a receiving agent to be appointed; for large issues, many locations may be used as receiving points in order to make application by the public as convenient as possible. Application forms may be posted, delivered in person to the receiving agent, or increasingly, application may be made through the applicant's Internet broker.

Closing Date (No. 6)

All applications must be received by a date as specified within the application form; this is known as the closing date.

Share Allotment Announcement (No. 7)

Following the receipt of applications on the closing date, the total quantity of shares applied for is calculated and compared with the total number of shares available for issue. In the event of oversubscription (see below), the basis of share allotments is normally announced shortly after the closing date.

Oversubscription (No. 8)

If the total number of shares applied for exceeds the available quantity, the issue is said to be oversubscribed.

Pro-rata or Ballot (No. 9)

Where oversubscription has occurred, a method of scaling back will need to be applied in order to equalize the quantity of shares applied for versus the available shares. This is normally achieved in one of two ways, either by pro-rata (the proportional reduction of all applications), or by ballot (the random selection of successful applications). Monies relating to unsuccessful or scaled-back applications are refunded to the applicant.

Undersubscription (No. 10)

If the total application quantity is less than the available quantity, the issue is said to be undersubscribed.

Take-up by Underwriters (No. 11)

Where the issue is undersubscribed, the underwriters are obliged to subscribe for the residual quantity of shares, pro-rata to their underwriting commitment.

3.4.3   Registration & Settlement

Public offers for sale are usually not settled on a DvP basis, as applicants are normally required to make payment in advance of receiving the shares.

Following successful application, owners of the new security will have their name and address recorded on the issuer's *register* of holders, by a *registrar* or transfer agent; this topic is explored further within Chapter 6. Where securities are being held in *safe custody* by an agent for investors on behalf of the beneficial owner (see Chapter 2, section 2.3.2.), the shares are likely to be registered into the agent's *nominee name*. In turn, the agent maintains records internally of each of its clients (the beneficial owner) whose securities are held within the nominee name. Operating in this manner makes the agent's management of the beneficial owner's holding more efficient; for example, payment of dividends may be made to the agent, who in turn distributes the appropriate amount of dividend to all its entitled beneficial owners.

The owner of the shares (or the owner's nominee) will remain as the registered holder, until such time as the shares are sold, at which point the buyer's name (or its nominee's name) will replace the seller's name on the issuer's register of holders. Note that registration practices differ between countries; such points will be explored further in Chapter 6.

Historically, new issues of equity resulted in the creation of a share *certificate* in the registered holder's name; such certificates represented the holding on the issuer's register and led to a relatively inefficient method of transfer, following sales. Today, normal practice is for holdings in equity issues to be held and maintained in electronic form upon issue, either directly in the owner's name or in a nominee name, providing a far more efficient means of holding and transferring. Dependent upon local practice, an investor may be allowed to opt for a share certificate.

3.5   POST THE LAUNCH OF SECURITIES

Following the completion of a new issue, the issuer will have received its cash and the securities will have been successfully brought to the marketplace; at that point in time, the primary market for the particular security ceases to exist.

An owner of such securities may choose to hold them for days, months or years, or may choose to sell them immediately; all such trades will be effected within the secondary market.

In the case of a bond, secondary market trading will cease upon maturity of the bond, but in the case of equity secondary market trading will continue perpetually, or until an event occurs (such as a takeover or the company going into liquidation) that causes the shares to cease to exist.

3.6   SETTLEMENT OF TRADES IN THE SECONDARY MARKET

As mentioned in Chapter 2, individuals that wish to buy or sell securities (including newly issued securities) typically execute trades via an agent for investors, who in turn is likely to trade with an STO. The settlement of trades involving the STO, whether with other STOs, agents for investors or with institutional investors, is very likely to occur on a DvP basis.

3.7   FURTHER ISSUES OF EQUITY

Companies that have existing shares in issue may choose to issue further shares to their existing shareholders.

Examples of such situations include the raising of further capital through a *rights issue*, and the (free of cost) increase to shareholdings through a *bonus issue*. Both rights and bonus issues are explored in Chapter 26.

3.8 SUMMARY

The specific operational implications for an STO when involved in a new security issue focus on the extended period between trade date and value date (compared with trading in securities in the secondary market). The implications are that trades in such securities require specific treatment, for example particular wording on trade confirmations issued to counterparties.

Having described within this chapter the fundamental aspects of bringing bond and equity securities to the marketplace, from this point forward the primary focus of attention will be on securities traded after their launch (within the secondary market), and the subsequent operational implications.

4

Structure of a Securities Trading Organisation

4.1 INTRODUCTION

Presenting an overview of the way a typical STO is structured internally aids understanding of how operational processing is achieved; however, it is important to note that no two STOs are structured identically, as the management of each organisation will create a structure to suit its specific method of operation.

Note: the focus of this book is primarily from the perspective of STOs, which includes trading and market-making activities and subsequent operations, rather than the activities of other organisations (such as retail broking or asset management companies). However, many of the operational aspects covered within the book are common to all organisations that trade in or manage the processing of securities.

4.2 THE GROUP OF COMPANIES

Where a number of STOs, each one an individual trading entity, have a single parent company or a hierarchy of companies to which each STO reports, all companies within that structure are known as the group of companies.

It is also possible for the companies within a group to be involved with securities marketplace activities in various capacities, such as trading and market making, investment management, asset management or retail broking. Furthermore, some companies within the group could be involved with non-securities related activities such as retail banking, although all activity within the group is likely to be focused on financial services generally.

Whichever business a trading entity may wish to become involved with, it is usual for licences (to conduct business in a specific capacity) to be granted by the local financial authorities. This means that, for example, a company may be granted permission to trade as a retail broker, but not as a bank, for which a separate licence must be granted.

Figure 4.1 represents conceptually how a group of companies may be structured, taking into account the various activities of each company:

- the individual company (level 1),
- the country in which the company resides (level 2),
- the geographical region in which the collection of companies reside (level 3), and finally
- the overall group level (level 4 and highest level of hierarchy).

The significance of the group structure is that each of the companies is likely to be required to provide reporting of profit and loss (P&L) to the next level up within the hierarchy, so that the P&L of XX Bank and XX Asset Management (both located in Sydney) is combined to form the total P&L for the group's Australia operation. Australia's P&L is combined with Japan's and Hong Kong's to form the P&L for the Asia/Pacific region, which is combined with both Europe and the Americas to form the P&L of the entire XX group.

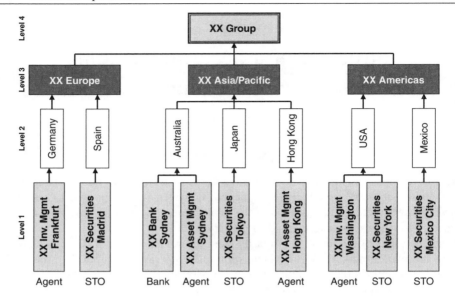

Figure 4.1   The group of companies: typical hierarchical structure

Specifically from the perspective of the STOs within the group (in this example located in Madrid, Tokyo, New York and Mexico City), it is normal for trading to be conducted between the various STOs on a daily basis, in order to fulfil orders from clients located in, say, Japan, where that client wishes to buy or sell a security where the normal trading location is elsewhere (e.g. IBM Corporation shares normally trading in New York).

4.3   COMPANIES WITHIN A GROUP

An individual STO is a distinct company in its own right, the business it undertakes needing to be recorded separately from the business of any other trading entity.

The typical characteristics of STOs are that they:

- are members of one or more exchanges/markets;
- may trade in securities of their choice;
- may operate in a market-making capacity for some securities;
- will hold securities positions for their own account;
- will need to borrow cash in order to fund their securities positions;
- may trade in securities locally (e.g. Italian securities), regionally (e.g. European securities) or globally;
- may specialise in equities or bonds or trade in both;
- will be required to operate according to the rules laid down by the regulatory authority where the STO is resident and in accordance with their trading capacity (e.g. market makers, as opposed to traders, are typically required to abide by additional regulations);
- normally appoint custodians of their choice in the normal place of settlement of the securities in which they trade (rather than use a global custodian, for instance) and communicate with *custodians* and *central securities depositories* directly for the purpose of settling trades.

4.4   DIVISIONS WITHIN A COMPANY

The larger of the STOs typically employ hundreds and in some cases thousands of staff in the major financial centres. The business of an STO may include both bond and equity trading and market making; specialist knowledge is usually necessary to operate successfully in the equity marketplace and different, but still specialist knowledge is required for bond trading and market making, demanding different skills and a fundamentally different understanding of how these markets operate.

In addition, it is not uncommon to find that an individual STO splits the business internally into two main divisions; the Equity Division and the Bond Division (also known as Debt or Fixed Income or Fixed Interest Division).

The P&L of the STO will comprise the P&L from the respective divisions; in the case of a global group of companies which has each of its STOs organised along similar lines, it is possible for the P&L of the entire group to be identified for the equity business, separately from the bond business.

Deregulation in many financial centres around the globe has given the incentive for some STOs to merge with or to acquire other STOs. Although a merger of two STOs may take place, it is not uncommon to find that, years later, the unification of personnel undertaking similar tasks has not occurred; the reason for this is typically due to the continued use of the original (and different) software systems. Where this is the case, those involved may still be part of a separate division.

Some, but not all, of the departments within an STO fall within their respective divisions, but others are neutral from a divisional perspective.

4.5   DEPARTMENTS WITHIN DIVISIONS

The nature of the securities trading business means that certain activities are common to all STOs; however, the ways in which individual STOs are structured internally to manage the business does differ.

Consequently, the structure illustrated within Figure 4.2 should be regarded only as an example of how an STO may be structured. Whatever the internal structure of an

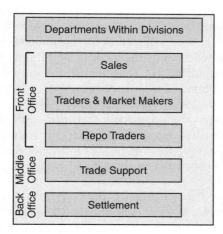
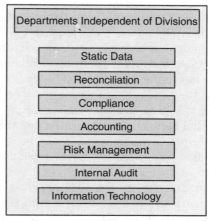

Figure 4.2   Structure of a securities trading organisation: departments typically within and independent of divisions

STO, trading and operational activities must be catered for; the remainder of this chapter describes those activities.

4.5.1 Front Office

The term 'front office' is a collective term used to describe those who are involved with trading and market making, directly or indirectly.

Sales

As mentioned within Chapter 2, institutional investors may utilise the services of an agent through whom orders to buy or sell securities are placed; alternatively, the institutional investor may have a direct relationship with one or many STOs. Where the latter is the case, an institutional investor may have a preference for placing orders for Spanish equities through one STO and orders for Spanish government bonds through another.

Institutional investors are powerful organisations that are the originators of a large number of trades with large cash values; when an institutional investor has a direct relationship with an STO, much revenue can be made by the STO as long as the services it provides to the institutional client are of a high standard. (The various aspects of these services will be covered throughout the book.) If the service levels provided by an STO fall below the required standard, an institutional client is likely to take its business to another STO.

In order to ensure that the institutional client is given top quality service by the STO, salespeople (also known as account or client managers) are typically employed by the STO to act as the primary contact point between the STO and the institutional client.

In a day-to-day sense, *orders* will be placed by institutional clients with the STO's salesperson either over the telephone or via an order management system to which the institutional client has access. The salesperson is responsible for managing the order internally within the STO, which involves the forwarding of the order to the trader or market maker (within the STO) to decide whether to trade or not. The salesperson usually has no authority to execute a trade on behalf of the STO.

If the trader or market maker agrees to the terms of the order, a trade will have been executed between the STO and the institutional client. The trader will record the details of the trade and advise the salesperson, who in turn will inform the institutional client that the order has been executed. This will be followed by the issuance of a formal *trade confirmation* from the STO to the institutional client, via a medium of the institutional client's choice, for example telex or fax. The topic of trade confirmation is explored in Chapter 14.

Figure 4.3 illustrates the relationship between the salesperson and their institutional clients, and between the salesperson and the traders and market makers within the STO. Each salesperson within an STO may be responsible for a number of institutional clients with similar characteristics, for example all insurance companies based within the same country.

The management of the STO require a mechanism to judge the performance of the salesperson and normally employ a method known as 'sales credits', whereby a percentage of the value of each trade is calculated so that the greater the number of trades and the cash value of each trade, the greater the accumulated sales credit for the individual salesperson. The accumulated sales credit is used to calculate the compensation payable

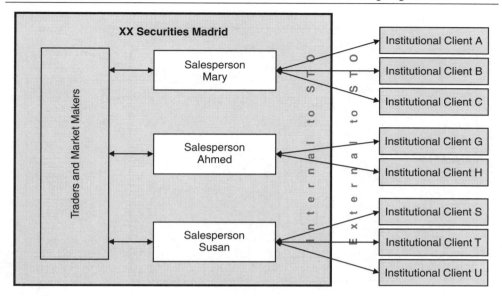

Figure 4.3   Structure of a securities trading organisation: salespeople within an STO

to the salesperson by the STO, so it is in the salesperson's personal interest to generate as many orders as possible, to maintain relationships with existing institutional clients and to bring new clients to the STO.

To summarise, salespeople are employed by STOs to act as intermediaries between institutional clients and traders and market makers within the STO.

Traders and Market Makers

Further to the description of traders and market makers in Chapter 2, traders and market makers execute trades with the following types of counterparty:

- institutional clients (via their own internal salespeople)
- agents acting on behalf of individual or institutional investors
- other STOs
- other companies within the STO's group

and whereas salespeople are the primary contact with institutional clients, traders and market makers have direct contact with other STOs and agents, such as retail brokers. Figure 4.4 provides an overview of the relationship between an STO's traders and market makers and the other parties with whom they communicate.

Traders and market makers involved with *proprietary trading* (i.e. trading on a principal basis) within an STO are responsible for the profitability of their particular trading portfolio (typically referred to as a *trading book*), which may be operated by an individual or by a small team of traders or market makers. Each trading book contains a number of individual securities in which the trader or market maker trades; the trading book contains the primary record of a trader's current and historic trades and trading positions.

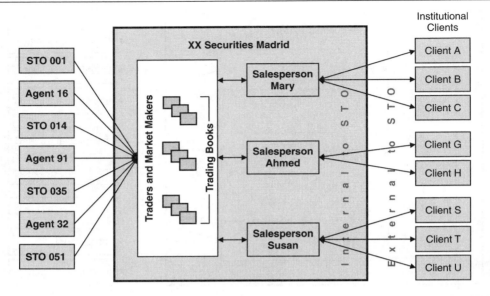

Figure 4.4   Structure of a securities trading organisation: traders and market makers within an STO

Trading books may be defined according to:

- individual or groups of traders, to which securities are assigned;
- groups of securities (e.g. shares in chemical companies), to which traders are assigned;
- currency of securities (e.g. Japanese Yen denominated bonds), to which traders are assigned;
- trading strategy (e.g. short or long-term), to which traders are assigned.

To enable the management of an STO to assess the profitability of its trading activity, the trading department typically contains a number of trading books, whereby each trade executed is 'owned' by a specific trading book. Trades are recorded against the relevant trading book and therefore P&L can be calculated at trading book level, from which performance of individual or groups of traders can be derived.

Within some STOs, individual securities are traded exclusively by an individual or group of traders within a specified trading book and trading by other traders in that same security may not be allowed by the management of the STO, although the view of management in other STOs may differ.

One way of looking at trading book structures is to make an analogy with a department store. The management of the store require frequently updated information regarding the P&L of each department (for instance furniture, perfume and sports goods) in order to make informed business decisions. For example, if the last three months' figures are very good for sports goods and the outlook remains positive, the management may choose to transfer resources from the furniture department if that area has not met its recent targets and the outlook is not positive.

Figure 4.5 provides an example trading book structure within an STO. The hierarchy can be explained as follows.

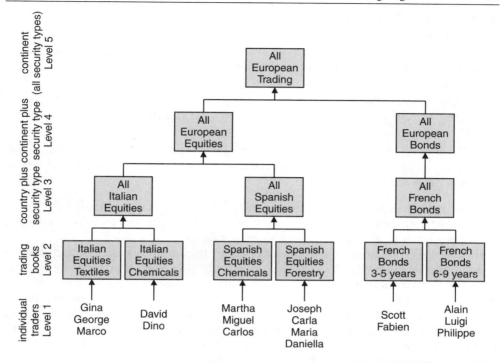

Figure 4.5 Structure of a securities trading organisation: trading books (example hierarchical structure)

Level 1: trades executed by individual traders or market makers may need to be recorded as belonging to that individual, requiring that the basic components of a (principal) trade:

- trade date
- trade time
- value date
- operation (buy or sell)
- quantity
- security
- price
- counterparty

be captured along with the name or code representing the individual trader or market maker. Some STOs record trades inclusive of individual trader or market maker, but others do not. If this information is captured, the management will be able to assess the profitability of individual traders over a specified period.

Level 2: trades executed over a trading book need to be recorded as such, so in addition to the basic trade detail listed above, the trading book will always be recorded. It is reasonable to assume that an STO will operate a trading book structure for its proprietary trading and market-making business and that it would want to capture the trading book name or code when a trade has been executed (but it may or may not want to capture the individual trader in addition to the trading book). This allows the profitability of each trading book for a given period to be reported to management.

Level 3: combining the P&L for all trading books falling within similar categories of business for a specified period; for instance, the profitability of all Italian equity business can be reported.

Level 4: merging the P&L for all categories of business for a specified period; for instance, combining all Italian and Spanish equities enables the reporting of profitability for the entire European equities operation.

Level 5: bringing together the profitability of, for instance, all European equities and the European bonds business enables reporting of profitability of the complete European operation of an STO.

The trading book structure of an individual STO is specific to that organisation and cannot be predicted from outside the STO, but it is reasonable to assume that all STOs conducting proprietary business will operate a trading book structure.

However, it is essential to remember that trades form *trading positions*, and where a trader or market maker has, for instance, a positive trading position in a specific security, it may be that the trades which make up that trading position were executed months ago; for example as set out in Table 4.1, where today is 17th July. In other words, the trading position of +15,000,000 has not changed in over five months. In summary, the two trades that were dealt on 7th January and 2nd February would have been recorded in the STO's books and records as belonging to the specific trading book, and on 17th July the resultant trading position still belongs to the same trading book.

Table 4.1

Operation	Quantity	Trade date	Trading position
		6th January	zero
Buy	10,000,000	7th January	+10,000,000
Buy	5,000,000	2nd February	+15,000,000

By the end of September, four more trades had been executed (including three sales), (see Table 4.2), all of which have been recorded as belonging to the specific trading book. So, for example, as at 14th December, the trading position has remained constant for over two months and still belongs to the same trading book.

Table 4.2

Operation	Quantity	Trade date	Trading position
		6th January	zero
Buy	10,000,000	7th January	+10,000,000
Buy	5,000,000	2nd February	+15,000,000
Sell	13,000,000	21st July	+2,000,000
Buy	40,000,000	16th August	+42,000,000
Sell	6,000,000	14th September	+36,000,000
Sell	12,500,000	29th September	+23,500,000

Only where a sale follows a purchase, or vice versa, is it possible to calculate true (known as 'realised') trading P&L, as calculation of realised P&L on, for example, a positive trading position with no sales is impossible. However, calculation of 'unrealised' P&L can be performed by use of current market prices, which informs the management of the profit (or loss) which could be made if the positive trading position were to be sold 'today'. P&L is explored in Chapter 28.

Once the management of an STO have P&L information over a period of time, such as weeks or months, informed decisions can be made and used in the formulation of trading strategies. For instance, whether to reallocate trading and market-making personnel from one trading book to another (so as to maximise a predicted profitable opportunity).

Traders and market makers within STOs are normally required to trade and take positions within predefined trading limits set by the management, in an attempt to avoid over-enthusiastic individuals trading and taking positions on a scale which is regarded as excessively risky (i.e. the risk of financial loss to the STO).

When a trader receives an order to trade, for example from an internal salesperson on behalf of an institutional client, the terms of the order will be assessed and, if felt to be a reasonable price, a trade will be executed. Market makers are obligated to trade providing the counterparty is prepared to trade at the market maker's published price.

Following execution, the details of a trade will be recorded by the trader in order to update the trading position and so that the various subsequent tasks, such as settlement and P&L calculation, can begin. Historically, trade details would have been recorded and trading position would have been updated manually onto paper. Today, trading systems are used by many STOs, whereby the input of a trade automatically adjusts the trading position.

It is important to note that all trades, including those with STOs and institutional clients, must be recorded against the relevant trading book.

From this point forward, the term 'traders' will be synonymous with 'traders and market makers'.

Repo Traders

The subject of repos is one of the more challenging areas to convey at this early stage, so for the moment only the high level concepts will be explained.

As mentioned previously, when an STO buys a security and takes a positive trading position in that security, once settlement has occurred the relevant custodian will be holding the securities in safe custody on behalf of the STO. Conversely, the purchase cost will be represented by a debit on the STO's nostro account at the custodian.

The rate of interest charged by the custodian (to the STO) to remain overdrawn on the nostro account may not be as low as borrowing rates in the money market. Unless action is taken to minimise the overdraft cost, the rate of interest payable will have an excessive detrimental impact on the STO's trading profits. Clearly, there is a cost to borrowing funds, but it need not be an excessive cost.

The cheapest method of borrowing cash is for the borrower to place some form of security (also known as *collateral*) with the cash lender. The cash lender charges a high rate of interest if the risk of not being repaid his cash is high, which is the case where cash is lent on an unsecured basis. However, if cash can be lent on a secured (or collateralised) basis, the risk to the lender is much reduced as the lender can recover the cash owed by selling the collateral, and therefore the rate of interest charged by the cash lender to the borrower is much reduced.

A mortgage taken out by an individual to buy a house is a form of secured borrowing. The cash borrower signs a legal agreement that if they fail to repay the cash amount borrowed in accordance with the terms of the loan, the cash lender may sell the house in order to recover the cash which it is owed.

An STO has collateral in the form of securities that it has purchased and which are held by the STO's custodian. In order to cover the overdraft at the custodian at minimal cost, cash may be borrowed by the STO on a secured basis by delivering securities (as collateral) to the cash lender in exchange for the required cash.

Repo traders are employed by STOs to manage the flow of collateral and cash in order to minimise the cost of borrowing cash that is needed to fund positive trading positions. Transactions are effected by repo traders (on behalf of the STO) with other STOs and institutional clients, to borrow cash against simultaneous delivery of securities (as collateral) on an agreed value date, with the return of the cash (plus interest) and the collateral at an agreed later date.

Repos are covered in detail in Chapter 23.

4.5.2   Middle Office

The middle office (also known as trade or trader support) within an STO is typically responsible for a number of tasks relating to the servicing and support of the traders, market makers and salespeople.

These tasks can include:

- the keying of trade details to trading systems (on behalf of the traders), thereby allowing the traders to focus on trading;
- the agreement of trade details with counterparties;
- the investigation of trade detail discrepancies between the STO and its counterparties;
- new counterparty and security set-up within internal systems;
- production of the daily trading P&L reporting from the STO's formal books and records, and agreement with the trader's view of their P&L; note that this task is managed by the accounting function in some STOs;
- the reconciliation of trading positions (i.e. the quantity of specific securities within each trading book) between the STO's books and records, and the trading system.

However, the responsibilities of this area are likely to vary from STO to STO. Note that many of the tasks listed are explained later in this chapter.

4.5.3   Operations (Back Office)

The term 'operations' or 'back office' are collective terms to describe those operational areas within an STO that deal with the result of trading by the front office.

Settlement Department

Following the execution of a trade within the front office and subsequent recording of the trade within a trading system, trade details are typically fed through an interface between the trading system and the settlement system.

Having received details of the trade, the back office is typically responsible for the following actions. Note that some of the activities listed below may be dealt with in other areas (such as the middle office) within some STOs; no two STOs are structured identically. All the topics listed will be explained fully in subsequent chapters:

- capturing the details of the trade within the settlement system,
- updating the trading position within internal books and records,
- applying additional details to the trade,
- applying custodian details to the trade,
- validating the details of the trade,
- gaining agreement to trade detail with the counterparty,
- providing details of the trade to regulatory authorities,
- issuing a settlement instruction to the relevant custodian,
- ensuring the trade settles on value date,
- updating internal books and records as a result of settlement,
- operating a custodian service to clients,
- ensuring that income due is received.

In general, to minimise operational costs and ensure the STO's assets are not put at risk.

Capturing the Details of the Trade within the Settlement System. The back office normally maintains the formal *books and records* of securities trades and positions within an STO. Trades are first recorded in the front office trading system, but the responsibility for updating the formal books and records lies with areas such as the settlement and accounting departments. The starting point for the settlement of trades and all subsequent activities is the capture of the trade details within the settlement system.

In situations where an STO has not invested in a trading system, the details of trades must be recorded by traders and market makers on paper, with manual input to the settlement system; Under these circumstances, there is a real possibility of input error with resultant trading position differences (the effect of such errors will be discussed in subsequent chapters).

In the modern era, the formal books and records are very tightly interlinked with software systems; having been fed from the trading system, trades are recorded in the settlement system (which forms part of the STO's formal books and records) automatically, and accounting entries for both securities and cash are derived from the trade detail of the individual trades.

The information regarding trades that is normally fed by a trading system and required to be captured within the settlement systems is listed in Table 4.3.

Updating the Trading Position within Internal Books and Records. The moment the details of a trade are captured within the settlement system, the trading position for both securities and cash, at a trading book level, must be updated.

For example, on 15th June trading book A had an existing trading position of +3,000,000 Xerox shares, all of which were held at the custodian (as the underlying trades had settled). The ownership versus location position would appear as in Table 4.4.

The following day, trading book A purchased a further 1,000,000 shares from ABC, Frankfurt; the trade was entered into the trading system and was fed to the settlement system where the capture of the trade resulted in the ownership versus location position in Table 4.5.

Table 4.3

	Example
Trading book	Book A
Trade date	16th June
Trade time	10:22
Value date	19th June
Operation	Buy
Quantity	1,000,000
Security	Xerox shares
Price	USD 10.03
Counterparty	ABC, Frankfurt

Table 4.4

Xerox Shares (as at 15th June)			
Ownership		Location	
Trading book A	+ 3,000,000	− 3,000,000	Custodian L, New York
	+ 3,000,000	**− 3,000,000**	

Table 4.5

Xerox shares (as at 16th June)			
Ownership		Location	
Trading book A	+ 4,000,000	− 3,000,000	Custodian L, New York
		− 1,000,000	ABC, Frankfurt
	+ 4,000,000	**− 4,000,000**	

Equivalent entries for the relevant cash amounts would also need to be made.

Passing these entries into the STO's formal books and records provides a complete and updated view of the STO's business, also enabling confirmation that the trading position agrees with the trader's and market maker's view of their position. The books and records show the STO's view of the securities that are under its control (at the custodian) and those that are not, as settlement is yet to occur (the example shows that 1,000,000 Xerox shares are owed to the STO by ABC). The equivalent cash entries would show the exact amount owed to ABC for the STO's purchase of the shares.

Applying Additional Details to the Trade. Trading systems cater primarily for the needs of traders and market makers and do not typically provide all the information on a trade that is needed for complete operational processing by the back office.

The typical trade information fed by a trading system and captured by the settlement system (refer to 'Capturing the Details of the Trade within the Settlement System') could be described as the 'trade skeleton'. This is the minimum detail a trader or market maker must provide as these items are variable and cannot be guessed by the settlement department, with the exception of trading book, trade date and value date, as in most cases it is possible to derive this detail from other information contained within the trade skeleton. This and other aspects of trade capture are described in Chapter 11.

However, for trades to settle successfully and for other operational activities to be completed, all trades require additional information to be attached over and above that contained within the trade skeleton. Examples of this are:

* mandatory charges—cash amounts that are imposed by law, for example stamp duty at a fixed percentage rate is payable on purchases of UK equities. The STO will charge a buying client the purchase cost inclusive of stamp duty, and the STO must in turn pay the stamp duty to the tax authorities;
* STO imposed charges—cash amounts that the STO chooses to charge, for example administration fees charged to clients are added to the buyer's purchase cost and deducted from a seller's sale proceeds;
* accrued interest—when trading in an interest bearing bond, the value of the interest payable by the issuer, up to the value date of the trade, is paid by the buyer to the seller in addition to the agreed trade price.

Such calculations are described in Chapter 8.

Applying Custodian Details to the Trade. Many years ago, business was typically transacted by STOs only in securities marketplaces of their 'home' country, with resultant trades always settling at the same custodian within their home country, meaning that there was little or no choice as to where to settle a trade.

Now, in high volume environments where STOs transact business in securities marketplaces worldwide, it is necessary to decide exactly which location and custodian are relevant for an individual trade. This information is essential in order for the trade to settle.

Therefore, when a trade is input to the settlement system (whether manually or by feed from a trading system), such as the above-mentioned purchase of 1,000,000 Xerox shares, the system will derive the STO's relevant custodian by a series of links. For example, the individual security (Xerox shares) is linked to the nationality of security (USA), which is linked to the relevant financial centre (New York), which is linked to the relevant custodian (Custodian L, New York). This is represented pictorially in Figure 4.6.

However, it is important to note that the STO must also derive the counterparty's relevant custodian. With regard to an individual trade, the STO's custodian is required to act (i.e. deliver or receive securities, pay or receive cash) on the STO's behalf only after the custodian has received a direct and specific communication from the STO.

The STO communicates with the custodian by issuing a *settlement instruction* directly to the custodian. The settlement instruction tells the custodian to:

* either receive or deliver
  * a specific quantity
  * of a specific security
  * from/to a specific counterparty (or the counterparty's custodian)
  * on a specific value date
  * against a specific amount of cash

but in order for the trade to settle, settlement instructions must match between the STO's and the counterparty's custodians. A match cannot occur if the counterparty's custodian on the settlement instruction issued by the STO is incorrect, and this may lead to *settlement failure*, which in turn may lead to monetary loss incurred by the STO. For this reason,

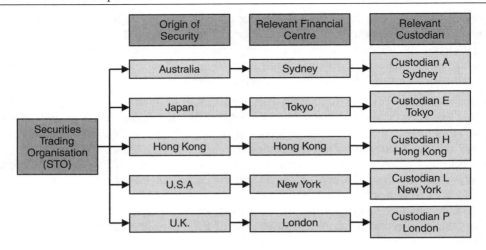

Figure 4.6   Example STO to custodian relationships

timely and accurate calculation of both the STO's and the counterparty's custodian is vitally important.

Validating the Details of the Trade. Though the basic details of a trade may appear very clear-cut, the inaccurate recording of the details can lead to unnecessary costs being incurred and risks being taken by the STO.

For instance, settlement instruction matching between the seller's and buyer's custodians must happen before settlement can occur, therefore inaccurate trade recording either by the trader when entering trade details to the trading system or when writing the details of a trade, or by middle or back office personnel inputting trades manually into the settlement system, is likely to result in a mismatch of settlement instructions, which can cause delays in settlement (i.e. the trade fails to settle on value date). Settlement failures usually result in cash losses being incurred by the seller or buyer.

Another example is where an STO's counterparty to a trade is an institutional client who expects a high quality service from the STO; part of the service that the STO provides is the issuance of a formal trade confirmation that lists all details of the trade. If the information contained on a trade confirmation is inaccurate, the STO increases the risk of losing that client's business.

In an attempt to prevent inaccurate information being sent to the outside world, the process of validating trade information is adopted by many STOs.

Historically, this would have been a manual task undertaken by those within the settlement department with an 'experienced eye'. In modern settlement systems, rules can be written and then compared with individual trade details as each trade is received, resulting in the trade either passing or failing this internal check. Validation failures can then be investigated, resulting in:

- continued processing of the trade in its original state, or
- amendment of trade detail

followed by transmission of trade details to the outside world.

Gaining Agreement to Trade Detail with the Counterparty. Failure of the STO and its counterparty to agree the details of the trade, immediately after trade execution, can result in monetary losses if the discrepancy remains unresolved as at value date. Consequently, it has become standard practice in many markets to strive for *trade agreement* as soon as possible after trade execution.

Today, electronic *trade matching* mechanisms exist in some marketplaces; in other markets trade agreement is reached by the STO issuing an advice of trade execution (commonly known as a *trade confirmation*) by more conventional methods, such as paper or fax.

From the perspective of an STO, there are two main reasons for wishing to achieve trade agreement and issuing a trade confirmation to the counterparty:

- client service—those counterparties that are institutional clients are likely to require a formal written or electronic notification of trade detail from the STO, within a specified deadline following trade execution;
- risk reduction—the issuance of a trade matching message or a trade confirmation by the STO provides the counterparty with the opportunity to agree or disagree with the details of the trade. It is in the STO's interests to remove any doubt that the counterparty agrees to the terms of the trade as soon as possible after trade execution, as there is always the possibility that the counterparty disagrees with the details (e.g. price or quantity differences) or that they executed the trade at all. The risk comes with the trader potentially having to amend or cancel a trade that was executed some time before, in which case a loss can be incurred, particularly in volatile markets; historically, days and in some cases weeks have passed between trade execution and the discovery that a trade needs amendment or cancellation.

The topics of trade matching and trade confirmation are explored in Chapter 14.

Providing Details of the Trade to Regulatory Authorities. In many securities market-places, in order for the local regulator to monitor all trades executed by STOs, individual trade details must be sent to the regulator by a specified deadline, typically during or at the end of the trade date; this is known as 'transaction reporting'.

Methods of achieving transaction reporting vary; in some marketplaces the trade detail is conveyed to the regulator as an individual message serving no other purpose, or sent as part of a 'trade matching' message, or is derived from the receipt by a *central securities depository* of the STO's settlement instruction.

The subject of transaction reporting is dealt with in Chapter 15.

Issuing a Settlement Instruction to the Relevant Custodian. Once the STO has determined which of its custodians to use for the settlement of an individual trade (and which custodian the STO believes the counterparty wishes to use for settlement), a settlement instruction must be issued by the STO to its custodian in order for settlement to occur.

Custodians are required to remove securities or cash from their client's accounts (an STO is a client of a custodian) only after receipt of a specific *settlement instruction* from the client. To make an analogy with an individual's own bank account, the individual expects the bank to remove cash from his/her account only after the bank has received specific authorisation from the account holder. Examples of authorisation in a personal banking sense are direct debits, standing orders and cheques. In each case, the account holder expects the bank to ensure that the true account holder has given authorisation for the payment; if not, cash may be removed from the individual's account fraudulently.

From an STO's perspective, there is a risk that its custodians may inadvertently act upon an instruction to remove assets (i.e. securities or cash) from the STO's account where someone other than the STO has sent the instruction.

However, the responsibility for minimising the possibility of fraud and error lies with both the account holder and the custodian. The STO and the custodian must agree the method of communication of settlement instructions; the choices include electronic methods (e.g. *S.W.I.F.T.*, which will be described in later chapters) and less automated methods such as telex and fax. The chosen method is extremely important to the STO, as it will impact:

- the ability to achieve *straight-through processing*;
- the speed and accuracy with which a settlement instruction can be generated and transmitted to the custodian;
- the extent of internal checking necessary prior to transmission to the custodian;
- the deadline imposed by a custodian for the receipt of settlement instructions (relevant to the value date of the trade);
- the type and extent of checking necessary by the custodian to prove the authenticity of the settlement instruction.

By whatever method settlement instructions are transmitted, the STO should seek (from the custodian) an acknowledgement of receipt of each individual instruction. If an STO does not know whether the custodian has in fact received an instruction that has been transmitted, the STO takes a risk that the instruction has not been received. Where a custodian has received no instruction, the trade cannot settle and, if this situation is not rectified on or before the value date (dependent upon how settlement operates in the individual market), settlement will not occur on value date and the STO will incur a cost.

Assuming that a settlement instruction sent by the STO has been received by the custodian and the custodian is satisfied that the instruction is authentic, before settlement can occur the settlement instruction must be matched with the counterparty's settlement instruction.

This topic is covered in Chapter 16.

Ensuring the Trade Settles on Value Date. The exchange of securities and cash (*settlement*) between buyer and seller is due to occur on value date. Generally, it is reasonable to expect a trade to settle on value date, but it is also common to have *settlement failures* in some markets, with settlement occurring at a later date.

The settlement of securities trades involves risk to both seller and buyer, unless measures are taken to prevent losses. If a seller delivers securities to the counterparty without receiving the sale proceeds from the counterparty at the same time, or if a buyer pays cash to the seller without receiving securities at the same time, the risk is that receipt of the counter-asset will be delayed or never arrive at all. This is no different from an individual's personal dealings, where, for instance, most people would feel at risk if they were to hand over a car that they were selling without receiving the buyer's payment at the same time; or when buying a car, to pay 100% of the cash to the seller without taking possession of the car immediately.

The desired method of settlement is DvP, meaning simultaneous exchange of securities and cash where neither seller nor buyer is at risk, regardless of whether the trade settles on value date or later.

Where securities have been sold and the trade is due to settle on a DvP basis, the seller has a further risk; unless the seller is able to deliver the securities on value date, the seller will not receive the buyer's cash at the earliest opportunity and there will be a loss of interest on cash, which is not recoverable. For example, the difference between USD 20 million due to be received by a seller on 16th February, but not actually received until 17th February, is the loss of interest on USD 20 million for one day (using an interest rate of 5%, this amounts to approximately USD 2500.00). Settlement failures are normally caused by the seller not having the securities available for delivery on the value date.

Taking into account all of the above, the first step in ensuring that settlement occurs on value date is to achieve a match of settlement instructions between the custodians of the seller and buyer. Both parties to the trade should proactively seek the status (i.e. matched or unmatched) of their settlement instruction from their respective custodian and, where unmatched, take immediate action in order to achieve a match. If settlement instructions are not matched settlement cannot occur.

On value date, providing settlement instructions are matched, settlement will occur if the seller has the securities to deliver and the buyer has the cash to pay. Should the seller be deficient in securities, it may be possible to borrow securities in order to settle the sale.

These subjects are described in Chapters 18, 19 and 20 respectively.

Updating Internal Books and Records as a Result of Settlement. Once settlement has occurred, the STO's custodian will advise the STO.

In order to bring the STO's internal books and records up-to-date to reflect the true position in the outside world, the appropriate trade within the STO's settlement system must be identified and updated, so as to reflect the external movements of securities and cash.

The successfully updated settlement system will reveal that the trade is no longer awaiting settlement with the counterparty, and that, in the case of a purchase by the STO, securities have been credited to and cash has been debited from the STO's account with the custodian (and vice versa for a sale by the STO).

This topic is explored in Chapter 21.

Operating a Custodian Service to Clients. Following the execution of a trade, STOs typically expect to settle externally with counterparties that are STOs; this means exchanging securities and cash between seller's and buyer's custodians.

However, where the counterparty to the trade is an institutional client, that client may not have a custodian relationship to enable external settlement to occur.

For clients such as these, an STO may offer to hold the client's securities (and possibly cash) in safe custody. This means that when an STO sells securities to the institutional client, the STO:

- externally moves the securities to a segregated account (from the STO's own account) at the custodian, whilst retaining control (but not ownership) of the securities;
- internally maintains records of the client's securities holdings (and possibly cash balances).

The reverse flow must occur when the STO buys securities from a safe custody client.

This subject is described in Chapter 25.

Ensuring that Income Due is Received. Issuers of most securities pay income period-ically, in the form of *coupon* on bonds and *dividends* on equities. Those who invest (including STOs) may or may not be entitled to these benefits.

The first step in collection of the benefit is for the STO to become aware that the issuer is making a specific income payment; income on most bonds is predictable and can be diarised months and years in advance of the payment date. However, income on equities is subject to announcement by the *issuer* and therefore the STO must seek this information in order to minimise the risk of not receiving income to which it is entitled.

Secondly, at the appropriate time, the STO must calculate whether it is in fact entitled to the income and, if so, must assess by whom the payment of income will be made and monitor the receivable amount until full payment is received.

Where an STO offers a safe custody service to clients, the STO is expected to collect income on behalf of its clients.

Furthermore, other events may occur on securities that generate additional monies or securities; such events are collectively termed *corporate actions*.

This topic is explored in Chapter 26.

In summary, the skill of the personnel within a settlement department is in being able to identify and anticipate problems and take measures to minimise cost and risk. A well-run settlement department enables the profit from trading to be retained as much as possible, as the operating costs are kept to a minimum and potential cost and risk reducing measures are identified and taken at every opportunity.

4.6   DEPARTMENTS INDEPENDENT OF DIVISIONS

Certain departments within STOs typically do not operate within the confines of a division within the company, but carry out their responsibilities across all divisions. See Figure 4.7. The activities of these departments are described below.

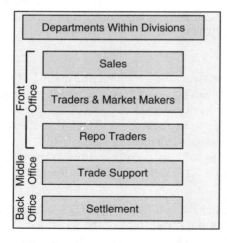
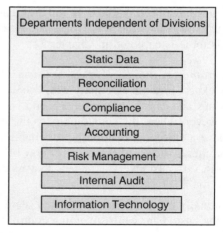

Figure 4.7   Structure of a securities trading organisation: departments typically within and independent of divisions

4.6.1 Static Data Department

Static data (sometimes referred to as 'standing data') is a term used within the securities industry to describe data that changes occasionally, or not at all. The two principle components are:

- securities static data, and
- counterparty static data.

The responsibilities of the static data department are the input of new and the update of changed securities and counterparty details to one or many systems (such as settlement systems and corporate actions systems).

If an STO wishes to achieve the highest possible automation of trade throughput (commonly known as Straight-Through Processing (STP), refer to Chapter 10) it must have complete confidence in the static data input to the settlement system. Two main types of data are fed to the settlement system, namely trade data and static data; if both are of high quality, STP is achievable. It is therefore essential that securities and counterparty static data are totally accurate and complete at all times.

Many components form security static data, but for instance, if the *coupon rate* on a bond is not set up correctly, incorrect trade cash values will result. Likewise, static data relating to counterparties involves a number of attributes; for example, the setting up of an incorrect counterparty postal address could result in an institutional client failing to receive a *trade confirmation*.

Where static data is not accurate, monetary losses can be incurred by the STO through settling trades against the incorrect cash values; where it is incomplete, delays in the throughput of trades are likely and this can result in a reduced service to institutional clients and may jeopardise the future relationship with such clients.

This subject is dealt with in Chapter 9.

4.6.2 Reconciliation Department

A vitally important process for the well-being of any company is proving that its books and records are accurate, meaning that they are up-to-date, complete and reflect reality, as good business decisions are dependent upon accurate information. Reconciliation is achieved through the comparison of specific pieces of information within the STO's books and records, and between the STO's books and records and the outside world.

Frequent reconciliation is extremely important in order to minimise the number of discrepancies requiring investigation. For example, if there are, on average, 10,000 individual security movements per day at one of the STO's custodians, to conduct reconciliation of those movements only once a week could result in a large number of discrepancies between the custodian's records and the STO's internal books and records, with the investigation of any discrepancies taking an inordinate length of time. However, if reconciliation is undertaken on a daily basis, the number of exceptions requiring investigation and resolution is much more manageable.

The various types of reconciliation and the methods of performing them are described in Chapter 27.

4.6.3   Compliance Department

The compliance officers within an STO are responsible for ensuring that the various rules and regulations, as laid down by the local regulatory authority, are adhered to by the STO. This includes ensuring that:

- only qualified personnel execute trades on the STO's behalf;
- reporting of trade and positional information to the regulatory authorities is complete and effected within the stated deadlines;
- methods of investigating trade disputes between the STO and its counterparties are carried out in a thorough and correct manner;
- measures are taken to prevent unlawful activities within the STO, such as *insider trading*.

The STO's compliance officers are seen as representing the STO from the standpoint of adherence to the regulator's rules, and they are employed to ensure that the STO is compliant with the terms of its operating licence, which may be revoked if the STO fails to comply consistently. Given this responsibility to the organisation as a whole, it is necessary to position the compliance function independent of a division. Various personnel within the STO (e.g. traders) view the compliance department as a source of information regarding what is and is not allowed in specific circumstances.

4.6.4   Treasury Department

From the perspective of an STO, the treasury department is responsible for obtaining funds as cheaply as possible, in order to finance the traders' positive trading positions. The treasury department typically has prior cash borrowing arrangements with other banks, on an unsecured and a secured basis; the activities of the repo trader and the treasury department are normally closely linked.

The treasury department may form a department within the STO, or be part of the banking arm within a group of companies where both the STO and the bank form part of the group.

Where the treasury department is part of a bank, that bank's main business may be high volume lending and borrowing of cash or buying and selling of currencies, for business reasons completely outside the sphere of securities trading. In this situation, securities related cash borrowing on behalf of the STO may form only a part of the bank's daily activity.

The topic of obtaining funds to cover negative cash positions is described in Chapter 23.

4.6.5   Accounting Department

For any trading entity, there is a need to keep formal accounting records of the company's business, including:

- assets; any item of value to the owner
- liabilities; any item actually or potentially owing to others
- profit and loss
- income, such as
  - interest on bank balances
  - commission earned

- ○ dividends and coupons
- ○ trading revenues
- expenditure, such as
  - ○ payroll
  - ○ buildings
  - ○ furniture
  - ○ heating and lighting.

Accounting entries representing all the STO's trading activity are typically provided within a 'trading ledger' supplied by the settlement system to the accounting department's 'general ledger'. The trading ledger forms part of the overall content of the general ledger, which additionally contains information such as payroll costs.

The formal P&L of trading books is calculated by the accounting department and is supplied to the STO's management (although in some STOs this task is performed by the middle office).

4.6.6   Research Department

The function of the research department is to analyse the performance of securities markets, companies and individual securities and to produce forecasts of performance.

The information produced from such analysis is supplied to institutional clients, to enable them to make informed judgements in terms of trading decisions. The research material is usually considered to be part of the overall service that an STO is required to provide to the institutional client.

The accuracy of forecasting by the STO can influence an institutional client's view as to whether it wishes to continue utilising the services of the particular STO.

4.6.7   Risk Management Department

The risk management department is responsible for assessing the STO's risk, which arises in a number of different ways.

Trades

Having executed a trade, there is a risk that the counterparty may fail to honour its contractual obligation to settle the trade; the risk is that profit will be lost if the trade has to be cancelled. This is known as counterparty risk.

Besides assessing open trades by individual counterparties, trades with counterparties within certain countries or regions may be regarded as risky. In the event of, for instance, the outbreak of war or the occurrence of a natural disaster in such an area, the risk to the STO is that settlement may not occur as a result of the counterparty's offices not being manned.

A different risk exists regarding the method of settlement of a trade. If an STO agrees to settle a trade on an FOP basis and:

- on a sale, delivers securities to the counterparty before receiving the counterparty's cash, or
- on a purchase, pays the cash owing to the counterparty before receiving the counterparty's securities

there is a risk that the asset owed to the STO may be delayed, or never be received at all.

Risk on open trades may be assessed differently dependent upon whether the trade has a value date in the future, or in the past (i.e. settlement failure).

Throughout subsequent chapters, reference to operational risk mitigation measures on open trades will be made.

Positions

An STO that holds a positive securities position for its own account risks that the price of the securities will fall due to market volatility; this is known as market risk.

A settled position at a custodian may be regarded as risky, as the issuer of the bond or equity may go out of business. Additionally, the custodian may go out of business and, although the STO may be protected from financial loss of the assets that the custodian holds on behalf of the STO, there is a chance that settlement of any sales will be delayed and that income due to the STO may be delayed.

4.6.8   Internal Audit Department

Some STOs have set up a function that is responsible for examining and critically reviewing the books and records kept by the STO's operational areas, to ensure that adequate controls are in place and are being practised. In addition, the internal audit area ensures that an external auditor will ratify the STO's practices of bookkeeping and reconciliation, for the regulatory bodies.

Such audits are carried out in addition to the regular inspection by external auditors.

4.6.9   Information Technology Department

Today, IT has become central to taking the securities industry forward in many respects. At the time of writing, the industry is undergoing huge changes in order to reduce risk, reduce cost, provide better service to clients and in general rationalise and streamline working practices.

Many of the planned (and as yet unplanned) changes will impact the entire industry, not just STOs. Furthermore, catering for such changes will require alteration to existing systems or the introduction of new systems both internally to the STO and in the STO's communication methods to and from the outside world.

Consequently, many STOs employ specialists in the world of IT, including programmers, business analysts and project managers.

Today, it is normal to find that an STO has a number of projects running concurrently to support business areas, such as:

- static data
- order management
- trading
- settlement
- corporate actions
- risk management
- reconciliation

where either new systems are being implemented or existing systems are being upgraded. STOs are frequently assessing and reassessing which project or projects are to be undertaken next, amongst a plethora of high priority projects that typically arise as a result of the STO needing to keep pace with market developments, some of which are forced upon all market participants by regulators or exchanges/markets. Other projects are driven from a need that is internal to the STO, such as rationalising static data across various systems.

Some STOs choose to develop software systems themselves, whilst others may select an external system from a software supplier. Either way, a successful project usually requires a mixture of talents that blend the skills and knowledge of those who:

- understand the business need, for example trading or corporate actions;
- can interpret the business need and successfully communicate the need to the IT staff;
- can develop or adapt the software to meet the business need;
- can plan and manage the project within agreed timeframes and budget.

The industry-wide changes referred to above are explored in Chapter 29.

5
Transaction Types

5.1 INTRODUCTION

STOs buy and sell securities many times during each day, but in addition, an STO executes other types of transactions in order to manage its business properly on a day-to-day basis.

In general terms, the purchase (or sale) of goods is one type of transaction, whereby an agreement is made to exchange one asset for a different asset. This transaction is intended to be a single action that does not involve the return of the assets to the original seller and buyer at some later date.

To make an analogy with a car dealer, it is expected that the main type of transaction would be the purchase and sale of cars. However, the cars that have not yet been sold could be rented to customers prior to being sold; a rental transaction has characteristics that differ from a sale transaction, in that there would be a rental start date and end date with a fee payable by the customer. In addition, the car dealer could use a car as *collateral* against a borrowing of cash and the features of this transaction would differ from the previously mentioned transaction types.

Each of the above transactions by the car dealer involves two assets, the car and the cash, with each transaction being effected for different reasons, namely:

- buying a car—the car dealer gains possession of the car, but loses the cash permanently;
- renting a car—the car dealer loses possession of the car temporarily, but gains the rental fee;
- using a car as collateral—the car dealer loses possession of the car temporarily, but gains cash temporarily.

This shows that the same asset (in the above example one car) can be involved in a number of transaction types; this concept is important to understand, as it is directly applicable to an STO's business.

The transaction types described within this chapter have been placed under two main headings, namely:

- securities transaction types—those transaction types applicable to securities and cash, or securities only;
- cash transaction types—those transaction types applicable to cash only.

In order to aid understanding, the transactions covered are described from the perspective of a fictitious STO, namely World Securities International, London (WSIL).

5.2 SECURITIES TRANSACTION TYPES

The following transaction types are typically used by STOs, each one involving securities:

- principal
- repurchase (repo)

- securities lending and borrowing
- trading book transfer
- depot (custodian) transfer.

It is important to note that an individual security could be used in one, some or all securities transaction types.

5.2.1   Principal Transactions

A principal transaction represents either a purchase or a sale by an STO on a *proprietary trading* basis (that is, on its own behalf, rather than on behalf of a client). A purchase of a security at one price followed by a sale at a higher price, with each trade being effected by the STO 'as principal', will reap a profit for the STO.

Table 5.1 represents the basic information relevant to a principal transaction. The associated characteristics are given in Table 5.2.

Table 5.1

Principal transaction	Example
Trading book	Book A
Trade date	16th June
Trade time	10:22
Value date	19th June
Operation	Buy
Quantity	3,000,000
Security	News Corporation ordinary shares
Price	AUD (Australian Dollars) 46.30
Counterparty	RST, Hong Kong

Table 5.2

Characteristics	Principal transaction
Securities only, securities + cash, cash only?	Securities + cash
Origin?	Front office (traders or market makers)
Trading position affected?	Yes
External securities movement?	Yes
External cash movement?	Yes
Number of external counterparties?	One
Issue a trade confirmation?	Yes
Issue a settlement instruction?	Yes

Figure 5.1 illustrates two independent principal transactions, one purchase and one sale, which have resulted in a trading profit for the STO. Within STOs, these transactions are executed by traders and market makers and will result in a change to their *trading position*. The STO's counterparty in a principal trade is usually another STO, an institutional client or an agent acting on behalf of an investor.

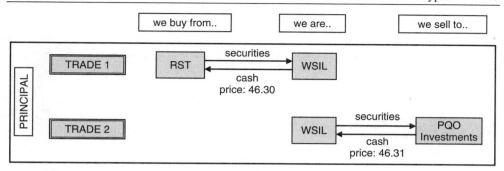

Figure 5.1   Securities transaction types: principal

Settlement instructions will need to be issued to the STO's custodian, with settlement normally occurring on a DvP basis. Principal trades involve one movement of securities and one movement of cash at the same time (the value date).

The STO will be required to provide some form of *trade confirmation* to its counter-party, whether electronically or via, for example, telex or fax. The wording on a trade confirmation is generally required to reflect the capacity in which the STO has acted; there-fore, for a principal trade, the wording 'As principal, we confirm having bought/sold. . .' (or similar) is used.

A principal transaction between two parties results in an outright exchange of securities and cash (without agreement to return the assets at some later point in time).

5.2.2   Repurchase (Repo) Transactions

The settlement of a principal purchase by an STO will result in a debit of cash and (usually) a negative cash position on the STO's nostro account at the custodian. As mentioned in Chapter 4, the interest on a cash overdraft at the custodian may not be as low as borrowing rates in the money market.

An STO wishing to minimise the cost of borrowing cash may have arrangements with banks, to borrow cash on a secured or unsecured basis; secured cash is cheaper to borrow than unsecured cash as the lender has less risk. A repo is a form of secured cash borrowing where the STO utilises the securities it has purchased and which it holds at the relevant custodian to deliver to the cash lender as security for the cash that the STO is borrowing.

Table 5.3 represents the basic information relevant to a repo transaction. The associated characteristics are given in Table 5.4.

Figure 5.2 illustrates a single repo transaction, where the STO receives cash on the opening value date against delivery of securities, and repays the borrowed cash plus interest (based on the repo rate) for the period of the loan on the closing value date against receipt of securities.

The trade is executed with an external counterparty and two settlement instructions need to be issued by the STO, pertaining to the movements of securities and cash on the opening and closing value dates.

The STO will normally be required to issue a trade confirmation to its counterparty, detailing every component of the transaction, inclusive of all dates and the repo rate.

Table 5.3

Repo transaction	Example
Trading book	Repo book D
Trade date	16th June
Trade time	10:22
Operation	Repo (deliver securities, receive cash)
Cash amount	USD 20,650,000.00 (to receive)
Quantity of securities	USD 20,000,000 (collateral to deliver)
Security	World Bank 6.75% 15th February 2025
Price	102.25% (price of collateral)
Counterparty	DEF, New York
Opening value date	18th June (value date of cash receipt)
Closing value date	28th June (value date of cash repayment)
Interest (repo) rate	4.5%

Table 5.4

Characteristics	Repo transaction
Securities only, securities + cash, cash only?	Securities + cash
Origin?	Front office (repo trader)
Trading position affected?	No
External securities movement?	Yes
External cash movement?	Yes
Number of external counterparties?	One
Issue a trade confirmation?	Yes
Issue a settlement instruction?	Yes (one for opening value date, one for closing)

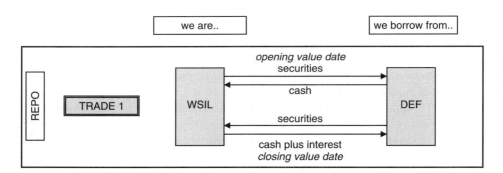

Figure 5.2   Securities transaction types: repo

Repo transactions involve a minimum of one movement of securities and one movement of cash at the same time, on two separate occasions (the opening followed by the closing value dates).

The delivery of securities used in a repo transaction does not result in a change to the trader's or market maker's trading position, as from their perspective ownership is retained.

The subject of repo is considerably deeper than the extent to which it has been covered in this chapter; repo is covered in detail in Chapter 23.

5.2.3   Securities Lending and Borrowing Transactions

Any investor in securities, including individuals, institutions and STOs, is able to increase the return on their investment if they lend their securities. STOs and other investors borrow a lender's securities, for which the lender receives a fee agreed with the borrower.

With regard to securities borrowing, where an STO has sold securities and the value date of the sale has been reached, the STO will lose interest on the cash amount due from the buyer unless the sold securities are delivered to the buyer on value date. Assuming that the sale is due to settle on a DvP basis, the seller will not receive the incoming cash until the securities are delivered to the buyer; the reasons for sellers having a shortfall of securities is explained in Chapter 19. Under such circumstances, the normal method for the seller to avoid delayed delivery of securities and therefore delayed receipt of the sale proceeds is to borrow the necessary securities.

Table 5.5 represents the basic information relevant to a securities lending or borrowing transaction, using other securities as collateral (with both securities having a notional cash value). The associated characteristics are given in Table 5.6.

Table 5.5

Securities lending and borrowing transaction	Example
Trading book	Securities lending and borrowing book
Trade date	16th June
Trade time	10:22
Operation	Lend
Quantity of securities lent/borrowed	GBP 12,000,000
Security lent/borrowed	IADB 6.2% 1st December 2015
Price of security lent/borrowed	98.625%
Quantity of collateral	GBP 12,500,000
Collateral	Denmark 6.5% 15th May 2020
Collateral price	99.10%
Counterparty	JKL, London
Opening value date (securities delivery)	18th June
Closing value date (securities return)	25th June
Fee.	4.2% (of market value)

STOs seek to maximise income opportunity and minimise costs, whilst remaining conscious of the risks involved; securities lending and borrowing transactions are undertaken to achieve these objectives.

Securities Lending

Figure 5.3 illustrates a securities lending transaction (from the STO's perspective), where the STO's securities have been lent and delivered to the counterparty against receipt of collateral from the counterparty, on the opening value date. The lent securities are subsequently returned to the STO by the counterparty against delivery of the collateral on the closing value date.

Table 5.6

Characteristics	Securities lending and borrowing transaction
Securities only, securities + cash, cash only?	Securities only or securities + cash
Origin?	Front office or back office
Trading position affected?	No
External securities movement?	Yes
External cash movement?	Yes
Number of external counterparties?	One
Issue a trade confirmation?	Yes
Issue a settlement instruction?	Yes (two for opening value date, two for closing)

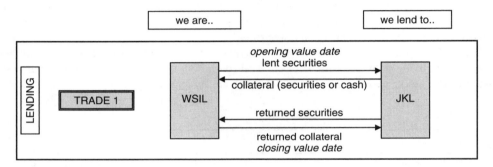

Figure 5.3   Securities transaction types: securities lending

The lending of securities does not result in a change to the trader's or market maker's trading position, as from their perspective ownership is retained. The counterparty to an STO's securities lending transaction is typically another STO or an institutional client of the STO.

As a safeguard to the lender of securities, the borrower is required to provide collateral that has a market value greater than the market value of the lent securities; the collateral may be in the form of cash or other securities. Settlement instructions need to be issued to the STO's custodian, with settlement normally occurring on a DvP basis and sometimes on an FoP basis. Securities lending transactions normally involve a minimum of one movement of securities and one movement of collateral (either securities or cash) at the same time, on two separate occasions (the opening followed by the closing value dates).

The STO may be required to issue some form of trade confirmation to the counterparty, whether an institutional client or another STO.

Securities lending transactions result in a temporary exchange of assets between the parties to the transaction.

Securities Borrowing

Figure 5.4 illustrates a securities borrowing transaction (from the STO's perspective), where the counterparty's securities have been borrowed and received from the counterparty against delivery of collateral from the STO, on the opening value date. The borrowed

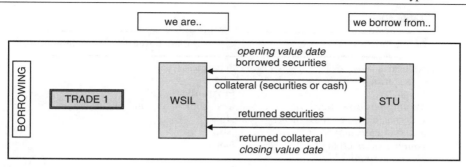

Figure 5.4   Securities transaction types: securities borrowing

securities are subsequently returned by the STO to the counterparty against receipt of the collateral on the closing value date.

Following a sale of securities, if the seller does not have securities available to deliver as at the value date of the sale, the necessary quantity of securities may be able to be borrowed from a securities lender.

The borrowing of securities does not result in a change to the trader's or market maker's trading position, as from their perspective the securities received have not been purchased.

The subject of securities lending and borrowing is covered in depth in Chapter 24.

5.2.4   Trading Book Transfer Transactions

An STO's traders and market makers trade on a principal basis with other STOs and institutional clients. Within some STOs, two (or more) trading books within the same legal entity may be allowed to trade and hold trading positions in the same security.

Under these circumstances, one trading book may agree to execute a trade with another trading book (a counterparty that happens to be internal to the STO). This trade will be executed at a price that is agreeable to both parties and the P&L of both trading books will be affected by the price at which the trade is executed. The executed trading book transfer trade results in the need for the trading positions for each trading book to be updated.

Table 5.7 represents the basic information relevant to a trading book transfer transaction. The associated characteristics are given in Table 5.8.

Table 5.7

Trading book transfer transaction	Example
Selling trading book	Book A
Buying trading book	Book B
Trade date	16th June
Trade time	11:17
Value date	16th June
Quantity	2,000,000
Security	ICI ordinary shares
Price	GBP 3.80

Table 5.8

Characteristics	Trading book transfer transaction
Securities only, securities + cash, cash only?	Securities + cash
Origin?	Front office
Trading position affected?	Yes (both selling and buying books)
External securities movement?	No
External cash movement?	No
Number of external counterparties?	None
Issue a trade confirmation?	No
Issue a settlement instruction?	No

Figure 5.5 illustrates a trading book transfer transaction between two trading books within an STO. These transactions are effected by the recording of independent trades by each of the trading books. Within both the trading and settlement systems, this trade needs to update the trading positions for both trading books.

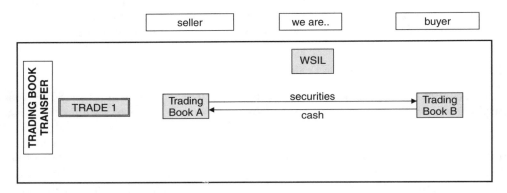

Figure 5.5 Securities transaction types: trading book transfer

Assuming that the securities positions for both trading books are held externally within the same account at the STO's custodian, no securities or cash movement is necessary; therefore no settlement instructions need to be issued. As there is no external counterparty involved in the transaction, there is no requirement to issue a trade confirmation.

5.2.5   Depot (Custodian) Transfer Transactions

An individual STO typically appoints one custodian in each financial centre to settle transactions and to hold the resultant securities on behalf of the STO.

Normally, an STO will hold securities in one custodian per financial centre, however certain securities may be held at more than one custodian or financial centre. For example, Italian Government bonds are able to be settled in Milan, but are also able to be settled in the international clearing systems, *Euroclear* (Brussels) and *Clearstream* (Luxembourg).

However, on occasions, the STO may need to switch securities from one custodian to another.

Table 5.9 represents the basic information relevant to a depot (custodian) transfer transaction. The associated characteristics are given in Table 5.10.

Table 5.9

Depot (custodian) transfer transaction	Example
From depot	Custodian Q, Milan
To depot	Custodian S, Brussels
Quantity	EUR 2,000,000
Security	Italy 6.0% 1st September 2012
Value date	19th June

Table 5.10

Characteristics	Depot transfer transaction
Securities only, securities + cash, cash only?	Securities only
Origin?	Back office
Trading position affected?	No
External securities movement?	Yes (both delivering and receiving custodians)
External cash movement?	No
Number of external counterparties?	None
Issue a trade confirmation?	No
Issue a settlement instruction?	Yes (to both delivering and receiving custodians)

Figure 5.6 represents a depot (custodian) transfer where securities are being moved between two of the STO's custodians.

An STO trading in such securities may have reason to transfer all or part of a holding from one custodian to another. For instance, an STO has an existing settled securities position of EUR 15 million Italian Government 6.0% bonds held at the STO's custodian, Custodian Q, Milan. A trader within the STO decides to sell EUR 2 million of the bond to counterparty BCD, for delivery to BCD's account with Custodian S, Brussels. In situations where the seller holds securities in one custodian and the buyer wishes to take delivery in a different custodian, there is normally a choice of effecting a *cross border settlement*, or of effecting settlement within the same custodian as the buyer following a depot (custodian) transfer (resulting in a *realignment* of securities) by the seller.

Should the STO choose to deliver the securities on a DvP basis within Custodian S, Brussels, the securities need to be moved to the STO's account with Custodian S, Brussels, ready for exchange between seller and buyer on value date. The movement of securities between two custodians belonging to the same STO is known as a depot transfer.

A depot transfer is not a transaction with a counterparty; it is a movement of securities between two of the STO's custodians in different locations, or between two accounts of the STO held by the same custodian. The STO's settlement department typically decides to effect a depot transfer, however, the underlying reason for doing so is likely to be trade related, as per the example above.

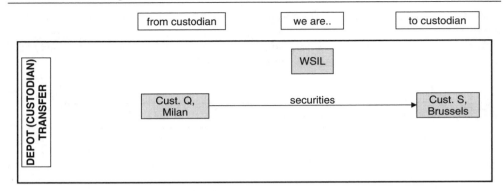

Figure 5.6   Securities transaction types: depot (custodian) transfer

FoP settlement instructions will usually need to be issued to both the delivering and the receiving custodian to effect the transfer. A trade confirmation will not be issued, as there is no counterparty in a depot transfer transaction.

5.3   CASH TRANSACTION TYPES

The following transaction types are typically used by STOs, each one involving cash:

- repurchase (repo)
- unsecured borrowing and lending
- nostro transfer
- foreign exchange.

In general terms, cash transaction types are used for the purpose of covering actual or projected overdrafts of cash at the STO's custodians, resulting from the settlement of purchases; these activities are commonly referred to as *funding*. This topic is described in detail in Chapter 23.

5.3.1   Repurchase (Repo) Transactions

For completeness, repo transactions are listed here as a cash transaction type, as well as in the previous section as a securities transaction type. Many repo transactions are executed by STOs from the perspective of the need to borrow cash, against which securities are given as *collateral*.

The borrowing or lending of cash on a secured basis is very similar in structure to a repo transaction, and so will not be specifically described within this section.

5.3.2   Unsecured Cash Borrowing and Lending Transactions

The settlement of a principal purchase by an STO will result in a debit of cash and usually a negative cash position on the STO's nostro account at the custodian. As the rate of overdraft interest charged by a custodian may be out of line with market rates, an STO will reduce its costs if it can borrow cash more cheaply from another source.

In order to cover a cash overdraft at the custodian, an STO may choose to borrow cash on an unsecured basis; this transaction type is similar to repo transaction types in that cash is borrowed from an external counterparty, but is different from repo in the respect that no collateral is provided by the cash borrower to the cash lender, as security for the loan. As a consequence of no security being given, the cost of borrowing cash on an unsecured basis is greater. Unsecured borrowing and lending transactions are typically executed by the treasury department on behalf of the STO.

Table 5.11 represents the basic information relevant to an unsecured cash borrowing or lending transaction. The associated characteristics are given in Table 5.12.

Table 5.11

Unsecured cash borrowing/lending transaction	Example
Trade date	16th June
Trade time	10:22
Operation	Borrow
Currency	HKD
Amount	22,500,000.00
Counterparty	Bank 'X'
Start date (opening value date)	18th June
Maturity date (closing value date)	25th June
Interest rate	6.4%

Table 5.12

Characteristics	Unsecured cash borrowing/lending transaction
Securities + cash, cash only?	Cash only
Origin?	Treasury department
Trading position affected?	No
External cash movement?	Yes
Number of external counterparties?	One
Issue a trade confirmation?	Yes
Issue a settlement instruction?	Yes (one for opening value date, one for closing)

Figure 5.7 illustrates both the borrowing and lending of cash on an unsecured basis. An unsecured cash borrowing transaction is executed on a trade date; the borrower is due to receive the borrowed cash on the start date and due to repay the cash plus interest at an agreed rate on the maturity date. A trade confirmation is issued by the STO to its counterparty, containing all details of the transaction, including the bank and account number to which the STO requires payment.

Typically, a settlement instruction is required to be issued by the STO to its receiving bank, so that the bank is alerted to the impending receipt of funds; this type of instruction is known as a 'pre-advice' of funds.

However, at maturity of the borrowing, the STO must issue a settlement instruction to its bank requesting repayment of the borrowed cash, plus interest, to the lender.

Most of the time, STOs have positive securities trading positions and consequently need to borrow cash in order to fund their purchases of securities. On occasions, however, the

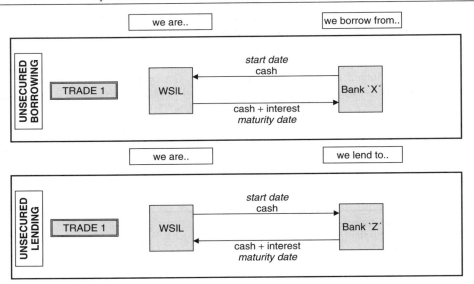

Figure 5.7 Cash transaction types: unsecured cash borrowing and lending

cash value of settled sales may be greater than that of settled purchases, resulting in a credit cash balance on the STO's account at a custodian. The interest rate (given by custodians) on credit cash balances is typically lower than can be obtained in the money markets, and in some cases can be zero. The STO will not be maximising a cash earning opportunity if no action is taken to receive a better rate of credit interest.

An STO wishing to maximise this opportunity can therefore become a cash lender; in this situation, the STO must assess the risk of lending cash on an unsecured basis and charge an appropriate rate of interest to the borrower.

Unsecured borrowing and lending transactions involve one movement of cash on two occasions.

The topic of unsecured borrowing and lending is covered in Chapter 23.

5.3.3 Nostro Transfer Transactions

Where an STO has an overdraft (or anticipated overdraft) at a custodian as a result of settlement of trades and the STO wishes to cover that overdraft, one of the options open to the STO is to transfer cash (in the same currency) from:

- another account with the same custodian, or
- an account held at another bank

where the accounts involved belong to the STO.

Table 5.13 represents the basic information relevant to a nostro transfer transaction. The associated characteristics are given in Table 5.14.

Figure 5.8 represents the movement of cash in a nostro transfer transaction.

The use of a nostro transfer to cover the overdraft at the custodian, particularly if the STO has a credit balance in an account elsewhere, may well be the cheapest method of funding the overdrawn account.

Table 5.13

Nostro transfer transaction	Example
From nostro	Custodian S, Brussels
To nostro	Custodian H, Hong Kong
Currency	HKD
Amount	37,800,000.00
Value date	25th June

Table 5.14

Characteristics	Unsecured borrowing/lending transaction
Securities + cash, cash only?	Cash only
Origin?	Treasury department or back office
Trading position affected?	No
External cash movement?	Yes (both paying and receiving nostros)
Number of external counterparties?	None
Issue a trade confirmation?	No
Issue a settlement instruction?	Yes (both paying and receiving nostros)

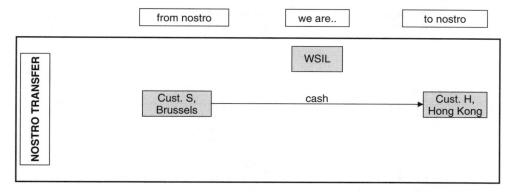

Figure 5.8   Cash transaction types: nostro transfer

There is no counterparty involved in a nostro transfer; the STO decides to effect a movement of cash between two of its cash (also known as 'nostro') accounts in the same currency. As there is no true counterparty, no trade confirmation is issued by the STO.

A settlement instruction will need to be issued by the STO to the 'paying' nostro (to request payment to be made) and a pre-advice of funds should be issued to the 'receiving' nostro (to expect receipt of the payment).

A nostro transfer involves one movement of cash between two nostros (or two accounts at the same nostro), on one occasion.

5.3.4   Foreign Exchange Transactions

A further option for an STO to cover an overdraft is to execute a foreign exchange (FX) transaction. Where the STO has a credit balance in a nostro account in one currency (e.g.

Japanese Yen), but has an overdraft in another currency (e.g. US Dollars), the STO can effect an FX transaction that sells the appropriate amount of Yen in exchange for the required amount of Dollars.

It is important to note that an FX transaction is not a temporary loan or borrowing of cash, but an outright sale of one currency and purchase of another, at an agreed exchange rate.

Table 5.15 represents the basic information relevant to a foreign exchange transaction. The associated characteristics are given in Table 5.16.

Table 5.15

Foreign exchange transaction	Example
Trade date	16th June
Trade time	08:35
Value date	18th June
Selling currency	Japanese Yen (JPY)
Selling amount	JPY 2,000,000,000
Buying currency	US Dollars (USD)
Exchange rate	124.075
Buying amount	USD 16,119,282.69
Counterparty	Bank 'Y'
From nostro	Custodian E, Tokyo
To nostro	Custodian L, New York

Table 5.16

Characteristics	Foreign exchange transaction
Securities + cash, cash only?	Cash only (two currencies)
Origin?	Back office or treasury department
Trading position affected?	No
External cash movement?	Yes (both paying and receiving nostros)
Number of external counterparties?	One
Issue a trade confirmation?	Yes
Issue a settlement instruction?	Yes (both paying and receiving nostros)

Figure 5.9 represents the movement of cash in a foreign exchange transaction.

The cash management function within the treasury department normally executes FX transactions with the counterparty to the trade being a bank or another STO, and a trade confirmation will need to be issued, listing all the relevant details of the transaction, including the STO's paying and receiving nostros.

The STO will need to issue a settlement instruction to its paying nostro (where the sold currency will be paid from) and a pre-advice may need to be issued to the STO's receiving nostro, in order for the STO to receive 'good value' on the incoming funds.

FX transactions involve the movement of two currencies at the same time, on one occasion.

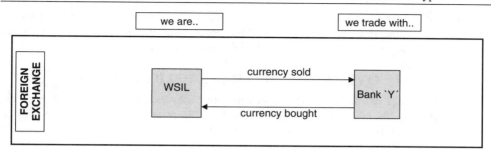

Figure 5.9   Cash transaction types: foreign exchange

Cross-Currency Securities Settlement

FX transactions are required to be effected by STOs on a daily basis, for a different reason from covering an overdraft (as mentioned above).

Cross-currency settlement typically occurs where an STO has executed a securities transaction with an institutional client who wishes to pay or receive cash in a currency other than the usual 'traded' currency of the security.

The following is applicable to both equities and bonds, but a bond will be used to describe an example. Most bonds are traded in the currency of issue; for example, a bond issued in Euros, that pays interest in Euros and which will repay the capital in Euros at maturity, will also be traded in Euros in the secondary market during its life. If an STO trades that bond in a currency other than Euros, an FX position and consequent risk will be taken by the STO, unless the STO takes action to negate the risk.

For example, if an STO buys the bond denominated in Euros, the STO is highly likely to pay for the purchase in Euros. If the STO then sells, the STO will normally want to receive the same currency as it paid for the bond. However, it is normal for an STO to execute trades with some institutional clients who wish to always pay or receive in the same currency; for example, a pension fund based in Singapore may wish to pay or receive the cash associated with bond transactions in Singapore Dollars (SGD), regardless of the issue currency of the bond.

If the cash paid by an STO on its purchase of the bond was Euros (EUR) 5,000,000.00, and it then sold the bond for a value of EUR 5,001,000.00, the trading profit made by the STO would be EUR 1000.00. However, if the counterparty to the sale were the Singapore-based pension fund that wished to pay for the bond in SGD, the STO would request the pension fund to pay the SGD equivalent of EUR 5,001,000.00, say SGD 7,600,000.00.

To summarise the STO's overall currency situation following settlement of its purchase and sale, the STO has an overdraft of EUR 5,000,000.00 from its purchase, but has a credit of SGD 7,600,000.00 from its sale. If the STO allowed this situation to continue, the EUR 1000.00 trading profit may increase, reduce or disappear completely, as a result of movements in the exchange rates between the two currencies. The movements in exchange rates are not controllable and therefore the trading profits (or losses) made by STOs are at the mercy of exchange rate movements, unless the STO takes action to remove the risk.

In the example quoted above, removing the risk would require the STO to sell the SGD 7,600,000.00 in exchange for Euros, thereby enabling P&L to be properly assessed, as payments and receipts of cash would be in the same currency. The management of an STO may impose internal rules banning the traders and market makers from taking FX positions, as the risk may be considered too great. Note that it is normal practice for STOs to cover any FX exposure at the time of trade execution.

5.4 OVERVIEW OF TRANSACTION TYPES

To bring a number of the transaction types together into a sequential flow so as to aid understanding of the circumstances under which different transaction types are utilised by STOs, Figure 5.10 will be used as a basis for the flow.

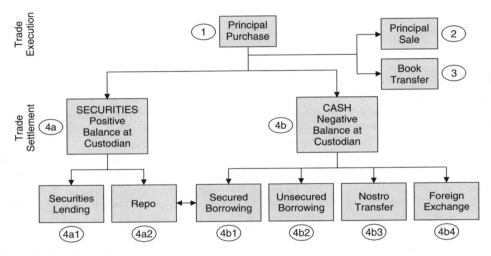

Figure 5.10   Transaction types: summary

The starting point is that the STO purchases a bond from another STO, as in Table 5.17, for a total cost of USD 15,220,000.00, for settlement at the STO's Clearstream (Luxembourg) account on a DvP basis.

Table 5.17

Principal transaction	Details of purchase
Trading book	Book A
Trade date	14th October
Trade time	08:47
Value date	17th October
Operation	Buy
Quantity	USD 15,000,000
Security	XOX 8.25% 1st June 2020
Price	98.35%
Counterparty	JKL, Amsterdam

Point 1 (14th October): the trade is executed and a principal purchase for trading book 'A' is recorded within the STO's books and records.

Point 2 (on or after 14th October): trading book 'A' could sell the securities to an 'external' counterparty via a principal sale, or to an 'internal' counterparty (another trading book) via a trading book transfer (Point 3). However, in our example, a sale will not be executed until after settlement of the principal purchase trade.

Points 4a and 4b (17th October): the principal purchase settles at the custodian Clearstream and results in a credit of securities and a cash overdraft on the STO's accounts at Clearstream.

With regard to the cash overdraft at the custodian, one option is to take no action, resulting in a continued overdraft at an interest rate that may be higher than market interest rates. However, the STO decides that the priority is to cover the overdraft by borrowing cash at a cheaper rate, for which there are a number of options:

- Points 4a2 and 4b1—execute a repo transaction to borrow cash versus delivery of one or many securities (as a form of secured cash borrowing);
- Point 4b2—borrow cash on an unsecured basis (i.e. unsecured borrowing transaction);
- Point 4b3—transfer cash from another of the STO's cash accounts (i.e. nostro transfer transaction);
- Point 4b4—sell a different currency in exchange for the required amount of US Dollars (i.e. foreign exchange transaction).

One or a combination of the above-mentioned transaction types could cover the entire overdraft amount.

Point 4a1: the STO could choose to lend the securities, if a borrower could be found. This is not an option, however, if the securities are used in a repo, as the STO will lose possession of the securities.

As a general comment, cash borrowing and lending and foreign exchange transactions are executed on a vast scale within the world's money and FX markets on a daily basis. Despite the magnitude of business transacted in the securities industry in its own right, the requirement for STOs to borrow cash to cover their overdrafts resulting from securities trading and from maintaining positive trading positions forms only a part of the overall volume of cash lent and borrowed in the money markets and foreign exchange markets.

To give an idea of scale, a large STO may have a daily funding requirement in various currencies with an aggregate value running into billions of USD, but satisfying the requirement to borrow funds may result in a relatively low number of cash borrowing transactions executed on a daily basis.

5.5 AUTOMATION

In a modern STO environment, the settlement system plays a major role in allowing the STO to settle and process the trades that the front office has executed.

The transaction types that a settlement system is capable of processing determine the extent of automation within the STO's back office, as each transaction type should contain characteristics allowing specific processing actions to be achieved.

Differences in the various transaction types includes the following:

- whether the transaction originates in the front office or back office
- the information to be captured
- whether the trading position is affected
- what accounting entries are required

- the additional information to be added to the skeleton trade details
- whether external movements of securities and cash will occur
- whether there is a need to issue a trade confirmation
- whether there is a need to issue a settlement instruction

and the settlement system should provide the essential characteristics of each transaction type, resulting in the appropriate actions occurring automatically.

5.6 SUMMARY

STOs typically effect many or all of the transactions described within this chapter.

It is normal to find that principal transactions account for the majority of trades in any one business day, with repos and securities lending and borrowing trades being the next largest category, in terms of daily volume.

However, handling transactions manually (even if only the lower volume transactions) from an operational perspective can place constraints on the STO's ability to grow the business, or to grow it profitably.

If an STO's settlement system is able to cater for the nuances of the various transaction types, the processing of all trades can be automated and controlled according to the STO's needs, and *STP* of a very high percentage of trades is much more likely. Under these circumstances, the business can be grown in the knowledge that it can be controlled, operationally.

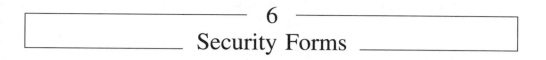

6

Security Forms

6.1 INTRODUCTION

Historically, issuers printed paper *certificates* in order to represent equity and debt issues. When purchasing a security, an investor would receive a certificate from the issuer (when buying a new issue) or from the seller (when buying in the secondary market). The certificate was intended to provide proof of ownership.

For an individual issue, certificates were usually designated as being in either *registered* or *bearer* form; the similarities and differences of each are highlighted towards the end of this chapter.

The following sections describe the characteristics of registered and bearer securities, as it is important to understand their nature in order to appreciate how settlement procedures differ, thereby increasing the probability of operational efficiency.

The two main forms of securities are registered and bearer form.

6.2 REGISTERED SECURITIES

The holders of a registered security will have their name and address recorded on a register of holders typically maintained by a *registrar* or transfer agent on behalf of the issuer.

The purpose of the register is to hold a complete list of all holders of the issue; most equity issues are in registered form, as the issuer of equity must be able to identify the owners of the company (refer to Chapter 2). Some bonds are issued in registered form.

The register contains:

- the name of the holder
- the address of the holder
- the quantity of shares or bonds held
- the date of registration and of changes to holdings

and the registrar is responsible for keeping the register updated following sales, or following the transfer of ownership (for example, between family members).

When a registered security is first brought to the marketplace, the issuer appoints a registrar who creates the register containing the above-mentioned details.

For some registered securities, certificates of ownership are issued, but for other issues no certificate is issued.

6.2.1 Certificated Form

Some issues in registered form are represented by certificates (also known as 'scrip'), which are printed and sent to the registered holders shortly after the security has been brought to the marketplace.

An example of a registered security certificate is shown in Figure 6.1.

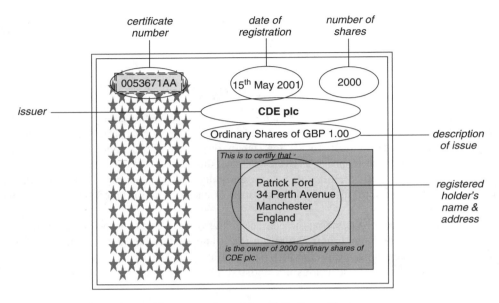

Figure 6.1   Registered securities: example registered share certificate

A registered certificate typically contains the following information:

- the name of the issuer—this identifies the entity that has issued the security;
- the description of the issue—equities are typically described as *common stock* in the USA and Canada and *ordinary shares* in Australia, India and the UK. The *par value* of shares also forms part of the description, for example 'common stock of par value USD 0.10' or 'ordinary shares of AUD 1.00'. Par value of equity issues bears no relation to market value, but does form part of the issue's formal description (e.g. CDE plc, Ordinary Shares of GBP 1.00);
- the certificate number—a unique number given to each certificate issued;
- the date of registration—the date on which the register was updated with the information contained on the certificate. Note that this date is important with regard to payments of dividends (refer to Chapter 26);
- the number of shares—represents the amount of ownership in the issue, as represented by an individual certificate. Note that individual certificates do not necessarily represent a holder's entire holding in an issue; an investor who has purchased the same registered security on five separate occasions is likely to have a single holding but five separate entries on the register and therefore will have five separate certificates;
- the registered holder's name and address—the investor's name and address which clearly identifies the owner, whether an individual or a company. Registered securities held by a company such as an STO, agent or custodian, on behalf of the investor, are likely to be registered in a nominee name for all clients. Nominee names appear on the issuer's register of holders, and represent the holdings of the underlying clients; this enables more efficient administration of subsequent sales by clients and the collection of income on behalf of the clients.

6.2.2   Uncertificated Form

The registered owner's holdings in some securities, although issued originally in certificated form, may today be held electronically via a method known as *book entry*, whereby holdings are maintained centrally within a *central securities depository* (CSD), as this facilitates more efficient holding (and faster transfer of ownership). The global trend is moving away from certificated form and towards electronic book-entry holdings and settlement.

Securities that have been transformed from certificated form to book entry are either:

* dematerialised—certificates are replaced by book entry, or
* immobilised—certificates exist but are held centrally in secure storage.

Where a specific security is usually held by book entry, and there is an option for the holder to receive a certificate from the issuer (instead of book entry), the transformation of the holding from book entry to certificated form is said to be *rematerialised*.

The holders of an uncertificated security will have their name and address recorded on a register of holders maintained by the issuer or registrar, but no certificate will be issued.

6.3   BEARER SECURITIES

The holders of a bearer security have no means of having their name and address recorded on a register of holders maintained by the issuer (or by a registrar on behalf of the issuer), as no such register exists.

6.3.1   Standard Certificated Form

For bearer securities, proof of ownership is physical possession of the certificate; holding bearer securities is effectively the same as holding banknotes, in that absolute proof of ownership without physical possession is extremely difficult to establish. (The wording on banknotes issued by many countries around the globe states 'I promise to pay the bearer on demand, the sum of . . .'.)

When a bearer security is first issued (refer to Chapter 3), the issuer prints bearer certificates representing the entire issue, in specific denominations. The certificates are issued to the investors, via the lead manager and the relevant syndicate member.

The nature of bearer securities requires the investor to safeguard their certificates, by having them held securely; individual investors' certificates could be held in safe custody by an STO, an agent or a custodian. The physical movement of bearer securities introduces the risk of theft or loss, so it is common to have such securities held within vaults by a custodian or *CSD*. Failure to have bearer securities held in a secure place could result in direct financial loss to the investor where, for instance, the certificates are lost or stolen, as there is no centrally held register containing a list of the owners. Despite the fact that, at the point of launch of a new issue, the issuer and lead manager know who the syndicate members are, as the issue is sold in the secondary market (throughout the following months and years until maturity of the bond), the issuer maintains no formal track of who the owners are; this makes bearer securities just like cash. Although the responsibility for making payments of interest and maturity proceeds lies with the issuer (or its appointed

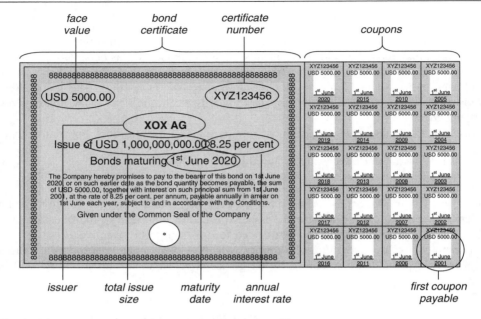

Figure 6.2   Bearer securities: example bearer bond certificate

agent), payments are not made automatically; the bearer certificate holder (or its custodian) is responsible for initiating these payments via the presentation of coupons (for interest payments) and the bond itself (for maturity proceeds).

An example of a bearer security certificate is shown in Figure 6.2.

A bearer bond certificate contains the following information:

- the name of the issuer—this identifies the entity that has issued the security
- the description of the issue
  - the annual interest rate, expressed as a percentage of the face value
  - the maturity date, the date when the issuer will repay the capital sum to the holders, after which the bond no longer exists
  - the total issue size, the cash amount and currency raised by the issuer
- the certificate number—a unique number given to each certificate issued
- the face value—represents the amount of ownership in the issue, as represented by an individual certificate. In the example of the XOX issue (refer to Chapter 3), bonds had been issued in USD 5000.00 and USD 20,000.00 denominations
- a sheet of coupons—each coupon represents one of a number of interest payments due during the life of the bond. Interest payments may be made once per year (annually), every six months (semi-annually), every three months (quarterly) or even monthly, dependent upon the type of bond. Each coupon contains the following information:
  - the certificate number of the bond to which the coupon relates
  - the face value of the bond to which the coupon relates
  - the interest rate or interest amount payable per coupon (hence the term *coupon* when referring to the rate of interest on a bond)
  - the specific interest payment date

○ the *coupon paying agent* (usually printed on the reverse of the coupon) appointed by the issuer

and in addition, measures must be taken to protect against counterfeiting and forgery, by the use of, for example, paper of a certain weight and watermarked paper.

In order for the bondholder to receive payments of interest on the due date, the relevant coupon must be detached from the bond and presented to the coupon paying agent at the appropriate time. Similarly, in order for the bondholder to receive the capital repayment on the due date, the bond must be surrendered to the issuer (or its agent) at the appropriate time. Investors will not be maximising their use of cash if coupons and bonds are presented after the coupon and maturity dates respectively, as the issuer does not pay compensation when the cash due is not claimed on time.

Note: bearer certificates contain no details of the owner of the security, unlike registered certificates.

6.3.2   Global Certificated Form

The holders of a security in global certificated form will not have their name and address recorded on a register of holders maintained by the issuer, but a single (global) certificate representing the entire issue is lodged with an independent agency (known as a common depository). The record of owners is maintained by the relevant central securities depository (CSD), requiring holders to be a participant of the CSD, or to utilise a custodian that is a participant.

Global certificates may be issued as:

* a permanent global certificate—no physical certificates will be issued and an investor's holding must continue to be maintained within the relevant CSD;
* a temporary global certificate—physical certificates will be issued, but not until a specified future date. Until that time the investor's holding must be maintained within the relevant CSD.

Through automation, for the issuance of some types of bond (for example *eurobonds*), the trend is moving away from standard certificated form and into permanent global form. From the issuer's perspective the cost of printing certificates is reduced, whilst the relevant CSDs are able to maintain the record of holders solely on an electronic basis, without having to store, deliver or receive physical certificates. Holding certificates in this manner reduces (if not eliminates) the likelihood of forged certificates, and makes the collection of income and redemption payments far more efficient.

6.4   METHODS OF TRANSFER OF REGISTERED AND BEARER SECURITIES

6.4.1   Introduction

When securities are sold or transferred, the method of transfer of the securities from seller to buyer is closely linked to the form of the security being sold, needing to take account of whether there is a requirement to re-register the security, or not.

6.4.2   Transfer and Re-registration

The transfer and re-registration process is applicable to registered securities in certificated form, where:

- the book entry with re-registration method does not exist in the specific marketplace, or
- the book entry with re-registration method does exist, but is not available for all securities within a marketplace.

When an investor physically holds and then sells registered securities in certificated form, the holder is required to deliver the registered certificate to the buyer in order to effect settlement. The steps involved in this process are represented in Figure 6.3 and are described below.

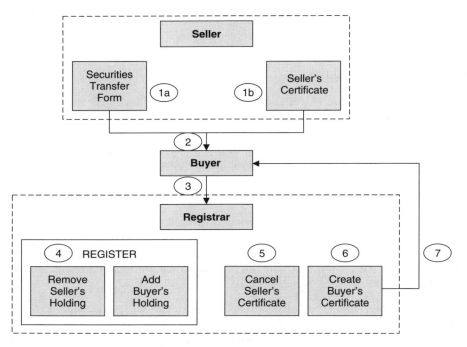

Figure 6.3   Registered securities: transfer and re-registration process

Step 1a: before the buyer can regard the registered certificate as valid for re-registration into the buyer's name, the seller is required to complete a securities transfer form (or in some markets to endorse the reverse of the certificate), thereby indicating that the registered holder authorises the removal (or reduction) of their holding in the specific security.

Step 1b: the seller's certificate plus the signed securities transfer form must be available for delivery together, in order for the buyer to accept the delivery.

Step 2: the seller's certificate plus the transfer form are delivered to the buyer, against payment.

Step 3: the buyer's name and address are added to the securities transfer form and both the seller's certificate and the securities transfer form are forwarded to the registrar.

Step 4: on the register, the registrar effects the

* removal of the seller's holding
* creation of the buyer's holding.

Step 5: the registrar cancels the seller's certificate, so it is no longer valid.

Step 6: the registrar creates the buyer's certificate.

Step 7: the registrar sends the buyer's certificate to the buyer.

It is important to remember that a registered certificate is a reflection of the information on the master record, the register. There is a fundamentally important distinction in this respect, between registered and bearer securities. Consequently, if a registered certificate is lost, the registrar charges a fee for the generation and issue of a duplicate certificate.

In the past in some markets, and still in some markets today, an investor would not be allowed to sell registered securities unless the investor had physical possession of a valid certificate of ownership. Under these circumstances, the efficiency of the registration process can impact the trading of securities.

The transfer and re-registration process was the historic method used in a number of countries around the globe. As a manually intensive method of transfer, it was (and still is) prone to cause major difficulties in operational efficiency across the marketplace, when trading volumes increase.

This was exemplified when, after *deregulation* in the London Stock Exchange in 1986, trading volumes increased dramatically and within 3 years many registrars and settlement departments of many STOs were completely inundated with transfer forms and sellers' certificates. The registration of buyers' securities and the resultant issuance of new certificates in some cases took many weeks to complete, which had major knock-on effects for settlement due to share certificates not being available.

6.4.3   Book Entry without Re-registration

The book entry (without re-registration) process is applicable to bearer securities in standard form and in global certificate form.

STOs buying a bearer security typically request that their securities are delivered to a relevant *CSD* where the STO is a participant, and where other STOs are likely to require their securities to be delivered.

Bearer securities are normally held by the CSD in secure storage, where it may hold securities only, or securities and cash on behalf of its participants. Although possible in most cases, bearer securities are not normally held outside the relevant CSD, due to the risk of theft and the need to have the securities located in the normal place of settlement. The CSD must maintain records of the total quantity of an individual security that it holds, and the quantity held by all relevant participants. For example, see Table 6.1.

CSDs do not normally maintain records of which of their participants are the owners of which specific certificates of the bearer issue. Just like banknotes held by a bank for all its account holders, where an individual account holder has no need or desire to have specific banknotes held for his account, bearer certificates are normally co-mingled (such holdings are said to be *fungible*) amongst all participants of the CSD holding the security. (However, CSDs may offer to hold *non-fungible* certificates for participants, where specific certificates are held by the CSD to the order of an individual participant;

Table 6.1 A CSD's record of its holding of XOX AG 8.25% Bonds 1st June 2020 (as at any point in time during the life of the bond)

Participants	Holding per participant	Total holding at the CSD
WSIL	5,000,000.00	
RST	15,000,000.00	
MNO	3,000,000.00	
GHI	5,500,000.00	
JKL	1,000,000.00	
DEF	550,000.00	
ABC	12,000,000.00	
Total	**42,050,000.00**	**42,050,000.00**

most participants of CSDs do not make use of this facility, as there is normally no advantage in holding specific bearer certificates of a security.)

Sales and purchases of bearer bonds are executed as a minimum of, and multiples of, the smallest denomination (in the example of the XOX bond this is USD 5000.00), otherwise it would be impossible to deliver the bond from seller to buyer, as it is not possible to split a bond into a quantity that is less than the lowest denomination. The seller is required to deliver the bearer certificate(s) representing the quantity sold to the buying STO's custodian. The steps involved in this process are represented in Figure 6.4 and are described below.

Step S1: having executed a sale, the selling STO issues a *settlement instruction* directly to the relevant CSD (which is holding the bearer securities to the STO's order, in safe custody) to deliver securities to the buying participant's account (within the CSD), versus receipt of cash, on the value date.

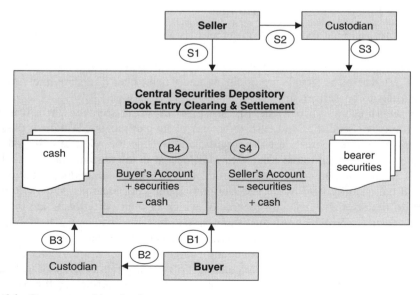

Figure 6.4   Bearer securities: book entry process

Step S2 and S3 (alternative to S1): if the seller has no account with the CSD, the seller issues a settlement instruction to its custodian, who in turn issues a settlement instruction to the CSD (which is holding the bearer securities to the custodian's order) to deliver securities to the buying participant's account, versus receipt of cash, on the value date.

Step B1: having executed a purchase, the buying STO issues a settlement instruction directly to the relevant CSD (where the STO typically has cash borrowing facilities) to receive securities from the selling participant's (or its custodian's) account, versus payment of cash, on the value date.

Step B2 and B3 (alternative to B1): if the buyer has no account with the CSD, it will request its custodian to settle on its behalf, as in step S2 and S3.

On value date, the following will occur if the seller has sufficient securities to deliver and the buyer has sufficient cash to pay:

Step S4: the seller's (or its custodian's) account will be debited with the securities and credited with the cash.

Step B4: the buyer's (or its custodian's) account will be credited with the securities and debited with the cash.

Note that in the case of sales of bearer securities, the original certificate remains live and valid throughout the life of the issue, as there is no registration or re-registration process.

As a result of settlement, the CSD will need to update its records of securities holdings for its participants. It is important to note that the total of all the holdings for all the participants has not changed, and there has been no physical removal from or addition to the securities in the CSD's vaults. The *ICSDs* Euroclear (Brussels) and Clearstream Banking (Luxembourg) are examples of CSDs that operate in this manner.

On occasions, an STO may buy securities from a counterparty who holds the securities outside the normal CSD. Besides being able to settle transactions in bearer securities on a book-entry basis, CSDs typically have the capability to accept incoming certificates and add them to the existing holding in their vaults, whilst at the same time updating the balance for the buying STO. This normally requires the STO to receive the physical certificates from the seller, then to deliver the certificates to the CSD accompanied by an instruction to the CSD requesting them to credit the account of the STO. The CSD is expected to take measures to ensure that any securities that it receives physically are checked for authenticity at the time of receipt; otherwise it may take months or years for the CSD (and its participants) to discover that it holds counterfeit securities.

Conversely, an STO may sell securities to a counterparty who requires physical delivery of securities, requiring the STO to issue a specific type of settlement instruction to the CSD. This will result in the CSD needing to reduce its records of physical holding of certificates and the holding for the relevant participant, the STO.

6.4.4   Book Entry with Re-registration

The book entry with re-registration process is applicable to registered securities in uncertificated form, and is also applicable to registered securities in certificated form, where the seller holds the securities in certificated form, but the buyer requires the securities in uncertificated form.

This method of transfer is effectively the same as the book entry method described above, but with the addition of one vital component, namely re-registration into the buyer's name.

In some marketplaces, the traditional transfer and re-registration process remains in use as the sole method of transferring holdings from the seller's to the buyer's name. However, in other marketplaces, a 'hybrid' of the transfer/re-registration and book entry method of transferring holdings has been introduced; this will be referred to as the 'book entry with re-registration' method and involves the transfer of registered holdings by electronic means (Figure 6.5).

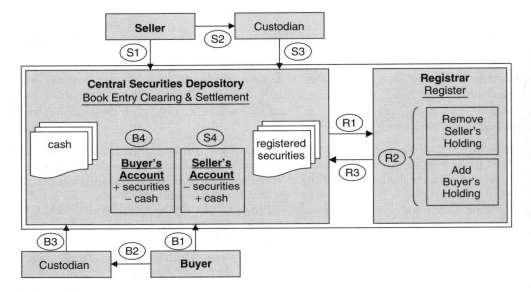

Figure 6.5   Registered securities: book entry with re-registration process

The seller and buyer each input a settlement instruction directly to the CSD or via their custodian, and on value date settlement will occur if the seller has sufficient securities to deliver and the buyer has sufficient cash to pay. The additional steps are:

Step R1: the CSD sends an electronic message containing details of the change in holding as a result of settlement to the registrar.

Step R2: the register is updated electronically.

Step R3: the registrar sends an electronic message confirming that the register has been updated to the CSD.

Note that in some countries, where the seller's holding is registered in a nominee name (a name that represents the seller's holding), the buyer's holding may remain in that same nominee name. Under such a system, the holder on the company's register (the nominee name) remains the same upon settlement, the record of the owner of securities being held within the CSD's records. However, if the seller holds securities in his own name, then re-registration will need to occur into the buyer's name (or into a nominee name that represents the buyer's holding).

Table 6.2 gives examples of systems that are used for the book entry with re-registration process.

Table 6.2

Country	System acronym	System full name
Australia	CHESS	Clearing House Electronic Subregister System
Hong Kong	CCASS	Central Clearing and Settlement System
Japan	JASDEC	Japan Securities Depository Center
UK and Ireland	CREST	Crest
USA	DTC	Depository Trust Company

Note: these systems may not be the only systems in use in the countries listed.

In some marketplaces, all records are kept in electronic form and it is not possible for registered certificates to be issued at all; under these circumstances, holdings are said to be in *dematerialised* form.

In other marketplaces, the aim is to have as much of a security as possible kept in electronic form, but to allow physical registered certificates to be held, when required (typically by individual investors). Under these circumstances, the CSD and the registrar must be able to accept incoming and to create outgoing physical registered certificates, in a similar fashion as described in Section 6.4.3.

6.5 REGISTERED AND BEARER SECURITIES: SIMILARITIES AND DIFFERENCES

A comparison of the characteristics of:

- registered securities in certificated form (1 in Table 6.3),
- dematerialised registered securities (2 in Table 6.3), and
- bearer securities in certificated form (3 in Table 6.3)

would reveal the similarities and differences as listed.

6.6 SUMMARY

STOs need to be aware of the methods by which settlement occurs in each of the financial centres in which they trade, in order to avoid delays and associated costs.

For example, where trades are typically settled via book entry within a specific country, the STO should be aware whether physical certificates are allowed and if so, the timing

Table 6.3

Subject	1. Registered (certificated)	2. Registered (dematerialised)	3. Bearer (certificated)
Issuer's knowledge of holders' identity	Yes (via register)	Yes (via register)	No
Frequency of issuing certificates	Recurring (upon sale or transfer of holding)	not applicable	Once when new issue
Normal method of holding	Register & certificate	Register & book entry	Certificate & book entry
Normal method of transfer	Transfer & re-registration	Book-entry & re-registration	Book-entry transfer
Income payment method	To holders on register at specified date	To holders on register at specified date	Following presentation of coupon by holder

and sequence of steps involved when physical certificates are being received from the seller, or are required to be delivered to the buyer.

If this is not understood in advance of such trades being executed, the STO may suffer unexpected costs through delays in settlement.

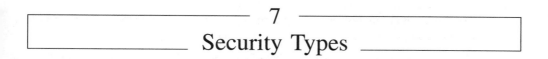

7
Security Types

7.1 INTRODUCTION

Further to the description of equity and debt securities in Chapter 2, many variations of securities exist with varying characteristics that are designed to meet the needs of both issuers and investors. This chapter aims to convey the essential characteristics of each type.

7.2 EQUITIES

Companies issue equity, some companies issuing solely *common stock* or *ordinary shares*, others issuing a variety of the following types.

7.2.1 Types of Equity

Common Stock/Ordinary Shares

Issuers of common stock or ordinary shares are able to raise long-term capital. The units of ownership in a publicly owned company are typically named common stock (the term used in the USA) or ordinary shares (UK); these securities carry no undertaking by the issuer to repay an investor's cash. The vast majority of daily trading volume in equities is effected over such securities, as opposed to other types of equity.

Such shareholders (also known as stockholders in the USA) have the right to vote on issues such as the appointment of directors and the payment of *dividends*. However these rights do not apply to shareholders in non-voting shares (where issued by a company). Some companies issue A and B shares that typically represent voting and non-voting shares.

If a company becomes insolvent, ordinary shareholders/common stockholders rank lower in the hierarchy of those due any assets than, for example, preference shareholders.

In North America, the everyday term in use for this type of security is 'stock', whilst in the UK and Australasia, the term 'share' is used.

Preferred Stock/Shares

Issuers of preferred shares are able to raise capital without diluting the rights of the common stockholders or ordinary shareholders. Preferred stock/shares are similar to common stock/ordinary shares regarding ownership in a publicly owned company, but with certain differences, such as:

- dividends are potentially payable at a different rate in comparison with ordinary shares; they are usually paid at a predetermined percentage (similar to a bond). Such payments may or may not be favourable when compared with dividends payable on common stock/ordinary shares;

- holders have no voting rights
- in an insolvency situation, holders have priority over ordinary share/stockholders regarding the liquidation of assets

although it is important to note that the rights of preference share/stockholders can differ between different companies, and between different countries (according to differing laws of incorporation).

Not all companies issue preferred stock/shares and the number of shareholders is typically much lower than for common stock/ordinary shares.

Cumulative Preference Shares

A variation of the preferred stock/share is the cumulative preference share; such securities give the holder similar rights as per preference shareholders, with the exception of payments of dividends.

If the company fails to make sufficient earnings within a given period to pay dividends on ordinary and preference shares, the company is not obliged to make payments in arrears (once the company's financial position has improved) to the ordinary and preference shareholders.

However, cumulative preference shares entitle the holders to receive the accumulated dividends retrospectively.

Equity Warrants

Warrants entitle the holder to subscribe to the equity of the issuing company:

- in a proportionate amount to the number of warrants
- at a fixed price set at the time of issue
- at or before a prespecified date or before the closure of a stated period

whereafter the warrant expires. The act of subscribing to the equity is achieved by *exercising* the warrant.

Depository Receipts

Depository receipts are documents representing shares in a foreign company, in a fixed ratio to the underlying security; such receipts are typically created so as to enable investors to effectively acquire securities in overseas companies in a tax efficient manner.

For example, in order for US investors to overcome certain difficulties in investing in overseas securities (including the avoidance of paying stamp duty on UK securities), residents of the USA can hold *American Depository Receipts* (ADRs), which may be bought and sold within the USA at a USD price. ADRs are created (commonly known as 'issuance') for underlying shares in numerous countries. The underlying shares that ADRs represent are converted and held by depository banks in the USA; ADRs may be reconverted (commonly known as 'cancellation') to the underlying share at any time. The example of a UK equity is used in Figure 7.1 to illustrate the conversion of shares to ADRs and vice versa.

Although ADRs are aimed at the US market, UK investors may buy ADRs in order to reconvert the ADR to the underlying share, thereby taking advantage of any price differential (commonly known as 'arbitrage') between the US and the UK marketplaces.

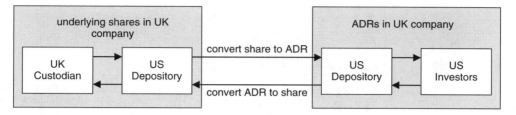

Figure 7.1   Security types: American depository receipts

Conceptually similar to ADRs, *Global Depository Receipts* (GDRs) represent shares in a foreign company which residents of various countries are able to purchase. GDRs allow issuers to receive capital in overseas currencies, whilst the purchase cost to the investor is typically paid in the investor's local currency.

7.2.2   Equity Characteristics

Board Lots

Some equities are traded in standard quantity parcels, commonly referred to as *board lots* or round lots; amounts traded are in multiples of the board/round lot, whilst amounts other than a board/round lot are known as *odd lots*.

Share for share, it is normally cheaper for investors to trade in the standard quantities, as a premium may be charged for executing non-standard quantities.

Par Value

Some equities are given a 'par value' (e.g. USD 5.00), which is part of the formal description of the issue, but has no bearing on the price of the share and is used only in the issuer's accounting. Some equities are issued as 'no par value' securities.

7.3   BONDS

Companies, governments, government agencies and supranational organisations (amongst others) issue bonds, with most types of bond paying interest (commonly known as *coupon*), some at a fixed rate and others at a variable rate.

However, numerous variations of bonds exist as a result of issuers in many locations offering bonds with characteristics that match investors' needs with their own needs; the following should not therefore be regarded as an exhaustive list.

7.3.1   Types of Bonds

Straight Bonds

Bonds that pay coupon on prespecified dates at a fixed rate, and which mature on a fixed date, are known as straight bonds. Such bonds are not convertible into any other form of security (Figure 7.2). A straight bond typically pays coupon annually or every six months; in the example of the fictitious XOX bond, the primary value date (the date the investors paid for the bonds and the date the issuer received its cash) was 1st June 2000. The first

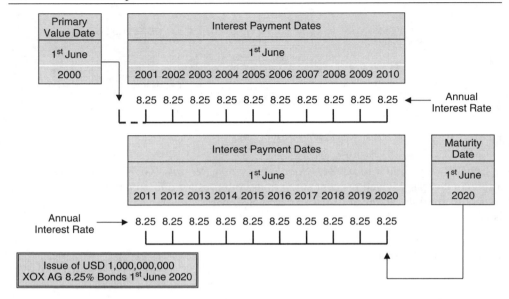

Figure 7.2   Security types: straight bonds

payment of coupon is due exactly 1 year after the primary value date, with the last coupon payment date on 1st June 2020. Between those dates, coupon is payable on 1st June in each year. On a straight bond, the rate of coupon payable at all coupon payment dates remains the same, in this case 8.25%. Finally, the capital sum is repayable by the issuer to the bondholder on maturity date (also known as redemption date); this date is typically the same date as the last coupon payment date.

Floating Rate Notes

Floating Rate Notes (FRNs) are a type of bond that pay coupon at variable rates (Figure 7.3):

- the coupon rate is relevant to a specific coupon period (the time between the latest and the next payment of coupon);
- coupon is typically paid every six months, or every three months, or monthly;

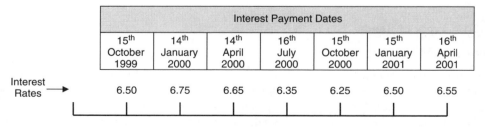

Figure 7.3   Security types: standard floating rate note

- the rate of coupon for each coupon period is calculated immediately prior to the coupon period according to prespecified criteria, for example a reference or benchmark rate (such as LIBOR, the London Interbank Offered Rate), which is an average rate calculated from rates provided by a specific group of banks. Consequently, the physical coupons attached to the FRN certificate do not have a stated coupon rate (unlike a straight bond). The calculation of the rate for each coupon period is known as rate refixing. More complex rate refixing structures may apply to index-linked bonds, which are another form of FRN;
- the coupon rate may have a minimum rate payable (known as a 'floor' FRN);
- the coupon rate may have a maximum rate payable (known as a 'cap' FRN);
- individual FRNs may be convertible into a fixed rate bond.

FRNs are brought to the marketplace in a similar fashion to fixed rate bonds. During the life of an FRN, the issuer pays interest at the end of each coupon period (unless the issue is a mismatch FRN, see below). In the example of Figure 7.3, the coupon rate is calculated at the beginning of each quarterly coupon period, and that coupon amount is payable at the end of each coupon period. Working from the left side of the example, coupon for the quarter ending on 15th October 1999 was payable on the same date, at a rate of 6.50%. On or immediately before 15th October, the rate for the next quarter would be calculated (according to the predefined method for the specific issue), and so 6.75% would be paid for the quarter ending on 14th January 2000. Unlike straight bonds, coupon payment dates on FRNs are not fixed. If the coupon payment date falls on a non-working day, the date will be brought forward or moved back to the nearest working day; therefore coupon payment dates as well as coupon rates on FRNs are variable.

Mismatch FRNs

One type of FRN is known as a mismatch FRN, where coupon may be payable after a series of coupon periods, as represented in Figure 7.4. Mismatch FRNs differ from standard FRNs in the respect that the dates of coupon rate refixes, and coupon payment dates, are not the same. For example, Figure 7.4 shows that coupon is calculated at the beginning of each monthly coupon period, starting with the month ending on 20th February 2001; however, coupon is not paid on that date. Instead, coupon for three consecutive monthly periods, namely:

- to 20th February (rate 5.75%)

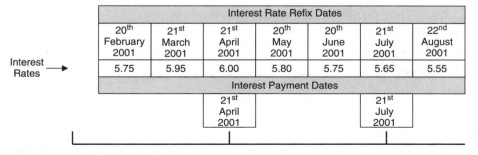

Figure 7.4   Security types: mismatch floating rate note

- to 21st March (rate 5.95%)
- to 21st April (rate 6.00%)

is aggregated and the coupon is paid quarterly, in this case on 21st April. Therefore in this example, coupon rates are recalculated each month, but payments of coupon occur on a quarterly basis.

Zero Coupon Bonds

Issuers borrowing cash to fund a project that will not generate income for ten years (for example), are unlikely to want to make regular payments of interest to the bondholders during that period. Consequently, the issuer may issue a zero coupon bond to attract investors that prefer no income, but a large capital gain (for tax purposes).

Zero coupon bonds are a type of bond that does not pay coupon, but the price at which an investor acquires the bond at issue launch is at a deep discount to the capital repayment price at maturity. During the life of the bond, the market price gradually increases towards maturity (Figure 7.5). For example, a bond with a face value of USD 10,000.00 may have been issued at a price of 40%, meaning that an investor would pay USD 4000.00 at issue launch. Bonds typically mature at a price of par (meaning 100% of the face value), which would result in the holder receiving redemption proceeds of USD 10,000.00. Zero coupon bonds are also known as accrual bonds.

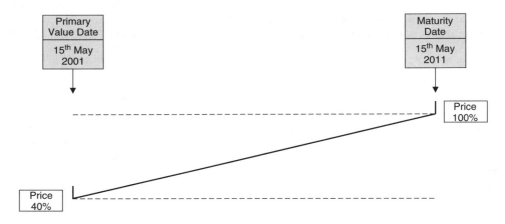

Figure 7.5   Security types: zero coupon bond

7.3.2   Other Types of Bond

Split Coupon Bonds

Bonds that are issued as zero coupon bonds, but which during the life of the bond become coupon paying bonds.

Step-up Bonds

Bonds that are issued with an initial lower than average coupon rate, and at some later point the rate is increased to a higher than average coupon rate.

Eurobonds

A type of bond that is usually sold to investors outside the country relating to the currency of issue.

Dual Currency Bonds

Bonds that are denominated in one currency, but which pay coupons in another currency at a fixed exchange rate.

Perpetual/Undated Bonds or FRNs

Bonds or notes that have no maturity date (usually because the issuer has the need for capital on an ongoing basis), but which pay coupon on a regular basis.

Flip-Flop FRNs

Perpetual notes issued as an FRN, becoming a fixed interest security and then reverting to an FRN, usually at the bondholder's option.

Stripped Bonds

Bond stripping is the practice of detaching all the coupons from the bond, then treating as separate securities the bond (without coupons attached) and the individual coupons. The resultant bonds and coupons are then regarded as having the characteristics of zero coupon bonds, since the original bond and each individual stripped coupon entitles the holder to receive an amount of cash at a specified future date, without payments of interest. These elements are usually referred to as IO (Interest Only) or PO (Principal Only).

Bonds with Warrants Attached

Warrants entitle the holder to subscribe to another security, at a fixed ratio to the face value of the bond set at the time of issue, before a prespecified date, whereafter the warrant expires. Warrants are issued attached to a host bond, but during their life the warrants may be detached from the bond and traded separately. The bond in its issued state is described as 'cum-warrant' (with warrant attached to the bond), the bond after the warrant has been detached is known as 'ex-warrant', and the detached security is described as the warrant.

Convertible Bonds

Convertible bonds are equity related, interest bearing bonds that entitle the holder to convert the bond into the underlying equity of the issuer, at a fixed ratio to the face value of the bond, during prespecified periods during the life of the bond. Holders of unconverted bonds at maturity date will receive repayment of capital, as per straight bonds. Convertible bonds usually pay a lower rate of interest than straight bonds.

Mortgage-backed Bonds

Issuers in the business of providing mortgages to the public for the purchase of residential properties may issue bonds as a means of raising the necessary cash. Such issuers include the Government National Mortgage Association in the USA.

The mortgages serve as the guarantee that the bond investor will be repaid its capital. Some interest and some capital are typically repaid to investors periodically, according to the type of issue. The method of capital repayment may result in amortisation; see Amortising Bonds.

Brady Bonds

'Brady bonds' is a collective term to describe bond issues of varying types that represent the restructuring of debt in Less Developed Countries (LDCs), primarily centred on Latin America. In 1989, a restructuring plan was implemented by the US Treasury Secretary Nicholas Brady to recover some of the debt owing (to banks who were the original lenders) by LDCs, in acknowledgement that repayment of the full monies owing by the LDCs was no longer realistic.

Brady bonds are of varying types, and include:

- par bonds—issued at the full face value of the original debt, but at a reduced interest rate
- discounted bonds—issued with a face value discounted from the original debt

issued in numerous currencies.

Certificates of Deposit (CD)

A type of bond issued by a bank as a notice of the deposit of funds for a fixed period and with maturities up to 5 years.

Commercial Paper (CP)

A type of interest bearing bond that usually has a life of no more than 1 year.

Medium-term Notes (MTN)

A type of bond that can be issued according to the investor's requirements in terms of lifespan, currency of issue and whether floating rate of interest or fixed, typically maturing within 2 and 6 years.

Note that CDs, CPs, MTNs and FRNs of less than five years to maturity are collectively known as Money Market Instruments; they are bought and sold in the same fashion that money is traded.

Debenture

A certificate issued by a company that represents long-term loans, normally paying a fixed rate of interest and maturing on a fixed date; some debentures are convertible into the underlying equity of the company.

7.3.3 Bond Characteristics

The following are distinctive features of bonds that may be applied to the various types of bond listed above.

Amortising Bonds

Bonds (such as a mortgage-backed bonds) that pay coupons and partial repayment of capital to investors in instalments over a period of time in a specific manner.

The capital repayment results in the face value of the bond remaining unchanged, but a percentage is applied to the bond price and to interest payments, in order to represent the decrease in cash owing by the issuer.

Callable Bonds

An attribute of a bond issue that allows the issuer to give notice that bondholders are required to present their bonds for redemption, prior to the maturity date.

Capitalising Bonds

Bonds that have a percentage of their coupon payments converted into capital. This typically occurs where the issuer cannot make interest payments at the scheduled time, but resulting in the capital amount outstanding on a bond being increased in recognition that the cash amount will eventually be repaid by the issuer.

Partly Paid Bonds

Bonds requiring investors to pay an initial instalment (for example 40% of the full cost) followed by one or more later instalments, until fully paid.

Purchase Fund

Should the price of an issue in the secondary market fall below the price at which the bond was issued, a purchase fund allows the issuer to buy the issue in the market place in order to sustain the price.

Puttable Bonds

A characteristic of a bond that allows the bondholder to invoke the redemption of bonds prior to the maturity date, at a predefined price and time.

Secured

Bonds issued whereby the issuer has pledged assets to support the bond; in the event of issuer default, the pledged assets are used to repay capital to the bondholders.

Subordinated

Some bonds are issued as specifically being lower in rank (compared with other bonds issued by the same issuer) in relation to the repayment of capital, in a default situation.

Tranches of Bonds

A single bond security may be issued in a series of sub-releases, commonly known as tranches.

Unsecured

Bonds issued where the issuer has pledged no assets to support the bond; for such issues, the investor must be able to ascertain the issuer's ability to pay coupons and repay capital on maturity. This is typically achieved through the use of issuer ratings by *ratings agencies*.

7.4   GROUPING OF SECURITIES

Within the securities marketplace, securities are not only referred to individually, but also in groups; treatment of securities in groups enables automated identification of a security's features which can provide operational advantages.

Individual securities normally have the same or similar characteristics as other securities issued in the same marketplace. They are also treated by the marketplace as behaving similarly and can therefore be grouped together, from an operational processing perspective.

Examples of such groups are:

- Argentinian equities
- Canadian equities
- New Zealand equities
- Swedish equities

- Australian corporate bonds
- *Eurobonds*
- Japanese Government bonds
- US Treasury bonds

and further sub-groupings may be necessary, for example:

- Canadian equities traded on the Toronto stock exchange
- Canadian equities traded on the Vancouver stock exchange

- Eurobonds—straight
- Eurobonds—floating rate

in order to maximise efficiency in operational processing. The operational benefit of placing individual securities into groups is described below.

An individual security that is referred to as a UK equity (for instance, Marks & Spencer plc, Ordinary Shares) is expected to behave in a very similar fashion in an operational sense to all other securities in that group. Table 7.1 compares typical characteristics of UK equities, US Treasury bonds and Eurobonds.

These and other security group characteristics are generally known by those who invest and trade in such securities, enabling market-wide understanding of, for instance, how to calculate the cash values of trades in such securities (which will be explored in Chapter 8) and how to settle them. Such information is also used within STOs in order to automate the throughput of trades.

Table 7.1

Characteristic	UK equities	US Treasury bonds	Eurobonds
Value date	Three days after trade date*	One day after trade date*	Three days after trade date*
Security form	Registered	Registered	Bearer
Settlement location	Crest**	FBE***	Euroclear or Clearstream****
Transfer method	Book entry with re-reg'n	Book entry	Book entry
Settlement terms	DvP	DvP	DvP

*The topics of value date calculation and *settlement cycles* are explored in Chapter 11.
**Crest is the settlement system for UK and Irish equities.
***FBE (Federal Reserve Book Entry) is the CSD for US Treasury securities.
****Euroclear and Clearstream Luxembourg are the two ICSDs.

However, within these security groups by market, variations in the characteristics of securities are likely to occur. For example, Eurobonds can be issued in various guises, such as straight bonds, FRNs and zero coupon bonds.

In an automated environment, the placement of individual securities into groups can assist in the efficiency of operational processing. Within settlement systems, individual securities can be related to a group that can then trigger appropriate processing for trades in that security. This will be described in Chapter 9.

7.5 DERIVATIVES

The term derivative is a generic term to describe financial instruments that relate to an underlying asset, such as a security. The subject of derivatives is a major topic in its own right, about which numerous books have been written. As this book primarily focuses on the operational aspects of equities and bonds, the topic of derivatives is not covered.

7.6 SUMMARY

Understanding the nature of the securities in which an STO trades is a vitally important factor in calculating associated trade cash values correctly. If not well understood, the STO stands the risk of calculating too little cash on sales, and too much cost on purchases, leading to payments and receipts of incorrect monetary amounts.

Furthermore, appreciating the subsequent actions that can occur to the various types of security at particular times or under certain circumstances is likely to result in the STO taking advantage of profitable opportunities.

8
Trade Cash Value Calculation

8.1 INTRODUCTION

For nearly all trades that an STO needs to manage and process, it is necessary to calculate the cash value in order to know the cash cost to pay upon receipt of securities from counterparties, and cash proceeds to receive when delivering securities to counterparties.

It is necessary to calculate trade cash values (a process also known as figuration) for all transaction types (refer to Chapter 5), with the exception of depot (custodian) transfers as this requires only a movement of securities. Due to the differing components within each transaction type, trade cash values for each transaction type will differ, even where the same security and the same quantity of securities are used.

The need for accuracy and speed in calculating trade cash values is paramount, enabling an STO to function efficiently and to realise the following benefits:

- avoid losses through the payment of too much cash (for example on purchases) and the receipt of too little cash (for example on sales);
- avoid mismatches of trade details with counterparties, requiring additional handling by the STO (and therefore administrative cost);
- provide high quality service to clients by communicating the correct trade cost or proceeds calculations within the required timeframe following trade execution.

The details recorded by front office personnel following trade execution are typically limited to a few essential pieces of information; in the case of a principal trade:

- trading book
- trade date
- trade time
- value date
- operation
- quantity
- security
- price
- counterparty

and there is a high probability of calculating trade cash values accurately if the information is well understood and interpreted correctly. The responsibility for the calculation of trade cash values for operational purposes typically resides within the middle office/trade support area, or the settlement department.

In a situation where an STO executes trades in, for example, bonds of one type and solely using one transaction type (e.g. trading on a principal basis in the Italian Government bond market), the understanding within the relevant area of the organisation as to how to calculate trade cash values correctly can remain focused on that specific situation. However, to take the other extreme, an STO trading in a large number of the world's market places, in a range of security types, using a variety of transaction types, increases the necessary range and depth of understanding of the STO's personnel.

The final cash amount of trades is described in this book as the Net Settlement Value (NSV). Two sets of information are necessary to calculate the NSV, namely:

- the Gross Cash Value (GCV)
- any additional trade amounts

and Figure 8.1 illustrates example routes in the calculation of trades.

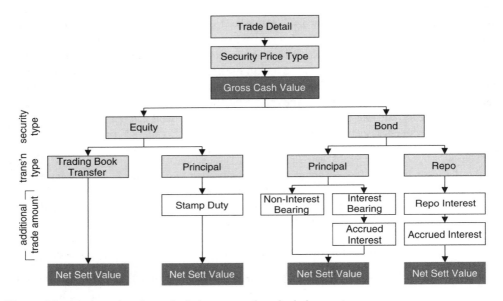

Figure 8.1   Trade cash value calculation: example calculation routes

The calculation of the GCV is dependent upon the trade quantity and price (contained within the trade detail) and the type of price applicable to the security; this topic is expanded upon in Section 8.2.

The calculation of any additional trade amounts is dependent upon the type of security (e.g. equity or bond) and the transaction type. The calculation of accrued interest will depend upon whether the security is an interest bearing bond (e.g. a straight bond) or a non-interest bearing bond (e.g. a zero coupon bond). The calculation of stamp duty on equities, for instance, depends upon the security group (e.g. UK equity as opposed to French equity).

The NSV is the sum of the GCV and the additional trade amounts.

The following sections explore the necessary calculations that need to be understood by those in operational areas, so that as individual trade details are received, they can be dealt with accurately and efficiently.

8.2   GROSS CASH VALUE CALCULATION

The type of price at which securities are traded differs according to whether the security is an equity or a bond.

This concept is important to understand, as the calculation of the correct cash values of trades begins with applying the price to the quantity traded, in order to derive the GCV.

8.2.1 Equity Price Types

The price at which equities are normally traded is a currency and cash amount for each share purchased or sold.

For example, a pension fund wishes to buy PQR shares from an STO resulting in a sale by the STO of 100,000 PQR Common Stock at a price of USD 54.75 to the pension fund. This requires a straight multiplication of the quantity of shares and the price, giving a GCV of USD 5,475,000.00. The term used in some parts of the globe for the GCV of equity trades is the 'gross consideration'.

8.2.2 Bond Price Types

Different types of bonds can be traded using different pricing conventions.

Percentage Prices

Bond prices are, in general, traded at a percentage price relevant to the currency and face value of the bond.

For example, an STO buys JPY 1,000,000,000 Japanese Government 3.60% bonds, maturing 1st September 2022 (a fictitious bond) at a price of 98.125%; this requires a calculation of:

$$\frac{\text{Face value} \times \text{Price}}{100} = \frac{1,000,000,000 \times 98.125}{100}$$

giving a GCV of JPY 981,250,000. The GCV of a bond trade is commonly known as the 'principal' or 'principal value'.

Bonds trading at a price of 100% are said to be trading at par; those trading above par are trading at a premium, whilst those trading below par are trading at a discount.

Yield Prices

The price of bonds can be quoted on a yield basis. Yield can be calculated using different measures but, for example, the 'yield to maturity' on a bond is the annual return on an investment taking into account:

- the purchase price
- the projected income (coupon) over the remaining life of the bond
- the time to maturity of the bond
- the proceeds at maturity

and expressed as a percentage of the capital invested.

If a bond is purchased at a price below par and the buyer retains the position until maturity of the bond, the yield will be greater than the annual coupon rate. The converse is true if the bond is purchased at a premium; note that both cases assume the bond repays at par on maturity.

8.2.3   Aspects Relevant to Both Equity and Bonds

Certain aspects of prices are relevant to equity and bonds.

Fractional Prices

In some marketplaces equities and bonds trade at whole prices plus fractions, where each fraction represents a known fractional amount (also known as tick value). For example, if a bond trades in fractional increments of 32nds, a trade in such a bond at a price of 99-5 means that the trade has been executed not at 99.50%, but at 99 5/32nds. As each 32nd equals 3.125% of a whole percentage point, 5/32nds equates to 15.625% of a whole percentage point. Therefore, where the relevant tick value is in 32nds, a price of 99-5 equates, in percentage terms, to 99.156 25% (99.00 plus 0.156 25).

During 2001, US equities moved from trading on a fractional basis to decimal based prices; this has resulted in trades being tradable in increments of one cent, rather than $1/16^{th}$ of a dollar.

8.3   ADDITIONAL TRADE AMOUNTS

Following the calculation of the GCV, any additional trade amounts must be calculated in order to derive the NSV of a trade. Such trade amounts can be categorised as follows:

- compulsory trade amounts,
- optional trade amounts, and
- internal trade amounts.

8.3.1   Compulsory Trade Amounts

Compulsory trade amounts can be defined as cash values that STOs are obligated to charge (by bodies such as stock exchanges, regulators and tax authorities) to counterparties, or because of market practice, that will affect the NSV of trades.

When an STO trades in certain markets, it may be required to charge its counterparties amounts imposed by authorities located in the country of issue of the security, or to pay amounts resulting from market practice.

Types of compulsory trade amounts include:

- stamp duty
- purchase and sales taxes
- transaction levies
- registration costs
- accrued interest.

Examples of compulsory trade amounts are:

- Hong Kong: stamp duty of 0.125% and transaction levy of 0.007% is payable on equity purchases and sales
- India: stamp duty is payable when registering physical securities, and is not payable on purchases registered via a book entry mechanism

- Ireland: stamp duty of 1% is payable on equity purchases
- Japan: registrars may charge a fee for registration of securities
- UK: stamp duty of 0.5% is payable on equity purchases, and PTM Levy (Panel on Takeovers & Mergers) at a fixed GBP 0.25 is payable on purchases and sales over GBP 10,000.00
- USA: S.E.C. (Securities and Exchange Commission) fee of 1/300th of one per cent is payable by sellers of equity securities.

Note that the description of accrued interest follows this section.

When trading in appropriate securities, STOs must calculate the value of such amounts, usually based upon the GCV of the trade.

The cash amount that would be payable by a buyer of 1,000,000 Marks & Spencer plc, Ordinary Shares (a UK equity), purchased at a price of GBP 2.46 per share, would be calculated as follows: GCV is GBP 2,460,00.00, stamp duty at 0.5% amounts to GBP 12,300.00, plus PTM Levy of GBP 0.25. The STO is obligated to charge these amounts to the buyer as part of the total sale proceeds; the amounts collected from the buyer must be paid to the relevant authorities.

Automation of these calculations can occur where the calculation details are held within an STO's settlement system. These amounts are typically required to be charged on groups of securities, such as on Australian equities but not on Australian Government bonds. Providing that individual securities can be classified as forming part of a group of securities, the amounts should be automatically calculated only when relevant.

Accrued Interest

Interest on bonds (also known as *coupon*) is payable by the issuer at the prespecified *coupon payment dates*. When executing a transaction in an interest bearing bond, normal practice in many of the world's markets is for the buyer to compensate the seller for the proportion of coupon earned since the previous coupon payment date, for which the seller has not been paid, as the next coupon payment date is in the future. This coupon amount is commonly referred to as *accrued interest*.

Having executed a trade, it is essential to calculate the accrued interest component accurately in order to avoid paying too much cash when buying, or receiving too little cash when selling.

In order to convey the concepts of calculating accrued interest on trades, the example of the fictitious XOX bond (refer to Chapter 3) that pays coupon annually on 1st June, beginning in 2001 and ending in 2020, at a fixed rate of 8.25%, will be used.

In example 1 (Figure 8.2), WSIL (a fictitious STO) purchased USD 10 million of the XOX bond at a price of 100%, for value date 1st June 2000, the same date as the *primary value date*. Interest typically begins to accrue from the close of business on the primary value date of a new bond issue, therefore no accrued interest was payable on this trade by WSIL. The cost of the purchase was therefore as in Table 8.1. Should WSIL decide to hold the bonds until maturity, they will be entitled to all payments of coupon falling on 1st June each year, until the last coupon payment in 2020, at which point WSIL will also be entitled to the maturity proceeds. Each payment of coupon will be USD 825,000.00 (USD 10 million × 8.25%).

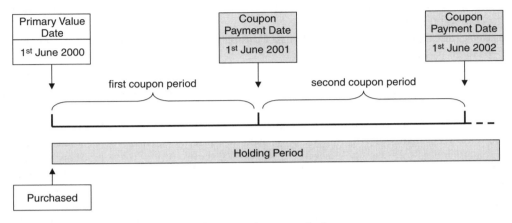

Figure 8.2   Accrued interest calculation on trades: example 1

Table 8.1

Operation	Buy
Quantity	USD 10,000,000.00
Price	100%
Principal	USD 10,000,000.00
Accrued days	nil
Accrued interest	0.00
NSV	**USD 10,000,000.00**

In example 2 (Figure 8.3), following the purchase on value date 1st June 2000 at a price of 100%, WSIL decide to sell for value date 25th June 2000, at a price of 100.25%. For each day that WSIL have held the bond, they are entitled to coupon for that day; but unlike example 1 where WSIL were compensated in the form of coupon payments made by the issuer on the coupon payment dates, market practice states that when a trade is executed, the buyer must compensate the seller as part of the buyer's purchase cost, to be included in the cash amount to be paid upon settlement of the trade. In order to ensure that they will be paid the correct sale proceeds, WSIL need to calculate the cash value of accrued interest owed by the buyer.

Focusing on the accrued interest from WSIL's perspective, they would expect to be compensated for holding the bonds for the period between 1st and 25th June 2000.

The first step in calculating the cash value of accrued interest on trades is to calculate the number of days of accrued interest; the first day to be counted is the latest coupon payment date or, where the first coupon payment date is in the future, the primary value date. The last day to be counted is the day prior to the value date (i.e. 24th June), therefore the correct number of days is 24.

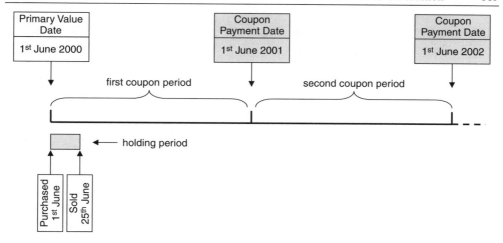

Figure 8.3   Accrued interest calculation on trades: example 2

The second step is to calculate the cash value of the accrued interest, for which the equation is:

$$\frac{\text{Face value} \times \text{Coupon rate}\%}{\text{Annual divisor}} \times \text{Number of days}$$

$$\frac{\text{USD } 10,000,000 \times 8.25\%}{360} \times 24 = \text{USD } 55,000.00$$

which produces WSIL's sale proceeds as in Table 8.2. Note that with regard to the annual divisor (shown above as being 360), different conventions exist according to the type of bond; this is explained in more detail later in this chapter.

Table 8.2

Operation	Sell	
Quantity	USD 10,000,000.00	
Price	100.25%	
Principal		USD 10,025,000.00
Accrued days	24	
Accrued interest		USD 55,000.00
NSV		**USD 10,080,000.00**

It is essential to remember that accrued interest calculations on trades are not related to the price at which a trade is executed. Instead, the calculations are directly related to the face value of the bond, as it is on this basis that the issuer pays interest.

WSIL will need to record all the trade details within their internal *books and records*, inclusive of all calculations, and then issue a *settlement instruction* to their relevant *custodian*, as will the buyer. The seller's and buyer's custodians then need to compare settlement instructions to ensure they match, before settlement can occur.

In example 3 (Figure 8.4), step 1: WSIL choose to buy USD 25 million of the XOX bond, at a price of 99.125%, for value date 7th February 2007. The cost to WSIL is given

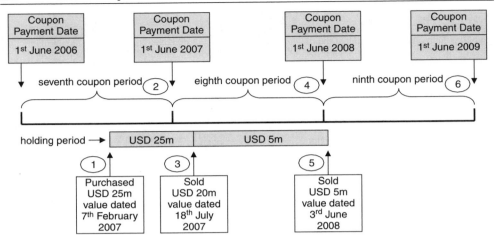

Figure 8.4   Accrued interest calculation on trades: example 3

Table 8.3

Operation	Buy
Quantity	USD 25,000,000.00
Price	99.125%
Principal	USD 24,781,250.00
Accrued days	246
Accrued interest	USD 1,409,375.00
NSV	**USD 26,190,625.00**

in Table 8.3. The seller will be compensated, from an accrued interest perspective, via the payment of USD 1,409,375.00, as part of the total cost payable by WSIL.

Step 2: As none of the bonds purchased by WSIL had been sold with a value date prior to 1st June 2007 coupon payment date, WSIL would be entitled to receive interest at 8.25% on all USD 25 million bonds, amounting to USD 2,062,500.00. WSIL is therefore being compensated by receiving the entire year's coupon payment; at first, this may appear to be incorrect, as WSIL has held the bond only for the period between 7th February and 1st June 2007. However, WSIL paid the seller USD 1,409,375.00 for the accrued interest component of the trade. The difference between the accrued interest paid on 7th February 2007 and the interest received on 1st June 2007 coupon payment date represents the bond interest income earned by WSIL during that period.

Step 3: WSIL decides to sell USD 20 million of the XOX bond, at a price of 99.10%, for value date 18th July 2007. The proceeds due to WSIL are given in Table 8.4. The reason that the number of days of accrued interest has dropped to 47, compared with the (step 1) purchase of 246 days, is that between the dates of the purchase and sale there has been a payment of coupon; this causes the day count to begin again from the latest coupon payment date (1st June 2007), for any trades with a value date within the new coupon period. Therefore, for each coupon period, holders of bonds are entitled to an amount of accrued interest that grows daily (A1 in Figure 8.5), until the coupon for that period is paid (B1). The count begins again after each coupon payment, until the next payment of coupon.

Table 8.4

Operation	Sell	
Quantity	USD 20,000,000.00	
Price	99.10%	
Principal		USD 19,820,000.00
Accrued days	47	
Accrued interest		USD 215,416.67
NSV		**USD 20,035,416.67**

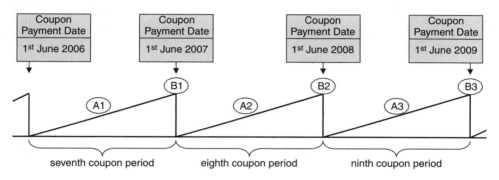

Figure 8.5   Accrued interest calculation on trades: bond accruals

Step 4: As WSIL is still the holder of USD 5 million bonds as at 1st June 2008 coupon payment date, WSIL would be entitled to receive coupon at 8.25% on that number of bonds, amounting to USD 412,500.00.

Step 5: WSIL decides to sell the remaining USD 5 million bonds at a price of 99.25%, for value date 3rd June 2008. The proceeds due to WSIL are given in Table 8.5.

Table 8.5

Operation	Sell	
Quantity	USD 5,000,000.00	
Price	99.25%	
Principal		USD 4,962,500.00
Accrued days	2	
Accrued interest		USD 2291.67
NSV		**USD 4,964,791.67**

Step 6: WSIL has no position in the bond as at 1st June 2009 coupon payment date and is therefore not entitled to receive that coupon payment.

Accrued Interest Annual Divisors and Day Count. The method of counting days of accrued interest and the annual divisors used when calculating the accrued interest on bond trades varies according to the type of security traded; these differences stem from evolution of working practices in the world's bond markets.

The XOX bond that this book uses as an example is intended to be a US Dollar denominated Eurobond; a comparison of such Eurobonds with, for example, Hong Kong Government bonds reveals that the day count and divisor conventions differ.

In the case of a US Dollar denominated Eurobond, the day count is based on a 360-day year consisting of 12 equal 30-day months (regardless of the calendar days in a month); the divisor is 360, which is used to calculate the accrued interest amount for a single day. This accrued interest basis is commonly referred to as '30/360'.

In example 3 earlier in this chapter, the purchase of USD 25 million bonds on value date 7th February 2007 resulted in 246 days of accrued interest being calculated; this was derived as in Table 8.6 (counting from the previous coupon payment date of 1st June 2006).

Table 8.6

Month	Day count
June 2006	30
July	30
August	30
September	30
October	30
November	30
December	30
January 2007	30
February	6
Total	**246**

The number of days and the divisor are then used as part of the calculation to determine the accrued interest cash amount on a trade, namely:

$$\frac{\text{Face value} \times \text{Coupon rate}\%}{\text{Annual divisor}} \times \text{Number of days}$$

$$\frac{\text{USD } 25,000,000 \times 8.25\%}{360} \times 246 = \text{USD } 1,409,375.00$$

The upper line of the formula produces the amount of coupon for the entire year, whilst the lower line provides the amount for one day, which when multiplied by the number of days relevant to the value date of the trade results in an accrued interest amount of USD 1,409,375.00.

If, instead of a Eurobond, the above-mentioned purchase were of a Hong Kong Government bond with a coupon rate of 8.25% and a coupon payment date of 1st June, for exactly the same value date (7th February 2007), the following differences would be evident:

- the annual divisor is 365 (this is the Hong Kong Government bond market convention);
- coupon payment dates—Hong Kong Government bonds pay coupon semi-annually, so the latest coupon payment date for a trade with a value date of 7th February 2007 is 1st December 2006 (coupon is payable 1st June and 1st December each year);
- the day count is the number of actual (calendar) days in the month (Table 8.7).

Table 8.7

Month	Day count
December 2006	31
January 2007	31
February	6
Total	**68**

Due to the above-mentioned differences, the calculation would therefore be:

$$\frac{\text{HKD } 25{,}000{,}000 \times 8.25\%}{365} \times 68 = \text{HKD } 384{,}246.58$$

resulting in an accrued interest value of HKD 384,246.58. This accrued interest basis is commonly referred to as Actual/365.

Table 8.8

Day count	Divisor
30	360
Actual	360
Actual	Actual
Actual	365
Actual	366

Other day count and divisor combinations are used, including those listed in Table 8.8, in various marketplaces and for specific types of bonds, according to:

- the type of issuer (e.g. government or corporate)
- whether a straight bond, convertible bond or an FRN.

Coupon Payment Dates. Fixed rate bonds typically pay coupons on dates that are aligned with the maturity date of the bond. For instance, a bond with a maturity date of 1st June 2020 will typically have been brought to the marketplace with a primary value date of 1st June, then pay coupons on 1st June each year (if the bond pays coupon annually) or 1st June and 1st December each year (if the bond pays coupon semi-annually).

A minority of bonds have coupon payment dates that are permanently not aligned with their maturity date. For example, a bond may have a maturity date of 1st October with an annual coupon date of 1st February, throughout its life.

As a general rule, straight bonds issued by corporations (e.g. Eurobonds) typically pay coupons annually, whilst many government issues pay semi-annually.

Short and Long Coupon Periods. Some bonds are issued with a primary value date that is not aligned with the bond's regular coupon payment dates. For example, a bond that is due to pay coupon semi-annually on 15th March and 15th September each year may have been brought to the marketplace with a primary value date of 15th January. In this situation, the first payment of coupon could occur on either 15th March or 15th September in the year of issue.

Table 8.9

The bond coupon rate	On a straight bond the rate remains static throughout the life of the bond On an FRN, the rate is subject to periodic change
The accrual basis	The annual divisor and day count information relevant to the specific bond group
Schedule of past and future coupon payment dates	On a straight bond the coupon payment dates remain static throughout the life of the bond (some bonds pay coupon semi-annually, others annually) On an FRN, some pay coupon semi-annually, others quarterly or monthly
Start accrual date	The date from which coupon begins to accrue; this is typically the primary value date
Short first coupon period	The period between the start accrual date and the first coupon payment date, where the regular payments of coupon will be a greater period
Long first coupon period	The period between the start accrual date and the first coupon payment date, where the regular payments of coupon will be a lesser period

If the issuer chooses to pay coupon on 15th March, for the period 15th January to 15th March, this is known as a 'short' first coupon period, as this coupon period is less than the regular coupon periods during the life of the bond.

If instead, the issuer chooses to make the first coupon payment on 15th September, for the period 15th January to 15th September, this is commonly referred to as a 'long' first coupon period, as this coupon period is greater than the bond's regular coupon periods.

Holding Accrued Interest Data. Accurate calculation of accrued interest involves gathering, storing, maintaining and utilising information such as that listed in Table 8.9. This information is normally published within the issue prospectus (a document that describes the detail of the issue), or is available from securities information service providers, such as Reuters, Bloomberg and Telekurs.

Regardless of whether an STO uses systems or calculates trade cash values manually, this information must be immediately available in order for the STO to operate in an efficient manner.

Negative Accrued Interest. In some markets (such as the UK Government bond ('gilt') market), negative accrued interest is applied to trades executed within a specified period leading up to a coupon payment date. This occurs once a point has been reached where it is no longer possible for a buyer to take delivery of the securities so as to receive the imminent coupon payment directly from the issuer. Cash values of trades in such markets result in the deduction of the accrued interest value relating to the remainder of the accrued interest period.

8.3.2 Optional Trade Amounts

Optional trade amounts can be defined as cash values that STOs choose to charge, that will affect the NSV.

Author's Comment

A low level of attention given to the calculation of accrued interest on trades can lead to incorrect cash value calculations and under these circumstances, the error:

- may be identified through the trade agreement and settlement instruction matching processes, which will take operational time and effort to rectify, requiring amendment of trades and the issue of amended trade confirmations and settlement instructions;
- may not be identified and a monetary loss to the organisation can result.

It is dangerous practice to rely upon the counterparty for accurate accrued interest calculation on trades; the cash value of accrued interest can be a significant amount in its own right, an amount worth protecting.

Administration Fee

An STO may choose to charge an additional amount to its counterparty where, for instance, an unusual method of settlement is necessary, such as the processing of physical certificates rather than the normal process where book entry with re-registration is used.

Under these circumstances, the STO may opt to charge the counterparty a 'one-off' cash amount for special handling of the trade.

Commission

Those companies acting as agents for investors typically make profit by charging their client *commission* on executed trades.

However, STOs may charge commission to their institutional clients even when the STO executes a trade on a principal basis; the commission charged can depend upon a number of factors, such as:

- the monetary value of trades—typically, the greater the size and frequency of trading, the lower the rate of commission
- the location of the market—STOs are likely to charge a lower rate of commission if the investor wishes to trade in a security in which the STO usually trades, as opposed to trading in a security rarely, where the costs of trading and settlement may be greater
- availability of the security—trades in securities which are popularly traded are more likely to be charged at a low rate of commission compared with securities that are rarely traded and which may prove more difficult to buy or sell

and is often negotiable on a trade-by-trade basis. Commission is normally charged as a percentage of the gross cash value of the trade, but can also involve scales of commission. Whatever calculation method is used, the STO may choose to charge a minimum commission amount per trade, in order to ensure that basic costs are covered and that a profit is made.

8.3.3 Internal Trade Amounts

Internal trade amounts can be defined as cash values that STOs will not charge to the counterparty, which will not affect the NSV.

In order to make provision for trade costs or revenue that may be charged or received at a later time, an STO may wish to calculate cash values on individual trades, without affecting the NSV (the purchase cost or sale proceeds to be settled with the counterparty). For internal purposes, the STO may calculate such items as:

- sales credits—where the STO's salesperson has been responsible for the client's order, a percentage sales credit can be applied and the cash amount derived
- anticipated external costs—where the STO expects to be charged by an external entity on a per-transaction basis, such as the cost of:
  - processing a settlement instruction by a custodian
  - transmitting a trade confirmation
- internal operating costs—the management of an STO may take the view that the trader or market maker should bear the internal operational cost of processing each transaction. The total cost of operation (including items such as office space, systems and payroll) over a given period of time can be divided by the STO's average number of trades over the same period, in order to derive the average cost per trade.

For all relevant trades, such amounts can be calculated and accounting entries can be passed so, for example, in the case of the anticipated external costs, the amounts accrued to the internal account can be compared with the invoices received from external entities, to ensure the costs are reasonable.

However, in order to achieve accuracy in undertaking this exercise, it will be necessary to apply these amounts only when relevant; for example, although it makes sense to apply the anticipated external costs and the internal operating costs to all principal trades with external counterparties, the sales credit should only be applied for trades with institutional clients. In the case of book transfer transactions, there are typically no external costs and no sales credits.

Taking these measures can aid the control of operational costs for an STO; however, the manpower required to perform this task manually on every relevant transaction may prove to be costly and time-consuming, but these tasks can be automated through the use of a settlement system.

8.4   NET SETTLEMENT VALUE

The NSV is the final cash amount of a trade, which is to be paid by a buyer, or received by a seller. The NSV is derived by:

A. calculating the GCV
B. adding or subtracting any additional trade amounts.

For example, the sale by an STO of 1,000,000 Marks & Spencer plc, Ordinary Shares (a UK equity), at a price of GBP 2.46, to an institutional client would be calculated as in Table 8.10.

Table 8.10

A	1,000,000 × GBP 2.46	GBP	2,460,000.00
B	Add commission	GBP	+1,500.00
B	Add stamp duty at 0.5% of GCV	GBP	+12,300.00
B	Add PTM levy	GBP	+0.25
C	**NSV (to be received by the STO)**	**GBP**	**2,473,800.25**

Table 8.11

A	1,000,000 × GBP 2.46	GBP	2,460,000.00
B	Deduct commission	GBP	−1,500.00
B	Deduct PTM levy	GBP	−0.25
C	**NSV (to be paid by the STO)**	**GBP**	**2,458,499.75**

Table 8.12

A	USD 30,000,000.00 × 103.65%	USD	31,095,000.00
B	Add accrued interest (200 days)	USD	+875,000.00
C	**NSV (to be paid by the STO)**	**USD**	**31,970,000.00**

Had the STO purchased from the client the same number of shares at the same price, the calculation would be as in Table 8.11.

To take a different example, the purchase by an STO of USD 30,000,00.00 City of Oslo 5.25% bonds 15th February 2015 (a Eurobond), at a price of 103.65% for value date 5th September, from another STO, would be calculated as in Table 8.12. A point to note is that whether buying or selling bonds (on a positive rather than a negative accrued interest basis), the accrued interest is added to the GCV in order to derive the NSV. Had the STO sold the same number of bonds for exactly the same price and for the same value date, the NSV for the sale would be exactly the same figure as the NSV for the purchase; this is because the buyer of a bond is required to pay an additional cash amount (the accrued interest), whilst the seller is due to receive it.

Some counterparties (usually institutional clients) may wish to pay or receive the NSV of trades in a currency other than the trading currency; this is commonly known as cross-currency settlement, for which a foreign exchange transaction is effected resulting in the NSV in the required currency. Cross currency settlement is described in Chapter 5, Section 5.3.4.

8.5   SUMMARY

It is recommended that all those who trade need to make themselves aware of the true costs of trading in each marketplace, and have the capability of calculating the correct amounts whenever a trade is executed.

9
Static Data

9.1 INTRODUCTION

The use of static data is a significant factor in enabling an STO to achieve *STP*. Static data is the commonly used term to describe a store of information that is used to determine the appropriate actions necessary to achieve successful processing of each trade.

Static data is necessary to set up at six major levels, namely:

- trading companies within the STO
- counterparties of the STO
- trading books within a trading company
- currencies
- securities
- security groups.

In each case, the necessary static data is explored, within this chapter.

Such data can be held entirely manually, or within a systems repository. The use of static data is not confined to the settlement department, as other areas including:

- order management
- equity, bond and repo trading
- corporate actions
- reconciliation
- risk management

also make use of this information.

The term 'static data' implies that the information does not change. The majority of static data items are static and not subject to change; however, certain aspects of static data are subject to periodic change or updating, and such areas of static data are highlighted within this chapter.

The challenge for an STO is to:

- gather the relevant data
- store it securely
- update it when necessary
- utilise it appropriately

ensuring that for every individual trade, only the appropriate information is attached to the trade from the entire store of data. Typically, the amount of information held within an STO's static data store is vast. Large STOs may be holding within their systems database thousands of securities, and hundreds of counterparties. It is essential to select the correct information in a timely fashion if delays and costs are to be avoided.

In an automated environment, when a trade has been executed and recorded onto a trading system, the trade will be received by the settlement system (via an interface) and will, at that point in time, typically contain only the essential trading information, which is normally (in the case of a principal trade):

- trading book
- trade date
- trade time
- value date
- operation
- quantity
- security
- price
- counterparty.

In order to process the trade in an operational sense, the trade requires enriching with much more information. Fully functional settlement systems not only hold the necessary static data, but also have the capability to automatically enrich trades with the appropriate data (refer to Chapter 12).

Note that this chapter contains examples of static data items that are necessary to be held, but are not an exhaustive list of static data contents. In addition, only some of the items of static data listed have been described in the book as at this point; other items listed have not yet been described, but will be covered within subsequent chapters.

Where necessary, tables are used to highlight the type of data that is held under each of the six main areas of static data; where this is the case, the typical use of each component is described within the table.

9.2   TRADING COMPANIES

In order to automate the processing of trades, it is necessary for static data to be held regarding the trading company's (i.e. the STO's) own details.

Furthermore, an STO may be required to process the business of more than one trading company, so information that is specific to each trading company will require setting up within static data. For example, the trading activity of each company must remain segregated and separately identifiable for regulatory purposes, and the management would require separate accounting and P&L for each of the companies.

Table 9.1 contains typical attributes of an STO that are necessary to hold within static data. For ease of understanding and for later reference, the STO has been given a name; that is World Securities International, London (WSIL).

9.3   COUNTERPARTIES

STOs need to hold static data relating to all their counterparties, to enable automated enrichment of trades and subsequent actions, such as the production of *trade confirmations* and *settlement instructions* containing the counterparty's custodian details.

Table 9.1 lists some of the information held within WSIL's static data for two of its counterparties, an STO and an institutional client.

Table 9.1

Static data item	Example of a trading company (the STO)	Example of a counterparty (an STO)	Example of a counterparty (an institutional client)	Typical use of data
Full name and location of trading company	World Securities International, London (WSIL)			The STO's heading on trade confirmations and any automated communication issued to counterparties
Full name and location of counterparty		Professional Traders Inc., 22 Bahnhofstrasse, Frankfurt	Solar Fund Managers Pte., 105 Western Road North, Singapore	The addressee on trade confirmations and any automated communication issued to counterparties
Short name of counterparty		PTIF	SFMS	The abbreviated counterparty name used on the STO's internal reports
Counterparty reference number		STO255098	IC106588	The unique counterparty identifier within the STO's books and records
Type of counterparty		STO	Institutional client; fund manager	Categorises counterparties for statistics and management reporting within the STO
Associated counterparties			IC106588A: Solar Far East Fund IC106588B: Solar Pacific Income Fund	Other counterparties that are linked to this counterparty, enabling automated processing
Relationship with associated counterparties			Fund Manager	The basis for allocation of executed trades to the associated counterparties

(continued overleaf)

Table 9.1 (continued)

Static data item	Example of a trading company (the STO)	Example of a counterparty (an STO)	Example of a counterparty (an institutional client)	Typical use of data
Custodian names and locations	C1: Cust. A, Sydney C2: Cust. E, Tokyo C3: Cust. H, Hong Kong C4: Cust. L, New York C5: Cust. P, London C6: Cust. S, Brussels	C1: Cust. B, Melbourne C2: Cust. F, Tokyo C3: Cust. I, Hong Kong C4: Cust. L, New York C5: Cust. Q, London C6: Cust. S, Brussels	C1: Cust. C, Sydney C2: Cust. G, Osaka C3: Cust. J, Hong Kong C4: Cust. M, New York C5: Cust. P, London C6: Cust. S, Brussels	The complete list of an STO's custodians, one of whom will be issued a settlement instruction on an individual trade, containing the counterparty's appropriate custodian (relevant to the security group, such as Japanese equity)
Securities account numbers at each custodian	C1: 5023598 C2: A0078802 C3: 111693XM C4: 334RR126 C5: 9455B1 C6: XA3396269	C1: 5532896 C2: A9096220 C3: 110242TP C4: 339RR098 C5: 2967D2 C6: XA8824179	C1: 5900329 C2: A2022451 C3: 101584GL C4: 331RR443 C5: 7765V3 C6: XA6061349	The specific securities account number over which a securities trade will settle; the relevant account number will be quoted on a settlement instruction sent to the STO's custodian
Cash account numbers at each custodian (and currency of account)	C1: 5023598 (AUD) C2: A0078802 (JPY) C3: 111693XM (HKD) C4: 334RR126 (USD) C5: 9455B1 (GBP) C6: XA3396269 (various)	C1: 5532896 (AUD) C2: A9096220 (JPY) C3: 110242TP (HKD) C4: 339RR098 (USD) C5: 2967D2 (GBP) C6: XA8824179 (various)	C1: 5900329 (AUD) C2: A2022451 (JPY) C3: 101584GL (HKD) C4: 331RR443 (USD) C5: 7765V3 (GBP) C6: XA6061349 (various)	The specific cash account number over which a securities trade will settle; the relevant account number will be quoted on a settlement instruction sent to the custodian

Settlement instruction communication method to each custodian	C1: S.W.I.F.T. C2: S.W.I.F.T. C3: Tested Telex C4: S.W.I.F.T. C5: Proprietary C6: Euclid	The medium by which settlement instructions are transmitted to each custodian and bank; typically, there are choices as to the method of transmission (refer Chapter 16 Settlement Instructions)
Trade confirmations	Not required (trades to be compared and matched electronically)	Fax	The medium by which trade confirmations are to be issued to the counterparty (if required)
Trading company membership numbers	ISMA Trax: WSI44662 LSE firm code WS7934	Identification numbers used when, for example, issuing details of trades for regulatory reporting to a regulatory authority
Counterparty membership numbers	ISMA Trax: PT230871	Identification numbers used in the transmission by the STO of trade matching messages (see Chapter 14)

The following should be noted:

- counterparty type—provides the base from which, for example trade volume statistics can be run from the information held within the settlement system, by type of counterparty;
- associated counterparties—in the case of a fund manager, it is likely that individual trades will initially be recorded against the 'parent' counterparty (e.g. counterparty reference IC106588), before being allocated to the underlying funds.

9.4 TRADING BOOKS

As described in Chapter 4, *trading books* within an STO represent groups of traders (whether one or many traders) who trade in individual securities within specific security groups.

The STO's trading P&L may be calculated at a number of levels, beginning with the trading book level, followed by increasingly higher levels, as represented in Figure 9.1.

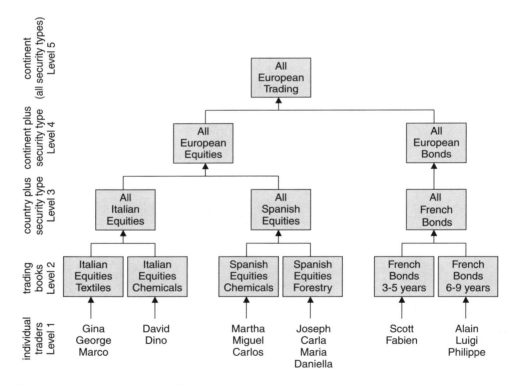

Figure 9.1 Structure of a securities trading organisation: trading books (example hierarchial structure)

It is normal for each trading book to be set up within the STO's static data, and to have individual securities or security groups attached. An example of such a structure is given in Table 9.2, thereby enabling automatic defaulting of the relevant trading book onto individual trades.

Table 9.2

Trading book	Security group	Individual securities
Italian equities textiles	Italian equity textiles class 1	MM ordinary shares PP ordinary shares
	Italian equity textiles class 2	TT ordinary shares VV ordinary shares
Italian equities chemicals	Italian equity chemicals class 1	BB ordinary shares DD ordinary shares
	Italian equity chemicals class 2	LL ordinary shares RR ordinary shares

9.5   CURRENCIES

Historically, where an STO may have executed and settled trades only in its domestic marketplace, there would typically have been little need to hold a database of currencies.

A modern STO normally operates in a multicurrency environment, executing and settling trades in numerous currencies. Consequently, many of the world's currencies need to be set up within the STO's systems, in order to automate and provide consistency in the currency related aspects of, for example:

- trade cash value calculation,
- recording trades and updating the trading company's books and records,
- issuing trade confirmations to counterparties,
- issuing settlement instructions to custodians and banks.

The *ISO* (International Organisation for Standardisation) have standardised references to currencies by producing a three character code for most, if not all, currencies in use around the globe.

The ISO currency codes are recognised internationally and can therefore be used by, for example, an STO in Japan that transmits settlement instructions to its agent in Toronto, without the need for interpretation of the currency in question by the receiving party.

Table 9.3 lists a selection of ISO currency codes as at January 2002, by country within continent.

It is important for an STO to be aware of public holiday dates around the globe, which if overlooked could cause monetary losses through being unable to move cash amounts when required. An additional important aspect of static data, therefore, is the holding of holiday dates for all currencies that can be used to highlight automatically any trades that may be affected.

9.6   SECURITIES

In order to automate the processing of trades, STOs need to hold the description, attributes and characteristics of securities allowing, for example:

- accurate trade cash value calculation, and
- exact description of the security appearing on trade confirmations issued to counterparties.

Table 9.3

Continent	Country	Currency	ISO code
Africa	Ghana	Cedi	GHC
	Ivory Coast	Franc	XOF
	Kenya	Shilling	KES
	South Africa	Rand	ZAR
	Zimbabwe	Dollar	ZWD
Americas	Argentina	Peso	ARS
	Bermuda	Dollar	BMD
	Brazil	Real	BRL
	Canada	Dollar	CAD
	Mexico	Peso	MXN
	USA	Dollar	USD
	Venezuela	Bolivar	VEB
Asia	China	Renminbi	CNY
	Hong Kong	Dollar	HKD
	India	Rupee	INR
	Indonesia	Rupiah	IDR
	Japan	Yen	JPY
	Korea	Won	KRW
	Malaysia	Ringgit	MYR
	Pakistan	Rupee	PKR
	Philippines	Peso	PHP
	Singapore	Dollar	SGD
	Taiwan	Dollar	TWD
	Thailand	Baht	THB
	Vietnam	Dong	VND
Australasia	Australia	Dollar	AUD
	New Zealand	Dollar	NZD
Europe	Czech Republic	Koruna	CZK
	Denmark	Krone	DKK
	Euro	Euro	EUR
	Norway	Krone	NOK
	Poland	Zloty	PLN
	Russia	Ruble	RUR or RUB
	Slovenia	Tolar	SIT
	Sweden	Krona	SEK
	Switzerland	Franc	CHF
	UK	Pound	GBP

Security static data is publicly available data. Each security has specific and unique attributes that an STO must make itself aware of, as financial losses may occur if information is not held accurately. For example, whether an equity issue is an *ordinary share* (*common stock* in North America) or a preference share. In the case of bonds, numerous types exist with many having substantially different features (refer to Chapter 7).

Static data for securities that have changing attributes (for example FRNs that have different coupon rates for each coupon period) will need to be updated at the time at which the change occurs in the outside world.

Table 9.4 lists the primary information held within WSIL's static data for two securities, a bond and an equity (initially described in Chapter 3).

9.6.1 Securities Identification Code Numbers

In order to enable unambiguous identification of securities, each individual security is given a unique identification code number.

The securities numbering convention that is used globally is *ISIN* (International Securities Identification Number), a 12 character code where:

- the first two characters are a country code relating to the country of the issuer,
- the next nine characters are the national securities identification number, and
- the last character is a check digit (which verifies the code).

In addition to the ISIN code, securities identification numbers are given and used locally within the world's financial centres; see Table 9.5.

Securities identification code numbers are used in various ways, including:

- the communication of trade details between an STO's trading systems and settlement system,
- the issue of transaction reporting messages to regulators,
- the issue of trade confirmations to counterparties,
- the issue of trade matching messages to trade matching facilities,
- the issue of settlement instructions to custodians,

mainly for the purpose of ensuring the correct security is ultimately exchanged between buyer and seller.

9.7 SECURITY GROUPS

Individual securities typically have characteristics that are similar to other securities, and can therefore be treated as forming part of a security group (as mentioned in Chapter 7).

Security groups (as defined by an individual STO) are normally held as part of static data, where the attributes pertaining to each group are set up, maintained and changed (if and when there is a need, which should be rare).

It is normally operationally advantageous to the STO to attach the relevant security group to an individual security at the point of setting up the individual security within static data, as thereafter, when processing a trade in each security, the relevant security group attributes can be attached to the trade automatically.

Table 9.6 contains static data held by WSIL for two of the security groups in which it trades. The attributes of a security could, in theory, be set up and held within static data against individual securities. However, a major advantage of holding this information by security group is that when any changes to the attributes are necessary, the changes need only be made against the single security group, rather than every relevant security. This provides a great saving in operational effort to effect the change.

For example, settlement cycles (described fully in Chapter 11) are reducing in many markets around the globe; when an individual market changes its settlement cycle, for instance from T+5 to T+3, only the relevant security group(s) would require to be changed within static data. Trades executed (in securities relating to the changed settlement

Table 9.4

Static data item	Example of a bond	Example of an equity	Typical use of data
Full name of the security	XOX AG 8.25% bonds 1st June 2020	CDE plc GBP 1.00 Ordinary Shares	The formal description of the issue, used on trade confirmations and other correspondence with clients
Short name of the security	XOX 8.25% 1.6.20	CDE Ord	The informal description of the issue, used on the STO's internal reports
Security internal reference	BD00757339	SH00463815	The identifier of the individual security, used internally within the STO
Security external reference	ISIN: XS1234567893	ISIN: GB9876543215	The commonly known security identification number, used for external communication, such as on trade confirmations and settlement instructions
Issued currency	USD	GBP	Quoted on trade confirmations and settlement instructions. Internally, represents the currency of the trading position and the cash owed to/by counterparties
Issued quantity	USD 1,000,000,000.00	100,000,000	Provides a measure of the STO's holding as a percentage of total issued (can have regulatory implications)
Security type	Bond	Equity	Provides internal statistics and reporting by type of security
Security group	Eurobond (USD)	UK Equity	Enables distinguishing of security for static data defaulting
Coupon rate type	Eurobond fixed rate		Enables attachment of attributes such as accrued interest divisor and day count (e.g. 30/360)
Coupon rate	8.25%		Enables calculation of cash value of accrued interest (on trades) and coupon payments
Coupon frequency	Annual		Enables calculation of accrued interest (on trades) and coupon payments
Coupon payment dates	1st June		Enables calculation of accrued interest (on trades) and coupon payments
Primary value date	1st June 2000	16th January 2000	Earliest value date of a new issue and the point from which accrued interest begins to accrue (on a bond)
First coupon payment date	1st June 2001		Enables determination of short, long or regular coupon period
Maturity date	1st June 2020		Identifies the date of capital repayment
Maturity price	100%		Identifies the price of the bond payable by the issuer at maturity
Denominational values and board lots	USD 5000.00 and USD 20,000.00	500 shares	Ensures trades are executed in acceptable denominations
Default trading book	Trading book 'Y'	Trading book 'D'	Enables defaulting of the internal trading book that typically trades this security
Credit rating	AA		Enables calculation of collateral values of this security

Table 9.5

Country	Identification code name
Australia	ASX
Belgium	SVM
Canada	*Cusip*
Germany	WKN
Japan	Quick
Switzerland	Valoren
UK	Sedol
USA	*Cusip*

Table 9.6

Static data item	Example of a bond	Example of an equity	Typical use
Name of the security group	Eurobond (USD)	UK equity	The name that an STO chooses to give to a security group, which will be attached to the static data of relevant individual securities
Settlement cycle	Trade date plus 3 business days (commonly referred to as T+3)	Trade date plus 5 business days (T+5) changed to T+3 in February 2001	The normal period between trade date and value date, used to calculate the value date of a trade
Custodian	Euroclear	Crest	The custodian used by the STO for settlement
Transfer method	Book entry	Book entry with re-registration	Indicates whether additional time will be taken for registering of purchases
Accrual basis	30/360		The day count and divisor convention for calculation of accrued interest

cycle) after the effective date of a change such as this would automatically have the correct information applied.

Another example is that if an STO chooses to change its custodian for the settlement of Eurobonds from Euroclear to Clearstream Luxembourg, the new information need only be set up against the security group static data, and not the relevant individual securities.

9.8   TIMING OF STATIC DATA SET-UP

The point at which static data is set up within the STO's static data repository has a direct impact on the STO's ability to process trades on an *STP* basis.

As settlement cycles reduce in markets around the globe, the deadlines by which STOs must act in order to:

- service their clients (for example, issuing trade confirmations)
- report trades to regulators
- ensure settlement occurs (for example, issuing settlement instructions)

are becoming increasingly aggressive.

As static data plays such an important role in helping to meet these deadlines by providing defaults for most events in the trade lifecycle, any failure to have the necessary data set up in advance of trading is increasingly likely to result in missing the above-mentioned deadlines. This can result in unhappy clients, fines from regulators and direct monetary loss through failure to issue settlement instructions within the necessary deadline.

9.8.1   Securities

Some STOs take the view that securities static data will be set up as and when trades have been executed; others take the view that all securities of a given type (e.g. all New Zealand Government bond issues, or all equities forming the Hang Seng (Hong Kong) index of securities) should be set up at the earliest opportunity, in anticipation and expectation of executing trades at some point in the future.

9.8.2   Counterparties

It should be expected that all STOs adopt a method of credit assessment prior to trading with a counterparty that the STO has not traded with previously.

If a salesperson, trader or market maker wishes to trade with a new counterparty, the credit control department is contacted in order to assess their creditworthiness. This assessment should occur prior to any trade being executed between the STO and the counterparty in question.

It could be considered as a safety measure not to set up counterparties until the assessment has been completed and the credit controller has given approval for trading to commence.

However, it is recommended that wherever possible STOs set up their static data in advance of trading, whether or not an STO subscribes to the services offered by providers of counterparty information (such as Alert), or *securities data providers* (see below).

9.9   SOURCES OF STATIC DATA

Various options exist for an STO to obtain static data.

9.9.1   Counterparties

When an STO trades with a counterparty for the first time (whether another STO or institutional client), it is usual for the STO and the counterparty to swap custodian details directly, for each market in which trades may be executed between the two parties. Better still, exchanging information in advance of the first trade between the two parties allows immediate STP.

Additionally, the STO will need to gather all other appropriate pieces of information from the counterparty, in advance, in order to avoid halting processing of trades whilst the missing information is sought. This information, for example, would include counterparty membership numbers and the required medium of trade confirmation.

Counterparty information should be considered as private information, whereas security information is publicly available. Consequently, the information as to which custodian a particular STO or institutional investor uses for settlement of, for example, Swedish equity is unlikely to be freely available.

There is one main reason why this information is regarded as private; openly publicising the custodian is the equivalent of an individual publicising his or her bank account or credit card details; generally, it is not possible to control how someone who discovers the information will use it. The ultimate concern is that assets may be removed from an account without authorisation by the account holder.

Consequently, it is normal for information such as custodian details to be swapped only when it is agreed by two parties that they will trade with one another.

Historically, the process of gathering this information has been a manual exercise. However, such information is available nowadays for those organisations (including STOs and institutional investors) that choose to subscribe to a service known as 'Alert', by Thomson Financial (now Omgeo). Counterparty custodian details are available electronically via Alert; the advantage of this being that the updating of an STO's counterparty static data can be automated, thereby removing errors typically associated with manual input of data.

9.9.2   Securities

For those STOs that trade in numerous markets around the globe, the details of securities in which they trade will derive from many sources in numerous locations. The accurate collection of relevant data is a task that should not be underestimated. As for counterparty information, if losses are to be avoided, the accuracy of the information is paramount, as is the timeliness of setting up the data.

The decision as to which method(s) to employ regarding the gathering of accurate and timely security static data is typically a difficult one to make.

When a security is being brought to the marketplace, it is normal for the issuer (or his agent) to produce a prospectus or offering circular; a document detailing the terms of the issue. The information contained in the prospectus is publicly available, at which point the relevant custodians and *CSDs* typically set up the details of the issue in their own static data systems (enabling STP in their own environment).

Some STOs gather their securities static data directly from the prospectus, but this may not always be available within the urgent timeframes that an STO typically requires the information. Another option is to request the necessary information from a custodian or CSD. If the relevant information is gathered from either of these sources, the details of the security will be input to the STO's static data system manually, or automatically if a feed is available from the CSD.

However, there is an alternative; a number of companies specialise in gathering and distributing securities static data to those who are prepared to subscribe to such a service. These companies are known as *securities data providers* or data vendors, and include:

- Reuters
- Telekurs
- Standard & Poor's
- J.J. Kenny
- Bloomberg
- FT Interactive Data

who typically provide data by electronic feed, or via the Internet.

Some STOs subscribe to one service provider, others subscribe to many to enable a comparison of data received from two or more providers in an effort to ensure that only completely accurate securities information is updated within the STO's own static data repository.

Associated with the supply of securities data is the provision of current securities prices and the details of corporate actions; these topics will be covered within a number of subsequent chapters.

9.10   MANAGEMENT OF STATIC DATA

It is not only important to gather, store and update static data when processing trades in the settlement system, it is also essential to have consistent and compatible data held between internal systems, such as between order management, trading and settlement systems.

For instance, if bond denominational values are held within the trading system's static data as USD 1000.00 and USD 10,000.00, but the settlement system holds the equivalent information as USD 5000.00 and USD 10,000.00, the trader or market maker could execute a trade for a quantity of bonds (e.g. USD 1,502,000.00) that will not be accepted by the settlement system. Furthermore, if the settlement system holds the factually correct information, the traders and market makers will have traded in a quantity of bonds that does not exist; this will result in the need to amend the trade to an acceptable quantity urgently, in order to avoid settlement failure.

Static data can be obtained independently by a number of departments within an STO, without having a coordinated approach. In Figure 9.2, each trading area and the settlement area are obtaining security and counterparty data separately, and potentially from different sources.

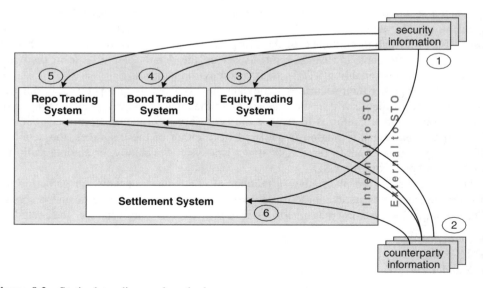

Figure 9.2   Static data: dispersed method

Points 1 and 2: there are various sources of security and counterparty static data, external to the STO.

Points 3 to 5: the three trading areas are obtaining static data from different sources.

Point 6: the settlement system is obtaining its static data from the same sources as some, but not all, of the trading systems.

With this method of operation, the cost and effort required to gather the necessary information across the STO may be considerably greater than is necessary. It should be noted, however, that some security static data providers focus more on equities and less on bonds, so an STO may make a conscious decision to continue with more than one source.

Additionally, unless there is an attempt to reconcile the static data between trading systems and the settlement system (where static data has not originated from the same source, or has been updated manually), when trades are executed, recorded in the trading system and sent to the settlement system, the trade could be rejected by the settlement system and could result in missed deadlines and costs being incurred.

Figure 9.3 shows an alternative method of gathering, storing and updating static data, which includes the use of an internal central repository, thereby reducing the risk of conflicting data in the various processing systems.

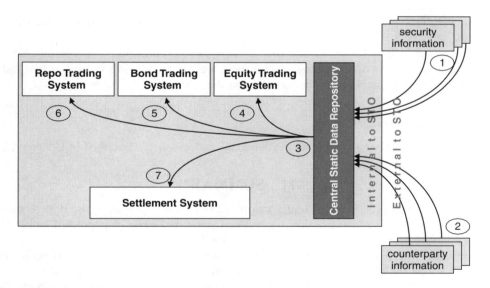

Figure 9.3   Static data: central repository method

Steps 1 and 2: securities static data is obtained from a number of sources, as is counterparty information.

Step 3: the STO stores all static data centrally, and compares the information received (e.g. from two sources of information for the same security) for any discrepancies. The process of comparing static data is known as data cleansing.

Steps 4 to 7: the Central Static Data Repository then releases the same static data to the relevant internal systems.

With this method of operation, the STO can focus its efforts on gathering all static data in a controlled fashion. When trades are executed and recorded in the trading system, there should be no reason for the trade to be rejected within the settlement system, thereby maximising the chances of meeting the various deadlines and minimising costs.

9.10.1 Controlling Access to Static Data

The effort and cost of setting up accurate static data makes the protection of that data very worthwhile. In an environment where any member of staff is allowed to change static data, with the best of intentions mistakes can be made, such as inaccurate:

* changes to the coupon rate on an FRN—incorrect trade cash value calculations will result;
* changes to the address of a counterparty—trade confirmations will not be received by institutional clients within an acceptable timeframe;
* changes to a counterparty's custodian details—settlement instructions issued by the trading company will not match with the counterparty's instruction, and if not rectified in time will cause delayed settlement and monetary losses.

In order to guard against such errors, many STOs protect their static data by restricting access to static data systems to a limited number of staff; unauthorised staff should be denied access if any attempt is made to enter such systems.

Any changes made by those staff who are given access rights to static data would ideally be subject to verification by a colleague, prior to the change being fully accepted by the system; this is known as the *'four-eyes' principle*. Following a successful change to static data, details of the change should be traceable by keeping records of the staff members, the time and date of the change, and the items that were changed.

9.10.2 Static Data Defaulting

The method of applying static data to individual trades will be described in Chapter 12.

9.11 SUMMARY

The very efficient processing of trades can result only from applying static data to trade data automatically. To facilitate this, the relevant static data must be populated within all relevant systems, from a reliable source, at the earliest opportunity.

Any situation that differs from this ideal is likely to result in fundamental problems impacting service levels to clients and the cost-effectiveness of processing trades.

As the window for the processing of trades becomes ever smaller (refer to Chapter 29), the timeliness and accuracy of static data will play an increasingly important role.

10

The Trade Lifecycle and Straight Through Processing

10.1 THE TRADE LIFECYCLE

All the steps involved in a trade, from the point of order receipt (where relevant) and trade execution through to settlement of the trade, are commonly referred to as the 'trade lifecycle'.

The management of all *STOs* require that trades are processed in the most proficient manner, and this is reflected in their desire to achieve *STP*. This is only achievable if the trade lifecycle is begun by recording the details of each trade in a timely and accurate fashion within the front office, and is handled efficiently, cost-effectively and within the various deadlines in the operational areas of the STO.

A problem created early on in the trade lifecycle will cost more to correct the further it flows through the operational process, the effect of the error being replicated and magnified.

The trade lifecycle can be regarded as a series of logical steps, which are represented in Figure 10.1 (however, it should be noted that some of these steps can occur in parallel, or in a different order to that stated).

The following 11 chapters, beginning with Chapter 11 and ending with Chapter 21, focus on each major step in the trade lifecycle.

As the reader completes each chapter, a logical sequence of steps should become apparent.

10.2 STRAIGHT THROUGH PROCESSING

STP is a securities industry-wide term to describe the objective of managing trades throughout the trade lifecycle automatically and without human intervention.

Historically, within many STOs there was little or no connectivity between the various systems, thereby necessitating rekeying (manual input) of individual trade details, at various points. Even where connectivity existed between an STO's internal systems, a lack of consistent reference data (primarily security and counterparty identifiers) prevented automatic passing of trade details from system to system.

From the STO's perspective, the objective is as follows. Following trade execution, input the details of individual trades once only, and from that point until the complete settlement of the trade, manage each of the steps in a fully automated fashion.

The trade lifecycle involves a series of steps, including both the internal and external management of trades.

With regard to STOs communicating externally, similar concepts apply. For example, once a *settlement instruction* is transmitted by an STO, the management of the instruction by the custodian should ideally be effected on an STP basis.

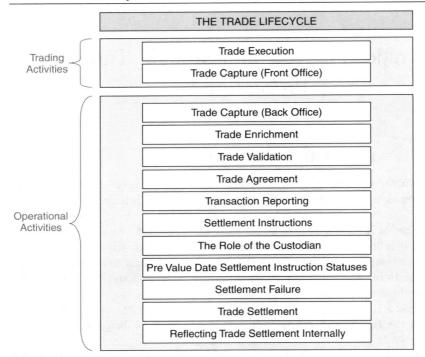

Figure 10.1   The trade lifecycle

10.2.1   The Need to Control Straight Through Processing

Achieving STP is a major challenge in its own right, but STP may not address the issues of risk, from the STO's perspective. Unchecked, STP may raise issues of risk.

Once the infrastructure (both within and outside the STO) supports STP, potential risks remain, which the STO must mitigate. Such risks will be highlighted throughout the following chapters that focus on the trade lifecycle.

When processing trades, ideally all trades should be scrutinised from a risk mitigation and error reduction perspective, resulting in individual trades:

- being processed on an STP basis, where no risk or error has been detected, or
- being treated as an exception, where the scrutiny has detected a potential risk or error.

In order to enable trades to be scrutinised in such a manner, business rules would be set up within the settlement system, which should be compared automatically with the relevant trade components. For example, a business rule may be set up to compare the current market price with the trade price, from a risk mitigation perspective (this and other such business rules are explained further in Chapter 13).

10.2.2   Treatment of Exceptions

When the process of scrutiny has detected an exception, this must be investigated and resolved without delay, in order to meet various deadlines (which are described within the subsequent chapters).

Because the investigation must occur at once, the appropriate staff (according to the nature of the exception) should be alerted immediately and automatically. The exception should be investigated, and the trade is then either:

- validated as being acceptable, and processing of the trade should continue, or
- amended or cancelled at the point of origin of the trade (typically by the traders and market makers).

10.3 SUMMARY

STP throughout the securities industry will enable the management of trades to be handled in a far faster and efficient way than has been the case historically.

From an STO's perspective, however, operating on an STP basis 'without due care and attention' may result in unnecessary costs being incurred (albeit in a much more efficient manner!).

11
Trade Execution and Capture

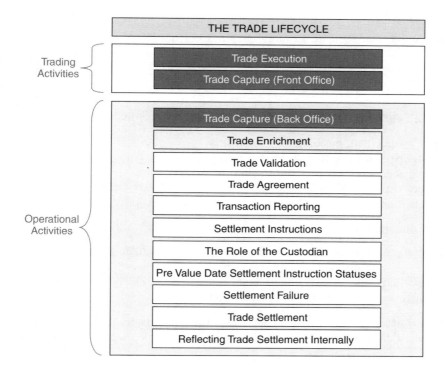

11.1 INTRODUCTION

Trading began in meeting points such as coffee shops; it became more formalised when stock exchanges were formed, where trading would be conducted on a face-to-face basis. For some marketplaces that have been formed in more recent times, telephone has been the sole medium for conducting trading. Today, some face-to-face marketplaces still exist, others have become mainly telephone based, and some marketplaces operate on an electronic basis.

This chapter describes:

- the flow and management of *orders* from clients
- trade execution, and the components that form a trade
- trade capture within the front office
- trade capture within the back office

in order to convey the sequential steps involved in trade execution and capture.

11.2   ORDERS FROM INSTITUTIONAL CLIENTS

An order is a request to buy or sell securities, given by an investor (such as an institutional client) to an STO, or to an *agent for investors*. Usually, some (but not all) of the trades executed by STOs are originated by orders from its institutional clients.

11.2.1   Order Features

Orders contain a number of standard features, such as the request to:

* buy or sell
* a specific quantity of
* a specific security

and will contain a number of features that are relevant to the price, including:

* Limit—a price is specified, meaning
  ○ when buying, pay no more than the stated price
  ○ when selling, accept no less than the stated price
* At Best—at the best available price, also known as an At Market Order
* Stop Loss—sell if and when the market price falls to the stated price

and a number of time related features, such as:

* Fill or Kill—complete the entire order in full, or reject it immediately, without partial execution
* Good Till Cancelled—the order remains open until it is executed, or the order is cancelled by the client, also known as an Open Order.

Orders can remain open until executed, or until an expiry date is reached, or until the order is cancelled; additionally, partial executions may be possible, dependent upon the type of order.

11.2.2   Order Flow

Further to the description in Chapter 4, Figure 11.1 represents the typical steps in an institutional client placing an order with an STO.

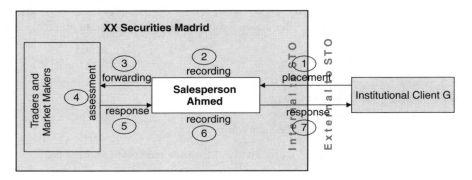

Figure 11.1   Trade execution and capture: orders from institutional clients to STOs

Step 1: the institutional client decides to buy or sell a specific security, and contacts one of the STOs with whom it normally trades; the details of the order are normally placed with the STO via the relevant salesperson (within the STO).

Step 2: the STO's salesperson records the details of the client's order, either manually or electronically within an order management system.

Step 3: the order details are forwarded by the salesperson or are fed automatically by an order management system to the relevant trader or market maker (usually according to the specific security).

Step 4: the trader assesses the order, to decide whether they wish to execute the trade on such terms; on the other hand, a market maker must execute the trade, providing that the order price is within the market maker's published price. Should the trade be executed, the trade details are recorded by the trader or market maker within the relevant *trading book*.

Step 5: the trader or market maker responds to the salesperson who placed the order on behalf of the client, advising whether they have or have not executed the trade, and if so, on what terms (the trader or market maker may have executed the trade at a more advantageous price (for the client) than the order price, or for a lesser quantity, known as a partial execution (if the terms of the order allow it)).

Step 6: the salesperson records the detail of the execution, thereby closing the open order; in the case of a partial execution, the outstanding order amount would need to be kept open by the salesperson.

Step 7: the salesperson contacts the institutional client (typically by telephone) to advise whether the order has been fulfilled fully, partially, or not at all. Note that a formal advice of trade execution (known as a *trade confirmation*) will be required to be issued by the STO to the client via a medium of the client's choice, and within a specified deadline (this is described in Chapter 14).

Points to note are:

- the trader or market maker does not normally contact the institutional client directly. This is usually the responsibility of the salesperson (the primary point of contact between the institutional client and the STO);
- the above-mentioned order flow is similar, but not identical to, the order flow for an individual client placing an order with an agent, such as a retail broker, where the broker may forward the order directly to an STO or to an exchange;
- incorrect communication of order details is likely to lead to incorrect trade recording by the traders and market makers, in turn requiring amendments or cancellations of trades (the scope for error making is described later in this chapter).

However, not all trades executed by an STO begin with an order from institutional clients; traders and market makers deciding to buy or sell securities on behalf of the STO result in trades being executed directly with other STOs.

11.3   TRADE EXECUTION

11.3.1   Types of Securities Markets

Further to the description of securities markets in Chapter 2, individual markets around the globe tend to operate in one of three ways, where sellers and buyers execute trades:

- on a face-to-face basis on the trading floor of a stock exchange (the traditional method of trading),
- via telephone,
- via computerised exchanges.

Furthermore, markets are either quote-driven or order-driven.

Quote-driven Markets

In markets where market makers publicise (quote) prices at which they are prepared to buy and sell with the intention of attracting a counterparty, the market is said to be 'quote-driven'.

Examples of quote-driven markets where quoted prices are displayed on computer screens are Nasdaq (US), SEAQ (UK) and the Eurobond market; trade execution typically occurs by telephone or electronically.

Order-driven Markets

In markets in which orders from sellers are compared and matched with buyers' orders electronically, the market is said to be 'order-driven'.

Examples of order-driven markets are:

- SEATS (Australia)
- Xetra (Germany)
- SETS (UK)

all of which match orders by computer.

Electronic Communications Networks

At the time of writing, a number of organisations categorised as Electronic Communications Networks (ECNs) or 'electronic trading platforms' or 'alternative trading systems' have emerged as another route by which trades may be executed.

ECNs operate on a solely electronic basis, where trades are executed directly following orders placed with the ECN. Such organisations include Euro-MTS, Brokertec, Archipelago and Island ECN. These types of organisation usually differ from computerised exchanges in the respect that ECNs may not have acquired the status of a stock exchange.

From an STO's perspective, trades can be executed through a number of methods:

- orders received from institutional clients (via the STO's salespeople),
- the trading floor of face-to-face stock exchanges,
- computerised exchanges,
- ECNs,
- by telephone direct with other STOs.

11.4 TRADE CAPTURE (FRONT OFFICE)

Regardless of their origin, all trades executed by an STO must be recorded formally, within the STO's books and records, without delay.

Typically, the first step in achieving this is for the traders or market makers to record the basic detail of each trade. This is necessary in order to:

- update the trading position for the specific security (typically within a trading book), so that the factual trading position is reflected in the trader's records. Table 11.1 illustrates individual trades having updated a trading position, within an individual security;

Table 11.1

Operation	Quantity	Trade date	Trading position
		6th January	zero
Buy	10,000,000	7th January	+10,000,000
Buy	5,000,000	2nd February	+15,000,000
Sell	13,000,000	21st July	+2,000,000
Buy	40,000,000	16th August	+42,000,000
Sell	6,000,000	14th September	+36,000,000
Sell	12,500,000	29th September	+23,500,000

- update the average price of the current trading position so that when the next trade is executed, the trader or market maker knows whether a trading profit or loss will be made. Note that trading P&L does not take account of operational costs.

Thereby enabling trading to continue, from a revised standpoint.

Traders and market makers normally use trading systems designed specifically for the purpose of managing their positions, and applying updated prices to those positions. However, regardless of whether trading systems are in use or not within an STO, the basic trade detail must be conveyed immediately to the middle or back office (refer to Chapter 4) to allow operational processing to commence.

11.4.1 Trade Components

The following elaborates on the description of trade components within Chapter 1 and describes the impact of each component being incorrect.

The responsibility for the content of the core detail of a trade, in terms of its individual components, lies with the trader. In the case of a principal trade, the basic components that are typically recorded by the trader or market maker are:

- trading book
- trade date
- trade time
- value date
- operation
- quantity
- security
- price
- counterparty.

For each of these components, the following describes how traders and market makers typically input trades into a trading system, at the very beginning of the trade lifecycle.

Trading Book

The trading book on a trade has only internal implications. The purpose of an STO apply-ing a trading book to a principal trade is to assign internal responsibility and ownership for the trade, resulting in an update to the trading position within the specific security, and trading profits within the trading book. If the incorrect trading book is applied to a trade, amendment of the trade will have no external impact.

Trading systems are typically segregated by security within trading book; when a trader records a trade, the system should automatically default the relevant trading book accord-ing to, for example, the specific security or the system 'log-in' of the trader.

Trade Date

The trade date on a trade has both internal and external implications. The trade date is the day that the parties to the trade agree to execute the trade. It has an impact on:

- the date that a trading position is updated—if an executed trade is not recorded by the trader or market maker on the trade date, the trading position (the running quantity of securities in the trader's inventory) will remain incorrect until the trade is recorded. Furthermore, because the trade is not recorded, risk exposure with the counterparty cannot be assessed;
- trading P&L calculation—the P&L impact of a trade cannot be calculated if the trade has not been recorded. If the trade is recorded one day late, for example, the trading P&L would be incorrect as at close of business on the trade date;
- the calculation of accrued interest on a bond—the trade date is normally linked with the value date of trades, and value date is (in most markets) used to calculate accrued interest on trades. If the trade date is incorrect, it can affect value date, in turn affecting the number of days of accrued interest, in turn affecting the cash value of accrued interest and, ultimately, the net settlement value of a trade;
- entitlement to income on equity—in most markets, entitlement to dividends on equity is directly related to trade date. Where trade dates are incorrect, a buyer may lose entitlement, as could a seller.

Trading systems typically assume the trade date to be the same date as the trade input date; this causes no problems, providing trade date is overridden when necessary, such as when a trade is being recorded on a day after the trade execution date (commonly known as a 'late booking' or an 'as-of' trade [meaning 'as-of' yesterday; for example]).

Trade Time

The regulators of many markets around the globe require that STOs record the exact hour and minute that a trade was executed, this enables:

- the monitoring of an STO's trading activity to ensure that trades have been traded at 'best execution' price at the time of trade execution, for the protection of investors;
- the settling of disputes between counterparties regarding the basic detail of trades (e.g. quantity differences).
- market surveillance; identification of price fluctuations relative to trade time, with a view to identifying abnormal trading activity.

Regulators also insist that all telephone conversations made by traders and market makers are taped; the tapes are then stored in a secure environment. When a dispute arises, the trade time is used to quickly identify and retrieve the relevant tape from storage, thereby enabling the original conversation to be replayed in order to resolve what was actually agreed. Note that access to the secure environment is under the control of the compliance officer, rather than front office personnel.

In some cases, the trade time is used as a measure for trade reporting. In the Eurobond marketplace, the regulator requires that all trades executed by UK based members of the Eurobond industry body (International Securities Market Association, ISMA) report details of trades to ISMA, via their system Trax, within 30 minutes of trade execution. Fines are imposed on ISMA members who fail to meet the 30-minute deadline.

Industry Anecdote

When Trax was first introduced in 1989, the front office of some STOs were still using manual methods to record trades and to transmit messages to Trax. Meeting the 30-minute deadline was proving to be a challenge, and sizeable monthly fines were being incurred by some STOs. Attempts were made to falsify the trade time, in order to avoid being fined; unfortunately, the senders of the false information did not appreciate that Trax made a comparison of trade time between buyer and seller. This comparison revealed that certain STOs were regularly reporting trades with trade times that were 10 or 15 minutes later than the corresponding trade times of many of their counterparties. The detection of these attempts means that STOs must record the trade time accurately, and report trades to Trax within the 30-minute deadline, if fines are to be avoided.

If the trader or market maker records the trade onto the trading system immediately upon trade execution, the assumption by the trading system that trade time should be the same as input time will be accurate. Unless trade capture occurs immediately, trade time will be incorrect, unless overridden.

Value Date

The value date of a trade is the intended date of exchange of securities and cash; this is also known as the 'contractual settlement date'. (*Note*: it is important not to confuse this date with the 'actual settlement date', as this refers to the date securities and cash were actually exchanged, which can be known only after the event.)

The period between trade date and value date is commonly referred to as the *settlement cycle*.

Generally speaking, the greater the number of days between trade date and value date, the greater the potential risk of one of the parties to the trade defaulting. This is a concern because where, for example, a buyer executes a trade, but is not required to make payment for that purchase for many days or weeks, the buyer may be tempted to *default* from paying, should the market price of the security fall dramatically before the value date.

In addition, if all other methods fail to confirm that the buyer and seller agree the details of the trade, the attempt to match *settlement instructions* immediately prior to value date is regarded as the ultimate point at which agreement (or disagreement) becomes apparent. Clearly, attempting to resolve a disagreement of the detail of a trade executed many days or weeks previously is not necessarily in keeping with an efficient marketplace.

In the majority of markets around the globe, standard methods are used to derive the value date of trades. In each market, one of two main conventions is used, namely:

- account settlement, or
- rolling settlement.

Account Settlement. Historically, some markets operated their settlement cycle on an *account settlement* basis, meaning that all trades with a trade date within a given period (sometimes referred to as an account period) would have a value date on a fixed future date. This means that neither cash nor securities are exchanged between buyer and seller during the account period; the exchange is intended to occur on value date, the fixed future date.

Figure 11.2 illustrates the concept of account settlement. For example, in the UK, the account settlement convention was used until 1994; until that point in time, account periods were normally periods of two weeks, with the value date being on the Monday, ten days after the close of the account period. In India, weekly account periods are in operation (for securities not settled via *book entry*) and until recently in France, the settlement cycle was on a monthly account settlement basis.

The trend, however, is for markets to move towards a rolling settlement convention.

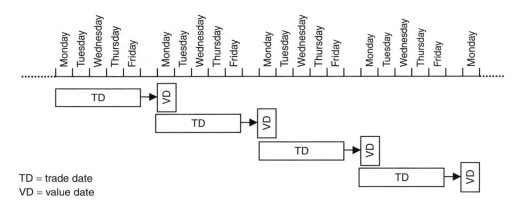

TD = trade date
VD = value date

Figure 11.2   Trade execution and capture: account settlement

Rolling Settlement. Rolling settlement refers to the practice of applying the value date to trades, a fixed number of business days after trade date. For example, the equity markets in Australia, the UK and USA operate on a trade date plus 3 business days settlement cycle; this is commonly referred to as 'T+3'.

Figure 11.3 illustrates the concept of rolling settlement (on a T+3 basis).

In 1989, an organisation known as the *Group of Thirty* made a series of recommendations regarding the methods of operation within the securities industry globally. One of its recommendations was that all markets should adopt rolling settlement, and that settlement cycles should be reduced to T+3 by 1992. This is important for the entire securities industry from a risk reduction perspective, as the shorter the settlement cycle, the fewer the number of open trades with counterparties at any one point in time, thereby reducing

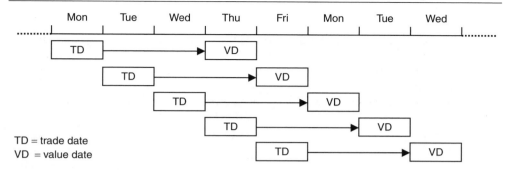

Figure 11.3 Trade execution and capture: rolling settlement

the risk of counterparties defaulting on their contractual obligation to settle executed trades.

An ongoing challenge for the entire industry will be to strike an acceptable balance between the desire to reduce settlement cycles globally, against a background of increasing trading volumes and the practicalities of communication within shortening deadlines. Clearly, automation will play a major role in realising the objective.

Indeed, many markets have reduced, and continue to reduce, their settlement cycle; for example, in 1994 the UK equity market initially moved from account settlement to T+10 rolling settlement, then in 1995 moved to T+5. The move to T+3 occurred in February 2001. In the USA, at the time of writing, T+3 is in operation for equities, and the desire is to move to T+1 in 2005.

Points to note are:

- if a party to a trade wishes for a value date earlier or later than the current standard for the particular market in question, a trader or market maker may agree, providing this is stated at the time of trade execution;
- some countries have different settlement cycles for equities and government bond markets.

Value Date of New Issues. Because new issues of securities are, in many cases, announced weeks in advance of the *primary value date*, trading can commence, for example, three weeks in advance of the primary value date. As it is not possible to have a legitimate value date prior to the primary value date, care must be taken to ensure that the primary value date is the earliest value date that can be applied to trades in new issues of securities.

Providing the trading system has the capability to hold settlement cycles at individual market level, and to associate individual securities with the relevant market, the correct value date should be defaulted from trade date, unless a trade has been executed for an earlier or later value date than the standard period, in which case the value date must be overridden.

Trading systems that have the capability to hold the primary value date within their security static data should be capable of deriving the correct value date of trades in new issues. If this is not the case, the value date must be overridden.

Operation

The term 'operation' refers to the direction of the trade; quite simply, whether an STO is a buyer or a seller. However, 'buy' or 'sell' is not relevant to all transaction types, as in the case of a securities lending and borrowing transaction, the relevant choice of operation is 'lend' or 'borrow'.

The trader or market maker will need to record whether the trade is a purchase or a sale.

Quantity

For a principal transaction, the quantity refers to the number of shares or bonds that have been bought or sold.

Standard tradable quantities may be relevant to both equity and bonds, depending upon the individual security. In the case of equity, the number of shares relating to a trade may be traded in *board lots* (refer to Chapter 7), whilst bonds are typically tradable in accordance with their denominational values.

Furthermore, the management of an STO may impose their own minimum quantities, to avoid trading in amounts that are too small on which to make trading in such a quantity viable.

Industry Anecdote

Care must be taken regarding trade quantities; on one occasion 50 million of a particular bond was sold (over the telephone) at a good price to a counterparty. Once the counterparty had received the trade confirmation (on the day following trade date), they questioned the content immediately as they thought they had bought 15 million. The dealing tapes were, unfortunately, inconclusive. The counterparty insisted their intention was to buy only 15 million, so the seller was forced to amend the trade to 15 million, resulting in a dramatically reduced trading profit, with 35 million bonds remaining unsold.

The quantity will require inputting by the trader or market maker, but the trading system should prove its validity (regarding board lots and denominational values) by reference to static data.

Security

When a trade is being executed, it is essential to be precise as to exactly which security is being traded.

On equities, confusion between parties to a trade can arise where the original security and a second security, with superficially identical details, are validly in existence at the same time. An example of this is where an issuer has created new shares in addition to the original shares; the two sets of shares need to be identified separately, in a situation where the new shares may not be equal in all respects, until some later point in time. For example, the next dividend may be payable only on the original shares, and not on the new shares. Following the payment of the dividend, both the original shares and the new shares can be merged, as they will at that point in time become equal in all respects.

Some issuers of bonds, such as the World Bank (official title International Bank for Reconstruction and Development), may have hundreds of bonds with details that are extremely similar, such as:

- issues with identical coupon rates and maturity dates, differentiated by their currency of issue;
- issues with identical coupon rates and currency of issue, differentiated by their maturity dates;
- issues with identical maturity dates and currency of issue, differentiated by their coupon rates.

It is essential that, at the time of trade execution, the two parties to a trade are precise as to which security they wish to execute a trade in.

To help avoid errors in the identification of the correct security, securities identification code numbers such as *ISIN* and *Cusip* (refer to Chapter 9) are assigned to each security.

The security over which the trade was executed should be held within the trading system's static data repository. Trading systems normally display only those securities that are pertinent to the particular trading book; the trader needs only to select the correct security from the list.

If the relevant security has not already been set up within the trading system's static data, trade capture will be held up at the very beginning of the trade lifecycle, causing delays and potential cost.

Price

The price is obviously an essential component of a trade and it is therefore crucial to be exact when executing a trade.

As described in Chapter 8, the price of equities is typically expressed as a cash amount for each share, whereas bonds are normally traded at a percentage price relevant to the currency and face value of the bond; in some markets, a fractional price is used.

The price at which a trade has been executed will require being input (with care) by the trader or market maker.

Industry Anecdote

Some traders and market makers communicate security prices in 'small' digits only; for example, a bond with a current market price of 88.25% may be communicated by some traders and market makers as 8.25%. No damage was done by this alone except when, for example, a trade was recorded as 98.25%. The trader stated that the small digit was perfectly correct; they just couldn't remember the 'big' digit correctly. Unfortunately, the consequence of this error on a medium-sized purchase of USD 20 million bonds is that an overpayment of USD 2 million is in danger of being made!

Counterparty

Identifying the counterparty with whom a trade has been executed is also vitally important; a securities trade is a contract to exchange securities and cash, and as such it is essential to know precisely with whom a trade has been executed.

Confusion can arise where, for instance, an STO trades with a group of companies containing numerous trading entities in different locations. Under these circumstances, it is insufficient to know that it is Counterparty 123, if the location of the counterparty remains unknown. For example, the STO may have actually traded with Counterparty 123, Frankfurt office but the STO may also trade on a regular basis with the counterparty's offices in Paris, Vienna, Rome and Madrid. Being uncertain of the counterparty and its location is highly likely to lead to delays in settlement processing, unmatched settlement instructions and delayed settlement, all of which are operationally time-consuming and costly.

When an STO trades with a mutual fund manager (also known as a unit trust company) it is common to find that at the point of placing an order, and at execution of the order, the mutual fund manager has yet to decide to which of its underlying funds the trade should be allocated. It may take a number of hours for the fund manager to respond to the STO with the allocation details. Under these circumstances, the STO has executed the trade with a counterparty, knowing that the final counterparty details will differ from the counterparty known at trade execution. Normally, the trade is recorded as executed with the parent counterparty, and when, at a later time, the quantities and allocation details are known, the original trade is replaced.

Industry Anecdote

Traders and market makers are naturally very eager to secure a transaction at a good price; this is good for the STO as well as the trader. On occasions, however, over-eagerness results in trading with a counterparty prior to knowing exactly which counterparty a trade has been executed with. The dealing tapes may be inconclusive in identifying the counterparty. Under these circumstances, the trader or market maker may wish the trade to be recorded to a 'dummy' counterparty, in the hope that time will reveal the identity of the real counterparty through, for instance, a settlement instruction from the counterparty. On some occasions this approach works: the counterparty would be identified and the trade rebooked to the true counterparty, and a settlement instruction issued in order to match the counterparty's instruction. On other occasions the counterparty cannot be traced, and ultimately the trade would need to be cancelled outright, occasionally resulting in cancelled profit, but on other occasions resulting in cancelled loss!

The counterparty with whom the trade was executed should be held within the trading system's static data repository, as for securities. The trader needs only to select the correct counterparty, inclusive of location, from the list.

If the relevant counterparty has not already been set up, trade capture will be held up at the very beginning of the trade lifecycle, causing delays and potential cost.

11.4.2   Front Office Trade Reference

The trading system should perform validation that all necessary components of a trade are present, before assigning a trade reference number to the trade. Storage of the trading system trade reference number allows efficient identification and inspection of the details of each trade, at any time after trade capture. Efficient trade amendment and cancellation primarily relies upon identification of the trade, via its reference number.

11.4.3   Following Successful Capture in the Front Office

The successful capture of a trade within a trading system should result in the trade details being sent to the back office immediately, via an interface, for operational processing.

Where an STO has no trading system (nowadays a rare circumstance), the trade detail is usually recorded manually, by the trader or market maker, onto a 'dealing slip'; this will require collection by, or delivery to, the middle office or settlement department for operational processing. Under these circumstances, the trader or market maker will need to maintain their trading position manually, keeping it updated with any new trades.

11.4.4   Accuracy and Timeliness of Trade Capture

It is imperative that traders and market makers maintain up-to-date and accurate records of all trades executed, and the impact on their trading positions, regardless of whether the information is held manually or a trading system is used.

In volatile market conditions, a large number of trades may be executed in a short space of time, leading to healthy trading profits being made.

However, under any market conditions, if the trader or market maker records trades accurately, and at the time of trade execution, the chances of achieving *STP* of trades is high, the risk of operational loss is low, and unnecessary operational effort is avoided.

A trading error relates to any trade where the basic trade information requires amendment, or outright cancellation, following the original recording of the trade.

Measures can be taken (refer to Chapter 13) in an attempt to detect errors before any information is sent externally; however, it is unrealistic to expect that such measures will successfully detect all errors.

Incorrectly recorded trades (that are not detected prior to transmission of information to the outside world) will inevitably lead to an STO sending:

* inaccurate trade confirmations to counterparties; where the counterparty is an institutional client, the STO will jeopardise its relationship with the client unless errors are minimised or stopped completely. Ultimately, the institutional client may choose to take his business elsewhere
* inaccurate settlement instructions to its *custodian*
  o this is highly likely to lead to unmatched settlement instructions with the counterparty, investigation as to which is correct, and (if the STO is incorrect) subsequent amendment of the trade detail by the trader
  o furthermore, this can lead to direct monetary loss by the STO, if the counterparty matches the STO's instruction, and the trade settles (even though the details are incorrect).

Only where an error has been detected will it be possible to treat it as an error and take action to correct it, and to recognise the cost of the error. In the case where the counterparty matches the STO's instruction, and the trade settles for the incorrect cash value, the STO may never be aware that there was an error!

Some front office personnel have acquired a good understanding as to why it is essential to minimise errors, and how profits are retained and lost operationally as a result. Others are less aware and have appear not to been trained in the fundamental aspects of settlement, or of general operational pitfalls.

Understanding the impact of failing to record trades accurately or on time, or both, is an essential element in becoming a successful salesperson, trader or market maker.

Some people hold the view that persistent front office offenders should have the cost of each error charged directly to the trader or market maker, resulting in a direct negative impact on their trading profits, or increased trading losses. In the case of salespeople, the cost of errors originated by inaccurate order details should be deducted from their sales credits. As the management of STOs typically judge the performance of traders and market makers on their P&L, and salespeople by their sales credits, it is in their own interests that salespeople, traders and market makers aim for 100% accuracy when recording details of orders and trades, and to record them without delay.

However, taking those actions internally cannot conceal the probability that unnecessary costs have been incurred by the STO, and that its profits have been reduced as a result.

11.5   TRADE CAPTURE (SETTLEMENT SYSTEM)

In an automated environment, where the trade has been sent by the trading system to the back office system electronically, although it is to be expected that the trade will arrive successfully in the receiving system, it is possible that the trade fails to arrive in the back office system. As it is vital to recognise these circumstances immediately, it is recommended that a trade-by-trade reconciliation is conducted, to ensure that the trades sent by the trading system have in fact been received successfully by the back office system, within an appropriate timeframe. A procedure needs to be in place to take corrective action once a missing trade has been identified.

As soon as the back office system receives a trade, validation should be performed to confirm that static data items, including trading book, security and counterparty, are known, and that the quantity is in accordance with the information held within static data. Where this check reveals a problem (e.g. counterparty not known), this should be highlighted and treated as an 'exception', requiring corrective action; this will have the impact of temporarily halting operational processing of the trade.

As mentioned in Chapter 9, it is imperative that static data is consistent (and correct) between trading systems and settlement systems, if there is a desire to achieve *STP*.

Some STOs require the trading system to pass minimal trade data, for instance, excluding value date, requiring the back office system to perform the 'calculation'. This particular situation should not prove problematic, providing that the trader or market maker did not agree to a non-standard value date with the counterparty; in that situation, the value date should be input within the trading system, thereby overriding any default calculation in the back office.

Once the trade details have been checked for validity, a settlement system trade reference number (in addition to the trading system trade reference number) will be assigned, at which point the trade is accepted into the settlement system.

The trade is now in a condition to be 'enriched'; in other words, to have additional information added.

Where a handwritten dealing slip has been received from a trader or market maker, this will require manual input to the settlement system. However, this situation demands an additional step, in comparison with an automated trade capture mechanism. Manual input of trades creates the possibility of human error, and so the quality of input is normally validated to ensure that no 'keying' errors have occurred. Lack of clarity when handwriting the trade details can also lead to problems.

11.5.1 Position Updating in the Settlement System

Upon successful receipt of a trade by the settlement system, whether from a feed from a trading system or by manual input, the updating of ownership and location positions (refer to Chapter 1) must occur immediately.

Table 11.2

Trading book	A
Trade date	14th April
Trade time	11:22
Value date	17th April
Operation	Buy
Quantity	4,000,000
Security	TUV Corporation, HKD 1.00 shares
Price	HKD 2.922125
Counterparty	PTIF (Professional Traders Inc., Frankfurt)

Table 11.3

TUV Corporation, HKD 1.00 shares			
Ownership		Location	
Trading book A	+ 4,000,000	− 4,000,000	Counterparty PTIF
	+ 4,000,000	− 4,000,000	

For example, once the trade detail in Table 11.2 has been received by the settlement system, the position update in Table 11.3 should occur, thereby enabling a complete current view of the trading position at trading book level, and outstanding trades with counterparties. Note that the equivalent cash position updating will need to occur, as soon as the net settlement value is known (refer to Chapter 12).

11.6 SUMMARY

The efficiency of an STO, in an operational sense, is extremely reliant upon the commitment of the front office personnel (i.e. salespeople, traders and market makers) to record each order and trade accurately and in a timely fashion.

As automation generates more competition for STOs in the marketplace, it is widely predicted that trading profits will become tighter, making it essential that errors in the recording of orders and in the recording of trades are minimised, and that 'late booked' or 'as-of' trades become a rarity.

Furthermore, the drive towards reducing settlement cycles (for example T+1) is very likely to require the very highest levels of efficiency within STOs, throughout the chain of steps, in order to avoid unnecessary costs.

12
Trade Enrichment

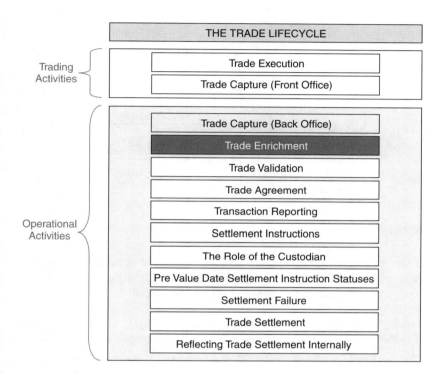

12.1 INTRODUCTION

Following trade capture within the settlement system, the details of a trade require enrichment.

Whether by manual or automated means, trade enrichment involves the selection, calculation and attachment to a trade of relevant information necessary to complete a number of essential actions, following capture of the basic trade details.

In an automated environment:

- *STP*
- efficient servicing of clients
- avoidance of operational risk
- minimising operational cost

cannot be achieved successfully unless trade enrichment is completed accurately and within the necessary deadlines.

In an automated environment, trade enrichment is achieved through defaulting relevant information automatically from the store of information within static data; this is commonly known as *static data defaulting*. Within this book, the term 'trade enrichment' refers

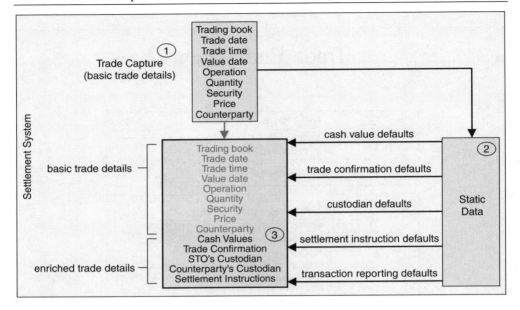

Figure 12.1   Trade enrichment: overview

generically to the enrichment of trades, whether achieved manually or automatically. The term static data defaulting refers only where trade enrichment is achieved automatically.

Figure 12.1 illustrates how trade enrichment is normally achieved.

Step 1: the basic trade details are captured within the settlement system, whether having been fed from a front office system or input manually.

Step 2: the basic trade details are compared with the information held within the static data repository and (if set up) the default information is selected.

Step 3: the selected defaults are attached to the basic trade detail to form the enriched trade.

12.2   TRADE ENRICHMENT COMPONENTS

In general terms, the trade components requiring enrichment are:

- calculation of cash values
- counterparty *trade confirmation* requirements
- selection of *custodian* details
- method of transmission of *settlement instructions*.
- determining the method of transaction reporting (for regulatory purposes)

However, the essential actions requiring to be added to an individual trade are initially dictated according to the specific transaction type, as the components pertaining to one transaction type may have only some similarities with another transaction type. For instance, the components requiring enrichment on a principal trade will have some similarities and some differences when compared with a custodian (depot) transfer. They will be similar in the following areas:

- the need to select custodian details
- the need to determine the method of transmission of settlement instructions

and differ as, for a custodian (depot) transfer, there is no requirement to:

- calculate cash values
- issue a trade confirmation to a counterparty
- report the transaction to a regulatory authority.

The basic components and attributes of each transaction type are detailed in Chapter 5; however, Table 12.1 summarises the typical trade enrichment components of each transaction type.

Table 12.1

Component	Securities transaction types					Cash transaction types		
	Principal	Repo	Securities lend and borrow	Trading book transfer	Depot (custodian) transfer	Unsecured borrow and lend	Nostro transfer	Foreign exchange
Cash value calculation	✓	✓	✓	✓	×	✓	✓	✓
Securities depot details	✓	✓	✓	×	✓	×	×	×
Trade confirmation	✓	✓	✓	×	×	✓	×	✓
Transaction reporting	✓	✓	✓	×	×	×	×	×
Settlement instructions	✓	✓	✓	×	✓	✓	✓	✓
Securities accounting	✓	✓	✓	✓	✓	×	×	×
Cash accounting	✓	✓	✓	✓	×	✓	✓	✓

Having assessed the components that are relevant to a trade based upon transaction type, further consideration must be given to each trade component, in order to determine what is relevant to enrich on an individual trade.

12.3 DETERMINING FACTORS IN TRADE ENRICHMENT

Before enrichment of individual trades can occur, consideration must be given to the choices an STO has for deriving the correct information to attach to a trade. Examples follow, but it should be noted that additional factors may determine the correct information.

12.3.1 Calculation of Cash Values

In order to calculate all the cash related components of a trade, it is necessary to consider the following, for example.

Operation

Buying or selling, or borrowing or lending, may determine cash values. For example:

- client purchases of UK equity attract stamp duty, but sales do not;
- only sellers of US equity are required to pay a Securities & Exchange Commission fee.

Security Group

Cash values will be determined according to security group, for instance:

- stamp duty is payable on Irish equities, but not on Japanese equities;
- accrued interest is applicable on straight bonds, but not on zero coupon bonds.

Counterparty Type

Different types of counterparty may determine different cash values, such as trade amounts that will not affect the net settlement value. For example:

- sales credits are normally calculated on trades with institutional clients, but not on trades with other STOs;
- sales credits may be calculated differently for different types of institutional client, such as pension funds and insurance companies.

12.3.2   Selection of Custodian Details

The selection of the relevant custodian details for both the trading company and the counterparty will be affected by the following, for example.

Trading Company

If an STO processes the business of more than one trading company:

- different custodians may be used by each of the companies, even for the same security group. For example, for settlement of their Spanish equities, company A may use custodian 'S', but company B may use custodian 'T';
- the same custodian may be used by both trading companies, distinguished by different account numbers for each company at the custodian.

Transaction Type

Different transaction types will determine the settlement location of a trade, for example:

- a principal trade will settle at a securities custodian, whereas a foreign exchange trade is likely to settle over a main bank account. The custodian and the bank may not be the same entity, for example, the trading company may use in Japan
  - Custodian E, Tokyo as securities custodian (for principal trade settlement for example)
  - Bank T, Tokyo as the main bank account (for foreign exchange trade settlement, for example).

Security Group

The custodian for a trade will be selected according to the security group, for instance:

- US equities will settle at the New York custodian;
- New Zealand Government bonds will settle at the Wellington custodian.

Counterparty

Where there is a choice of settlement location, a counterparty may choose, for example, *domestic settlement* as apposed to settling through an *ICSD*. Note that some counterparties select settlement location on a trade-by-trade basis.

12.3.3 Counterparty Trade Confirmation Requirements

In order to determine whether a trade confirmation should be issued to the counterparty, it is necessary to consider the following, for example.

Counterparty Type

An STO will normally issue a trade confirmation to its institutional clients, as part of the service it offers to those clients. However, the STO may not issue trade confirmations to other STOs with which it trades, particularly where other methods of agreeing the trade details exist. (Such trade agreement methods are described in chapter 14).

12.3.4 Determining the Method of Transaction Reporting

The method of transaction reporting to the STO's regulator will depend upon the following.

Security Group

The types of security in which an STO trades may require that the STO carries out its transaction reporting via different methods, for example:

- a UK-based STO may be required to report its UK equities via one route, and its international bonds via a different route.

12.3.5 Method of Transmission of Settlement Instructions

The methods used to transmit settlement instructions will depend upon the following, for example.

Trading Company

Where an STO processes the business of more than one trading company, each company may have a preferred (but different) method of transmission. For instance:

- company A may choose to transmit via telex, whereas company B may choose to transmit via *S.W.I.F.T.* (described in Chapters 14 and 16).

Custodian

Custodians typically have a preference for the method of communication between the STO and themselves. For example:

- custodian X may require all settlement instructions to be transmitted via a specific S.W.I.F.T. message type, whereas custodian Y may require the transmission of all such instructions via a different S.W.I.F.T. message.

12.4   STATIC DATA DEFAULTING

Given that there are choices for many of the essential actions, the selection of the correct and appropriate information, particularly in an automated environment, is of paramount importance.

For example, in order to automatically default the custodian details for both the trading company and its counterparty, the following rules could be used (refer to Chapter 9, from which the data in Table 12.2 is derived).

Column 1 contains the name of an individual security, whilst column 2 shows the security group in which the individual security belongs, and which has been defaulted from security static data. With that information, the settlement system can then default the custodian details for both the trading company and the counterparty, based upon predefined rules, such as whenever a trade is received by the settlement system

- for a principal trade with these conditions:
  - for the trading company WSIL (the settlement department may be processing business for more than one trading company, where the custodians used by each trading company may differ)
  - with a security within security group Australian equity
- select and default the following:
  - the custodian to be used by WSIL (the trading company) will be Custodian A, Sydney for the settlement of both securities and cash (it should not be assumed that securities and cash settle at the same custodian in all cases)
  - WSIL's account number at Custodian A, Sydney for both securities and cash is 5023598

and

- for a principal trade with these conditions:
  - where the counterparty is PTIF
  - with a security within security group Australian equity
- select and default the following:
  - the custodian to be used by PTIF (as counterparty to WSIL) will be Custodian B, Melbourne for the settlement of both securities and cash
  - PTIF's account number at Custodian B, Melbourne for both securities and cash is 5532896.

The above represents automatic defaulting of static data in order to calculate custodian details, from which a settlement instruction will be generated.

A similar sequence of steps is necessary in order to derive the defaults for all other trade components requiring enrichment.

Table 12.2

1	2	Custodians of Trading Company (WSIL)		Custodians of Counterparty (PTIF)	
Security	Security Group	Securities	Cash	Securities	Cash
News Corporation Ordinary shares	Australian Equity	Cust. A Sydney A/c5023598	Cust. A Sydney A/c5023598	Cust. B Melbourne A/c5532896	Cust. B Melbourne A/c5532896
Japanese Gov't. 4.2.% 1st May 2015	Japanese Gov't Bond	Cust. E Tokyo A/cA0078802	Cust. E Tokyo A/cA0078802	Cust. F Tokyo A/cA9096220	Cust. F Tokyo A/cA9096220
TUV Corporation Shares	Hong Kong Equity	Cust. H Hong Kong A/c111693XM	Cust. H Hong Kong A/c111693XM	Cust. I Hong Kong A/c110242TP	Cust. I Hong Kong A/c110242TP
IBM Corporation Common Stock	US Equity	Cust. L New York A/c334RR126	Cust. L New York A/c334RR126	Cust. L, New York A/c339RR098	Cust. L, New York A/c339RR098
British Airways Ordinary shares	UK Equity	Cust. P London A/c9455B1	Cust. P London A/c9455B1	Cust. Q London A/c2967D2	Cust. Q London A/c2967D2
XOX AG 8.25% 1st June 2020	Eurobond (USD)	Cust. S Brussels A/cXA3396269	Cust. S Brussels A/cXA3396269	Cust. S Brussels A/cXA8824179	Cust. S Brussels A/cXA8824179

12.5   FAILURE TO APPLY STATIC DATA DEFAULTS

In an automated environment, failure to fully enrich a trade may be intentional or unintentional.

12.5.1   Intentional Failure

In a situation where the default of a particular trade component is best applied manually, the STO may choose to set no automatic default of static data.

Some securities, such as Italian Government bonds, can settle domestically (in Milan) or internationally (in Euroclear or Clearstream Luxembourg). An STO may choose to settle an individual trade in one or other location, depending upon the circumstances at that time. If no rule can be applied, then it is not possible to automate the default.

Under these circumstances, whenever the settlement system cannot complete an action (such as applying company and/or counterparty custodian details), an exception should be raised automatically. Once corrective action has been taken (in this case attaching the relevant custodian details manually), the action can be completed by the system.

Therefore, under some circumstances, operational control may be enhanced by the intentional failure to apply defaults automatically.

12.5.2   Unintentional Failure

In an automated environment it is, of course, not possible to default static data automatically if, for a particular component, static data is missing.

For instance, a specific counterparty is set up within both the trading system and the settlement system, but no custodian details are set up within the settlement system for that counterparty trading in a particular security group. Consequently, as defaults cannot be selected and attached to the trade automatically, static data defaulting would fail. This situation requires that the trade is treated as an exception, the necessary information added to static data, at which point operational processing can continue.

12.6   ENRICHMENT OF COUNTERPARTY CUSTODIAN DETAILS

This section is intended to clarify the reasons for an STO needing to calculate its counterparty's custodian details (as well as its own custodian details).

When a trade is executed by an STO, particularly an STO that trades in many markets around the globe, it is necessary to determine where it wishes to settle the trade (from its choice of custodians). In addition, the STO must determine how the counterparty wishes to settle the trade, as this information will be required on the settlement instruction issued by the STO.

For example, if WSIL, an STO, has bought 5,000,000 News Corporation Ordinary Shares from PTIF, WSIL first needs to assess how it wishes to settle the trade from its own perspective. WSIL needs to determine its appropriate custodian based on the individual security, or the security group (in this case, Australian equity), resulting in the decision to settle the purchase at Custodian A, Sydney.

A similar decision needs to be taken by WSIL regarding where it believes PTIF will settle the trade, according to the information received from PTIF and held within the STO's static data. The custodian to be used by the counterparty will appear on the settlement instruction that will be sent by WSIL to its custodian. This is essential information, otherwise WSIL's custodian will not know with whom the trade is to settle. Stating 'PTIF' does not provide the answer, as the information required to match and settle the instruction sent by WSIL is the account number at the relevant CSD, of the Australian custodian being used by PTIF, namely Custodian B, Melbourne.

Figure 12.2 represents the basic steps involved in issuing and matching of settlement instructions, in order to emphasise the importance of holding correct static data, and enriching the trade with the correct data.

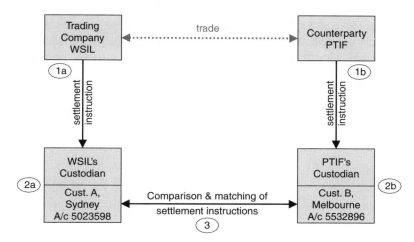

Figure 12.2   Custodian details on settlement instructions

Following trade execution between WSIL and PTIF, from WSIL's perspective, the trade would be captured within the trading system, then captured within the settlement system, followed by trade enrichment within the settlement system, where WSIL would have calculated:

- the custodian that they themselves wish to use for settlement of the trade
- PTIF's custodian

Step 1a: WSIL issues a settlement instruction to its custodian, telling Custodian A, Sydney to receive 5,000,000 News Corporation ordinary shares, against payment of the relevant cash amount, from Custodian B, Melbourne, account number 5532896, on the value date of the trade.

Step 1b: PTIF issues a settlement instruction to its custodian, Custodian B to deliver the shares against the relevant cash amount to Custodian A, account number 5023598, on the value date of the trade.

Step 2a: Custodian A should update its records with the details of the instruction received from its client, WSIL.

Step 2b: Custodian B should update its records with the details of the instruction received from its client, PTIF.

Step 3: each custodian should aim to achieve a match of their client's settlement instructions with the counterparty's custodian (at the relevant CSD), as soon as possible. If the information does not match, the custodians have no authority to change any aspect of their client's settlement instruction, but must advise their client of the status of the instruction, without delay. At that point, WSIL would need to investigate the reason for the mismatch of instructions, without delay. If WSIL's static data is accurate in all respects, and if trades are enriched with correct details, the number of unmatched instructions will be minimised (although settlement instructions may be unmatched for many other reasons, such as price or quantity differences).

12.7   SUMMARY

As mentioned in Chapter 11, as settlement cycles (the period between trade date and value date) continue to decrease in many markets around the globe, the quality of static data held by STOs, and the efficiency of use of static data in the trade enrichment process, becomes ever more important, particularly when settlement cycles around the globe move to T+1, or T+0.

13
Trade Validation

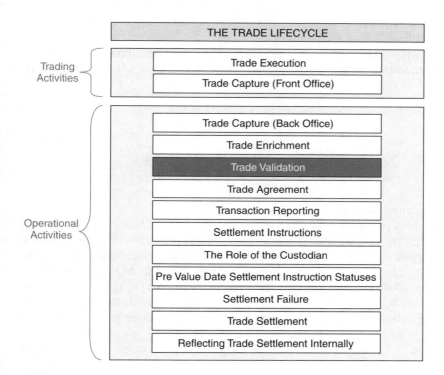

THE TRADE LIFECYCLE

Trading Activities {
- Trade Execution
- Trade Capture (Front Office)

Operational Activities {
- Trade Capture (Back Office)
- Trade Enrichment
- Trade Validation
- Trade Agreement
- Transaction Reporting
- Settlement Instructions
- The Role of the Custodian
- Pre Value Date Settlement Instruction Statuses
- Settlement Failure
- Trade Settlement
- Reflecting Trade Settlement Internally

13.1 INTRODUCTION

Having executed, captured and enriched a trade, it is now complete and the various tasks, such as:

- issuing a *trade confirmation*
- reporting the trade to the regulatory authorities
- issuing *settlement instructions*

could now be actioned.

However, many STOs adopt a final check of the data contained within a fully enriched trade, in order to reduce the possibility of erroneous information being sent to the outside world. This activity is known as trade validation, a mechanism to reduce risk and remain in control. Unless an STO performs validation of trade information at this stage of the trade lifecycle, there is a risk that:

- timely and accurate servicing of clients
- avoidance of operational risk
- minimising of operational costs

will not be achieved successfully.

Conversely, the desire to also achieve *STP* requires that an STO must decide upon an acceptable balance between the need to validate trades and the temptation to allow all operational activities to commence as quickly as possible.

13.2 STRAIGHT THROUGH PROCESSING

As stated in Chapter 10, STP is an objective, which is to manage the trade throughout its entire lifecycle without human intervention.

During the 1990s, 'STP' became an internationally recognised term, with many of the world's organisations having a role to play in the automation of trade processing, including:

- *institutional investors*
- STOs
- regulatory authorities
- stock exchanges
- *custodians*
- *registrars*

contributing to meeting the objective.

At the time of writing, much discussion within the securities industry revolves around the subject of STP. The historic and, in many cases, current efficiency of communication between such parties as listed above is typified by manual processes, different conventions (e.g. security identification codes), high percentage of error rates and settlement failure costs. The industry recognises that, as it continues to grow in terms of both volume and global reach, it must become more efficient. Not surprisingly, the means of achieving the STP objective lie with the automation of the various parts of the trade lifecycle.

The parts of the trade lifecycle that could be automated and handled on an STP basis include:

- order management
  - ○ via automated links to STOs or to order-driven exchanges
- trade execution
  - ○ via computerised stock exchanges and through *Electronic Communications Networks*
- trade capture (front office)
  - ○ from computerised stock exchanges and ECNs into a trading system
- trade capture (back office)
  - ○ from a trading system
- trade enrichment
  - ○ from static data
- trade validation
  - ○ through automated comparison of trade detail with validation rules
- issuing trade confirmations
  - ○ via electronic communication mechanisms
- reporting the trade to the regulatory authorities
  - ○ via electronic communication mechanisms
- issuing settlement instructions
  - ○ through electronic links to custodians

- matching of settlement instructions at the custodian
  - ○ through automated comparison mechanisms
- settlement of the trade by the custodian
  - ○ via the automated book entry method
- updating of internal records following settlement
  - ○ as a result of custodians communicating details of settled trades automatically
- reconciliation between internal records and externally held information
  - ○ as a result of custodians issuing statements of securities and cash balances automatically.

However, whilst attempting to achieve full automation of trade throughput, care must be taken to ensure that trades that give rise to risk, or trades containing errors, are detected and highlighted at the earliest opportunity, preferably prior to communicating details to the outside world.

13.3   FUNDAMENTAL RISKS

The basic risks associated with trades are that the STO can make a loss
- directly
  - ○ when buying by, for example:
    - ▪ paying more cash than the market value of the securities
    - ▪ paying the correct amount of cash, but without simultaneous receipt of securities
  - ○ when selling by, for example:
    - ▪ receiving less cash than the market value of the securities
    - ▪ delivering securities without simultaneous receipt of cash
- and indirectly
  - ○ by losing clients through provision of slow and inaccurate levels of service.

These risks can arise as a result of, for instance:
- trading error—the trader makes a mistake at the time of trade execution (e.g. the trader deals at a price that is significantly different from the market price, or agrees to settle on an FoP basis without realising the risk);
- trade recording error—the trade has been captured with one or more components that differ from those that were in fact executed (e.g. a quantity of 10 million was purchased, but has been recorded as 1 million);
- trade enrichment error—the calculation of trade cash values is incorrect (e.g. the number of days of accrued interest on a bond is incorrect, leading to erroneous cash values of accrued interest and consequently incorrect net settlement values).

Trade validation is a task that is designed to detect such situations, on a trade-by-trade basis.

13.4   BASIC TRADE VALIDATION

If a member of an STO's staff were asked to perform basic validation on a fully enriched trade, it is suggested that the trade components would be viewed from this perspective (for a principal trade).

Trading book:

- may be restricted to specific transaction types (e.g. principal only)
- may be restricted to specific instrument groups (e.g. Swedish equities)
- may be restricted to specific traders.

Trade date:

- should be 'today' for a new trade
- cannot be in the future
- should be today or in the recent past for an amended trade
- should be a business day (not a weekend day or public holiday)
- cannot be after the value date.

Trade time:

- cannot be in the future.

Value date:

- is normally the standard *settlement cycle* for the security group (e.g. T+3 for Canadian equities)
- may be shorter or longer than the standard (if the trader has agreed at trade execution and has recorded that date)
- should be a business day in the location of settlement
- cannot be earlier than the trade date
- cannot be earlier than the primary value date of a new issue.

Operation:

- typically this cannot be validated, as settlement personnel usually have no means of knowing whether the trader should be buying or selling, lending or borrowing.

Quantity:

- cannot be less than the minimum denomination of a bond
- must be multiples of the minimum denomination of a bond
- is normally in multiples of *board lot* on an equity
- may be *odd lot* on an equity.

Security:

- cannot be a matured bond
- cannot be an expired warrant
- must be clearly distinguishable from any other security.

Price:

- must be expressed according to the security group
  - share price must be an amount per share
  - bond price must be either a percentage relevant to face value or a yield.

Counterparty:

- must be clearly distinguishable from any other counterparty
- must include location of counterparty.

Trade Cash Value:

- must be quantity × price (unit or percentage) plus or minus other costs such as stamp duty, where relevant
- accrued days
  - ○ must be relevant to last coupon payment date and value date of the trade
- accrued interest
  - ○ must be relevant to quantity, accrued days, coupon rate and annual divisor.

Trade Confirmation:

- should be sent to institutional clients
- should not be sent to STOs (e.g. where electronic *trade matching* is in place).

Company's and Counterparty's Custodians:

- must be relevant to the security group.

13.5   ADDITIONAL TRADE VALIDATION

In order to have the ultimate level of control regarding the information on trades that are about to be sent to the outside world, the following types of validation measures are taken by some STOs, in addition to the basic trade validation as described above.

In each of the categories listed below (and in parallel with the items listed in Basic Trade Validation), any trade falling within one (or more) of the categories should be treated as an exception and held, pending validation. Taking this action means that such trades will not be handled on an STP basis.

Trades Due to Settle on an FoP Basis

As extreme caution needs to be taken when settling trades on an FoP basis (because an STO may be required, for example, to deliver securities to the counterparty prior to the receipt of cash from the counterparty), all such trades should be held for validation.

Trades with a Cash Value At or Above a Certain Figure

In order for an STO to give specific focus to all trades that it deems to be 'large', or larger than the average size (e.g. USD 35,000,000.00), all trades with a net settlement value of that figure or greater, or the currency equivalent of that figure or greater, should be held for validation.

Trades in a Specific Transaction Type

All trades in a particular transaction type may require to be held for validation, to ensure correctness before transmission to the outside world.

Trades with a Specific Counterparty

An STO may need to take special care of trades with a particular counterparty, in order to ensure that the trade detail is correct before being communicated externally. This is likely to be required for trades with institutional clients, rather than other STOs, and may be necessary because the institutional client is new to the STO, or because an existing institutional client may have complained about the accuracy of information or speed of service provided by the STO on prior trades.

Trades in a Specific Market or Security Group

Where an STO trades in a marketplace for the first time, it may wish to re-check that trade cash values are accurate, and that the custodian details are correct for all trades in securities within the security group, before transmitting information to the outside world. This may prove necessary for a limited period only, until it is proved that new trades are correct routinely.

Trades Due to Settle at a Specific Custodian

If an STO has recently changed custodians in a particular financial centre, it may wish to double-check all trades destined for settlement at that custodian, in order to ensure that the correct custodian has been applied, according to the security group.

Trade Price Outside of Market Price

As a precautionary measure, an STO may decide to validate all trades, to ensure that trade prices are reasonable; this is to guard against mistakes and attempts to defraud the STO. Because the price is a major factor in deriving the NSV of trades, there is a danger of an STO making overpayments on purchases, or receiving underpayments on sales. If the current market price of individual securities is accessible by the STO, and a tolerance set against the current market price [e.g. on bonds, 2% above and below; on equities, 4% above and below (to allow for typical volatility)], only those trades with a price falling outside the set tolerance should be held for validation.

When such trades are identified, the management may require to be informed as a matter of urgency. *Note*: the management of the STO will need to decide how 'tight' to make the tolerance relative to current market price. Too tight may well result in many trades being held for validation, requiring much effort to investigate and resolve, and preventing STP; too loose and incorrect prices may be processed undetected.

Trades in a Specific Trading Book

The management of the STO may wish to monitor the trading activity of a particular trading book, or trader, before new trades are conveyed externally; this can occur where the management have an underlying reason to scrutinise the business being executed.

Trades with Trade Date in the Past

Any new trade (as opposed to an amended or cancelled trade) that has a trade date in the past may be held for validation, to ensure that it is valid. Trade date is important for the reasons given in Chapter 11; for example on equities, entitlement to income is governed by trade date.

Trades with Value Date in the Past

Any new trade with a value date in the past should be held for validation, as this indicates that something has gone seriously wrong. If settlement of a trade should have occurred in the past, this is highly likely to result in a cost to the STO, for not only failing to settle, but also failing to have their settlement instruction with the custodian prior to value date (this is explained fully in Chapter 20).

All Amended Trades

Some STOs wish to monitor amended trades, for instance, to ensure that trades recorded originally with the incorrect quantity or price have been amended correctly.

All Cancelled Trades

The need for outright cancellation of trades should be minimal and, as for amended trades, an STO may wish to check the detail before issuing information, such as cancelling trade confirmations and cancelling settlement instructions, to the outside world.

Performing this type of validation may provide an STO with a high degree of control, almost certainly resulting in a reduction in the number of trade inaccuracies prior to communicating trade detail externally. However, an STO must decide for itself the compromise between STP and maintaining sufficient control.

13.6   METHODS OF TRADE VALIDATION

The validation of trades can be effected manually or automatically, according to the availability of systems.

13.6.1   Manual Trade Validation

Due to the number of trade components (as listed within this chapter), performing validation manually is likely to result in:

- a limited number of components being validated, so as not to adversely affect meeting external deadlines;
- occasional human error, resulting in a failure to identify a risk or an error.

Realistically, in order to identify potentially problematic trades, manual trade validation needs to be undertaken by the more knowledgeable members of the STO's middle or back office personnel, using their 'experienced eye' to scan the components of trades and their wealth of knowledge to sense whether a trade is acceptable or not.

However, the scale of this task should not be underestimated; a significant amount of manpower would be required to validate all trades to the fullest extent, even when using the more experienced staff, owing to the sheer volume of trades executed by an average sized STO.

In order to meet the combined demands of, for example:

- STP
- servicing clients accurately and speedily

- issuing settlement instructions by the necessary deadlines (particularly with decreasing *settlement cycles*)
- transaction reporting within required deadlines

it is suggested that performing extensive trade validation is only achievable by use of intelligent and efficient systems.

13.6.2   Automated Trade Validation

The processing of trades can be highly automated, whilst achieving satisfactory levels of STP and control over those trading situations requiring additional trade validation (as described above).

Quite simply, an STO could decide that all trades should be handled on an STP basis, unless identified as needing to be held for validation. Trades needing to be held for validation are commonly referred to as exceptions, and are therefore subject to 'exception handling'.

The trigger that causes trades to be treated as exceptions is the setting of rules within the settlement system. All or some of the rules mentioned within Sections 13.4 and 13.5 could be set up within the settlement system.

Then, after each trade has been enriched, the system would compare the trade detail with all of the relevant rules:

- if the trade passes this validation check, the trade would be allowed to continue immediately and can be regarded as having been processed on an STP basis (provided further actions, such as generation of the settlement instruction, do not fail);
- if, on the other hand, the trade fails the validation check (e.g. trade date is in the past), the trade will be treated as an exception and held for validation.

Where a trade is held for validation, it is temporarily suspended and no dependent actions (e.g. the issuance of a trade confirmation or settlement instruction) should occur until the trade has been released from its exception state.

The release of such a trade from exception handling should occur only after the relevant member of the STO's staff has authorised its release. This is achieved in some systems by categorising exceptions, then directing those exceptions to the appropriate individual or team, for investigation and resolution. Examples of this are:

- all trades due to settle on an FoP basis should be sent directly to the team of supervisors within the settlement department, whereas
- all trades with a price outside of market price (inclusive of a tolerance) should be sent to trading management.

Figure 13.1 summarises the flow of trades, where handled on an STP basis and where an exception is found.

Step 1: a trade has been captured and enriched, and is now subject to trade validation.

Step 2: the detail of the trade is compared with preset validation rules; if the rules include a 'price outside of market price and tolerance' check (see Trade Price Outside of Market Price earlier in this chapter), an incoming feed of current market prices may be used (see below).

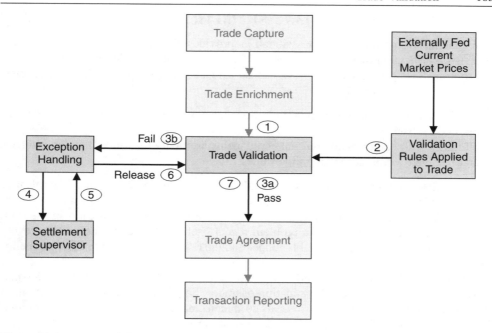

Figure 13.1   Automation of trade validation

Step 3a: if all validation rules are passed, the trade will be forwarded immediately for actioning of other operational tasks, such as trade agreement and transaction reporting.

Step 3b: if it fails validation, the trade will be held for validation, and routed for exception handling.

Step 4: the trade will be forwarded to the appropriate authoriser (one person or a group of people), according to the reason for validation.

Step 5: having been investigated and found to be correct, the trade is authorised.

Step 6: the trade within the exception handling system is updated, and then released to the settlement system.

Step 7: the trade is now forwarded for actioning of other operational tasks.

Note: at step 5, the investigation may have revealed that the trade should be amended or cancelled, requiring action by the front office (in the case of a principal trade).

Further automation may be employed where resolution of an exception has not occurred within an acceptable timeframe. The management of an STO may decide that unresolved exceptions that are, for example, 45 minutes old, should be escalated to a more senior member of staff.

If an STO decides to validate trade prices, price feeds are available from those companies that provide securities static data, commonly known as *securities data providers* or data vendors. As for securities static data, some STOs subscribe to a single vendor, others to two or more vendors in order to make a comparison of prices. Note that STOs typically use current market prices for multiple purposes, not just for trade validation. These topics will be covered within subsequent chapters.

13.7   SUMMARY

The practice of performing trade validation provides STOs with an independent and objective verification of trade detail, prior to transmitting information externally.

From an STP perspective, an STO can be said to manage a controlled and efficient operational environment if:

- all trades with normal and acceptable components (as defined by the STO) are processed on an STP basis;
- all trades with one or many unusual components are firstly identified, then investigated and resolved within acceptable timeframes.

Given that there will always be some trades with unusual components, identification of such trades very shortly after trade capture should be viewed as a positive act. The consequence of failing to identify, investigate and resolve such trades early in the trade lifecycle may mean that, should a problem reveal itself further along the trade lifecycle, resolution may well take considerably longer and the risks (as described in the introduction to this chapter) increase.

As trading volumes increase and settlement cycles reduce, the resultant pressures may cause a temptation to avoid full validation of trades; however, it is under these extremely demanding circumstances that errors can go undetected and generate greater operational costs in their eventual resolution than the cost of performing validation.

Some firms take the view that if a trade is incorrect, it will be highlighted by the counterparty (e.g. when attempting to match settlement instructions). A more sensible opinion is that if the trading company's profits are at stake, control should reside with that company, not its counterparty.

14
Trade Agreement

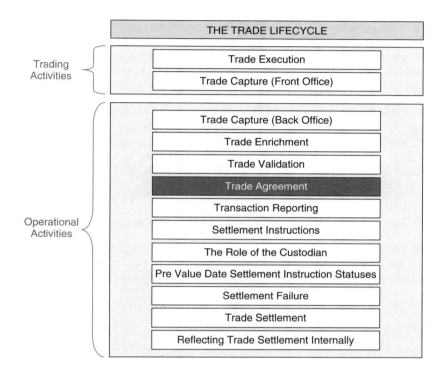

THE TRADE LIFECYCLE

Trading Activities
- Trade Execution
- Trade Capture (Front Office)

Operational Activities
- Trade Capture (Back Office)
- Trade Enrichment
- Trade Validation
- Trade Agreement
- Transaction Reporting
- Settlement Instructions
- The Role of the Custodian
- Pre Value Date Settlement Instruction Statuses
- Settlement Failure
- Trade Settlement
- Reflecting Trade Settlement Internally

14.1 INTRODUCTION

Once a trade has passed validation, a number of actions can commence. The action that is typically regarded as being most urgent to complete is the act of gaining agreement of the trade details with the counterparty. Trade agreement is necessary in order to reduce the STO's risk.

Trade agreement can be achieved through:

- the issuance of outgoing trade confirmations to the counterparty
- the receipt of incoming trade confirmations from the counterparty
- trade matching
- trade affirmation

and each of these methods will be explained within this chapter.

In a generic sense, trade agreement is achieved by the STO communicating the details of each trade to its counterparty, whereupon the counterparty should check the detail, and revert to the STO if:

- it recognises the trade, but the details differ (e.g. the price is different), or
- it does not recognise the trade at all.

The communication needs to contain all the basic trade details as a minimum, plus the cash value calculations and, optionally, the settlement details including both the STO's and the counterparty's custodian details, their account numbers and whether the trade is to settle on a *DvP* or an *FoP* basis.

Note: the matching of seller's and buyer's trade details is, in many cases, effected through two routes, namely:

- trade agreement—the agreement of trade detail between the STO and its counterparty, and additionally
- settlement instruction matching—the *custodians* of the buyer and seller attempt to match settlement instructions prior to delivery of securities and payment of cash.

These two exercises are similar in that the seller's and buyer's trade details are matched prior to the value date, but typically the timing may be different. Trade agreement is necessary immediately after trade execution to ensure that the correct counterparty has been recorded by the STO and that the details of the trade are agreed (from a risk mitigation perspective). However, settlement instruction matching is typically effected at any time between trade execution and value date. This topic will be described in Chapter 18.

14.2   REDUCING THE STO'S RISK

For each executed trade, the STO remains at risk of its trading P&L being incorrect if that trade (and its detail) has not been agreed or matched by the counterparty within a reasonable timeframe, as the P&L remains subject to change until it is proven that all trades have been agreed by the counterparties.

Because of that risk, the objective is to gain agreement of the trade detail as soon as possible after trade execution. To re-state the circumstances:

- the trader has just executed a trade with a counterparty
- the trader has recorded the trade within the STO's trading system
- the trade has also been captured within the STO's settlement system
- the trade has been validated (internally)

but unfortunately at that moment in time, there is no guarantee that:

- the counterparty with whom the trade has been captured by the STO is the counterparty with whom the trade was in fact executed, or
- the trade detail (e.g. quantity, price, net settlement value) will be agreed by the counterparty.

From an individual STO's perspective, failing to seek agreement of trades with its counterparties as soon as possible after trade execution will inevitably result in the identification of errors during the settlement instruction matching process which, for example in a T+3 environment, is unlikely to bring errors to light until the day following trade date, at the earliest. The longer a trade remains unmatched after trade execution, the greater the risk of price movement and subsequent loss.

Time is an important factor. For instance, a trader within an STO believes he sold 15 million shares at a price of HKD 22.59, on trade date 15th June, for value date on 18th June. If, on 17th June, it becomes apparent, through the settlement instruction matching process, that the counterparty believes it bought at HKD 22.55, and investigation proves that the counterparty is correct, the trader within the STO will need to amend the trade to the correct price. This will have an immediate detrimental effect on the trader's P&L.

Worse still, on 17th June it may come to light that the counterparty with whom the STO has recorded the trade did not recognise the trade at all. If this results in the trader within the STO cancelling the trade outright, the trader will now have regained a positive trading position of 15 million shares. If the market price of the share has fallen between the time of trade execution and the discovery of the erroneous trade, the trader (and his management) would have failed to realise a profitable opportunity.

In both cases above, the trader's P&L would have included the profit from the above-mentioned sale for two days (15th–17th June). Had the error been discovered on trade date, the factual profit (or loss) would have been known immediately and action taken where necessary.

14.3   TRADE AGREEMENT METHODS

Although the risk, and the requirement to minimise the risk, remain the same from an STO's perspective, the method of agreement of trade detail between the parties to a trade varies according to the local regulations, market practice and type of counterparty.

Generally, gaining agreement of trades executed with other STOs is likely to be handled differently from trades with institutional clients. This is illustrated in Figure 14.1.

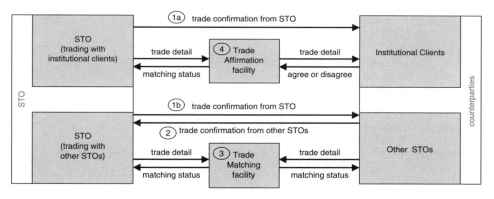

Figure 14.1   Trade agreement: trade agreement methods

Method 1: the issuance of outgoing trade confirmation to counterparties.

- 1a: it is highly likely that an STO will be required to issue a trade confirmation to its institutional clients, particularly where a trade affirmation facility is not being used (see method 4 below);
- 1b: it is likely that an STO will want to issue a trade confirmation to other STOs with which it trades, particularly where a trade matching facility is not being used (see method 3 below).

Method 2: the receipt of incoming trade confirmations from counterparties; the STO may receive trade confirmations from other STOs, but is very unlikely to receive confirmations from institutional clients, as institutional clients are the recipients of the service from the STO.

Method 3: trade matching; the term trade matching is normally used when referring to the mandatory electronic matching of trade details between STOs and other members of stock exchanges/markets (such as *agents for investors*), which excludes institutional clients. Both parties to the trade are required to input their details to a central trade matching facility, and matching results (e.g. matched or unmatched) are provided by the trade matching facility to both parties. Note that where trades have been executed electronically, the trade detail is usually considered to have been already compared and matched.

Method 4: trade affirmation; this relates to the optional electronic matching of trade details between STOs and institutional clients, where the trade details are input by the STO to a trade affirmation facility, and the institutional client agrees (affirms) or disagrees. Both the STO and the institutional client must elect to subscribe to such a service. This is regarded as distinct from trade matching as only the STO can trigger the act of achieving agreement on an individual trade basis.

Table 14.1 summarises typical methods of achieving trade agreement between an STO and its counterparties, whether institutional clients or other STOs. These methods are described below.

Table 14.1

	Trade agreement method	Counterparties	
		Institutional clients	Other STOs
1	Outgoing trade confirmation transmitted to...	✓	✓
2	Incoming trade confirmation received from...	✗	✓
3	Trade matching between STO and...	✗	✓
4	Trade affirmation between STO and...	✓	✗

Because the regulators of STOs and institutional clients are typically different bodies, they are not usually required to abide by the same rules. For example, the regulator of STOs in a specific country may require that all STOs input their trade detail electronically to a central trade matching facility, in order to effect trade agreement of trades between those STOs. As that regulator may not regulate institutional investors, no trade agreement will occur between STOs and their institutional clients through that trade matching mechanism. Therefore a different mechanism is necessary in order for an STO to gain trade agreement with its institutional clients.

14.4   OUTGOING TRADE CONFIRMATIONS

A trade confirmation is a formal statement of the terms of a transaction, issued by an STO to its counterparty, whether an institutional client or another STO.

The issues for consideration regarding the transmission of trade confirmations by an STO normally include:

- the need to provide a high quality service to institutional clients,
- the need to issue trade confirmations to other STOs,
- the content of the trade confirmation,
- the method of transmission,
- the number of copies required by the counterparty,
- the language in which the confirmation is issued, and
- the automation of the above.

14.4.1   Trade Confirmations to Institutional Clients

As mentioned in prior chapters, the relationship that an STO has with an institutional client is based upon the quality of service it provides. Amongst others, this is evident in such areas as:

- the competitiveness of prices quoted by the STO to the client;
- the speed of confirming trade details formally by the STO;
- the accuracy of information provided on trade confirmations by the STO.

As STOs are extremely eager to win and retain the business of institutional clients, the level of service that is provided by the STO is likely to determine whether the client chooses to remain a client of that STO, or whether the client will seek a better service with another STO.

Where an STO has executed a trade with an institutional client (for example, over the telephone), the institutional client is likely to require the receipt of a trade confirmation within a mutually agreed timeframe after trade time (the time of trade execution) of, say, 1–2 hours. This timeframe is likely to shrink as *settlement cycles* shrink. The trade confirmation represents formal confirmation of trade details, which must be received by the institutional client within the agreed timeframe and which must be completely accurate. The continued failure by an STO to provide such a service is likely to result in the institutional client taking his business elsewhere.

However, under some circumstances, it is not possible for the STO to issue a confirmation within the required timeframe to the ultimate counterparty. Certain types of institutional client (normally fund managers) usually place an order to buy or sell a specific quantity of a specific security within a limited price. Once an order becomes an executed trade, the STO's salesperson reports the detail of the execution to the fund manager [e.g. QRS Fund Managers (a fictitious fund manager)] informally, usually via telephone.

Following trade execution, it is normal for the fund manager to allocate the total trade to one or many of its underlying funds; for example, if an STO sold USD 50 million World Bank 6.5% bonds 1st February 2018 to QRS Fund Managers, at a price of 98.625%, QRS will require the total quantity of bonds to be allocated to its underlying funds along the lines of Table 14.2. A frequent occurrence is that the fund manager does not convey to the STO the names of the underlying funds until some time (in some cases many hours) after trade execution.

Table 14.2

Fund name	Quantity	Price
QRS Healthcare Growth Fund	12,000,000.00	98.625
QRS Global Bond Growth Fund	10,000,000.00	98.625
QRS European Income Fund	25,000,000.00	98.625
QRS Pacific Income Fund	3,000,000.00	98.625
Total	**50,000,000.00**	

The fund manager usually requires the receipt of trade confirmations for each of the underlying funds, in accordance with the quantity of securities allocated, as ultimately it is the underlying funds that have purchased or sold the securities, not the 'parent'.

Under such circumstances, the STO needs to decide whether to record the trade (internally, within its books and records) with the parent counterparty or not, knowing that the trade with the parent will be replaced by one or many trades with the fund manager's underlying funds at some point later in the day. Should the STO decide to record the trade details to the parent counterparty immediately after trade execution, the STO will have reflected the factual situation. If not, the settlement system will not reconcile with the trading system (the trading positions will differ).

Some STOs treat these situations in the following manner (following trade execution by the STO, and the STO's salesperson advising the fund manager of the executed trade over the telephone):

- the original trade is captured in the trading system and fed to the settlement system
  - e.g. sold USD 50 million to QRS Fund Manager (the 'parent') at a price of 98.625%
- the original trade is captured within the settlement system, but is treated as a trade with a 'parent' counterparty, awaiting allocation to the fund manager's underlying funds
  - the trade is simply held, in the knowledge that allocations will be advised by the fund manager at the earliest opportunity (no trade confirmation is usually issued to the parent)
- the fund manager advises the STO of the allocations (refer to Table 14.2)
- the original trade is effectively replaced by one or many trades (in the above example, it will be four trades), either in both the trading system and the settlement system, or only in the settlement system. The STO has effectively traded with the underlying funds and it is essential that the settlement system holds the detail of all trades at individual counterparty level, as it is the formal books and records of the company. (It may not be regarded as essential to hold the trades with the children within the trading system; if this is the case, the 'parent' trade remains intact within the trading system)
- from the settlement system, formal trade confirmations can now be generated and transmitted to the fund manager, for each trade, at underlying fund level.

Once the institutional client has received the trade confirmation(s) from the STO, the detail will be checked and, if found to be incorrect, should be communicated to the STO without delay.

14.4.2   Trade Confirmations to Other STOs

In order for an STO to gain agreement of trade details, the STO normally issues a trade confirmation to other STOs with which it has traded. Typical exceptions to this may arise where electronic trade matching occurs within a specific marketplace (this is described later within this chapter).

Unlike the transmission of trade confirmations to institutional clients, which is regarded as part of the service that an STO provides to its client, the transmission of trade confirmations to other STOs is primarily used as an attempt by the STO to confirm that its trade details are correct, as soon as possible after trade execution.

The issuer of the trade confirmation hopes that the recipient will check the detail upon receipt, and respond without delay if it is found to be incorrect (as is the case for institutional clients); however, this is not always the case (as described in Section 14.5).

14.4.3   Trade Confirmation Content

Table 14.3 describes the typical content of a trade confirmation, based upon a principal bond trade. Note that some of the detail would change dependent upon transaction type (e.g. a repo would need to include the repo rate, plus the opening and closing value dates)

Table 14.3

From	The name of the issuing STO
To	The name of the STO's counterparty
Attention	The relevant person/department at the counterparty
Subject	A heading that states the message purpose 'Trade confirmation'
Our trade reference	The STO's settlement system trade reference
Trading capacity	The capacity in which the STO has traded (principal or agent)
Transaction type	Whether principal, repo, foreign exchange, etc.
Operation	Whether buying or selling, lending or borrowing, etc.
Trade date	The date of trade execution
Trade time	The time of trade execution
Value date	The value date of the trade
Quantity	The quantity of shares, or quantity of bonds with currency
Security	The exact, unmistakable description of the security
Security reference	The security identifier code, e.g. *ISIN, Cusip, Quick*
Price	Quoted according to whether equity or bond (percentage)
Principal	The result of quantity multiplied by price
Accrued days	The relevant number of days of accrued interest
Accrued interest	The cash value of accrued interest
NSV	The cash value to be paid or received
Our depot	The STO's settlement location of securities (deliver to/from here)
Our nostro	The STO's settlement location of cash (pay from/receive into here)
Your depot	The counterparty's settlement location of securities
Your nostro	The counterparty's settlement location of cash
Settlement basis	Whether DvP or FoP
Exchange/market	The exchange or market over which the trade has been executed
Rules	Statement that the trade is subject to rules of the exch/mkt
Sign-off by the STO	Full name and location of STO
Transmission time	A clear statement of the date and time of transmission

and a principal equity trade would not include accrued interest, but may include charges such as stamp duty, dependent upon the security traded.

The regulators of markets typically insist upon specific wording being contained within the trade confirmation, such as a statement that the trade is subject to the rules of the exchange/market over which the trade has been executed (this is an important point, as such rules are made to ensure an 'orderly market' and that investors are given some protection in the event of a dispute).

14.4.4 Trade Confirmation Transmission Methods

The STO's counterparty typically has a preference for the medium by which trade confirmations are to be received. This information needs to be held as part of the STO's static data for the specific counterparty, to enable the automation of both the generation and the transmission of the confirmation by the STO.

Historically, before the electronic age, trade confirmations would be issued only on paper, and were commonly referred to as 'contract notes'; these were normally posted through the mail, or delivered by hand to the recipient.

In the modern era, trade confirmations are regularly required to be issued in a variety of media, such as:

- fax (facsimile)
  - an exact reproduction of a handwritten or typed message transmitted over a public telecommunications network, requiring that the STO and the counterparty each have a fax machine and a telephone line over which fax can be transmitted. Note that fax is sometimes used as an informal method of communicating trade details between salesperson and institutional client (pending transmission of the formal trade confirmation)
- telex
  - a printed message transmitted over a public telecommunication network, requiring that both the STO and the counterparty have their own, unique, telex numbers
- S.W.I.F.T.
  - 'Society for Worldwide Interbank Financial Telecommunication'; initially set up to manage the secure transmission of payments between banks, it now also transmits securities messages. Trade confirmation is one of a number of message types that S.W.I.F.T. is capable of processing, and requires that both the STO and the counterparty are S.W.I.F.T. subscribers. S.W.I.F.T. will be described further in Chapter 16.
- e-mail
  - with the advent of the World Wide Web, the popularity of electronic mail as a medium for the transmission of trade confirmations is increasing; however, at its relatively early stage of development, many STOs and regulators have concerns over the extent of security that the WWW provides
- paper
  - contract notes (as described above).

The format of a trade confirmation is, to some extent, governed by the transmission medium. Therefore, the appearance of a trade confirmation issued on paper would differ somewhat from the same trade issued by telex or S.W.I.F.T.; however, the content should remain unaffected.

It is important to note that the above-mentioned transmission media are 'one-way'; in other words, when the STO issues a trade confirmation to its counterparty, the counterparty may not be forced (by a regulator, for example) to check the detail and respond if it is incorrect, within a specified timeframe. However, as mentioned previously, from a risk perspective the STO is reliant upon the counterparty to check the confirmation and respond if incorrect, as quickly as possible. This puts the STO in a dilemma, particularly where the counterparty is an institutional client as, due to the nature of the relationship, STOs are not normally inclined to criticise their institutional clients for failing to check the confirmation at all, or failing to check it and respond (if incorrect) in a reasonable timeframe.

However, once the STO's counterparty receives the trade confirmation, if checked with its own records and found to be accurate, this fact is not normally communicated to the STO. Under these circumstances, the transmitting STO can only assume that the counterparty agrees the trade detail, until and unless the counterparty advises otherwise. From the STO's risk perspective, this is a very unsatisfactory state of affairs, as the STO is completely reliant upon communication from the counterparty. The STO's trading P&L can therefore be affected by how the counterparty acts operationally. (If the counterparty fails to check the trade confirmation received from the STO, any discrepancy regarding trade details is most likely to be revealed during the settlement instruction matching process. Unless trading within a T+0 or T+1 environment, the timing of the settlement instruction matching process may mean that the STO does not discover a discrepancy for a number of days after trade date, in which case the STO's P&L cannot be fixed until a match of instructions has occurred.)

Consequently, the issuance of a trade confirmation by an STO does not necessarily result in the STO being certain that the trade has been agreed with the counterparty. The sheer volume of trading usually precludes STOs from positively investigating whether the counterparty to each trade agrees or disagrees with the trade details. Instead, it is usual for the STO to be informed only when the counterparty disputes that they executed the trade or disputes the details of the trade. Agreement to the detail of a trade confirmation is not usually advised to the originator, by the recipient of the confirmation.

Fortunately, in some environments, 'two-way' trade matching occurs for certain types of trades, allowing an STO to be certain of the trade status with its counterparty, shortly after trade execution. See later in this chapter.

14.4.5   Number of Copies Required by the Counterparty

Some counterparties, typically institutional clients, may require the receipt of one or many copies of a trade confirmation, for each trade. Where many copies of a confirmation are required, the counterparty may require all copies to be sent to the same destination, or to different destinations and sometimes via different transmission methods.

The different destinations may include, for instance, the counterparty's head office, its bank and its accountant.

To enable automation of this service by an STO, this information needs to be held within the STO's static data.

14.4.6   The Language in which the Confirmation is Issued

An STO may be required to issue trade confirmations in the language of the counterparty's choice, regardless of the STO's location.

14.4.7   Automation of Outgoing Trade Confirmations

In modern settlement systems, the following aspects of outgoing trade confirmations can usually be automated:

- the decision to issue confirmations pre or post trade validation
- the selection of the content, according to the security group (e.g. equity or bond) and transaction type
- according to the counterparty's preference
  - the selection of the transmission media
  - the issuance of one or many copies
  - the language used.

The counterparty information is normally held within the STO's counterparty static data repository, and during processing of a trade, the relevant data will be selected as part of the trade enrichment process (refer to Chapter 12).

14.5   INCOMING TRADE CONFIRMATIONS

Some of the counterparties with whom an STO trades may issue trade confirmations. These are most likely to be other STOs, as opposed to institutional clients who typically expect only to receive confirmations from the STO through whom they have traded.

Upon receipt of incoming confirmations, an STO needs to decide whether to place resources on the task of checking the detail contained in each confirmation versus the STO's own records, or not. Note that where the STO has received a confirmation of a trade that has been or will be agreed by another means (such as trade matching), a decision may be made not to also expend effort on checking the confirmation.

14.5.1   Benefits of Checking

In order to gain trade agreement and for the avoidance of risk, it is clearly better to check the confirmation upon receipt, as this will highlight whether the STO and the counterparty agree or disagree with the details of the trade. Any discrepancies highlighted can be investigated immediately, and resolved at the earliest opportunity.

14.5.2   Risks of Failing to Check

Decisions are sometimes taken not to check incoming confirmations; for trades where agreement will not be achieved by another means, this decision could result in monetary losses for the STO.

A situation could occur where, say, a telex confirmation has been received by an STO from its counterparty on the afternoon of trade date, on a T+3 trade, and the STO decides not to check the incoming confirmation, but on the day prior to value date it comes to light (for instance through the settlement instruction matching process) that there is a discrepancy. Upon investigation of the events (e.g. by listening to the dealing tapes), it may transpire that the counterparty's price or quantity was incorrect, and that the counterparty will need to amend its detail to match with the STO's detail. At first glance, the STO may appear to have incurred no cost, as it was the counterparty that recorded the trade detail within its books erroneously. However, should the counterparty realise, during its investigation, that a trade confirmation was sent to and received by the

STO, and that the STO failed to highlight the discrepancy (as early as trade date), the counterparty may seek some form of compensation from the STO.

14.5.3 Updating Internal Records

When an incoming confirmation has been checked and agreed with internal records, ideally, the fact that trade agreement has been achieved should be recorded. Particularly in an automated environment, keeping a record of when an incoming confirmation was checked, and by whom, is likely to prove beneficial when requesting the settlement system to list all trades not yet agreed. Furthermore, if an investigation of events on a trade is necessary, the fact that an incoming confirmation had been received and checked is likely to be an important factor.

14.6   TRADE MATCHING WITH STOs

Trade matching is a generic term to describe any electronic method of comparing the trade detail of both seller and buyer.

The process of trade matching typically includes:

• the transmission of trade detail by both seller and buyer to a central trade matching facility, by a specified deadline, and
• the application by the trade matching facility of the current status (e.g. matched, unmatched, etc.)

thereby allowing the parties to a trade to know whether trade agreement has been reached, or not.

The following is an example of a trade matching facility.

14.6.1 Trax

The *ISMA*, based in Zurich, Switzerland, is a self regulatory organisation and trade association responsible for regulating and enforcing rules governing the orderly functioning of the international securities market. During the late 1980's ISMA (known then as the Association of International Bond Dealers), was primarily focused on the *Eurobond* market.

Within the Eurobond marketplace prior to 1989, where an STO traded with another STO, trade agreement was attempted but not necessarily achieved by the issuance of trade confirmations, normally in the form of telex. As described above, an STO issuing a telex confirmation does not guarantee that the STO becomes aware (within a reasonable time frame) whether the counterparty agrees the trade or not.

This situation was inefficient and not without risk, from the perspective of each STO that traded within the Eurobond marketplace, and in 1989, ISMA introduced its Trax system as a means of addressing these issues. Trax is a real-time trade matching mechanism covering all internationally traded debt and equity securities, whereby ISMA members are required to issue a message to Trax, so as to be received by ISMA within 30 minutes of trade execution.

If the message is not received by Trax within the 30-minute deadline, a fine is imposed by ISMA on the STO. This is on a sliding scale, so the later the message is received, the larger the fine, as illustrated in Table 14.4.

Table 14.4

Trax fines for late reporting of trades	
Period after trade time	Fine
0–30 minutes	zero
30–60 minutes	CHF 5.00
60–90 minutes	CHF 10.00
90 minutes–end of trade date	CHF 15.00
After end of trade date	CHF 50.00 per day
Failure to report at all	CHF 150.00

Source: International Securities Market Association

In addition, ISMA impose fines for other non-compliance reasons, such as failure to provide all necessary trade details, and failure to act upon a non-matching advice within a reasonable timeframe.

Despite the small size of the fine for a single trade reported between 30 and 60 minutes after trade execution, STOs have become very aware that the accumulated cost of Trax fines can run to thousands of CHF per month, and have a direct negative impact on the STO's P&L. However, such costs must be balanced against the benefits of early trade agreement.

A Trax message serves the objective of achieving trade agreement (and identifying trades that are not agreed by the counterparty) by conveying the details of a trade to a central matching facility that compares both seller's and buyer's trade details. Following the comparison within Trax, real-time reports are produced that detail the current status of each trade. However, it is important to note that a Trax message does not serve as a settlement instruction, and there is a need to issue a settlement instruction to the relevant custodian, independently of the Trax message, in order to effect the exchange of securities and cash.

In terms of when messages are sent to Trax, the STO needs to decide whether to transmit to Trax before or after trade validation. Issuing a message to Trax prior to trade validation introduces the risk and possibility that incorrect information may be matched by the counterparty, prior to the STO realising that a problem may exist with the trade. If an STO chooses to transmit messages to Trax prior to trade validation in order to meet the 30-minute deadline and avoid being fined, it is recommended that trade validation should still be conducted, albeit after the Trax message has been sent. This allows the STO to be made aware of potential issues on a trade, despite the fact that the trade may have already been matched at Trax. To reiterate the point made earlier in this chapter, an STO should be responsible for determining its own P&L, without the P&L being influenced by the counterparty.

Figure 14.2 represents the sequence of achieving trade matching within Trax, in the optimum fashion and in the fastest time.

Step 1: an STO executes a trade with a counterparty, both of which must be ISMA members (or non-member users of the system).

Step 2: both parties send their trade details to Trax, to be received by Trax within the 30-minute deadline.

Step 3: the Trax system searches for a match, and then applies the status (e.g. matched, unmatched) to each of the trades.

Step 4: the current trade status is then made available to each of the parties involved.

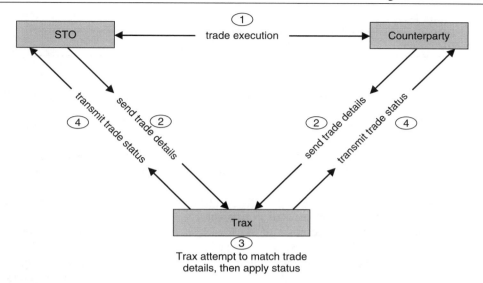

Figure 14.2   Trax trade matching

The receipt of a status other than matched requires immediate investigation by the STO, resulting in one of the following actions:

- the STO leaving its trade detail intact, and the counterparty amending its trade detail (resulting in a match);
- the STO amending its trade detail (resulting in a match);
- the STO cancelling the trade;
- the counterparty cancelling or denying the trade.

Trax will apply the trade statuses in Table 14.5 for those messages sent by the STO, and in Table 14.6 for those messages not sent by the STO.

Table 14.5

Trax status	Meaning
Matched	The STO's and the counterparty's trade details have been compared and agree
Unmatched	The STO has input its trade details, but the counterparty has not input matching trade details (the counterparty will see this status as their 'advisory')
Denied advisory	The counterparty does not recognise the (advisory) trade and has stated that it denies knowledge of the trade

STOs typically wish to maintain a full historic record of when each Trax message was sent, all the statuses applied (e.g. unmatched for 2 hours after trade time, then matched), in case of the need for later investigation. Additionally, as a means of assessing potential risk, an STO may, for example, wish to view all trades with a trade date of the previous

Table 14.6

Trax status	Meaning
Advisory	Trade detail has been input by the counterparty, awaiting either input of trade detail by the STO, or the STO to state 'denied'
Denied	If the STO does not recognise the 'advisory' trade (above), the STO can state 'denied'

day, without trade agreement to date. Clearly, that list of trades should not contain trades matched at Trax, or any trade for which an incoming confirmation has been checked and found to match.

Note: issuing messages to Trax serves the purpose of regulatory transaction reporting, besides trade matching. This is covered in Chapter 15.

Other trade matching services include, in the USA, the National Securities Clearing Corporation's (NSCC) Trade Comparison Service. For UK equities settling through Crest (but not traded over the London Stock Exchange's computerised order matching system SETS), there is no independent trade matching facility, and the settlement instruction issued to Crest serves as the mechanism by which trade agreement is reached. Note that trade execution effected electronically (where the details of each trade are reported to the STO and its counterparty) is likely to negate the need for independent trade matching.

14.6.2   Automation

In modern settlement systems, the following aspects of trade matching messages can usually be automated:

- the decision to issue the message pre or post trade validation;
- the decision whether to issue a message or not, according to the security group (e.g. Eurobond versus US Treasury bond);
- the decision whether to issue a message or not, depending upon the counterparty (e.g. ISMA members as opposed to non-members).

Much of this information is held within the STO's static data repository, and during processing of a trade, the relevant data will be selected as part of the trade enrichment process.

Furthermore, the following can be automated:

- the transmission of the message to the trade matching facility;
- the receipt of message statuses from the trade matching facility;
- the updating of the relevant trade record (internally within the STO's books and records) with its trade matching status;
- the highlighting of trades with a status other than 'matched'.

14.7   TRADE AFFIRMATION WITH INSTITUTIONAL INVESTORS

Around the globe, institutional investors are able to have trades confirmed to them (by STOs and those companies acting as *agents for investors*) electronically, via Omgeo's

Oasys Global system. This means that an institutional investor based in, for example, Tokyo, could have their trades confirmed electronically by an STO based in Toronto.

Unlike trade matching for STOs, which is typically regulated by an exchange/market or local regulator, it is the decision of each institutional investor whether they choose to subscribe to the Oasys Global system.

Strictly speaking, the method of gaining agreement of trade details with the counterparty via Oasys Global is not by trade matching (which implies that both parties input details at the same time, to a central facility) but by trade affirmation, where the organisation that has executed the trade on behalf of the institutional investor inputs its trade detail, to which the institutional investor responds (or affirms).

Those institutional investors that choose to subscribe to Oasys Global usually encourage its use by STOs, in an attempt to ensure that as many trades as possible are affirmed via this route and to realise the full benefit of its subscription. Institutional investors regard an STO's use of Oasys Global as part of the service level they expect. Similarly, subscribing STOs usually encourage their institutional clients to subscribe for reasons of automation and STP.

Figure 14.3 represents the sequence of achieving trade matching within Oasys Global, in the optimum fashion and in the fastest time. For the purposes of the following illustration, the underlying funds are referred to as the 'child' to the 'parent'.

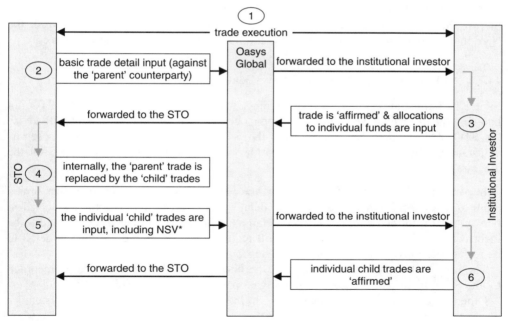

* NSV = Net Settlement Value

Figure 14.3   Trade affirmation for institutional investors via Oasys Global

Step 1: an STO executes a trade with an institutional client, in particular a fund manager. At this point in time, typically the STO knows only the name of the fund manager (not the names of the underlying funds to which the fund manager may later decide to allocate the trade).

Step 2: the basic trade detail for the 'parent' counterparty is input to Oasys Global, which forwards the detail to the specified institutional client (the fund manager).

Step 3: internally within the fund manager, the trade detail is checked versus its own records, and if found to be correct, the trade in Oasys Global is annotated as agreed and, at the same time, the detail of allocations to the underlying funds is input, as per the example in Table 14.7.

Table 14.7

Fund name	Quantity	Price
QRS Healthcare Growth Fund	12,000,000.00	98.625
QRS Global Bond Growth Fund	10,000,000.00	98.625
QRS European Income Fund	25,000,000.00	98.625
QRS Pacific Income Fund	3,000,000.00	98.625
Total	**50,000,000.00**	

Step 4: internally within the STO, the 'parent' trade is replaced by the trades with the underlying funds (see Section 14.4.1).

Step 5: the individual trades are input to Oasys Global, inclusive of the NSV for each.

Step 6: the fund manager checks the trade detail for each of the funds, inclusive of the NSV and, if found to be correct, each trade in Oasys Global is annotated as agreed.

14.7.1   'Block' and 'Confirmation' Level Matching

Figure 14.3 illustrates 'block' level matching, where the steps begin with the STO not knowing the underlying allocations. On some occasions, an institutional client will advise the STO of the underlying allocations at the point of trade execution. Under these circumstances, trade details can be input to Oasys at 'confirmation' level (step 5 on the diagram).

In parallel with trade matching via Trax, the receipt of a trade status other than agreed requires that the STO investigate without delay. This normally requires the STO's salesperson to be informed and, if the trade detail as recorded within the STO is found to be incorrect, the STO's books and records will require amendment and the revised detail to be re-input to Oasys Global (either from step 2 or step 5 above).

The use of Oasys Global requires that the history of each relevant trade be recorded by the STO, in case of the need to investigate past events, as for Trax.

Other trade affirmation services include, in the USA, Omgeo's TradeMatch system.

14.7.2   Automation

In modern settlement systems, the following aspects of trade affirmation messages can normally be automated:

• the decision to issue the message pre or post trade validation;

- the decision whether to issue a message or not, depending on the counterparty (e.g. Oasys Global subscriber, or not).

As for trade matching, this information is usually held within the STO's static data repository, and during processing of a trade, the relevant data will be selected as part of the trade enrichment process.

Furthermore, the following can be automated:

- the transmission of the message via Oasys Global;
- the receipt of message statuses from Oasys Global;
- the updating of the relevant (internal) trade record with its trade matching status;
- the highlighting of trades with a status other than 'matched'.

14.8 SUMMARY

The basic principle regarding trade agreement is: the longer a trade's detail remains unchecked after trade date, the greater the risk of price movement and subsequent loss.

The risk of financial loss to an STO cannot be eliminated on trades where it is unknown whether the counterparty agrees the trade at all, and if so, whether the counterparty agrees the detail, or not. The aim of achieving trade agreement is to minimise that risk as far as possible. (Procedures for the investigation and resolution of non-matching trade details are much the same as those for non-matching settlement instructions, which are described within Chapter 18).

Outgoing trade confirmations and trade matching messages should be issued as soon as possible, but it is recommended to do so after trade validation, to avoid issuing information to the outside world before it has been validated internally. This reduces the possibility that incorrect trade detail will be matched by a counterparty, to the financial detriment of the STO.

However, the timely and accurate servicing of clients is a major consideration, and therefore a sensible balance must be struck by the STO regarding the twin issues of risk and service.

It is recommended that incoming confirmations are checked upon receipt, as acceptance of trade detail is assumed, unless disputed. In other words, in the event of a trade detail dispute, the STO is not in a strong position if the counterparty can prove that it issued a trade confirmation, but the STO failed to check it and revert in a reasonable timeframe.

Transaction Reporting

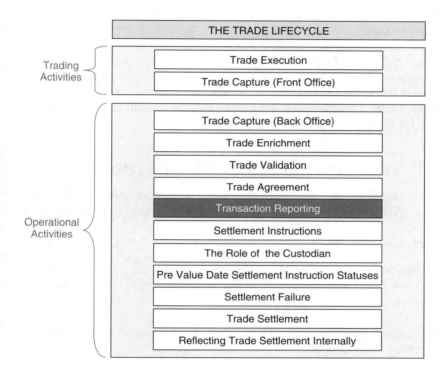

15.1 INTRODUCTION

Within each marketplace, a regulatory environment exists in order to ensure that the market operates in a fair and orderly manner. This encompasses a number of facets of operation relating to stock exchange/market members, including STOs, such as:

- transaction reporting
- trading rule breaches
- position taking disproportionate to the member's financial position (also known as *capital adequacy*).

The rules and regulations set up by marketplaces are designed to provide an efficient market environment based upon investor protection, the interests of its members and guarding the reputation of the marketplace.

This chapter focuses on transaction reporting, as it is a component of the trade lifecycle that stock exchange/market members must comply with and is an essential part of being a member firm.

15.2   PURPOSE OF TRANSACTION REPORTING

Following execution of a trade, stock exchange/market members are normally required to report to the appropriate regulator the details of each transaction undertaken, within a prestated timeframe from the time of trade execution. This information allows the regulator to assess and supervise the business being transacted by individual companies within the marketplace. This activity is commonly referred to as supervision or surveillance within the regulatory environment.

Marketplaces endeavour to be regarded as fair places to conduct business, requiring the integrity of the marketplace to be upheld through the regulator's independent monitoring, carried out via attentive and constant supervision. Potential investors in a marketplace are more likely to invest if that marketplace has a reputation for being a fair and just place to trade, where positive steps are taken to ensure that the rules and regulations are followed, and measures are taken against those who break the rules.

15.3   TRANSACTION REPORTING METHODS

Various methods exist for transaction reporting, usually dependent upon how the local regulator requires transaction reporting to be effected by the members of the stock exchange/market.

For instance, transaction reporting can be achieved by:

- the automatic forwarding of trade details to the regulator by a computerised exchange on behalf of the stock exchange member (requiring no further transmission by the stock exchange member), for example:
  - ○ SETS in the UK;
- transmission originated by the member of a specific message, part of which is used for transaction reporting, for example:
  - ○ Trax (ISMA's trade matching and transaction reporting mechanism, see Chapter 14) where a single message sent by an ISMA member serves the purpose of trade matching as well as transaction reporting, with the relevant information forwarded by ISMA to the regulator
  - ○ transmission of a settlement instruction to a *national central securities depository* (NCSD), that then forwards the necessary information to the regulator, for example:
    - ▪ Crest (UK).

Figure 15.1 illustrates two of the routes by which transaction reporting can be effected in the UK.

Step 1: those who must comply with transaction reporting requirements are UK-based regulated firms, including STOs.

Step 2: transaction reporting by the STO may be achieved through different methods, according to the type of security and exchange/market in which trading has been conducted, such as Eurobonds as opposed to UK equities.

Step 3: where Eurobonds have been traded under the rules of ISMA (as is standard), or where UK equities have been traded over the London Stock Exchange, then the following applies.

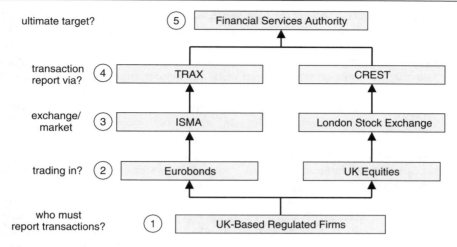

Figure 15.1   Transaction reporting: UK example

Step 4: Trax is used as the mechanism for transaction reporting of Eurobonds (as well as being used for trade matching purposes), whilst Crest is used for transaction reporting of UK and Irish equities (as well as being the settlement system for UK and Irish equities).

Step 5: once trade details have been received by ISMA and Crest, they are forwarded to the destination, the regulator.

The generation and transmission of transaction reporting messages (by STOs) to regulators can usually be automated from modern settlement systems; however, this is very dependent upon the reporting method.

15.4   TRANSACTION COMPONENTS

The usual trade information requiring submission to the regulator is:

- capacity
  - e.g. principal, agent
- trade date
- trade time
- value date
- operation
  - buy or sell
- quantity
- security
- price
- counterparty.

Upon receipt, the regulator analyses the transaction detail and attempts to identify unusual patterns of trading, which may have been caused by, for example:

- market manipulation, or
- insider trading, and
- significant errors (on the part of the STO).

One objective of surveillance is to identify trading activity that falls outside the norm, against a background of continual securities' price fluctuation. Another objective is the identification of breaches of trading rules. A further aim is the identification of insider trading; when someone obtains information about a company and trades in that company's shares when the information has not been made public and the information would affect the company's share price.

Some regulators are able to analyse trading activity very shortly after trade execution, dependent upon the transaction reporting methods in operation.

The scale of this operation is vast due to the ever-increasing trading activity in many marketplaces; however, regardless of the scale, regulators must be capable of differentiating between unusually large quantities of trades and securities' price movements caused by genuine market forces, as opposed to those caused by questionable activity.

In some marketplaces, automation is used to search for such trading patterns. At the New York Stock Exchange (NYSE), a computer system named StockWatch is used to identify abnormal trading activity. At the Australian Stock Exchange (ASX), the SOMA system is set up with limits representing normal market activity, thereby enabling any reported transactions that fall outside the limits to be identified automatically.

15.5   ACTIONS FOLLOWING DETECTION

When a regulator detects trading activity that is dubious, an investigation begins, involving the scrutiny of all transactions executed by the stock exchange member in the specific security. This may include the inspection of the exchange/market member's books and records and interviewing the member's personnel.

At the same time, the regulator may contact the issuing company (of the security in which trading has been executed) to establish whether any company notices are due for publication. If so, it is possible that 'insider trading' has occurred where, for example, an employee, or friend or relation of an employee, has executed one or many trades based on non-public information. Note that even if the employee is found to have passed information on for someone else to execute trades, the employee may still be regarded as guilty of insider trading.

If, after investigation is complete, the regulator uncovers suspicious trading practices by a member firm or its employees, disciplinary action can be taken; this is known as enforcement. Punishment in some countries can be quite severe, with prison sentences of up to seven years for those found guilty of insider trading.

Member companies, if found guilty of contravening membership rules, may be expelled, their licence to trade suspended, or they may be disciplined in a suitable manner.

Investors who have incurred financial losses as a result of incompetence or fraudulent activity by a member may be able to receive compensation.

15.6   SUMMARY

STOs are obligated to provide transaction reporting to the appropriate regulator(s), and by doing so they contribute towards upholding the integrity of the marketplace.

16
Settlement Instructions

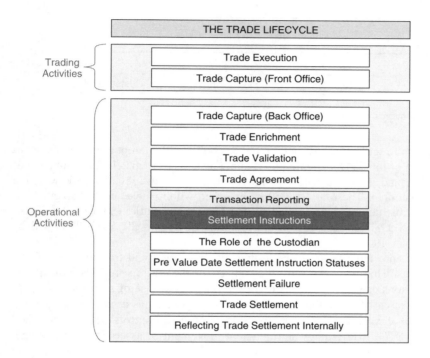

THE TRADE LIFECYCLE

Trading Activities

- Trade Execution
- Trade Capture (Front Office)

Operational Activities

- Trade Capture (Back Office)
- Trade Enrichment
- Trade Validation
- Trade Agreement
- Transaction Reporting
- Settlement Instructions
- The Role of the Custodian
- Pre Value Date Settlement Instruction Statuses
- Settlement Failure
- Trade Settlement
- Reflecting Trade Settlement Internally

16.1 INTRODUCTION

Having transmitted the necessary trade confirmations or trade matching messages, it is usual to then focus on the generation and transmission of settlement instructions.

Note that none of the actions as described up to this point will result directly in the movement of securities and cash at the custodian. Despite the fact that trade agreement has been reached on a particular trade (through trade matching, for example), securities and cash will not be exchanged unless a settlement instruction is issued to the custodian.

The term *settlement instruction* is a generic term used to describe the (only) mechanism by which trade settlement (the exchange of securities and cash) is initiated between seller and buyer. For each trade, an STO issues a settlement instruction to the relevant custodian (with the exception of those issued under Power of Attorney, described later in this chapter).

Note: the term *custodian* is used within this book as a generic term for the many types of organisation that provide custodial services, which are investigated further in Chapter 17.

Settlement instructions are normally generated by and transmitted from the STO's settlement system by a secure method, the destination being the appropriate custodian (to be selected from the range of the STO's custodians, depending upon the security that has been traded). This is illustrated in Figure 16.1.

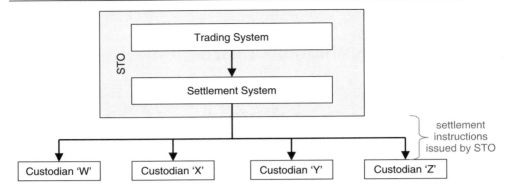

Figure 16.1   Settlement instructions: overview

Upon receipt of the settlement instruction, the custodian will attempt to match the detail with the custodian of the STO's counterparty, apply a status (e.g. matched or unmatched) to the instruction, and on value date attempt to exchange securities and cash with the counterparty's custodian. These topics will be explored within subsequent chapters.

If a settlement instruction is not issued by the STO, trade settlement would not take place, and this is very likely to cause a direct monetary loss to the STO. This will be described in Chapter 19.

A great deal of care must be taken regarding the generation and transmission of settlement instructions. This is a very sensitive subject for the entire securities industry, as settlement instructions cause assets to be delivered out (in the case of securities), or paid away (in the case of cash), from the control of the STO (as well as assets being received into the control of the STO). Consequently, safeguards and controls need to be taken seriously by each STO, if erroneous or fraudulent movement of assets is to be avoided. When considering that an average sized bond trade for a large STO may have a cash value of for example USD 10 million, one of the operational challenges is to ensure that the small, medium and large cash value trades have a consistently high level of control applied; a 'small' trade may have a cash value of USD 1 million!

To relate the security aspects to one's personal circumstances, an STO that does not take care of its assets by applying tight security to the generation and transmission of settlement instructions is the equivalent of an individual allowing other people to have free access to their cheque book or credit cards. Unless great care is taken regarding security, attempts to defraud an STO (from within or from outside) may be successful.

The automatic generation and transmission of settlement instructions is a major factor in an STO achieving *STP*, and the importance of this will become more critical as *settlement cycles* continue to shorten.

16.2   RISKS ASSOCIATED WITH SETTLEMENT INSTRUCTIONS

The generation and transmission of settlement instructions can be achieved in a controlled fashion, where an STO recognises the risk and takes measures to minimise the possibility of loss as a result of errors or fraud.

The types of measures that an STO can employ are as follows.

16.2.1   Generation and Transmission by Authorised Personnel

In a manual operational environment, the generation of settlement instructions should be restricted to a select group of people, with release of each instruction at a higher authority level. In an automated environment, trade capture within an STO's trading system should be restricted to authorised traders. Providing that trade validation is thorough, settlement instructions should be allowed to flow through in order to achieve STP, unless certain conditions are applicable, such as FoP settlement (see below). However, within an automated environment it may still be necessary to generate a limited number of settlement instructions manually, in which case measures such as those mentioned previously should be adopted. The reasons for manually produced settlement instructions are described later in this chapter.

16.2.2   Avoiding Settling on an FoP Basis

The majority of trades settle on a DvP basis, whereby simultaneous exchange of securities and cash is effected between buyer and seller. STOs typically wish to settle every trade on a DvP basis, as to settle in the alternative manner, namely FoP, means that STP is not achieved and that the possibility of risk is introduced.

Settling on an FoP basis requires that one (or both) parties to the trade will need to arrange delivery of the securities or payment of the cash prior to having possession of the other asset. However, from an individual STO's perspective, settling on an FoP basis can be with or without risk:

- with risk
  - where the STO has sold, delivering securities prior to the receipt of cash from the counterparty
  - where the STO has bought, paying the net settlement value prior to the receipt of the securities from the counterparty

- without risk
  - where the STO has sold, delivering securities only after confirmation of receipt of cash from the counterparty
  - where the STO has bought, paying the net settlement value only after confirmation of receipt of the securities from the counterparty.

Front office personnel (i.e. traders and salespeople) should be aware of the increased risk FoP settlement introduces, and should try to avoid agreeing to FoP settlement with counterparties whenever possible.

No back office should be seen to have made a unilateral decision that puts its company at risk; such decisions are best left to those with the appropriate level of authority, for instance the management of the trading area. From a back office perspective, one way of dealing with trades (advised by the trader or salesperson) that have been arranged to settle on an FoP basis is to assume that the STO is not to be put at risk, unless specifically advised to the contrary. When the back office is advised (typically by a trader or salesperson) to put the STO at risk, the operations areas of some STOs obtain written authorisation from the head of trading, for example.

However, placing a signature on a piece of paper, resulting in, for example, the payment of USD 30 million to a counterparty, without knowing for a fact that the purchased asset will be received on the due date, or at all, is a real concern regardless of the level of authority that a person carries. This often reduces the occurrence of such risky activities.

16.2.3   Transmitting via a Secure Means

Providing easy access to an STO's assets is likely to encourage attempts by an outsider to remove securities or cash from the STO's accounts with custodians. In a similar way to an individual wishing to avoid giving a stranger access to their on-line bank account via the Internet, STOs must minimise the possibility of the transmission channel between itself and its custodians being accessed by those in the outside world attempting to effect a fraud. Note that in some cases, custodians will stipulate the level of security required of their participants.

The STO's choice of custodian is dependent upon many service related attributes that the custodian may or may not be able to provide; one important attribute is the method of transmission of settlement instructions. An STO is likely to select a particular custodian if it is considered that the custodian's settlement instruction transmission method is sufficiently secure, where high levels of encryption are used in order to prevent an outsider from deciphering the coded message. The result of this measure is that even a successful break-in to an STO's transmission method is likely to result in the custodian receiving settlement instructions that cannot be deciphered, therefore implying that the message has not been issued by the STO.

16.2.4   Seeking Acknowledgement of Receipt from the Custodian

A settlement instruction that is issued, but not received by the custodian, is no different from an instruction not generated and transmitted at all. The risk is that a financial loss will be made by the STO as a result of the settlement instruction not being received by the value date, as settlement typically cannot occur until settlement instructions are matched with the counterparty's instruction at the custodian.

In order to minimise this risk, STOs typically require the relevant custodian to acknowledge the receipt of settlement instructions. In an automated environment, systems are capable of comparing settlement instructions issued versus acknowledgements received, and if a missing acknowledgement is detected, highlighting it as an exception.

16.2.5   Meeting the Deadline Imposed by the Custodian

Today STOs tend to trade and settle on a global basis. An STO is likely to have many custodians in different parts of the globe, some of which will be in a different time zone from the STO. Because the settlement process in the location of each custodian is very likely to differ in terms of timing (as well as in a number of other aspects), each custodian will impose their deadline upon the STO; the deadline is relevant to the value date of trades. For example, the deadline for the receipt of settlement instructions by an STO's Spanish custodian may be at 09:00 (Spanish time) on the value date, whereas the STO's Japanese custodian may impose a deadline of 16:00 (Japanese time) on the business day prior to the value date.

The STO must remain alert to the appropriate deadlines at each of its custodians around the globe, and where necessary, prioritise the transmission of settlement instructions according to the most urgent deadlines.

16.3   MAIN SETTLEMENT INSTRUCTION TYPES

Settlement of individual trades occurs in one of two ways:

- on a DVP basis, or
- on an FoP basis.

16.3.1   Delivery versus Payment

DvP is the simultaneous and irreversible exchange of securities and cash; this is a term that is used throughout the securities industry. Where trades are due to settle on a DvP basis, it is normal to issue a single settlement instruction to the relevant custodian, requesting the custodian to deliver securities versus payment, or to receive securities versus payment.

16.3.2   Free of Payment

Where the movement of securities and cash between buyer and seller is disassociated, settlement is said to occur on an FoP basis; this is the non-simultaneous exchange of securities and cash. For FoP settlement, it is normal for two settlement instructions to be generated.

Where the STO is buying:

- a settlement instruction needs to be issued to the STO's custodian to receive the securities, against nil cash value
- a separate settlement instruction needs to be issued to the STO's bank, requesting the bank (also known as 'nostro') to make the payment, according to whether settlement is to occur with or without risk, from the STO's perspective:
  - if the STO is not at risk, this instruction will be transmitted to the STO's bank only after having received confirmation of receipt of the securities by the STO's custodian (this is known as 'upon receipt')
  - if the STO has agreed to be at risk, this instruction will need to be transmitted in time for the cash to be paid to the counterparty, on value date (irrespective of receipt of securities).

Where the STO is selling:

- a settlement instruction needs to be issued to the STO's custodian to deliver the securities, against nil cash value
  - if the STO is not at risk, this instruction will be transmitted to the STO's custodian only after having received confirmation of receipt of the cash by the STO's bank (nostro)
  - if the STO has agreed to be at risk, this instruction will need to be transmitted in time for the securities to be delivered to the counterparty, on value date (irrespective of receipt of cash)
- a separate settlement instruction, a cash 'pre-advice', may need to be issued to the STO's bank, advising the bank to expect to receive the payment. From the STO's perspective, unless a pre-advice is issued, the bank may not credit the STO's account with 'good value' (this is covered in greater depth in Chapter 23).

16.4   CONTENT OF SETTLEMENT INSTRUCTIONS

A settlement instruction literally tells the custodian to carry out precise commands, such as:

- from whom securities will be received and to whom payment must be made, or to whom securities are to be delivered and from whom payment will be received
- the quantity of securities to be received or delivered
- the net settlement value to be paid or received
- the earliest date that the instructions are to be carried out

in exactly the same way that, having written a cheque, an individual expects nobody other than the payee to be paid, and to pay no more or less than the cash amount written onto the cheque.

Table 16.1

From	The name of the issuing STO
To	The name of the STO's custodian
Depot account no.	The STO's account number over which the securities movement is to be effected
Nostro account no.	The STO's account number over which the cash movement is to be effected
Trade reference	The STO's settlement system trade reference number
Deliver/receive	Whether securities are to be delivered or received
Settlement basis	Whether to be settled on a DvP or FoP basis
Value date	The value date of the trade (the earliest date that settlement is to be effected)
Quantity	The quantity of shares, or quantity of bonds
Security reference	The security identifier code, e.g. *ISIN, Cusip*, Quick
Settlement currency	The ISO code of the net settlement value currency
Net settlement value	The cash value to be paid or received
Counterparty depot	The counterparty's (securities) custodian details, including account number
Counterparty nostro	The counterparty's (cash) custodian details, including account number
Transmission time	A clear statement of the date and time of transmission

Table 16.1 describes the typical content of a settlement instruction, based upon a principal transaction. *Notes*:

- trade components such as trade date, price and accrued days are also usually included on a settlement instruction. In the event of the instruction being unmatched, this information allows the custodian to communicate with the counterparty's custodian in an attempt to identify the discrepancy
- an STO typically has a minimum of two securities accounts at each custodian:
  - ○ a main settlement account (in which the STO's purchases and sales are settled and the STO's settled positions are held)
  - ○ a safe-custody account (in which the securities owned by the STO's safe custody clients are held)

and so it is essential to quote the specific account number over which the movement is to occur

- at many custodians, each account has the capability of holding both securities and cash
- the settlement system trade reference number is vitally important for subsequent communication between the custodian and the STO
- it is usually not so important to a custodian to know whether its account holder has bought or sold, or lent or borrowed; it is however, vitally important to know whether securities are to be delivered or received, and whether cash is to be paid or received.

16.5   METHODS OF TRANSMITTING SETTLEMENT INSTRUCTIONS

Historically, when trading was confined to the domestic market of an STO, settlement would typically be conducted by physical delivery of share and bond certificates between the offices of those involved in the trade. Upon receipt of the seller's securities, the certificates would be inspected to ensure they were valid, and if found to be in order, the buyer would hand a cheque to the seller.

When *cross-border trading* and *cross border settlement* began, custodians were set up by the STO in the relevant financial centres; however, communicating settlement instructions on a risk-free basis was much more of a challenge than it is today. Prior to the *S.W.I.F.T.* network being available as a medium for transmitting securities settlement instructions (originally, S.W.I.F.T. catered only for cash), telex was the most popular method of transmission.

Telex was (and still is) usually regarded as being insufficiently secure in its own right as a settlement instruction transmission method; however, when a telex message contains a code number known only to the transmitting and the receiving parties (commonly known as a 'tested telex'), it does become more secure. This operates in the following manner:

- when an STO opens an account with a custodian, the latter would supply the STO with a 'test key'; a card containing a series of codes, such as:
  - if the transmission day of the month is 28th, use code 941
  - if the transmission month is October, use code 003
  - if the quantity is 1,000,000, use code 199
  - if the settlement currency is JPY, use code 627
  - etc., etc.
- the agreement between the STO and the custodian states that the test key must be kept locked and in a secure area, such as a safe
- when needing to issue a settlement instruction, the test key would be removed from the safe, and the details contained on the instruction used to produce a sequence of codes which, when added together produce a single code, such as: 941 + 003 + 199 + 627, total 1770. The total would be typed at the top of the telex as follows: 'Test Key 1770'
- all the details of the settlement instruction and the test key number would be checked independently by two authorised signatories of the STO
- the test key would be put back in the safe
- the telex would be transmitted
- when the telex was received, the custodian would then repeat the coding procedure to confirm that the test key was valid
- the custodian would now act upon the settlement instruction.

Although using a manual test key is a relatively secure method of transmission (but as it is not encrypted it is open to fraud), to process any reasonable volume of trades by that method is simply not feasible, due to the amount of manual effort involved in the creation and checking of the test key. Furthermore, a custodian is likely to impose a much earlier deadline for the handling of settlement instructions requiring manual intervention than for automated messaging. This then leaves a smaller 'window' of time between trade date and value date, in order to create and transmit settlement instructions. Such a method of transmission is unlikely to allow STOs to keep pace with the trend towards decreasing *settlement cycles*.

Another method used by some STOs is fax; this is not recommended at all, as it is regarded as being simply too 'open' and insecure. Some STOs have banned fax as a means of issuing settlement instructions, due to its lack of security.

16.5.1 Electronic Transmission Methods

Modern methods of transmitting settlement instructions include the following characteristics:

- the automatic generation of settlement instructions (by settlement systems);
- the automatic transmission of settlement instructions (either individually or in batches);
- the electronic exchange of test keys;
- settlement instructions in standardised formats;
- secure transmission environment due to high levels of message encryption;
- high speed of transmission;
- predictable cost of transmission;
- enables STP.

A widely used electronic settlement instruction transmission mechanism (for both domestic and cross-border settlement) is S.W.I.F.T. Note that this is the same organisation that carries trade confirmation messages (refer to Chapter 14). To be precise regarding the role of S.W.I.F.T., it is not a destination (in the same way that a custodian is a destination) but a communications network. In order to utilise the S.W.I.F.T. network, both the STO transmitting the settlement instruction and the destination custodian must subscribe to S.W.I.F.T.

For STOs that utilise the services of a global custodian (global custodians typically have an underlying network of sub-custodians in each financial centre), the global custodian may have developed a proprietary system. Alternatively, it is likely that S.W.I.F.T. is an acceptable mechanism for the transmission of settlement instructions.

For transmission of settlement instructions to the international central securities depositories (ICSDs) (Euroclear, Brussels and Clearstream, Luxembourg), there is a choice of:

- S.W.I.F.T.
- proprietary systems
  - Euclid (for Euroclear)
  - Cedcom (for Clearstream)
- tested telex, and
- mail.

Because STOs typically have relationships with a number of custodians around the globe, S.W.I.F.T. is often the preference. For settlement via the ICSDs, some STOs use S.W.I.F.T., thereby maintaining a consistent communication method for all their custodians, whereas other STOs prefer to use the proprietary systems.

It is important to note that whereas S.W.I.F.T. can be used by a subscribing STO in, say, Wellington, New Zealand to transmit a settlement instruction to another S.W.I.F.T. subscriber (its custodian in, say, Helsinki, Finland), the same cannot be said of Euclid and Cedcom. Only those who are participants of the Euroclear and Clearstream systems can use these proprietary systems.

Settlement instructions destined for some national central securities depositories (NCSDs) may be able to be issued via S.W.I.F.T., whereas some allow communication of settlement instructions only via their proprietary methods or by specific message types.

16.6 FORMAT OF SETTLEMENT INSTRUCTIONS

Cedcom, Euclid and S.W.I.F.T. transmission mechanisms all have standardised messages (incorporating mandatory fields) that are required to be used according to the action required of the custodian by the STO. However, note that S.W.I.F.T. also caters for optional information on messages. The following are examples of settlement instruction numbering conventions, with a description of their meaning.

16.6.1 S.W.I.F.T.

S.W.I.F.T. has numerous categories of settlement instructions and messages for different purposes, some of which relate to securities, while others relate to cash only movements. The use of optional information is normally at the request of the custodian and may differ from custodian to custodian. Therefore care needs to be taken to ensure that settlement instructions reflect the format requirements of each custodian. Table 16.2 gives examples of S.W.I.F.T.'s series 2 (cash) and series 5 (securities) messages used as settlement instructions.

Table 16.2

	Example S.W.I.F.T. cash settlement instructions
MT200	Transfer between two accounts of the same account holder
MT202	Payment of cash to a financial institution
MT210	Receipt of cash from a financial institution
	Example S.W.I.F.T. securities settlement instructions
MT540	Sent to a custodian to receive free of payment
MT541	Sent to a custodian to receive versus payment
MT542	Sent to a custodian to deliver free of payment
MT543	Sent to a custodian to deliver versus payment

Note: the MT540 series will fully replace the MT520 series by November 2002, as part of the *ISO15022* message standards.

16.6.2 Euclid

Euroclear's proprietary system Euclid uses a numbering convention that distinguishes between settlement with another Euroclear participant, as opposed to settlement with a

Clearstream participant. For example, an electronic 'bridge' exists between Euroclear and Clearstream Luxembourg that facilitates DvP and FoP settlement between cross-system participants. Table 16.3 gives examples of Euclid's available settlement instruction messages.

Table 16.3

	Example Euclid settlement instructions
E01	Receive free or versus payment from a Euroclear participant
E02	Deliver free or versus payment to a Euroclear participant
E03C	Receive free or versus payment from a Clearstream participant
E07C	Deliver free or versus payment to a Clearstream participant

Table 16.4

	Example Cedcom settlement instructions
41	Receive versus payment from a Clearstream or Euroclear participant
41F	Receive free of payment from a Clearstream or Euroclear participant
51	Deliver versus payment to a Clearstream or Euroclear participant
51F	Deliver free of payment to a Clearstream or Euroclear participant

16.6.3   Cedcom

Clearstream Luxembourg's proprietary system Cedcom has a settlement instruction numbering method that does not distinguish the system that the counterparty is using. See Table 16.4.

16.6.4   Crest

Crest, the system over which UK and Irish settlements are effected, uses a specific settlement instruction coding method, examples of which are given in Table 16.5.

Table 16.5

Example Crest settlement instructions	
ADVN	Delivery input
ASDN	Stock deposit input
ASWN	Stock withdrawal input

The following describes how such settlement instructions are used to settle a trade, for instance, when a participant of Euroclear purchases securities from a counterparty that is also a Euroclear participant, for settlement on a DvP basis:

• the buyer, when transmitting via Euclid, must send an E01 instruction
• the seller, when transmitting via Euclid, must send and E02 instruction

in each case, the sender needing to denote whether settlement is to occur on an FoP or DvP basis, by completion of certain 'tags' within the message.

If, instead, the buyer purchased securities from a Clearstream Luxembourg participant, the buyer, when transmitting via Euclid, must send an E03C instruction; this tells Euroclear to receive from a participant of Clearstream. The Clearstream participant, when transmitting via Cedcom, must send Clearstream a 51 instruction, telling Clearstream to deliver to a Euroclear participant.

Note that many NCSDs (including Crest) have electronic links with the two ICSDs, enabling settlement between participants in different systems. This is termed *cross border settlement*, for which specific instructions are normally used.

16.7   DEADLINES FOR THE RECEIPT OF SETTLEMENT INSTRUCTIONS BY CUSTODIANS

All custodians will quote a deadline by which settlement instructions must be received by them, relevant to the value date of the securities and/or cash movement; the method of transmission is also likely to affect the deadline imposed by the custodian.

For example, if the settlement processing (the actual exchange of securities and cash) occurs in Bangkok during daylight hours of the value date, a custodian in Bangkok will impose a deadline on its clients for the receipt of settlement instructions for that value date of, say, 08:00 (Bangkok time) on the value date, providing the instruction is transmitted in an electronic form (such as a S.W.I.F.T. MT540 series message). This deadline normally allows for matching of instructions with the counterparty's custodian, prior to the settlement process (there is little point in undertaking the settlement process if instructions do not match). If a New York-based STO buys shares in a Thai equity, for settlement on a T+3 basis, the STO will need to issue the instruction by close-of-business on T+2 (New York time) in order to meet the deadline imposed by the Bangkok custodian, taking into account the time difference between Bangkok and New York.

The ICSDs Euroclear and Clearstream Luxembourg begin to operate their overnight settlement processing during the evening of the day prior to value date, Central European Time (CET). The deadline for the receipt of settlement instructions imposed by, for instance, Euroclear is 19:45 CET, on the day prior to value date.

From the perspective of all custodians, the imposed deadlines exist so that the account holder (e.g. STOs) at each custodian are very clear as to the time by which settlement instructions must be received, in order to have a chance of settling on value date. If settlement instructions are received, for example, 30 minutes after the deadline, the custodian may still accept the instruction, but it simply cannot be processed on the value date. The detrimental effect of settlement instructions failing to be received by the custodian within the stated deadline will be explored within subsequent chapters.

Deadlines for the transmission of settlement instructions to the ICSDs (Euroclear, Brussels and Clearstream, Luxembourg) via S.W.I.F.T. or the proprietary systems are identical, because the standardised format allows the information contained in the instruction to be automatically captured into the custodian's systems. However, transmission via tested telex is not in a standardised format and therefore requires the custodian to rekey the information contained on the telex into the custodian's system. Consequently, a considerably earlier deadline is imposed.

STOs effecting cross border trading and settlement in numerous markets around the globe must be conscious of the deadlines imposed by each of their custodians. An STO would need to take particular care if it is using a mixture of electronic and non-electronic methods of transmission.

Nonetheless, it is recommended that settlement instructions are generated and transmitted as soon as possible after trade validation, on trade date, rather than leaving the transmission of the instruction until just prior to the custodian's deadline. Issuing the instruction shortly after trade execution gives the maximum available time to resolve any discrepancies prior to value date. If both the STO and its counterparty issue their instructions on trade date, the instructions will match, or be unmatched, in which case an investigation can begin, resulting in one of the instructions being amended, resulting in instructions matching prior to the value date. The other extreme is that neither the STO nor its counterparty input their instructions until just prior to the deadline, which leaves little or no window to resolve unmatched instructions prior to value date.

Another reason not to delay issuing settlement instructions is the possibility that a software or communication fault can occur in the period leading up to the deadline, thereby preventing automatic transmission.

16.8   AUTOMATIC GENERATION AND TRANSMISSION OF SETTLEMENT INSTRUCTIONS

In today's settlement systems, the trade enrichment process not only selects the appropriate custodian, but also determines the method of transmission of settlement instructions to that custodian.

Consequently, the appropriate settlement instruction (e.g. S.W.I.F.T. MT541 or Cedcom 41) is generated with the relevant trade data, and transmitted automatically via the necessary communication channels. Where the settlement system has failed to generate or transmit an instruction successfully, this should be treated as an exception automatically.

16.9   SETTLEMENT INSTRUCTION VALIDATION

As for trade validation, as an added safeguard some STOs wish to review and authorise settlement instructions of certain types, prior to transmission to the custodian. This requires the setting of settlement instruction validation rules within the settlement system.

At the point where each settlement instruction can be transmitted, the system would compare the trade detail with the relevant rules:

- if the settlement instruction passes this validation check, it will be allowed to continue immediately and can be regarded as having been processed on an STP basis
- if, on the other hand, the settlement instruction fails the validation check (e.g. settlement instruction is FoP), the instruction will be treated as an exception and be held, pending authorisation by the relevant member of the STO's staff.

Because of the risk implications, FoP settlement instructions are typically subject to specific authorisation; this may well be in addition to the trade validation process for FoP trades mentioned within Chapter 13.

16.10   MANUALLY GENERATED SETTLEMENT INSTRUCTIONS

Even in an automated environment, it may be necessary to generate settlement instructions manually, under certain circumstances.

For example, if a trader has executed a trade, but fails to record it within the trading system, there will be no trade within the settlement system either. On the day prior to value date, it may come to the attention of the STO that the counterparty has input their settlement instruction, which is unmatched. Once the situation is investigated (typically by listening to the dealing tapes), if the STO's trader did in fact execute the trade, the trader will need to record the trade within the trading system, and feed the trade to the settlement system, which in turn should generate and transmit a settlement instruction. However, if there is insufficient time to meet the custodian's deadline by allowing the settlement system to generate and transmit the settlement instruction (because the last batch of instructions may have already been sent, for example), the only option open to the STO is to input the instruction manually (directly into the transmission mechanism destined for the custodian, typically via a PC and not via the settlement system), so as not to incur *settlement failure* costs. If the trade has not yet been recorded within the settlement system, the trade reference number will not be known, so a dummy trade reference number will need to be applied to the manual settlement instruction. When the trade is captured within the settlement system, the (automatically generated) settlement instruction will need to be suppressed, in order to avoid duplication of instructions at the custodian.

When the custodian receives the manually sent instruction, it will be subject to all the normal settlement instruction events (refer to the list in Section 16.13). However, as there will be no connection between the settlement instruction and the trade within the settlement system, the trade record within the settlement system will not be updated automatically with these events, unless the settlement system allows an association between the instruction and the trade reference number.

It is recommended that manual settlement instructions be kept to a minimum, to enable the STO to maintain control. In subsequent chapters, the detrimental effect of manual intervention and failure to update trade information automatically will be explored.

16.11   SAFE CUSTODY RELATED SETTLEMENT INSTRUCTIONS

Following the execution of a trade, STOs typically expect to settle 'externally' with counterparties; this means issuing settlement instructions to custodians, who undertake the exchange of securities and cash on the STO's behalf, with the custodian of the STO's counterparty.

However, where the counterparty to the trade is an institutional client, that client may not have a custodian relationship that enables 'external' settlement to occur.

For clients such as these, an STO may offer to hold the client's securities (and possibly cash) in safe custody. This means that when an STO sells securities to the institutional client, the STO retains control (but not ownership) of the securities and issues a settlement instruction to the relevant custodian, to remove the securities from the STO's main account (in which the STO's own securities are held) to a segregated account at the custodian, in which the securities owned by the STO's safe custody clients are kept. The reverse flow must occur when the STO buys securities from a safe custody client.

Note that both the main account and the safe custody account are under the direct control of the STO at the custodian. By law in many countries an STO's own assets and the assets the STO holds on behalf of others must be segregated and held in different accounts at the custodian. However, there is no need to hold the accounts at separate custodians.

In an automated environment, such situations are able to be identified during trade capture and/or trade enrichment, by use of static data. In terms of settlement instructions, this can mean the need to generate and transmit (in the case of a sale by the STO to a safe custody client) either:

- two settlement instructions
  - one for the removal of securities from the STO's main account and delivery to the safe custody account
  - one for the receipt of securities into the STO's safe custody account from the STO's main account
    - with the instructions requiring matching (as usual) before settlement occurs, or
- a single settlement instruction
  - for the removal of the securities from the STO's main account and delivery to the safe custody account (commonly known as 'Own Account Transfer')

but whether one or two instructions are required to be generated depends upon the way the custodian wishes to operate movements between two accounts owned by the same STO.

16.12   SETTLEMENT INSTRUCTIONS ISSUED UNDER POWER OF ATTORNEY

A recent development in the marketplace is the concept that, where trades have been executed either:

- on a computerised stock exchange, for example
  - Xetra (Germany)
  - SEATS (Australia), or
- via Electronic Communications Networks (ECNs), 'electronic trading platforms' and 'alternative trading systems', for example:
  - Euro-MTS

the entity over which the trade has been executed issues the settlement instruction on behalf of the STO. In order for this to occur, the STO must give *power of attorney* to that entity; in other words, legal authority to act on its behalf.

Figure 16.2 represents the flow of information when settlement instructions are issued on the STO's behalf by an authorised third party, under power of attorney (in an automated environment).

Step 1a: trades that are executed in the traditional manner, via telephone or over a conventional stock exchange, are input manually to the trading system.

Step 1b: trades that are executed via a computerised exchange, ECN or trading platform are typically fed to the trading system automatically.

Steps 2a and 2b: the trading system feeds each trade to the settlement system automatically.

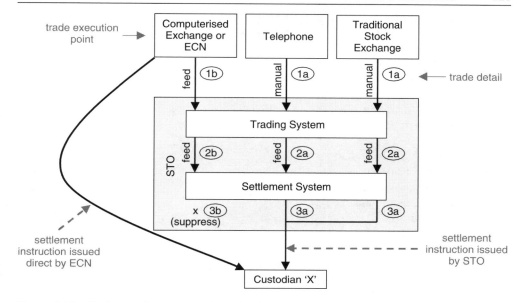

Figure 16.2   Settlement instructions: issued under power of attorney

Step 3a: the settlement system generates and transmits settlement instructions (where not already produced by another entity on behalf of the STO) to the relevant custodian.

Step 3b: where settlement instructions have been generated and transmitted directly to the custodian by a computerised exchange or ECN (under power of attorney granted by the STO), the STO will need to suppress the generation of settlement instructions by the settlement system, in order to avoid duplicate settlement instructions at the custodian.

However, any one of the STO's custodians can expect to receive settlement instructions from a third party (acting under power of attorney granted by the STO) and from the STO. Because an STO may execute trades in one security over, for example, an ECN and in the conventional manner, the STO will need to:

• suppress instructions where executed via an ECN, and
• issue settlement instructions where trades are executed in the conventional manner

to the same custodian, as the custodian will be required to settle all trades in the specific security, regardless of the origin of the trades.

Furthermore, settlement instructions are likely to be issued by the STO to custodians for other transaction types, such as depot (custodian) transfers, that will only originate from the STO; refer to Chapter 5.

Where settlement instructions are issued directly to the custodian by another entity, the STO benefits as settlement instructions are issued very shortly after trade execution, and the expense of issuing a settlement instruction is avoided. Additionally, since the settlement instruction has been issued from the point of trade execution, the risk of the STO issuing an incorrect settlement instruction (due to erroneous trade recording) is prevented. However, this situation requires the STO to recognise each individual trade that falls into this category, so as to suppress the production of settlement instructions from the settlement system for all appropriate trades.

16.13   MAINTAINING A LINK BETWEEN A TRADE AND ITS SETTLEMENT INSTRUCTION

As already stated, each trade within the settlement system should be represented by a settlement instruction at the relevant custodian (unless a transaction type, such as a trading book transfer, requires no external movement of securities and/or cash). STOs typically wish to maintain a history of settlement instruction events for each individual trade, such as the time and date of:

- transmission to the custodian
- receipt by the custodian
- achieving a status of 'unmatched'
- achieving a status of 'matched'
- settlement failure
- settlement completion

so as to be aware and to maintain control of events happening remotely (at the various custodians).

In order to update the appropriate trades within the settlement system automatically with the information received from the custodian, there is a necessity for a link between the settlement instruction reference and the trade residing within the STO's settlement system. Where the STO has issued the settlement instruction, the settlement system trade reference number is normally sent as part of the content of each settlement instruction.

However, where another entity such as an ECN has issued settlement instructions under power of attorney, the settlement instruction reference number may not be the same as the settlement system trade reference number. Nevertheless, there is still a need to update the appropriate trade within the settlement system with the current status, etc. of the settlement instruction. In some settlement systems, the settlement instruction reference (reported at the trade execution point) can be associated with the trade, thereby facilitating the automatic update of the trade with the various settlement instruction events.

Maintaining a link between the trade and its settlement instruction enables the STO to have a complete picture of all trades that require no action, such as those with:

- successful instruction receipt by the custodian
- matched instructions
- instructions that have settled

and all trades requiring investigation and action, such as those with:

- unmatched instructions
- instructions that have failed to settle on value date.

16.14   SUMMARY

Achieving the twin aims of:

- generating and transmitting settlement instructions on an *STP* basis
- minimising the various risks associated with issuing settlement instructions

requires that STOs operate this aspect of their business in a tightly controlled manner, resulting in their assets being properly protected and the management remaining in control.

17
The Role of the Custodian

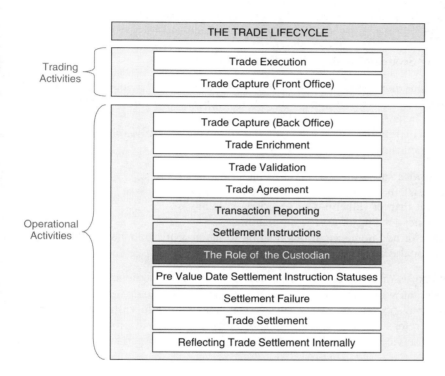

THE TRADE LIFECYCLE

Trading Activities
- Trade Execution
- Trade Capture (Front Office)

Operational Activities
- Trade Capture (Back Office)
- Trade Enrichment
- Trade Validation
- Trade Agreement
- Transaction Reporting
- Settlement Instructions
- The Role of the Custodian
- Pre Value Date Settlement Instruction Statuses
- Settlement Failure
- Trade Settlement
- Reflecting Trade Settlement Internally

17.1 INTRODUCTION

As stated in the previous chapter, the term *custodian* has been used in this book as a generic term to describe those organisations that effect settlement (the exchange of securities and cash) on behalf of STOs. In reality, a number of organisation types that are in similar roles fall within this heading, and the similarities of and differences between these types of custodian will be explored within this chapter, as will the services they provide. In addition, custodians provide services to individual investors, institutional investors and agents (e.g. brokers), as well as STOs; all of these will be described generically as the custodian's account holder.

As described in Chapter 2, a custodian is appointed by the account holder to take care of his assets (normally securities and cash) and to carry out his instructions to deliver or receive securities and to pay or receive cash. This is a comparable arrangement to an individual's relationship with his bank.

17.2 SERVICES PROVIDED BY CUSTODIANS

When an account holder first sets up an account with a custodian, in a situation where the account holder has had little or no prior involvement in the market(s) in which the custodian is focused, the custodian typically advises the account holder of local market procedures and practices.

In a day-to-day sense, the services usually provided by custodians relate to two main areas:

• the holding of securities and cash in safe custody, on behalf of the account holder
• the movement of securities and/or cash instructed by the account holder.

17.2.1   Holding Securities and Cash in Safe Custody

Following previous purchases of securities by the account holder, once settlement of those purchases has occurred, the custodian will hold the securities in safe custody on the account holder's behalf.

A custodian will provide some or all of the following services, relating to holding securities in safe custody:

• keep the securities safe from the threat of theft or loss
• provide daily statements of securities and cash holdings
• provide current market valuations of securities holdings
• provide securities lending or borrowing facilities
• collect income or additional securities relating to the account holder's entitlement
• advise of optional *corporate actions*.

Following purchases of securities by the account holder, upon settlement of those purchases the custodian will debit the cash account of the account holder.

A custodian may or may not allow an account holder to hold cash balances on an overnight basis (refer to Section 17.8). For those that do, they will provide some or all of the following services:

• keep the cash safe from the threat of theft
• pay interest on cash balances
• provide daily statements of cash balances.

17.2.2   Movements of Securities and Cash

When the custodian's account holder sells securities held by the custodian, or buys securities that will be held by the custodian, the account holder will issue a *settlement instruction* to the custodian in order to effect the appropriate movement of securities and cash. In addition, the account holder may issue settlement instructions relating to other transaction types, for example repo and depot (custodian) transfers.

The custodian will provide some or all of the following services, relating to the movements of securities and cash:

• acknowledge receipt of the settlement instruction to the account holder
• apply the current pre-settlement status of the instruction, e.g.
   ○ unmatched
   ○ matched
   ○ failed to settle

- transmit the current status of each instruction to the account holder
- effect the delivery or receipt of securities, and the receipt and payment of cash in accordance with the account holder's instructions
- upon settlement of each instruction
  - apply the status of 'settled' to the instruction
  - update the account holder's securities holding
  - update the account holder's cash account balance.

In addition, an account holder may wish to have cash paid away (from its account with the custodian) to another bank, or paid to its cash account with the custodian from an external source, for which the account holder will need to issue to the custodian an instruction to pay away or a pre-advice to receive cash (these points will be explored fully in Chapter 23). Once such instructions have been carried out, the holder's cash account will be updated accordingly.

17.3   TYPES OF CUSTODIAN

Various terms are used to describe those involved in the provision of trade settlement and custodial services on behalf of those that execute trades. Such terms include the ones listed in Table 17.1, each of which performs a specific custodian's role, and may be referred to generically as the account holder's settlement agent.

Table 17.1

Term	Description
Custodian	An organisation that holds securities and (usually) cash on its clients' behalf; and may effect settlement of trades on its clients' behalf
Global custodian	As per custodian above, but has a network of local (or sub-) custodians that hold securities and cash and effect settlement of trades on behalf of the global custodian
Local custodian	A custodian that operates within a specific financial centre
Sub-custodian	A custodian within a global custodian's network of custodians
Central Securities Depository (CSD)	An organisation that holds securities, normally in *book-entry* form; usually the ultimate place of settlement, effected through book-entry transfer.
National Central Securities Depository (NCSD)	A CSD that handles domestic securities of the country in which it is located
International Central Securities Depository (ICSD)	A CSD that handles domestic and international securities. Only two organisations are recognised as ICSDs, namely Clearstream (Luxembourg) and Euroclear (Brussels)
Settlement agent	An organisation that effects the exchange of securities and cash on behalf of its clients; resultant securities and cash balances may or may not be held

Figure 17.1 illustrates the roles of various custodians, following the execution of a trade. This example illustrates settlement ultimately occurring in a single CSD (not within two CSDs where cross-border settlement may occur). The trading related actions were as follows:

- an order to buy shares was placed by an institutional investor with an agent
- the agent forwarded the order to an STO
- the STO executed the order and recorded the details of the sale to the agent
- the STO issued an advice of execution to the agent
- the agent recorded a purchase from the STO and a sale to the institutional investor
- the agent issued an advice of execution to the institutional investor
- the institutional investor recorded a purchase from the agent

resulting in the actions shown to achieve settlement (note that these are examples only of how custodians may be utilised for settlement).

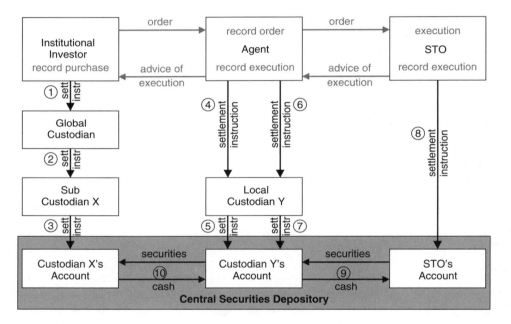

Figure 17.1   The role of the custodian: custodian roles and terminology

In each case, a settlement instruction must be issued in order to effect settlement (the exchange of securities and cash) ultimately at the central securities depository (CSD); each settlement instruction will request the recipient of the instruction to either:

- deliver securities to and receive cash from a specific account at the CSD, or
- receive securities from and pay cash to a specific account at the CSD.

Step 1: the institutional investor issues a settlement instruction to its global custodian.

Step 2: having received a settlement instruction from its client (the institutional investor), the global custodian issues a settlement instruction to its custodian in the relevant financial centre (sub-custodian X).

Step 3: having received a settlement instruction from its client (the global custodian), sub-custodian X issues a settlement instruction to its own account at the CSD.

Step 4: for its sale to the institutional investor, the agent issues a settlement instruction to its custodian (local custodian Y).

Step 5: having received a settlement instruction from its client (the agent), local custodian Y issues a settlement instruction to its own account at the CSD.

Step 6: for its purchase from the STO, the agent issues a settlement instruction to its custodian (local custodian Y).

Step 7: having received a settlement instruction from its client (the agent), local custodian Y issues a settlement instruction to its own account at the CSD.

Step 8: for its sale to the agent, the STO issues a settlement instruction to its custodian (the CSD).

Step 9: on value date, the CSD removes the relevant securities from the STO's account and adds them to custodian Y's account, and simultaneously debits the relevant cash amount from custodian Y's account and credits the STO's account; these actions have resulted in settlement being effected for the sale by the STO to the agent.

Step 10: on value date, the CSD removes securities from the agent's account and adds them to custodian X's account, and simultaneously debits the relevant cash amount from custodian X's account and credits the agent's account; these actions have resulted in settlement being effected for the sale by the agent to the institutional investor.

Following these movements:

- the securities are being held within custodian X's account at the CSD, on behalf of the global custodian, which in turn is holding the securities for the institutional investor:
  - there are no securities held in custodian Y's account at the CSD, on behalf of the agent
  - there are no securities held in the STO's account at the CSD
- the cash cost of the securities has been debited to custodian X's account at the CSD, on behalf of the global custodian, who in turn has debited the cash cost to its account with the institutional investor:
  - there is no cash amount held in custodian Y's account at the CSD, on behalf of the agent (with the exception of the commission paid by the institutional investor)
  - the sale proceeds have been credited to the STO's account at the CSD.

The view as to who is the client and who is the custodian depends upon the specific entity's perspective, for example:

- the institutional investor regards its custodian as being the global custodian;
- the global custodian regards its client as being the institutional investor, and its custodian as being sub-custodian X;
- custodian X regards its client as being the global custodian, and its custodian as being the CSD;
- the agent regards its custodian as being custodian Y;
- custodian Y regards its client as being the agent, and its custodian as being the CSD;
- the STO regards its custodian as being the CSD;
- the CSD regards its account holders as being custodian X, custodian Y and the STO.

An institutional investor, agent or STO may choose to set up arrangements for the settlement of trades and the holding of securities and cash with:

- local custodians in each financial centre
- CSDs within each financial centre
- a global custodian

or any combination of the three.

17.3.1 Global Custodians

Figure 17.2 illustrates conceptually how a global custodian operates. A global custodian is appointed by its client to facilitate trade settlement and the holding of securities and cash, by use of its existing worldwide network of sub-custodians, each of which is usually a member of its local CSD. The client issues settlement instructions to a single destination (the global custodian), which then directs its instruction to the appropriate sub-custodian, which effects settlement on behalf of the global custodian.

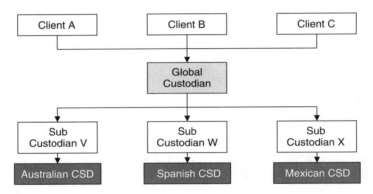

Figure 17.2   The securities marketplace: global custodians

The exchange of securities and cash resulting from a trade executed between buyer and seller occurs at the CSD, where accounts of the sub-custodians representing buyer and seller will be debited or credited with securities and cash.

17.3.2 National Central Securities Depositories (NCSDs)

An NCSD is typically set up and operated on behalf of the members of the national stock exchange of the particular country, as the core and primary repository of securities issued, traded and settled in that country. STOs and custodians located in the same country as the NCSD are likely to be direct members of the NCSD, whereas non-resident STOs may not be allowed to have a direct membership and therefore may be required to hold securities and cash, and settle trades via a member, such as a local custodian.

NCSDs typically provide DvP (and, if required, FoP) trade settlement capability for their members; securities can be held in safe keeping on behalf of members, but some NCSDs do not allow cash to be held overnight.

Examples of NCSDs are given in Table 17.2.

Table 17.2

Country	Depository abbreviation	Depository full name
Argentina	Caja	Caja de Valores
Australia	CHESS	Clearing House Electronic Subregister System
Brazil	CBLC	Brazilian Clearing & Depository Corporation
Canada	CDS	Canadian Depository for Securities
Denmark	VP	Vaerdipapircentralen
Finland	APK	Finnish Central Securities Depository
France	Euroclear France	Euroclear France (formerly Sicovam)
Germany	CLEARSTREAM BANKING	Clearstream Banking AG (formerly Deutsche Borse Clearing AG)
Hong Kong	CCASS	Central Clearing and Settlement System
India	NSDL	National Securities Depository Limited
Italy	MT	Monte Titoli
Japan	JASDEC	Japan Securities Depository Center
Korea	KSD	Korea Securities Depository
Malaysia	MCD	Malaysian Central Depository Sdn.Bhd.
Mexico	INDEVAL	Instituto para el Deposito de Valores
Netherlands	NECIGEF	Nederlands Centraal Instituut voor Giraal Effectenverkeer
New Zealand	NZCSD	New Zealand Central Securities Depository
Pakistan	CDC	Central Depository Company
Philippines	PCD	Philippine Central Depository
Poland	KDPW	National Depository of Securities
Portugal	Central	Central de Valores Mobiliarios
Singapore	CDP	Central Depository Pte. Ltd.
Spain	SCLV	Servicio de Compensacion y Liquidacion de Valores
Sweden	VPC	Vardepapperscentralen
Switzerland	SIS	SegaIntersettle AG
Taiwan	TSCD	Taiwan Securities Central Depository
Thailand	TSD	Thailand Securities Depository
UK and Ireland	CREST	Crest
USA	DTC	Depository Trust Company

17.3.3   International Central Securities Depositories (ICSDs)

An ICSD holds both international and national (domestic) securities; STOs, agents, institutional investors and custodians from around the globe can become members.

Securities are held (on behalf of the ICSD) by depository banks in numerous financial centres, and correspondent banks manage the external movement of currencies.

ICSDs provide DvP and FoP trade settlement capability on a multicurrency basis, with securities being held in safe custody and cash balances able to be held overnight.

Only two ICSDs exist, these are Clearstream in Luxembourg and Euroclear in Brussels. Settlement at the ICSDs falls into three categories:

- internal; settlement is between two participants in the same ICSD
- bridge; settlement is between a participant of Euroclear and a Clearstream International participant ('bridge' refers to the electronic link between the two ICSDs)
- external; settlement is between participants of an ICSD and an NCSD, via electronic links (this is known as *cross border settlement*).

17.4   RISKS ASSOCIATED WITH THE CUSTODIAN'S ROLE

From the account holder's perspective, the areas that a custodian must pay careful attention to include:

- the holding of securities (particularly bearer securities) and cash
- acting upon settlement instructions received by the custodian, professing to have been sent by the account holder
- the delivery and receipt of physical securities and cash
- the management of corporate actions (refer to Chapter 26)

as failure of the custodian to focus on these points introduces the risk of loss from both the account holder's and the custodian's perspective.

17.4.1   The Holding of Securities

As described in Chapter 6, certificates representing holdings in registered securities are, in many markets, *dematerialised* or *immobilised*; the holding with the custodian is secure as it is maintained in *book-entry* form. Where registered certificates remain in existence, following theft or loss, duplicate certificates are normally attainable from the registrar. In summary, there is typically less risk associated with the loss or theft of registered securities.

However, the nature of physical bearer securities requires that a custodian who holds such certificates keeps them extremely secure, normally within a vault. Unlike registered securities, there is no centrally held register containing the list of owners.

17.4.2   Acting upon Settlement Instructions Received

Custodians must remain vigilant regarding the authenticity of settlement instructions received, professing to have been sent by the account holder; this is of particular concern regarding instructions to deliver securities on an FoP basis, and for payments of cash.

The responsibility for a custodian acting upon an instruction that was not issued by the account holder is typically detailed within the agreement between the account holder and the custodian.

17.4.3   Receipt of Physical Certificates

Where an account holder has instructed a custodian to receive physical certificates (in particular bearer certificates) from the outside world, and upon receipt the custodian fails to check the authenticity of the certificates, there is a risk that the certificates are fraudulent and worthless, and that this fact will not be revealed until an event such as a coupon or maturity payment falls due.

This aspect of the custodian's responsibilities is usually detailed within the agreement between the account holder and the custodian; however, some custodians do not offer the receipt of physical certificates as part of the service that they provide, due to the risks involved.

17.5   CUSTODIAN SELECTION

For an STO wishing to set up one or many custodian relationships, there is a choice:

- set up direct relationships with CSDs or local custodians in all markets in which the STO is active;

- choose to have direct relationships with CSDs or local custodians only in the markets in which they are most active, whereas for markets in which the STO is less active and trading may be only occasional, they may choose to use a global custodian;
- opt to use a global custodian for all markets.

One consideration of course, is cost. In certain circumstances, it may be cheaper to set up and operate direct relationships with CSDs or local custodians, in comparison to say using a global custodian in all markets. Conversely, a global custodian may offer a premium service that an STO may consider operationally appealing.

The following criteria are typically used by an STO, in order to select a custodian:

- the custodian's credit rating (credit ratings will be described in Chapter 23)
  - o signifies the status and financial stability of the custodian as an organisation
- past performance
  - o levels and efficiency of services (listed in industry publications), for example
    - *STP* rates (as mentioned previously, STP is sought throughout the industry)
    - ability to process equity securities
    - ability to process debt securities
    - proficiency of cash management, for example
      - □ interest rates on cash balances
      - □ overdraft facilities
    - methods of processing corporate actions, for example
      - □ whether a default decision will be made in the case of an optional corporate action (refer to Chapter 26)
- cost of operating the service
  - o the cost of securities holdings
  - o the cost per settlement instruction
    - the cost per each type of settlement instruction, for example
      - □ a base charge for book-entry DvP settlement
      - □ a higher charge for cross border settlement
  - o the cost of non-STP (e.g. incomplete or incorrectly formatted instructions)
  - o whether volume discounts will be given if a number of the STO's offices use the same custodian
- ability to process multiple currencies
  - o this is provided within the ICSDs
  - o this is likely to be provided by global custodians
  - o this is less likely to be provided by a local custodian or an NCSD.

In the course of custodian selection, some STOs issue a document (known as a Request for Information) to likely custodians, containing questions regarding the services provided.

17.6   SETTLEMENT INSTRUCTION RELATED SERVICES

The following criteria are more specifically related to the custodian's capabilities regarding movements of securities and cash.

17.6.1   Method of Communication of Settlement Instructions

The settlement instruction communication method is an important consideration for the STO, as it has implications for security of messages and efficiency of operation. An STO is likely to select a custodian if the custodian's method of transmission is regarded as being adequately secure and compatible with the STO's communication capabilities.

If an STO is an existing user of an electronic settlement instruction communication method such as *S.W.I.F.T.*, it is clearly of benefit to the STO for any new custodian that it appoints to also use the S.W.I.F.T. network. This allows the STO to utilise existing operational practices to communicate with the new custodian, rather than having to introduce a new settlement instruction transmission method alongside the existing one.

As an example, a new operational practice may be necessary if the custodian has a proprietary mechanism for the communication of settlement instructions. In an automated environment, achieving STP would require the STO to develop an interface between its settlement system (responsible for generation of the instruction) and the custodian's proprietary communication mechanism. If the STO did not develop that interface (for whatever reason), settlement instructions would need to be input manually to the custodian's proprietary system.

Many STOs subscribe to S.W.I.F.T. for the purpose of settlement instruction transmission, and it is common to find that S.W.I.F.T. is an STO's preferred method of communication, on the basis that S.W.I.F.T. can be used globally by custodians. This enables an STO to operate a consistent and single method of settlement instruction transmission to all its custodians.

In the event of the normal communication link between an STO and its custodian becoming inoperative, the STO and the custodian need to agree upon back-up procedures, so as to ensure that settlement instructions are still sent by the STO and received by the custodian, within the necessary deadline. S.W.I.F.T. users are required to keep a spare communications line on standby, for use in such situations. In general, test keys (refer to Chapter 16) are used as a manual back-up in the event of an emergency.

Furthermore, should a real disaster befall the STO (e.g. the office is unusable due to fire or flooding), emergency measures will be required; this is commonly known as *disaster recovery* (DR). DR is a complete topic in its own right, but in summary involves the partial or complete duplication of the STO's live environment in order to maintain a presence in the marketplace, to complete outstanding contractual obligations and to sustain customer confidence.

17.6.2   Settlement Instruction Deadlines

The custodian will quote deadlines for the receipt of settlement instructions, relative to the value date of the required movement. Deadlines are likely to be earlier when transmitting instructions by a non-electronic mechanism, such as tested telex, that requires manual intervention (specifically checking of the test key and rekeying) by the custodian, compared with transmission via electronic means requiring no manual intervention.

Competing custodians may quote different deadlines for the receipt of settlement instructions by the same method.

17.6.3   Settlement Instruction Statuses

The current status of each settlement instruction is of vital importance to an STO, as it is a major mechanism by which an STO remains in control of its business. This is achieved through the monitoring of each stage in a settlement instruction's lifecycle, to reduce the chance of mismanagement resulting in financial loss.

An STO needs to know the various statuses applied by the custodian, the frequency of updating the instructions with statuses, and how the custodian intends to communicate statuses to the STO, whether electronically or non-electronically.

From an STP perspective, an STO will typically require settlement instruction statuses to be communicated electronically by the custodian, thereby facilitating the automatic update of the relevant trade within the settlement system.

Besides acknowledgement of receipt of settlement instructions, the minimum statuses that an STO would expect to receive are:

- for settlement instructions issued by the STO to the custodian
  - unmatched
    - including reason for failing to match
  - matched
  - settlement failure
    - including reason for failure
  - settlement completion
    - including specific information regarding the quantity of securities delivered or received, and the amount of cash paid or received
- for settlement instructions not issued by the STO to the custodian
  - advisory (for example, by a counterparty that believes it traded with the STO).

17.6.4   Settled Instructions

The detail of settled instructions, in terms of the quantity of securities delivered or received, and the amount of cash received or paid, is of paramount importance to the STO; the receipt of this information initiates the update of the STO's books and records. For example, where an instruction has settled fully, leaving no securities or cash outstanding with the counterparty, the relevant trade must be updated within the STO's settlement system to also reflect that the securities and cash have been exchanged, and that the trade is no longer outstanding with the counterparty.

The trade being updated (within the STO's books and records) in a timely and accurate manner in turn facilitates other activities being carried out against a background of correct and factual information. Such activities include:

- funding
- securities lending
- securities borrowing
- repoing

(each of these topics will be explored within subsequent chapters).

If the custodian can provide this information electronically, the STO can update its books and records automatically.

17.7   SECURITIES AND CASH HOLDINGS RELATED SERVICES

The following criteria relate to the custodian's holdings of securities and cash, on behalf of the STO.

17.7.1   Securities Lending and Borrowing

Some custodians provide a service whereby an account holder's securities can be lent to a borrower; this service is likely to be offered when a custodian has access to a large pool of its account holders' securities. Some account holders are prepared to lend their securities for additional income.

When an STO has sold securities that it cannot deliver to the buyer, some STOs are prepared to borrow securities; this enables the trade to settle with the buyer, but there will be a cost payable by the borrower.

Typically, the custodian acts as an agent between lenders and borrowers; the fee that is charged to the borrower is passed on to the lender, after deduction of the custodian's fee.

Some custodians provide a securities lending and borrowing service on a fully automatic basis, and on a request basis. This subject is described in Chapter 24.

An STO is typically interested to know whether the custodian can offer this service, and if so, the terms under which it operates.

17.7.2   Cash Borrowing Arrangements

The way in which the custodian allows its account holders to operate their cash accounts is crucially important to efficient and cost-effective settlement.

Typically, an STO needs to borrow cash in order to pay for purchases of securities. Some STOs borrow cash in anticipation of settlement occurring on the value date (and have that cash paid into their account at the custodian), while others borrow cash after settlement has occurred at the custodian. Generically, a custodian will not allow an STO to incur a cash overdraft as a result of securities settlement, unless the STO has sufficient cash or *collateral* (normally securities held by the custodian from previously settled purchases) against which the cash borrowing can be made. The collateral acts as a safeguard for the custodian, in that if the STO fails to repay an overdraft, the collateral can be sold to raise the cash amount owed to the custodian.

In addition, the STO will have a credit line or overdraft limit with the custodian, but that limit is typically only usable to the extent that the STO has collateral to support it.

Different custodians operate cash accounts for their account holders on different bases, for example:

* borrowing cash versus collateral up to an agreed credit line, where the credit line is only good up to the current value of the collateral in the account (collateral can be securities or cash);
* borrowing cash versus collateral held within a dedicated collateral account only (i.e. unless recently received securities are moved from a trading account into a collateral account, those securities will not contribute towards the collateral value for cash borrowing purposes);
* borrowing cash versus the STO's credit rating (the extent of the credit line is unknown by the STO, the STO being notified whenever the custodian calculates that more collateral is required);
* borrowing cash from the account holder's external bank, where the custodian allows only intra-day cash balances (within a credit limit) and the end-of-day cash balance becomes the external bank's responsibility.

Unless an STO understands the method of operation of its cash accounts at its custodians, settlement failure may well result. The STO will not only incur a financial cost, but may also earn a reputation for trading beyond its means, or of being inefficient.

17.7.3   Rates of Interest on Cash Balances

Following settlement of trades, an STO typically expects to be overdrawn at the custodian (unless funds had been paid into the STO's account as a result of cash borrowing from another source), as a result of a greater value of purchases settling, compared with sales. Occasionally, an STO may have a credit balance, where a greater value of sales had settled, compared with purchases.

Whether overdrawn or in credit at the custodian, the STO needs to know the basis of calculation, on which rates of interest will be charged by or received from the custodian, for each of the currencies that the custodian processes. Clearly, the STO hopes for competitive interest rates from the custodian.

17.7.4   Statements of Securities Holdings

As a result of settlement instructions settling, the quantity of securities held by the custodian for the STO will change. STOs normally require their custodians to issue updated statements of securities holdings including all movements since the close of the previous statement, for each of the STO's accounts with each custodian (e.g. main account and safe custody account), on a daily basis and by an electronic medium.

This facilitates automated reconciliation by the STO, between its own books and records and those of the custodian, without delay.

17.7.5   Statements of Cash Balances

An STO's cash account with a custodian is usually affected by:

- daily
    - ○ settlement instructions settling
- periodically
    - ○ income on securities holdings
    - ○ interest on cash balances
    - ○ custody fees (the cost of the custodian holding securities on the STO's behalf)
    - ○ service charges (for example, stock borrowing fees)

and as for securities holdings, statements of cash balances, with all relevant movements from the close of the previous statement, are usually required on a daily basis, electronically. This makes possible the automatic and timely reconciliation by the STO of its books and records versus the custodian's records.

17.7.6   Corporate Actions

When an event occurs which relates to an STO's securities holding, for which there may well be a benefit attached (e.g. a *dividend* on an equity), the custodian is normally the recipient of the benefit, but not the owner.

An STO with a securities holding on which a dividend (for example) is payable is entitled to the benefit. The STO expects the custodian to collect the dividend on its behalf, and to credit the STO with the value of the dividend on the dividend payment date.

Corporate actions of various types demand different actions by the STO. Some corporate actions give the owner an option to receive, for instance, securities or cash. In this case, the STO would be interested to know how the custodian deals with such situations, for example, whether the custodian would, by default, opt for securities in the event that the STO failed to advise the custodian by a deadline specified by the custodian. This topic is explored in Chapter 26.

Once the STO has decided to select a specific custodian, the method of operation between the two parties will be detailed within a Service Level Agreement (SLA).

17.8   COMPARISON OF CUSTODIAN SERVICES

Table 17.3 shows a brief comparison of the services offered by typical NCSDs and ICSDs, in order to highlight some similarities and differences.

Historically and in general terms, NCSDs have been geared more towards settlement of local equities rather than bonds, government bonds often being settled by the relevant central bank or a different NCSD in the same country. Conversely, ICSDs have historically been geared towards the settlement of bonds, rather than equities.

Recently, the merging of some NCSDs with ICSDs is blurring the distinctions mentioned above. Clearstream International was formed in 2000 following the merger of the

Table 17.3

	Typical NCSDs	Typical ICSDs
Securities coverage	National and (limited) international equities, and warrants. (Government bonds often processed by a central bank)	International equities, Government, corporate and convertible bonds, and warrants
Securities custody capability	Yes	Yes
Settlement instruction communication method	Proprietary, S.W.I.F.T.	Proprietary, S.W.I.F.T., telex
Settlement instruction statuses available	Yes	Yes
Settlement processing period	Overnight plus intra-day	Overnight plus intra-day
Automatic Securities Lending & Borrowing	Rarely available	Automatic and upon request
Accepted currencies	Local currency (rarely other major currencies such as USD and EUR)	Numerous currencies
Cash Borrowing Arrangements	Arrangements made with a 'payment bank'	Ability to borrow cash versus collateral up to agreed credit line
Cash Balances	Overnight cash balances assumed by payment bank	Overnight balances allowed; rates vary according to currency

NCSD Deutsche Borse Clearing (Frankfurt) with the ICSD Cedel International (Luxembourg). The French NCSD Sicovam was renamed Euroclear France following the merger with the ICSD Euroclear (Brussels). Consequently, the ICSDs' securities coverage has been extended to include the direct handling of international equities (in addition to the many existing links to NCSDs, as mentioned previously).

The characteristics listed emphasise the necessity for those using such services to understand how each custodian operates, if operational efficiency is sought.

17.9 SUMMARY

The safety of an STO's (and other account holders') securities and cash depend upon the care taken and vigilance practised by their custodians.

Furthermore, custodians play a major role in an STO achieving its objectives of STP, remaining in control of its assets (through the reporting provided by custodians), processing increasing trade volumes and minimising risk and costs.

18
Pre-Value Date Settlement
Instruction Statuses

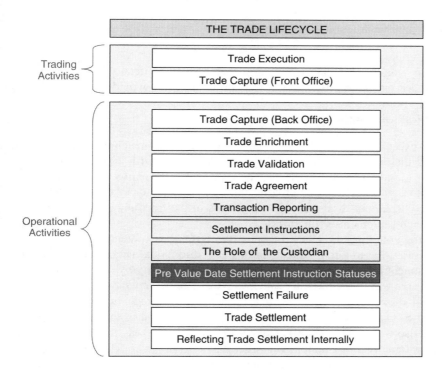

18.1 INTRODUCTION

Following the transmission of a settlement instruction to and the acknowledgement of receipt by the custodian, the next steps in the trade lifecycle are:

- the custodian's attempt to match the STO's instruction with the counterparty's instruction;
- the attachment of the current status of the instruction;
- the investigation and resolution of non-matching instructions;
- the updating of the current status within the STO's books and records.

Pre-value date settlement instruction matching is a very important component of the trade lifecycle, as in most cases *settlement* (the actual exchange of securities and cash) cannot take place without it.

Furthermore, *STP* can be achieved where the detail of the seller's and buyer's settlement instructions match first time, on or very shortly after trade date. Although STP is the objective, the reality is that a large number of settlement instructions typically remain unmatched at the end of the trade date; the reasons for this will be explained throughout this chapter.

18.2   TRADE MATCHING AND SETTLEMENT INSTRUCTION MATCHING

The processes of:

- matching trade details shortly after trade execution (as described in Chapter 14), including trade matching with other STOs (for example via Trax) and trade affirmation (for example via Oasys Global), and
- matching settlement instructions at custodians

are clearly very similar exercises.

Superficially, it would seem that achieving a match of trade details is precisely the same as achieving a match of settlement instruction details; this would very much be a desirable state of affairs.

However, the following must be considered.

- not all trades executed by an STO may be subject to trade matching; this may be the case where the counterparty is not required to trade match (in a regulatory sense) or chooses not to subscribe to a trade matching or trade affirmation mechanism. If a trade is executed with such a counterparty, the first opportunity to discover whether the counterparty agrees or disagrees with the details of the trade may well be through attempts to match settlement instructions.
- settlement instructions may be alleged against the STO by a (potential) counterparty who does not subscribe to a trade matching or trade affirmation mechanism; again the issue of a settlement instruction by that counterparty may be the very first occasion that the operations area within the STO is made aware that a trade may have been executed.
- where a match of trade detail has been achieved through trade matching or trade affirmation, an STO's settlement instruction may be unmatched at the custodian; this situation can arise where there are efficiency differences in the way that the seller and buyer operate internally. For example, the seller may operate on an STP basis, whereas the buyer may operate entirely manually and wait until the day prior to value date before issuing its instruction.

All of which can result in numerous non-matching settlement instructions.

18.3   SETTLEMENT INSTRUCTION STATUSES (PRE-VALUE DATE)

When an STO issues settlement instructions to its custodian, generically there are three main statuses that can be applied prior to value date, namely:

- matched
- unmatched
- advisory.

The following describes how such statuses occur. Note that in each case, in order to aid the reader's understanding, the focus is primarily on the settlement instruction status from the perspective of the STO, rather than the STO's counterparty.

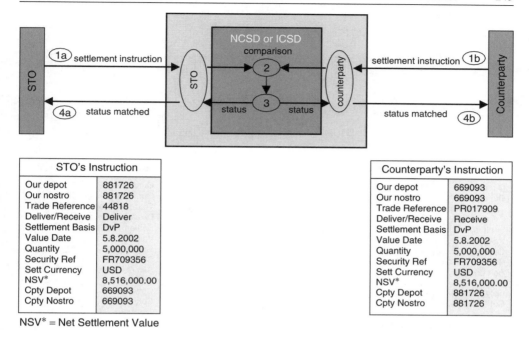

STO's Instruction	
Our depot	881726
Our nostro	881726
Trade Reference	44818
Deliver/Receive	Deliver
Settlement Basis	DvP
Value Date	5.8.2002
Quantity	5,000,000
Security Ref	FR709356
Sett Currency	USD
NSV*	8,516,000.00
Cpty Depot	669093
Cpty Nostro	669093

Counterparty's Instruction	
Our depot	669093
Our nostro	669093
Trade Reference	PR017909
Deliver/Receive	Receive
Settlement Basis	DvP
Value Date	5.8.2002
Quantity	5,000,000
Security Ref	FR709356
Sett Currency	USD
NSV*	8,516,000.00
Cpty Depot	881726
Cpty Nostro	881726

NSV* = Net Settlement Value

Figure 18.1   Pre-value date settlement instruction statuses: matched instructions

18.3.1   Matched Settlement Instructions

Figure 18.1 depicts the ideal sequence of events, resulting in an immediate match of settlement instructions.

Steps 1a and 1b: the STO and the counterparty transmit their settlement instructions to the CSD very shortly (e.g. within 60 minutes) after trade execution. The detail of the instructions sent by both the STO and the counterparty are displayed in Figure 18.1. Note that the majority of the components are identical, some are opposite (deliver and receive, and the depot and nostro account numbers), and one component is completely different (the trade references, where a match would not be attempted as they are not considered critical matching items).

Step 2: the CSD compares the detail of the two instructions to find that they match in all respects.

Step 3: the CSD applies a status of 'matched' to both the STO's and the counterparty's instructions.

Steps 4a and 4b: the STO and the counterparty are advised of the current status of their respective instructions and update the relevant trade record within their books and records, with the status.

Instructions that match immediately require no investigation, therefore not utilising the STO's valuable manpower.

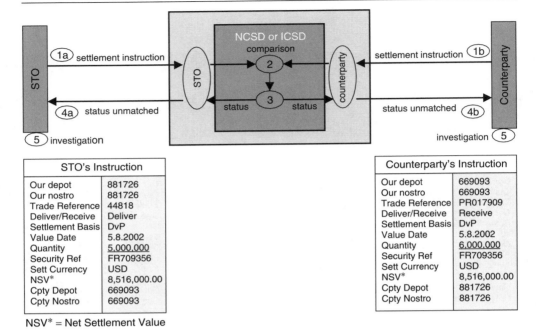

NSV* = Net Settlement Value

Figure 18.2   Pre-value date settlement instruction statuses: unmatched instructions (1)

18.3.2   Unmatched Settlement Instructions (1)

Figure 18.2 represents a sequence of events resulting in the STO having an unmatched settlement instruction (where both the STO and the counterparty have issued instructions).

Steps 1a and 1b: the STO and the counterparty transmit their settlement instructions to the CSD very shortly (e.g. within 60 minutes) after trade execution.

Step 2: the CSD compares the detail of the two instructions to find that they do not match in all respects, as the quantities of securities differ.

Step 3: the CSD applies a status to both the STO's and the counterparty's instructions:

- to the issuer of the settlement instruction in each case, the status is 'unmatched';
- to the counterparty in each case, the status is 'advisory'.

Steps 4a and 4b: the STO is informed that its instruction is 'unmatched', and is also informed of the 'advisory' (instruction alleged against the STO by the counterparty). Likewise, the counterparty is advised that its instruction is 'unmatched', and is also informed of the 'advisory' (the instruction alleged against the counterparty by the STO). For both the STO and its counterparty, their respective trade records will be updated within their books and records.

Step 5: because the settlement instruction status is unmatched and an advisory has been received, the STO needs to investigate whether it is they or the counterparty that are correct, as a matter of urgency. (Investigation and resolution of unmatched instructions are described later in this chapter.)

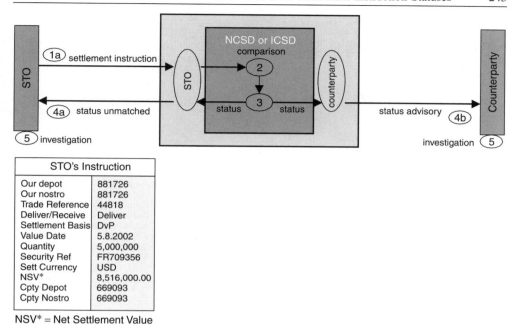

STO's Instruction

Our depot	881726
Our nostro	881726
Trade Reference	44818
Deliver/Receive	Deliver
Settlement Basis	DvP
Value Date	5.8.2002
Quantity	5,000,000
Security Ref	FR709356
Sett Currency	USD
NSV*	8,516,000.00
Cpty Depot	669093
Cpty Nostro	669093

NSV* = Net Settlement Value

Figure 18.3   Pre-value date settlement instruction statuses: unmatched instructions (2)

18.3.3   Unmatched Settlement Instructions (2)

Figure 18.3 depicts a sequence of events resulting in the STO's settlement instruction being unmatched with the counterparty (where only the STO has issued an instruction).

Step 1a: the STO transmits its settlement instruction to the CSD.

Step 2: the CSD attempts to compare the detail of the STO's instruction with the counterparty's instruction, to find that no equivalent instruction has been received from that counterparty.

Step 3: the CSD applies a status:

• to the issuer of the settlement instruction (the STO), the status is 'unmatched';
• to the counterparty, the status is 'advisory'.

Step 4: the STO and the counterparty are advised of the current status of the STO's instruction and the STO updates the relevant trade record within its books and records, with the status.

Step 5: because the settlement instruction status is unmatched, the STO needs to investigate whether the counterparty intends to match the STO's instruction, or not, as a matter of urgency. Having received an advisory status, the counterparty should also be investigating whether it recognises the trade or not, and if so, it should issue a settlement instruction subsequently.

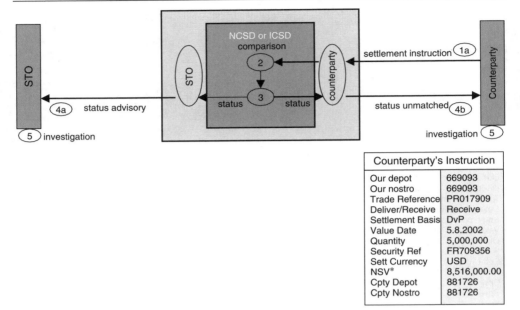

NSV* = Net Settlement Value

Figure 18.4   Pre-value date settlement instruction statuses: advisory instructions

18.3.4   Advisory Settlement Instructions

Figure 18.4 depicts a sequence of events resulting in the counterparty's settlement instruction being alleged against the STO (where only the counterparty has issued an instruction).

Step 1a: the counterparty transmits its settlement instruction to the CSD.

Step 2: the CSD attempts to compare the detail of the counterparty's instruction with the STO's instruction, to find that no equivalent instruction has been received from the STO.

Step 3: the CSD applies a status:

* to the issuer of the settlement instruction (the counterparty), the status is 'unmatched';
* to the STO, the status is 'advisory'.

Step 4: the STO and the counterparty are advised of the current status of the counterparty's instruction and the counterparty (only) updates the relevant trade record within its books and records, with the status.

Step 5: because the settlement instruction status is advisory, the STO needs to investigate whether it recognises the trade and will subsequently match the counterparty's instruction, or not, as a matter of urgency. Having received an unmatched status, the counterparty should also be undertaking an investigation to ascertain whether the STO intends to match the instruction, or not.

Notes:

* it is common for a settlement instruction to have two statuses, where the first status was unmatched, followed by a status of matched (for example, once the counterparty issues its instruction).

- a settlement instruction issued by an STO that has a status of matched will revert to unmatched (from the STO's perspective) if the counterparty cancels its instruction (for whatever reason).
- a different set of statuses are likely to be applied on and after value date to those described above (this will be covered in Chapters 19 and 20).

18.4   INVESTIGATION AND RESOLUTION OF UNMATCHED AND ADVISORY STATUSES

Having received settlement instruction statuses prior to value date, other than matched, each of the statuses should be investigated and resolved immediately. To delay investigation and resolution beyond a reasonable timeframe can:

- cause direct monetary loss to the STO, or
- provide the counterparty with a case for claiming compensation for any resultant loss it incurs.

However, in a situation where an STO has many such instructions to investigate, priority is given to those instructions with an imminent value date and/or high monetary value.

Consideration must also be given to whether the trade confirmation or trade matching processes resulted in agreement of trade details with the counterparty. Clearly, if a trade was successfully matched through, say, electronic trade matching on trade date, but now (on the day following trade date) the STO's instruction status is unmatched, the likelihood of eventually achieving a match of settlement instructions is expected to be greater.

STOs usually apply many resources to the investigation and resolution of non-matching instructions for very good reasons. The STO's P&L can be affected directly as a result of an investigation and resolution of a non-matching item, and therefore the quicker such discrepancies are resolved, the 'truer' the P&L becomes. The greater the period between trade execution and the finally agreed terms of a trade, the greater the likely impact on the P&L. To a large extent, minimising these uncertainties is in the hands of the STO itself. Careful recording of trade detail at the time of trade execution will go a long way to reducing the number of real problems that affect P&L. This in turn will reduce the level of resourcing (and associated costs) necessary to conduct such investigations.

In general, of great concern to the STO is whether the counterparty recognises the trade at all and whether the STO recognises the counterparty's trade at all (from the STO's perspective, unmatched and advisory statuses). It is still a concern, however, for the STO to resolve those trades that the counterparty recognises, but where there is some discrepancy (i.e. status of unmatched).

In order to aid understanding, each of these statuses will be viewed primarily from the standpoint of the STO, rather than the counterparty.

18.4.1   Unmatched Instructions (1)

A status of unmatched simply indicates that the instruction is not matched by the counterparty. However, the receipt of an advisory with the majority of the details being the same is likely to indicate that the trade is recognised by the STO's counterparty, but the details differ slightly.

From the list of trade components that typically constitute a settlement instruction, the majority are the responsibility of the front office, while others are the responsibility of the Middle/Back office (Table 18.1).

Table 18.1

Settlement instruction component	Trade detail from which settlement instruction component is derived	Primary responsibility
Depot account no.	Trading company	Front and/or Back office
Nostro account no.	Trading company	Front and/or Back office
Trade reference	Not applicable	Not applicable
Deliver/receive	Purchase or sale	Front office
Settlement basis	DvP or FoP	Front office
Value date	Value date	Front office
Quantity	Quantity	Front office
Security reference	Security	Front office
Settlement currency	Settlement currency	Front office
NSV	Price	Front office
Counterparty depot	Counterparty	Cpty = front office; Cpty a/c = BO*
Counterparty nostro	Counterparty	Cpty = front office; Cpty a/c = BO*

*Changes to the counterparty with whom the trade was executed are normally a front office responsibility; however, if a change is required to the counterparty's account number at its custodian, or if the counterparty wishes to settle at a different custodian (to the normal default from static data), this is typically regarded as a middle/back office responsibility.

The trader originates each trade, thereby affecting that trader's P&L. Any amendment or cancellation of trade components that affect P&L are typically actioned by the trader; it is not normal to find that back office personnel are allowed to change trade components 'owned' by the trader. Conversely, not all settlement instruction components are owned by the trader. Therefore when an amendment to a settlement instruction is required, a decision needs to be made as to whether the trader amends the original trade in the trading system, resulting in an automatically amended trade within the settlement system, or whether the amendment should occur in the settlement system only.

When an STO's settlement instruction is given a status of unmatched and an advisory is received with very similar details, the reason for the failure to match will be apparent (e.g. different quantity or value date). If the component is 'owned' by the trader, the person who is handling the unmatched item will need to advise the trader (or middle office or trade support personnel working on the trader's behalf) without delay. The trader needs to decide whether his detail is correct, or whether the counterparty is correct. This may necessitate listening to the dealing tapes, for which the STO's compliance officer is usually required to become involved.

If the STO's trader decides that his trade detail, as captured originally in the trading system, is correct, the person handling the unmatched item typically telephones his equivalent at the counterparty to advise that the STO's trader believes he is correct. Providing the counterparty's trader agrees, the counterparty will transmit an amended or replacement settlement instruction; this should result in a match of instructions.

Alternatively, if the STO's trader has captured the original trade detail incorrectly, the trader will need to amend the original trade within the trading system. This will be passed through the interface with the settlement system and the equivalent trade within the settlement system will be updated automatically. An amended trade confirmation may need to be issued, but an amended or replacement settlement instruction will definitely need to be transmitted to the custodian; this should result in matched instructions with the counterparty. From the perspective of the STO's trader, the amendment is likely to have impacted his P&L, particularly if the trade quantity or trade price were amended.

18.4.2   Unmatched Instructions (2)

A status of unmatched without having received an advisory instruction issued by the counterparty could be resolved as follows:

- the counterparty recognises the trade but has yet to issue its instruction;
- the counterparty does not recognise the trade.

When the STO first receives an unmatched status for its instruction, a telephone call to the counterparty's settlement department should confirm whether the counterparty recognises the trade, or not.

Where the counterparty does recognise the trade, the STO needs only to await its instruction to be matched. Where the counterparty does not recognise the trade, the investigation to be undertaken by the STO internally is to ascertain with which counterparty the trade was in fact executed. This may require listening to the dealing tapes and:

- if the investigation reveals that the trade was in fact executed with a different counterparty, the trade will need to be amended within the trading system which must then pass the amended trade to the settlement system, thereby amending the original trade within the settlement system and in turn issuing either an amended instruction, or a cancellation instruction plus a new instruction, following which a match should be achieved. Note that the STO may have received an advisory from the true counterparty, which should tell the STO the answer to the problem. Under these circumstances, the STO's original trade will need to be amended (as described previously) in order to issue the correct settlement instruction and to ensure that the STO's books and records are completely accurate;
- if the investigation reveals that the trade was in fact recorded against the true counterparty, the STO's trader will need to contact the counterparty's trader to confirm that the counterparty recognises the trade, and that they will be matching the STO's instruction.

18.4.3   Advisory Instructions

When an STO receives an advisory status [i.e. a (potential) counterparty has issued a settlement instruction, for which the STO has not issued a matching instruction], from the STO's perspective:

- the STO recognises the trade but has yet to issue its instruction;
- the STO does not recognise the trade.

The investigation will reveal whether in fact the STO did execute the trade; if so, the STO should input its instruction without delay, but if not, it must be communicated to the counterparty as soon as possible.

18.5   SETTLEMENT INSTRUCTION MATCHING TOLERANCES

At some custodians, the net settlement value of a pair of settlement instructions will be regarded as matched where either:

- all components match exactly, or
- all components, with the exception of the NSV, match exactly, and the NSVs of the two instructions differ by no more than a publicised cash amount.

This tolerance is designed to avoid small cash differences forcing settlement instruction amendments (or cancellation of the original instruction followed by a replacement instruction), in order to achieve a match of instructions.

Discrepancies that give rise to small cash differences occur through the seller's and buyer's NSVs being derived differently, for example:

- because of price decimal rounding differences
    - for instance, seller has a price of 97.9375, buyer has a price of 97.937
- because of accrued interest calculation differences
    - for instance, seller has used a divisor of 360, buyer has used a divisor of 365.

In Euroclear, the tolerance limit is USD 25.00, meaning that the payer's and the receiver's cash values can differ by up to this figure, or currency equivalent; under such circumstances, settlement occurs against the seller's NSV.

Within Crest, participants can opt for 'tolerance matching', where cash differences of up to GBP 10.00, USD 15.00 or EUR 15.00 will result in settlement against the seller's NSV, providing both seller and buyer have opted for tolerance matching. Where only one of the parties has opted for tolerance matching, such differences will be applied to that participant's cash value in order to achieve a match.

18.6   THE STO'S RISK

The following is stated in order to re-emphasise the importance of traders and market makers within STOs taking care to ensure they record trades accurately, under all circumstances. Although the examples point to potential erroneous, immoral and illegal actions by the STO's counterparties, it is incorrect to assume that these types of events are common.

Whenever a trade is executed, but the trade is recorded against the incorrect counterparty (although this is not realised at the time), and the STO issues a settlement instruction against that counterparty, the STO risks that the incorrect counterparty will match the STO's instruction, despite the fact that the incorrect counterparty has not executed the trade. Because the incorrect counterparty sees an advisory settlement instruction (and if able to derive the price of the trade through the information contained on the advisory), the incorrect counterparty could decide to issue a matching receipt instruction, for instance, where the price of the security has increased since trade date, with the intention of gaining securities cheaply (but illegally, as the incorrect counterparty will have no record of the contractual commitment). Although the STO should see an advisory instruction input by the correct counterparty, there is no guarantee that the correct counterparty will issue an instruction on trade date.

Similarly, a trade may be captured against the correct counterparty, but if a mistake is made in recording trade components such as quantity or price, or in the calculation of accrued interest on a bond trade, a risk to the STO is that its settlement instruction will be matched by the counterparty.

Some STOs rely upon their counterparties to provide correct NSVs; particularly in the area of accrued interest calculation, some organisations will amend the NSV of their settlement instruction because the counterparty tells them it's incorrect. This is an example of an STO's P&L being reliant upon its counterparty, when clearly the P&L should be under the STO's own control.

Creating a culture within the STO of being operationally efficient, from the moment a trade is captured, will minimise such risk of losses.

18.7   METHODS OF COMMUNICATING STATUSES FROM CUSTODIANS

As mentioned in previous chapters, many STOs use electronic communication links (e.g. S.W.I.F.T.) to transmit settlement instructions to their custodians in the various financial centres around the globe. Such links are typically two-way, thereby facilitating the electronic receipt of settlement instruction statuses from the custodian.

In the case of S.W.I.F.T., statuses are communicated by specific message types, namely:

* MT548 for instructions issued by an organisation to its custodian, and
* MT578 for advisory instructions issued by the (potential) counterparty.

Where an STO uses a custodian's proprietary system for the communication of settlement instructions, statuses are typically communicated via that same method.

If settlement instructions are communicated by manual means, such as by tested telex, statuses may be communicated by the custodian via telex, or by telephone.

18.8   UPDATING THE STO'S BOOKS AND RECORDS

The historic and current status of each settlement instruction is of vital importance to an STO, as it is a major mechanism by which an STO remains in control of its business.

Having the full history of an individual trade and its associated settlement instruction allows quick and efficient investigation (such as when investigating discrepancies when reconciling internal versus external positions). Reconstructing the full history of a trade can take a considerable length of time when the information is not consolidated.

STOs typically require each trade within their books and records to have a full history of settlement instruction events, including the time and date:

* the settlement instruction was transmitted by the STO;
* the settlement instruction was received by the custodian;
* the first status (e.g. unmatched) was applied by the custodian;
* subsequent statuses (e.g. matched) were applied by the custodian.

The link between the settlement instruction at the custodian and the relevant trade within the settlement system is the trade reference number (in an automated environment the settlement instruction is typically generated directly from the trade, therefore in most cases the settlement instruction reference number will be identical to the trade reference number).

From an STP perspective, an STO will typically require settlement instruction statuses to be communicated electronically by the custodian, thereby facilitating the automatic update of the relevant trade within the settlement system.

Settlement instructions transmitted without the settlement system trade reference number are very unlikely to be automatically updated within the STO's settlement system, unless specific action is taken. Examples of this are:

- manually input instructions, and
- instructions issued under *power of attorney* by a trading platform or an Electronic Communications Network (ECN), on behalf of the STO

for which the settlement instruction reference will need to be associated with the relevant trade reference, in order to update the trade automatically within the settlement system.

Following the updating of individual trades with the current settlement instruction status, some STOs drive their daily investigations of unmatched instructions from the information held within the settlement system (whilst other STOs operate directly from reports provided by their custodians).

Furthermore, statistics can be produced concerning the quantity of unmatched and advisory trades in a given period, compared with the number in a prior period. Additionally, reporting of all unmatched trades within two days of value date, due to settle in a geographical area (e.g. South East Asia) and at multiple custodians, should be possible. Management reporting providing much useful information can be gleaned from settlement instruction statuses, and used to improve operational efficiency within the STO.

18.9   SUMMARY

STOs give great emphasis to the resolution of non-matching settlement instructions, as without matching instructions settlement cannot (usually) occur.

Historically, the primary causes of non-matching instructions have been:

- inaccurate trade recording, and
- delayed transmission of settlement instructions

requiring vast amounts of manpower to investigate and resolve discrepancies.

Looking forward, as *settlement cycles* continue to reduce across the globe and particularly in a T+1 environment, there will simply not be sufficient time to investigate the sheer quantity of historic unmatched and alleged settlement instructions. Timely and risk-free settlement will depend upon accurate trade recording and timely settlement instruction transmission by both parties to the trade, requiring that the entire trading community operates on an STP basis.

19
Settlement Failure

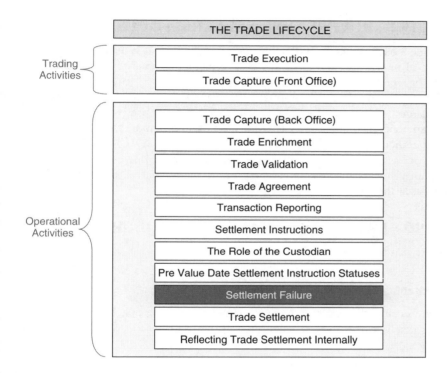

THE TRADE LIFECYCLE

Trading Activities
- Trade Execution
- Trade Capture (Front Office)

Operational Activities
- Trade Capture (Back Office)
- Trade Enrichment
- Trade Validation
- Trade Agreement
- Transaction Reporting
- Settlement Instructions
- The Role of the Custodian
- Pre Value Date Settlement Instruction Statuses
- Settlement Failure
- Trade Settlement
- Reflecting Trade Settlement Internally

19.1 INTRODUCTION

Having reached the value date, a trade will either settle successfully, or it will fail to settle (although partial settlement may be possible) on the due date and settle later.

Trade settlement is the act of buyer and seller (or their respective custodians) exchanging securities and cash, on or after value date, in accordance with the contractual commitment made upon trade execution on trade date. Settlement is successful when the seller is able to deliver the securities and the buyer is able to pay the cash owing.

Historically, a common occurrence in some markets was to find that a minority of trades had not settled months, or in some cases years, after value date, typically because the seller was awaiting delivery of the physical certificates from their purchase and could not therefore deliver the certificates in order to settle the subsequent sale.

In the modern era, because settlement is increasingly effected by electronic *book entry*, the rate of successful settlement is also improving. In some marketplaces, it is normal (even mandatory) for all trades to settle on their value date, and whenever there is a settlement failure, the authorities may impose penalties on those who cause the failure.

However, in other markets no such regime exists, resulting in the seller not being paid the cash amount due and the buyer not receiving the securities purchased, until the seller has the securities to deliver and the buyer has the cash to pay, whether on value date or later. In these markets, those who cause settlement failure will suffer the cost of failure.

19.2 BUYERS' AND SELLERS' FOCUS

In order to provide a background to settlement success or failure, it is useful to appreciate the focus of typical buyers and sellers of any goods, including securities, relevant to the cash being paid or received.

When buying goods, the buyer is normally concerned about both the goods being purchased (to ensure they are of good quality, whether for direct use by the buyer or for resale), but is also concerned about the cash (not wishing to pay more than the goods are worth, or to pay earlier than the due date).

When selling goods, however, the seller is usually no longer interested in the goods (unless their quality means that the buyer may reject them), but is solely focused on receiving the cash at the earliest opportunity.

19.3 CAUSES OF SETTLEMENT FAILURE

Settlement failure can be caused by a variety of factors.

19.3.1 Non-matching Settlement Instructions

Settlement failure occurs whenever settlement instructions are not matched by the settlement processing deadline for a given value date, at the relevant custodian (CSD). The causes of this include:

- instructions issued but not received by the custodian;
- instructions received by the custodian after the custodian's deadline;
- instructions remaining unmatched on and after value date;
- instructions remaining advisory on and after value date.

19.3.2 Insufficient Securities

Where settlement instructions are matched by the time of the custodian's deadline, and value date has been reached, delivery of the securities cannot occur if the deliverer has none of the specific securities in the relevant account at the custodian.

This situation arises from two circumstances:

- one or many deliveries by the selling counterparty to the STO have failed (thereby preventing onward delivery of the STO's sale);
- the trader has sold 'short', resulting in a negative trading position.

Where an STO has more than one account at a custodian, there may be a sufficient number of securities within one or a number of accounts to complete the delivery; however, if the STO instructs for delivery from the account that holds no (or insufficient) securities, settlement will fail. Custodians are required by account holders to follow instructions only from the account holder, therefore, the account holder will need to instruct the custodian to transfer the securities from one account to another, in this scenario, if settlement is not to fail.

Where an STO has some, but not all, of the necessary quantity of securities held within its account at the custodian, settlement of the partial quantity of securities may occur, providing agreement is reached between buyer and seller. When partial settlement occurs, it is normal for a pro-rata amount of cash to be settled. Following partial settlement, the remaining quantity of securities and cash amount remain open and will be settled as soon as possible.

19.3.3   Insufficient Cash, Collateral or Credit Line

Where settlement instructions are matched by the time of the custodian's deadline, and value date has been reached, payment of cash for the receipt of securities cannot normally occur if the account holder has insufficient cash, *collateral* or credit line (i.e. overdraft facility) at the custodian. This topic is explored in Chapter 20.

Where settlement fails for this reason, as a safeguard to the seller, the seller's securities will not be removed from his account at the custodian, until such time as the buyer is able to settle; note that this is only the case where settlement is due to occur on a DvP basis.

Where the buyer has some, but not all of the necessary cash available, partial settlement will not occur; partial settlement is driven from a securities (rather than a cash) perspective.

19.4   IMPACT OF SETTLEMENT FAILURE

The impact of settlement failure can be viewed from the securities and/or from the cash perspective.

With regard to the securities, legal ownership changes on trade execution, regardless of the date at which settlement occurs. Therefore, from a seller's perspective, ownership is not prolonged because of a failure to settle the sale on value date, and from a buyer's perspective, ownership is not delayed due to settlement failure.

With regard to the cash, it is important to note that in the event of settlement failure, the net settlement value (NSV) of a trade is not recalculated. For example, the sale proceeds of, say, EUR 10 million due to a seller of a trade will not alter if the trade fails to settle for, say, one week. In other words, the seller will receive EUR 10 million, whether the trade settles on value date, or at any later point in time. Even in the case of a bond that accrues interest, such as a straight bond, the accrued interest calculation is geared to *value date*, not *settlement date*, and therefore the NSV remains the same regardless of the settlement date.

The impact of failing to settle a trade on time is dependent upon the seller's or buyer's particular circumstances.

19.4.1   Selling

Focus on Cash

A seller of securities is very eager to settle the trade on value date, as this results in the sale proceeds being received at the earliest opportunity, thereby maximising the use of the incoming cash.

The first step in capitalising on this situation (after having achieved a match of settlement instructions with the counterparty) is for the seller to be in a position to deliver the securities on value date. Assuming this is the case, when value date arrives settlement should occur, providing the buyer has the cash.

Following trade settlement, the seller's cash account will have been credited at the custodian, at which point the seller may decide that this cash could be used for example:

• to fund new purchases of securities,
• to offset an existing overdraft (at the custodian or at another nostro), thereby reducing or nullifying debit interest, or
• to lend in the money market, thereby earning credit interest.

In any case, the seller will be maximising the use of the incoming funds.

The impact of settlement failure from a seller's perspective, therefore, is the loss of cash interest; this interest loss is directly detrimental to the STO. To provide an idea of scale, the cash interest for one day on EUR 10 million, at a rate of 5%, is approximately EUR 1,400.00, and the cash interest for seven days on USD 50 million at 5% is approximately USD 48,000.00. When compared with the amount of profit an STO may make on a single trade, these are significant amounts of cash to lose.

If the seller is able to deliver the securities on or after value date, but the buyer is unable to pay, the seller is usually able to claim compensation from the buyer, for the loss of cash interest, on the basis that the seller should not be penalised and the buyer should not benefit from a settlement failure caused by the buyer. Such claims for compensation are commonly referred to as *interest claims*, and in some marketplaces (e.g. *ISMA*), recommendations have been set for the minimum amount claimable and the deadline by which such claims should be issued to the counterparty.

Focus on Securities

An STO, when selling securities to an institutional client, typically focuses on ensuring that the securities are delivered to the client on or shortly after value date, as part of the service the STO provides to the client.

Where the STO has sold those securities out of its existing inventory of securities which are being held by the STO at its custodian (as a result of prior settled purchases), there should be no reason why settlement of the STO's sale should not occur on value date, assuming the buyer has the cash. Alternatively, if the STO has bought the securities in order to satisfy the sale to the institutional client, where the seller has failed to deliver the securities to the STO, the securities cannot be delivered to the institutional client, unless the STO borrows the securities (see Section 19.6).

In rare circumstances, the buyer may decide to force the seller to deliver the securities (see Section 19.7).

19.4.2 Buying

Focus on Securities

In a situation where an STO has bought securities:

• without selling those securities on, or
• selling those securities for a later value date than the purchase value date

failure of the seller to deliver the securities to the STO on the value date will not cause a problem as the securities are not needed by the STO on that date (unless the STO intends to lend or repo the securities). However, the fact that the STO has not had to pay for the purchase on value date means that the funds need not have been borrowed by the STO, thereby potentially saving the STO the interest on that cash, until such time as settlement does occur. This interest saving is directly beneficial to the STO (commonly known as a 'positive fail').

Alternatively, in a situation where an STO has bought securities and sold them for the same value date, the STO will receive securities and pay cash (on or after value date), then immediately deliver the securities and receive the sale proceeds. In this situation, from the STO's perspective there is no detrimental impact, other than where the counterparty who is buying the securities from the STO needs the securities urgently, in which case the buyer may decide to enforce delivery of the securities (see Section 19.7).

Focus on Cash

Should the buyer be unable to pay for a purchase at the time the seller is able to deliver the securities on or after value date, because the buyer has not used his existing funds or borrowed funds, the buyer has typically retained use of funds. However, as mentioned earlier, the seller in such a situation should not be penalised, therefore the buyer can expect to receive an interest claim from the seller, to compensate for loss of cash interest.

19.4.3 Fines Imposed for Late Settlement

In some marketplaces, the stock exchange will impose fines or penalties on those who cause settlement to fail. Examples of these markets and methods of fining are as follows.

* Australia: STOs due to deliver securities to other STOs (for trades executed within the Australian Stock Exchange) will be fined on a daily basis, from the value date to the date of settlement, based on the cash value of the trade (with minimum and maximum amounts), the charge being made direct to the STO's nostro account.
* UK: fines imposed by Crest result from a Crest member's failure to meet predefined settlement performance targets relating to the percentage of trades settling on any one day.

19.5 METHODS OF COMMUNICATING STATUSES FROM CUSTODIANS

Settlement failure is communicated by custodians to their account holders by attaching the current status to the relevant settlement instruction (in the same way that pre-value date settlement instruction statuses are attached), which is then transmitted to the account holder usually by the same method the account holder used to issue the settlement instruction.

Typical statuses are those that state:

* where the STO is selling
  * the STO has insufficient securities to deliver, or
  * the buyer has insufficient cash to pay

- where the STO is buying
  - ○ the seller has insufficient securities to deliver, or
  - ○ the STO has insufficient cash to pay.

In parallel with pre-value date statuses, STOs typically wish to record the full history of all settlement failure statuses in order to facilitate subsequent investigation of trades.

19.6   PREVENTION OF SETTLEMENT FAILURE

The points listed earlier in this chapter as the causes of settlement failure are addressed below, in terms of preventing such failures.

19.6.1   Instructions Issued but not Received by the Custodian

The main method of identifying settlement instructions that have not been received at all by the custodian is for the STO to actively seek acknowledgement of receipt by the custodian, for each individual instruction issued.

Some settlement systems, having issued the instruction, are programmed to check to ensure an acknowledgement is received; where not received within a specified timeframe of issuing the instruction, an exception is raised to alert the relevant personnel.

19.6.2   Instructions Received by the Custodian after the Custodian's Deadline

A number of operational measures could be instigated as a means of ensuring that missed settlement instruction deadlines are minimised, such as:

- recording of trade detail at or very shortly after trade execution;
- prioritising settlement instruction processing according to value date;
- taking account of time zone differences between sender and destination;
- minimising 'bottlenecks' where instructions are manually keyed for transmission.

19.6.3   Instructions Remaining Unmatched or Advisory on or after Value Date

It is important to treat settlement instructions having a status of 'unmatched' or 'advisory' with urgency, within the front, middle and back offices. Some STOs adopt a timing regime, where unresolved items older than a certain time, or with an imminent value date, are escalated to senior management for resolution.

19.6.4   Insufficient Securities

Settlement failure due to insufficient securities is predictable, where an STO has sold securities it does not own. This results in a negative trading position and is commonly referred to as 'short selling'. Settlement failure can also occur where the trading position is zero (also known as 'flat'). If an STO buys securities for a given value date from a counterparty, and sells the same quantity for the same value date to a different counterparty, and if settlement failure occurs on the STO's purchase, the sale will not settle either, due to the STO being insufficient of securities.

Under both these circumstances, it may be possible for the securities to be borrowed by the STO, thereby enabling settlement of the sale to be effected. The STO needs to decide whether to borrow securities in order to complete the delivery to the buyer, or not, as unnecessary costs would be incurred by the STO, if the borrowing and the purchase were to settle on the same date. The borrower of the securities incurs a cost for the privilege of borrowing, which is payable to the lender of securities.

In the first example above, if the decision is not to borrow, settlement of the sale cannot occur until the trader buys the securities, at which point settlement of the purchase will in turn settle the sale. In the second example, should the STO decide not to borrow, settlement of the sale will occur following settlement of the purchase.

However, if the decision is to borrow, the securities may be able to be borrowed from one (or both) of two main sources, either directly from another STO, or via a custodian who matches securities lenders to borrowers, at a cost to the borrower. The result of securities borrowing is that settlement of sales will occur (providing the buyer has the cash); the seller will therefore receive the sale proceeds, but will need to return to the securities lender equivalent securities to those borrowed, in the future. This topic is explored further in Chapter 24.

19.6.5   Insufficient Cash, Collateral or Credit Line

STOs typically hold positive trading positions in many securities; upon settlement of the purchases that constitute such a trading position, the securities will be held at the STO's custodian. These securities can be regarded as *collateral*, and therefore have a collateral value based on their current market price, less a margin for potential fluctuation in value.

Some custodians allow their account holders to borrow cash up to the collateral value of the securities held by that custodian, providing the borrowed cash does not exceed the credit line (also known as overdraft facility) set by the custodian. Where this is the case, the buyer needs only to ensure that sufficient collateral remains in his account at the custodian, relevant to the net settlement value of purchases due for settlement. If the account holder predicts that he will have insufficient collateral in order to settle one or many trades, urgent action needs to be taken, such as to add further securities into the account (this will increase the collateral value in the account), or to pay in cash to the account.

It may be that an account holder at a custodian has adequate collateral to settle trades, but the current credit line may be insufficient; this needs to be addressed by the account holder through urgent negotiation with the custodian, if settlement failures are to be avoided.

19.7   ENFORCING TRADE SETTLEMENT

Where a trade remains open after its value date, it is common to find that, in many markets, buyers and sellers are able to force the counterparty to settle a trade, providing that the defined procedure (as laid down by the relevant exchange/market) is followed. These procedures are commonly known as 'buy-in' and 'sell-out'.

The period of time before buy-in or sell-out can be effected is, for example:

- at ISMA, five days after value date;
- in Tokyo, one day after value date.

19.7.1 Buy-in

A buyer of securities who is in urgent need of the purchased securities may decide to initiate a buy-in procedure; typically, buy-in procedures are allowed to begin only after a minimum period following value date.

To initiate a buy-in, the buyer issues a written communication to the seller stating that unless delivery of the securities occurs by a specified date, a buy-in will be actioned; this communication is copied to the exchange/market over which the trade was executed, if necessary.

Should the seller deliver the securities to the buyer prior to the buy-in deadline stated on the written communication, no further action is taken.

If the seller has been unable to deliver the securities by the buy-in deadline, the buyer will execute the buy-in and will buy the necessary quantity of securities in the marketplace, at the current market price (usually via a buy-in agent). The securities purchased through the buy-in procedure are delivered to the original buyer; the buyer pays the net settlement value of the original trade as any additional cost of the buy-in purchase is charged to the original seller.

19.7.2 Sell-out

A seller of securities who is able to deliver the securities to the buyer, but where the buyer has been unable to make payment for his purchase, may opt to initiate a sell-out procedure. This is effectively the reverse of a buy-in, the focus of the sell-out being on the net settlement value due to the seller.

A specified number of days after value date, the seller must issue a written communication to the buyer, copying the relevant exchange/market, if necessary, stating that unless payment is made by the stated deadline, sell-out procedures will be actioned.

Should the buyer make payment prior to the sell-out deadline stated on the written communication, no further action is taken.

However, if the buyer has been unable to make payment by the sell-out deadline, the seller will sell the securities in the marketplace at the current market price (usually via a sell-out agent). The sale proceeds raised from the sell-out procedure are used to satisfy the original seller; any shortfall in proceeds between the original sale and the sell-out are borne by the original buyer.

19.8   SUMMARY

As most settlement failures involve a cost to the STO, it is imperative that adequate attention is given to the prevention of settlement failure.

Significant savings can be made by STOs if the necessary anticipatory actions resulting from the monitoring of:

- securities balances relative to value date,
- cash balances relative to value date, and
- settlement instruction statuses

are taken at the appropriate time.

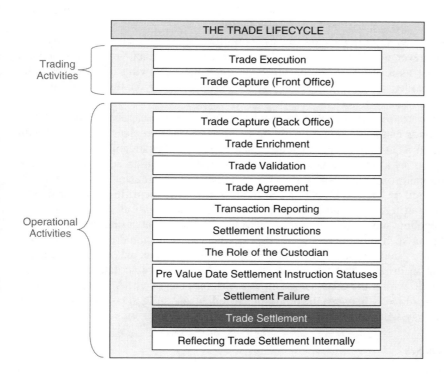

20.1 INTRODUCTION

Trade settlement is the act of exchanging securities and cash between buyer and seller. Due to the global nature of the securities industry, trade settlement typically occurs at the STO's custodians located in the various financial centres. Historically, trade settlement would have been effected by the physical delivery of certificates from seller to buyer, in exchange for cash.

In very general terms, it is to be expected that within each marketplace, the majority of trades settle on their value date (the intended date of delivery and payment, also known as the *contractual settlement date*), with those trades that do not settle on their value date settling at any later point in time. The date that the exchange of securities and cash is effected is known as the *settlement date*, or 'actual settlement date'.

20.2 ENABLING TRADE SETTLEMENT

In order to maximise efficiency and to minimise costs in relation to the act of settling trades, the following actions may be taken by STOs.

20.2.1 Sales

Providing the seller holds the relevant quantity of securities within the specific account from which delivery of securities is to occur, by the time the custodian operates its settlement processing on value date, settlement will occur (providing the buyer has the cash to pay). If the seller is in a position to deliver the securities but the buyer cannot pay, settlement will fail and the seller is normally able to issue an interest claim to the buyer, to be recompensed for the loss of cash interest.

If the seller is unable to deliver the securities on the value date, settlement of the sale will occur whenever a sufficient quantity of securities are available within the seller's account, whether as a result of purchasing or through the borrowing of securities. The sale will be regarded as failing to settle for the period starting on the value date and ending when the trade settles.

Because some securities can settle in more than one settlement location (e.g. Italian Government bonds can settle domestically or via the ICSDs, Euroclear and Clearstream Luxembourg), an STO may decide to settle a sale from its Clearstream account, but the securities may be held, on trade date of the sale, in the STO's Milan custodian. In order to enable settlement on value date within Clearstream, a depot (custodian) transfer will need to be effected by the STO, resulting in the movement of securities from the STO's domestic custodian to its account with Clearstream; this is known as *realignment*. The first step in enabling successful settlement on value date under such circumstances is to actively search for such situations. The STO's settlement system should be able to provide reports of all sales due for settlement from a specified custodian, where it is predicted that insufficient securities will be available at that custodian on value date, and the same securities are held within the STO's account at a different custodian. Alternatively, *cross border settlement* directly between the domestic custodian and an ICSD is usually possible, however there may be timing issues.

20.2.2 Purchases

If the buyer has sufficient cash, *collateral* or credit line within the specific account from which payment of cash is to occur by the time the custodian operates its settlement processing on value date, settlement will occur providing the seller has the securities to deliver. Conversely, if the buyer has insufficient cash, collateral or credit line in his account at the custodian on or after the value date, and the seller is able to deliver the securities, settlement will fail and the buyer can expect to receive an *interest claim* from the seller.

Typically, custodians are not prepared to be at risk by allowing account holders to have a cash overdraft on an unsecured basis. The custodian may well be prepared to lend cash (in the form of an overdraft) providing it is able to recover the lent cash amount from the account holder's other assets that the custodian holds, in the event that the cash overdraft is not repaid by the account holder.

In a situation where an STO sets up an account with a custodian, then the STO purchases securities for the first time in that marketplace, the STO will issue a settlement instruction to the custodian. Assuming that the STO's settlement instruction is matched with the counterparty's instruction prior to value date, the custodian will allow the STO to settle the trade providing sufficient cash or collateral is in the STO's account, and providing the credit line (overdraft facility) granted to the STO by the custodian is not exceeded. It can be seen that a number of options are usually open to the STO, to enable successful settlement of this purchase, namely having within the account sufficient:

- credit cash balance, or
- collateral, or
- a combination of cash and collateral.

Credit Cash Balance

If the account holder has a sufficient credit balance of cash on the specific account over which settlement is to occur, and providing there are no imminent payments of outgoing cash, there is no reason why the custodian should not settle the trade on the STO's behalf. This will result in a debit of cash to the STO's account, but the resultant balance will not be overdrawn, therefore the custodian is not at risk, as it has not lent funds to the STO.

Where the account holder has multiple accounts, the custodian may choose to aggregate the balances over all the accounts in order to determine the total credit cash position; this may be actioned over accounts in the same or different currencies.

Collateral

Having sufficient collateral within the account holder's account will enable settlement of purchases to occur at the custodian; the collateral effectively acts as a guarantee of repayment capability where the collateral holder owes cash. Note that some custodians may operate in a different manner regarding the use of collateral for the settlement of trades (refer to Section 17.7).

The securities that are held within the STO's account at the custodian (as a result of prior trades having settled) are typically valued by the custodian on a daily basis, in order to calculate the current market value, less a margin to allow for price fluctuation, thereby deriving a collateral value for each security held within the account. The total collateral value of all the securities in the account, as calculated by the custodian (and communicated to the STO), is the maximum amount of cash the custodian is prepared to lend to the STO. Figure 20.1 provides an example calculation method.

Step 1: the current market price of the individual securities is gathered, typically from one or many *securities data providers*.

Step 2: the current market price is applied to the holding, to calculate the gross cash value of the holding.

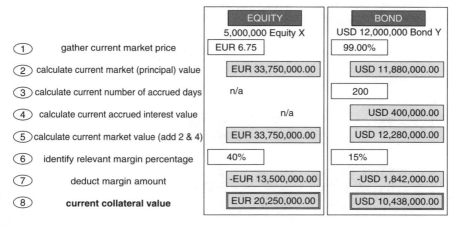

Figure 20.1   Calculation of collateral values by custodians

Step 3: where relevant, the current number of accrued days is calculated (this would, for example, be relevant to a straight bond, but not to an equity or zero coupon bond).

Step 4: from the number of days of *accrued interest*, calculate the current value of accrued interest.

Step 5: derive the current market value by adding the gross cash value and the current value of accrued interest (where applicable).

Step 6: identify the percentage margin to be deducted, according to the security type. In general, equities are more volatile than bonds, therefore the margin on equities is considerably greater than for bonds, as the custodian wishes to take no risk.

Step 7: calculate the amount of margin to be deducted from the current market value.

Step 8: derive the current collateral value, against which the custodian is prepared to lend cash.

From the custodian's perspective, it needs to ensure that it can recover a cash overdraft, should the account holder fail to repay the overdraft (an 'event of default'). The theory is that the custodian would recover the cash amount owed to it by selling the account holder's collateral in the market.

The custodian applies the margin to the collateral value calculation to allow for price movement of the securities held as collateral. The specific risk to the custodian is that, should it allow the account holder to go overdrawn today, by say CAD 3,000,000.00, because the market value of the collateral was CAD 3,000,000.00, tomorrow the overdraft may remain exactly the same, but the collateral value may increase or decrease (or stay the same), due to everyday securities price movements. Should securities prices fall, the custodian will be partially unsecured, in other words the custodian would not be able to fully recover the account holder's overdraft, in the event that the account holder fails to repay the overdrawn amount. In order to guard against the possibility of becoming unsecured, the custodian applies a margin as part of the collateral value calculation.

A margin of 15% applied to the market value of the collateral would reduce the collateral value by CAD 450,000.00, to CAD 2,550,000.00. This means that the market value of the securities would need to fall by at least 15% in order for the custodian to be at risk.

Figure 20.2 illustrates the circumstances under which the custodian is not at risk (and therefore will allow successful settlement), and also where the custodian will be at risk and will not allow settlement of further purchases.

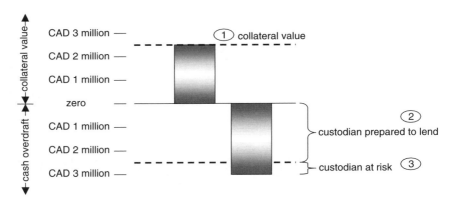

Figure 20.2   Cash overdraft and collateral management at custodians

Step 1: the collateral value of the securities within the account holder's account is calculated by the custodian to be CAD 2,550,000.00.

Step 2: the custodian is typically prepared to lend cash up to the collateral value of the securities (after margin considerations as already mentioned).

Step 3: should the custodian allow a cash overdraft beyond the collateral value of the securities, the custodian cannot be certain of recovering its funds in the event that the account holder does not repay the overdraft.

Following settlement of a trade, if, as in the above example, the overdraft amount is very similar to the collateral value, the custodian will again be at risk if it allows the account holder to remove securities from the account on an FoP basis. For instance, issuing a depot (custodian) transfer settlement instruction to the custodian requesting removal of the securities from the account and transferring to another custodian on an FoP basis will leave the custodian in an exposed position, as the account holder will have a cash overdraft but no (or insufficient) collateral within the account. Consequently, the custodian is likely to reject the settlement instruction, or at least not act upon it, until sufficient cash is credited to the account or further collateral is added to the account.

STOs need to actively manage the equation between cash overdrafts and collateral values at each custodian, if they wish their purchases to settle successfully.

Large STOs do not normally have such problems, as the amount of collateral they hold at custodians typically far outweighs the size of the cash overdraft in markets in which they are very active. Even so, in the markets in which they are not very active, the amount of collateral held at each custodian may be relatively small. Similarly, new account holders at the custodian may have problems settling trades if they have very little or no collateral within their account, and they do not actively manage their collateral.

For an STO to manage the equation successfully, the STO needs to think like each of its custodians. This means predicting the movement of securities and cash arriving into and leaving each of the STO's accounts for each value date in order to ascertain whether sufficient collateral is likely to be present, relevant to the likely cash overdraft, for the custodian to allow settlement of purchases to occur. The basic information allowing such a prediction is typically held within the STO's settlement system.

STOs need to take particular care where they remove securities from the account (for example when lending securities or executing repo trades) that sufficient collateral remains to settle normal purchases. The topic of collateral is explored further in Chapter 23.

Credit Line (Secured)

A credit line (also known as an overdraft facility) is the maximum amount of cash that a custodian is prepared to lend the account holder.

For example, the current collateral value within an STO's account at a custodian may be USD 1 billion, but if the credit line granted by the custodian to the STO is USD 600 million, the collateral value over the credit line (i.e. USD 400 million) cannot be used by the account holder for the purposes of borrowing cash from the custodian. However, it may be possible for the account holder to negotiate with the custodian to increase the credit line in order to make use of the excess collateral.

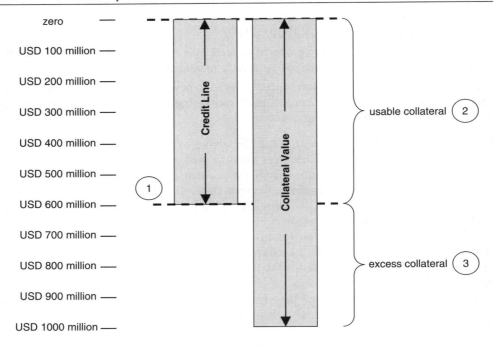

Figure 20.3   Credit line versus collateral at custodians

Figure 20.3 represents such a situation.

Step 1: the credit line granted to the account holder by the custodian, in this example, is USD 600 million. Cash may be borrowed by the account holder up to this limit, providing sufficient collateral is maintained within the account.

Step 2: the amount of usable collateral (for the purpose of borrowing cash from the custodian) is only that collateral that supports the size of the credit line.

Step 3: any excess collateral over and above the credit line, in this case USD 400 million, cannot be used for overdraft purposes.

Conversely, in a situation where the current collateral value within an STO's account at a custodian is USD 525 million, but if the credit line granted by the custodian is USD 600 million, the credit line over the collateral value (i.e. USD 75 million) cannot be used by the account holder for the purposes of borrowing cash from the custodian. The credit line is only of use to the extent that collateral is available to secure the cash borrowing (Figure 20.4).

Step 1: the credit line granted to the account holder by the custodian, in this example, is USD 600 million. Cash may be borrowed by the account holder up to this limit, providing sufficient collateral is maintained within the account.

Step 2: the amount of usable collateral (for the purpose of borrowing cash from the custodian) is in this case less than the credit line.

Step 3: any excess credit line over and above the collateral value cannot be used for overdraft purposes.

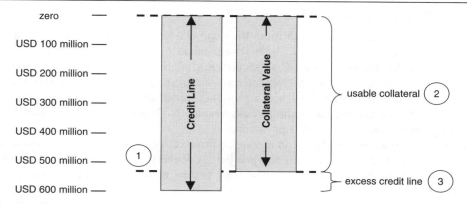

Figure 20.4 Credit line versus collateral at custodians

20.3 TRADE SETTLEMENT METHODS

Settlement at the various custodians is increasingly moving towards the DvP method (the simultaneous and irrevocable exchange of securities and cash), in order to minimise the seller's and buyer's risk of delivering one asset without receiving the contra asset at the same time. This is sometimes referred to as dependent deliveries of securities, or dependent payments of cash. In other words, the delivery of securities will not be effected without simultaneous payment of cash, and vice versa.

Care must be taken, however, to ensure that the method of settlement in each marketplace is well understood, preferably in advance of executing the first trade in a particular marketplace. Some marketplaces at first sight appear to operate on a DvP (truly simultaneous exchange) basis, but upon further investigation it may be found, for example, that there is a delay between the seller delivering the securities and the buyer paying the cash, although both occur during the same day. Under these circumstances, it may be perceived that the seller is at risk in the period between the securities having been removed from their account, and prior to the funds being received ('daylight risk').

Free deliveries and receipts of securities are able to be made, although over time the percentage of this method of settlement is likely to decrease compared to DvP, as the market becomes more sophisticated and increasingly risk averse.

Where a seller holds its securities in one location (e.g. domestically) and the buyer wishes to settle in a different location (e.g. an ICSD), settlement can occur in one of two ways:

- across the different locations, between the domestic system and the ICSD's system (this is known as *cross border settlement*)
- within the same location following *realignment* of securities by the seller.

20.4 TYPES OF TRADE SETTLEMENT

The movement of securities and cash can occur in different ways.

20.4.1 Full Settlement

Upon settlement of a settlement instruction, where the entire quantity of securities was delivered or received, and the full amount of cash was received or paid, thereby leaving no securities or cash outstanding and to be settled, the settlement instruction is said to be fully settled.

20.4.2   Partial Settlement

The settlement of an instruction in more than one delivery of securities and payment of cash is known as 'partial delivery', 'partial settlement' or 'settlement splitting'.

Where a seller has only some of the securities available for delivery on or after value date, the seller will maximise a cash interest earning opportunity if the buyer accepts a partial delivery of securities against a pro-rata amount of cash, on a DvP basis. The seller, for instance, can use the incoming cash amount to offset an existing cash borrowing, thereby reducing outgoing interest payments.

Partial settlement is usually not an automatic process, requiring the seller to contact the buyer to ask whether the buyer will accept a partial delivery of securities against payment of a pro-rata amount of cash, or not. The rules and regulations do not normally compel the buyer to accept partial deliveries. A buyer who is not in urgent need of securities purchased is within his rights to refuse the offer of a partial delivery, as accepting the delivery provides no immediate benefit, in fact the buyer retains the use of funds.

In order for a seller to offer a buyer a partial delivery, the seller must first become aware of such an opportunity. STOs typically run a report from the settlement system that identifies sales where value date is imminent or in the past, and some (but not all) of the securities are available for delivery at the custodian.

Should the buyer agree to accept a partial delivery, both seller and buyer will be required to cancel their respective (original) settlement instructions and issue two replacement instructions each; one instruction for the quantity of securities available for delivery versus a pro-rata amount of cash, the other instruction for the remaining quantity of securities versus the remainder of the cash. Each instruction is required to match with the counterparty's corresponding instruction, prior to effecting settlement. Figure 20.5 represents this sequence of steps.

Steps 1a and 1b: both the STO and the counterparty transmit their (original) settlement instruction.

Step 2: the instructions are matched at the custodian.

Steps 3a and 3b: the seller offers the buyer a partial delivery and the buyer accepts; both the STO and the counterparty transmit cancelling instructions relating to their respective (original) instructions.

Step 4: the original instructions are cancelled at the custodian.

Steps 5a and 5b: replacement settlement instructions are issued by the STO and the counterparty for the quantity of securities that are available for immediate delivery and settlement.

Step 6: the replacement instructions are matched at the custodian.

Steps 7a and 7b: replacement settlement instructions are issued by the STO and the counterparty for the remaining quantity of securities that are not yet available for delivery by the seller.

Step 8: the replacement instructions are matched at the custodian; settlement of this instruction will occur once the seller has the necessary quantity of securities to deliver.

It is important to note that from the STO's perspective the original trade remains intact, but instead of a single delivery and payment of cash (as occurs under normal circumstances),

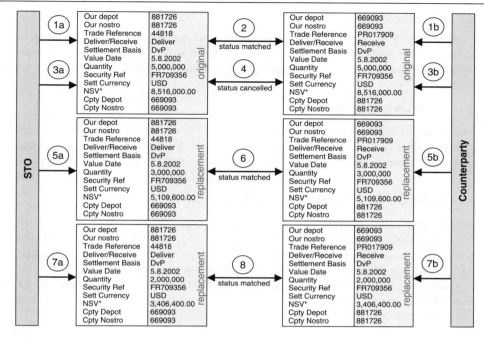

Figure 20.5 Partial settlement

partial settlement results in a minimum of two deliveries and payments of cash. Multiple partial deliveries to settle a single trade can occur where the seller, having already settled a partial amount of the trade, obtains a further quantity (but not the full remaining quantity) of securities.

Industry Anecdote

This story illustrates the impact of failing to partially settling a trade. Trader 'X' buys USD 50 million of straight bonds from five counterparties (USD 10 million from each), and sells the entire USD 50 million to a single counterparty for a large trading profit. All six trades were value dated the same day and all instructions were matched prior to the value date.

On value date, four of the five purchases settled, the fifth purchase failed; despite attempts, the shortfall of bonds could not be borrowed in order to complete delivery of the sale. The buyer was contacted to ask whether they would accept a partial delivery of USD 40 million of bonds versus a pro-rata cash amount; the offer was politely refused. Settlement of the sale of USD 50 million bonds could only occur once settlement of the fifth purchase occurred; until that time, trader 'X' had to unexpectedly fund the payment of USD 40 million bonds. The fifth purchase was delivered one week late, by which time the cost of funding the USD 40 million bonds turned the trader's trading profit into a loss. Buying in 'shapes' and selling as one amount is a common problem which is in the trader's interest to avoid.

20.4.3 Securities Only Settlement

The delivery or receipt of securities (independent of a cash payment) will occur on a trade where FoP settlement has been agreed between seller and buyer. Additionally, a securities only movement will occur in relation to a depot (custodian) transfer.

20.4.4 Cash Only Settlement

The cash side of a trade that settles on an FoP basis involves the receipt or payment of cash independent of a delivery or receipt of securities. Cash only settlement also occurs for example, in unsecured borrowing and lending and foreign exchange transactions.

20.4.5 Cross-Currency Securities Settlement

STOs and their counterparties usually wish to settle trades in the 'natural' or 'trading' currency of the specific security. This ensures that foreign exchange risk is not introduced by having, for example, an overdraft in one currency (as a result of a purchase) and a credit of cash in a different currency (as a result of a sale of the same security).

However, for example, some counterparties (typically institutional clients of the STO), require the settlement of all their trades in a single currency, regardless of the natural currency of the security. Refer to Section 5.3.4.

When a trade has been executed and the trading currency differs from the 'settlement currency' (the currency in which the counterparty wishes to settle), a foreign exchange ('FX') transaction will need to be effected. In the case of the STO selling securities, the FX transaction will result in the incoming currency from the STO's counterparty being exchanged for the natural currency of the security; the net result is that the STO should receive a credit of cash in the natural currency, thereby having no FX exposure.

Unless settlement of the securities versus the incoming currency can be processed by the central securities depository, a currency payment will need to be made by the counterparty, independent of the securities delivery by the STO.

20.5 SETTLEMENT NETTING

Historically, the settlement of trades between counterparties has been effected on a trade-for-trade (gross) basis at the custodian, resulting from the issue of settlement instructions for every individual trade.

However, instead of settling each open trade on a gross basis, the settlement of two or more trades may be effected by the single delivery (or receipt) of the net quantity of securities, and the single receipt (or payment) of the net amount of cash. This is known as *settlement netting*.

Settlement netting is beneficial as it:

• reduces costs through the transmission of a single settlement instruction, rather than individual settlement instructions, and
• enables settlement of multiple original trades by a single movement of securities and cash (typically on a DvP basis).

Note that the original trades remain intact as individual trades, as it is the settlement of those trades that is being netted.

Unless settlement netting were agreed between the sellers and buyers, each of the five trades listed in Table 20.1 (taken from the perspective of an STO, ABC) would typically have been settled individually. However, ABC has executed two trades (in the same security) with counterparty QRS, giving the opportunity to both ABC and QRS to effect *settlement netting* of the trades, providing both seller and buyer agree. Had agreement to net been made, ABC and QRS would each need to issue a settlement instruction for the net securities and cash amounts to their respective custodians, which would need to match before settlement could occur. Upon settlement, a single movement of 3000 shares against 14,500.00 cash would be made, resulting in the effective settlement of trades 1 and 5. This is known as *bilateral netting*.

Table 20.1

Trade number	Operation	Quantity of shares	NSV (HKD)	Security	Counterparty
1	Buy	+5000	−25,000.00	HSBC shares	QRS
2	Buy	+7500	−36,000.00	HSBC shares	XYZ
3	Buy	+4000	−20,500.00	HSBC shares	EFG
4	Sell	−6000	+31,000.00	HSBC shares	LMN
5	Sell	−2000	+10,500.00	HSBC shares	QRS
		+8500	**−40,000.00**		

The three remaining trades would need to be settled on a trade-for-trade basis.

Multilateral netting, which would involve the netting of all trades listed in the above example, is described in Chapter 29.

20.6   SETTLEMENT TOLERANCE

As mentioned in Chapter 18, at some custodians settlement instructions are regarded as matched even where the cash values of a pair of instructions do not match exactly, providing the cash difference is within a publicised tolerance.

Under such circumstances, the settlement instruction will settle against either the seller's or the buyer's cash figure, according to the specific custodian. At Euroclear, for instance, the settlement tolerance is USD 25.00, or currency equivalent, the instruction settling against the seller's figure, within the given tolerance.

This may mean that the instruction settles against a cash value at the custodian that is different from the of the STO's trade; the implications of such a situation will be explored in Chapter 21.

20.7   SETTLEMENT PROCESSING AT THE CUSTODIAN

The settlement processing at custodians, particularly CSDs, results in settlement success or failure for an STO's individual settlement instruction. The processing involves the identification of deliverers of securities that have sufficient securities to deliver to securities receivers (that have sufficient cash, collateral and credit line), to enable the optimum number of matched instructions to settle. This typically takes into account value date (normally oldest value date takes priority), the quantity of securities (largest takes priority) and any instructions prioritised by the issuer of the instruction (if permitted by the CSD).

The timing of the various CSDs' settlement processing is specific to each CSD; however, in general it is to be expected that national CSDs operate their settlement processing during daylight hours within their own time zone. The international CSDs Clearstream Luxembourg and Euroclear however have multiple processing periods (including overnight) and both have intra-day capability.

It is to be expected that automation will ultimately allow intra-day continuous settlement (rather than the historic predefined timetable) to become common amongst all CSDs.

20.8   RESULT OF TRADE SETTLEMENT AT THE CUSTODIAN

Following trade settlement, three main areas will be affected and require updating immediately by the custodian, within its own records:

* the settlement instruction,
* the securities position, and
* the cash position.

20.8.1   Settlement Instruction

Providing the settlement instruction has been fully settled in terms of both securities and cash, the settlement instruction is no longer outstanding and the custodian should not attempt to exchange any more securities or cash, relevant to the particular instruction.

The settlement instruction should be given a status of 'settled', and the detail of the exact quantity of securities received or delivered and the amount of cash paid or received must be communicated to the account holder, via the transmission method agreed with the account holder, as soon as possible.

Table 20.2 is an example of the information pertaining to a settled settlement instruction that a custodian would communicate to the account holder. Note that the settlement date for this instruction was one day later than value date; therefore settlement failed for one day.

Table 20.2

Detail of settlement instruction issued to the custodian by the STO		Detail of settlement as communicated by the custodian to the STO	
From	WSIL	From	Cust. H, Hong Kong
To	Cust. H, Hong Kong	To	WSIL
Depot account no.	111693XM	Depot account no.	111693XM
Nostro account no.	111693XM	Nostro account no.	111693XM
Trade reference	PR30184462	Instruction reference	PR30184462
Deliver/receive	Receive	Deliver/receive	Received
Settlement basis	DvP	Settlement basis	DvP
Value date	17th April	**Settlement date**	18th April
Quantity	4,000,000	Quantity	4,000,000
Security reference	HK1300848212	Security reference	HK1300848212
Settlement currency	HKD	Settlement currency	HKD
NSV	11,688,500.00	NSV	11,688,500.00
Counterparty depot	110242TP	Counterparty depot	110242TP
Counterparty nostro	110242TP	Counterparty nostro	110242TP
Transmission time	12:16 on 14th April	Transmission time	11:34 on 18th April

20.8.2 Securities Position at the Custodian

Following settlement of an instruction to receive securities, the custodian will credit the relevant securities account of the account holder. The account holder may have two or more securities accounts at the custodian, but the custodian must ensure it credits the specific account stated within the settlement instruction. Successful settlement of an instruction to deliver securities should result in a debit of securities by the custodian, to the relevant account.

Statements of the account holder's revised securities balance, inclusive of individual entries since the issuance of the previous statement, are required to be communicated to the account holder periodically. It is recommended that this period is daily, in order for the STO to attempt a reconciliation of positions on a daily basis. This subject is explored in Chapter 27.

Table 20.3 is an example of the resulting entries on the account holder's securities account at the custodian, following settlement of the instruction detailed in Table 20.2. The example shows the account holder's securities position in the specific security and within the specific account (the account holder may have multiple accounts), as at close of business on the settlement date 18th April (not the value date). The statement shows:

* a position balance of zero (at the custodian) as at close of business the previous day;
* the individual movements that occurred, whether delivered or received, on 18th April;
* the securities position as at the close of business on 18th April.

Table 20.3

	Custodian H, Hong Kong			
	Statement of *securities account* for World Securities International, London			
	Account number 111693XM for security HK1300848212			

Entry date	Narrative	Delivered from account	Received into account	Balance
	Balance brought forward from 17th April			*nil*
18th April	**Instruction reference PR30184462**		**4,000,000**	**4,000,000**
	Closing balance as at 18th April			*4,000,000*

20.8.3 Cash Account at the Custodian

In line with the actions to be taken by the custodian for securities, following settlement of an instruction to pay cash, the custodian will debit the relevant cash account of the account holder in the relevant currency (where there is a choice). The account holder may have two or more cash accounts at the custodian, but the custodian must ensure it debits the specific account stated within the settlement instruction. Cash receipts relating to trade settlement will result in a credit of cash to the account holder's appropriate account.

In parallel with securities, statements of the account holder's revised cash balance, inclusive of individual entries since the issuance of the previous statement, are required to be communicated to the account holder on a daily basis, to enable reconciliation to be attempted by the STO.

Table 20.4 is an example of the resulting entries on the account holder's cash account following settlement of the instruction detailed in Table 20.2. The example shows the account holder's HKD cash position within the specific account (the account holder may have multiple accounts), as at close of business on the settlement date 18th April. The statement shows:

- an overdraft (at the custodian) as at close of business the previous day;
- the individual movements that occurred, whether paid or received, on 18th April;
- the HKD position as at the close of business on 18th April.

Table 20.4

Custodian H, Hong Kong
Statement of *HKD cash account* for World Securities International, London
Account number 111693XM

Entry date	Narrative	Payments	Receipts	Balance
	Balance brought forward from 17th April			*−1,120,000.00*
18th April	**Instruction reference PR30184462**	**11,688,500.00**		**−12,808,500.00**
	Closing balance as at 18th April			*−12,808,500.00*

20.9   SUMMARY

In order to avoid settlement failure, minimise the cost of settlement and maximise opportunities to increase revenue, it is important for an STO to become fully aware of the characteristics of settlement in each location in which it settles. This includes market practices and the services provided by the custodian.

Such characteristics are likely to include:

- whether securities can be borrowed automatically in order to settle sales;
- whether the size of credit line granted by the custodian will be sufficient to settle all purchases;
- the margin applied to various types of securities for collateral valuation purposes;
- whether true DvP is practised;
- whether partial settlement is practised;
- whether a settlement tolerance is applied.

Although the custodian can assist the STO in understanding a market's method of working, the responsibility for ensuring efficient operation resides with the STO.

Reflecting Trade Settlement Internally

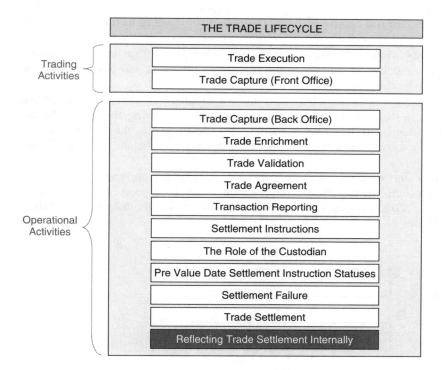

21.1 INTRODUCTION

Once a trade has settled at the custodian, it is essential for the STO to update its internal books and records immediately, with the detail of securities and/or cash movements.

To make an analogy, a small company trading in sports equipment is likely to have its purchases of goods from its wholesale supplier delivered to its premises, where the goods would be checked and a cheque given to the supplier's driver. Following the receipt of the goods and payment of the cash, the sports goods company would need to update its books and records to ensure that:

- the purchase is no longer showing as outstanding;
- the goods are showing as having been received and added to the inventory of goods held in the warehouse;
- the cash is showing as having been paid and deducted from the cash balance held at the bank.

Unless the sports goods company updates its internal records as above, its books and records will not reflect the factual situation, resulting in:

- the purchase still appearing as outstanding when it is in fact settled (thereby mis-stating the company's outstanding contractual commitment);

- the record of the quantity of goods in the warehouse appearing as fewer than the true number (potentially affecting future deliveries of goods from the warehouse);
- the record of cash within the bank showing as greater than the actual balance (potentially affecting decisions to borrow or repay cash borrowed previously).

Each of these pieces of information being incorrect within internal records means that the company is not in full control of its assets, potentially leading to incorrect business decisions.

The sports goods company has direct control over its purchases from the various wholesalers, as goods are delivered directly to the company's premises, and payments of cash are made directly by the company.

In contrast, an STO is reliant upon its various custodians to control deliveries and receipts of securities and payments and receipts of cash, following the receipt by the custodians of settlement instructions from the STO. Additionally, the 'warehouse' for the holding of goods (the securities) and the bank for the cash balance are the various custodians.

With regard to the updating of internal books and records, the sports goods company is itself the source of the information regarding receipts of goods and payments of cash, whereas the STO is reliant upon its custodians to provide the information. This is illustrated in Figure 21.1.

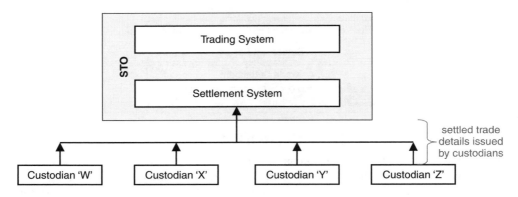

Figure 21.1   Reflecting trade settlement internally: overview

Upon receipt of settled trade information from the various custodians, the STO will attempt to locate the relevant trade record within its books and records, and then to update the detail with the specific quantity of securities delivered or received and/or cash paid or received, as advised by the custodian. At the same time, the STO's securities and cash positions must be updated in order to fully reflect the position at the custodian. This is shown in Figure 21.2.

Step 1: the STO receives settled trade information from one of its custodians, locates the relevant trade record within the settlement system and updates it accordingly.

Step 2a: the STO's internal record of its securities position held at the specific custodian (and within the specific account at the custodian, where the STO has multiple accounts) must be updated immediately.

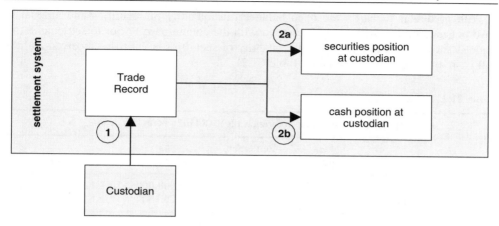

Figure 21.2   Reflecting trade settlement internally: overview

Step 2b: similarly, the STO's internal record of its cash position held at the specific custodian (and within the specific account at the custodian, where the STO has multiple accounts) must be updated immediately.

Besides many other benefits (described later within this chapter), effecting these entries internally will enable agreement of securities and cash positions with the statements of securities and cash issued by the custodian, through the reconciliation process (refer to Chapter 27).

The updating of internal books and records is a major mechanism by which an STO remains in control of its assets. Additionally, the automatic updating of the correct trade within internal books and records is an important component in achieving *STP*.

21.2   PRE-SETTLEMENT TRADE RECORD

Following the capture of a trade within the settlement system, the detail in Table 21.1 is typically held (for a principal trade) prior to settlement.

Table 21.1

Trade reference	PR30184462
Transaction type	Principal
Trading book	A
Trade date	14th April
Trade time	11:22
Value date	17th April
Operation	Buy
Quantity	4,000,000
Security	TUV Corporation, HKD 1.00 shares
Price	HKD 2.922125
Counterparty	PTIF (Professional Traders Inc., Frankfurt)
NSV	HKD 11,688,500.00

With particular focus on the open balance (the quantity of securities and amount of cash outstanding and still due to be settled with the counterparty) prior to settlement, this trade is shown as fully open. The full quantity of securities is yet to be received and the full cash amount is yet to be paid (Table 21.2).

Table 21.2

		Value date	Settlement date	Quantity	NSV
	Trade record for trade reference PR30184462: as at 16th April				

		Value date	Settlement date	Quantity	NSV
1	**Trade**	**17th April**		**4,000,000**	**HKD 11,688,500.00**
3	Open balance			4,000,000	HKD 11,688,500.00

The complete picture of the STO's position in the individual security (refer to Chapter 1) is shown in Table 21.3.

Table 21.3

TUV Corporation, HKD 1.00 shares			
Ownership		Location	
Trading book A	+ 4,000,000	– 4,000,000	Counterparty PTIF
	+ 4,000,000	**– 4,000,000**	

As a result of the purchase the ownership position is being shown as owned by trading book A (but this will not alter as a result of settlement of the trade). The location position (currently showing as being due from the counterparty) will however alter as a result of reflecting trade settlement internally.

The cash position is shown in Table 21.4.

Table 21.4

Hong Kong Dollars			
Ownership		Location	
Trading book A	– 11,688,500.00	+ 11,688,500.00	Counterparty PTIF
	– 11,688,500.00	**+ 11,688,500.00**	

Note that the convention used against location positions in these tables, for both securities and cash, results in a reverse sign when compared to the actual situation in the outside world. For example:

- a securities position held at the STO's custodian (as a result of a purchase) will be shown as a negative position within internal books and records, and

- an overdrawn cash position at the STO's custodian (as a result of a purchase) will be shown as a positive position within internal books and records.

This is owing to the *double-entry bookkeeping* principle (refer to Chapter 28).

21.3   POST-SETTLEMENT TRADE RECORD

Once settlement has occurred at the custodian, whether on or after value date, the trade record within the settlement system must be updated as follows. Note that:

- row 1 shows the original value date, quantity and NSV of the above-mentioned trade;
- row 2 shows the settlement date, the settled quantity and the settled cash amount;
- row 3 shows the open balance of securities and cash for the trade, as a result of settlement.

21.3.1   Full Settlement

Table 21.5 shows that settlement occurred one day later than value date, but the entire trade quantity and the entire cash amount have been settled, leaving no open quantity to be delivered from or cash to be paid to the counterparty.

Table 21.5

		Value date	Settlement date	Quantity	NSV
		Trade record for trade reference PR30184462: as at 18th April			
1	**Trade**	**17th April**		**4,000,000**	**HKD 11,688,500.00**
2	Settlement		18th April	4,000,000	HKD 11,688,500.00
3	Open balance			0	0

As a result of reflecting trade settlement internally, the securities location position has now been updated to that in Table 21.6, with cash position in Table 21.7 to mirror the situation in the outside world.

Table 21.6

TUV Corporation, HKD 1.00 shares			
Ownership			Location
Trading book A	+ 4,000,000	− 4,000,000	Custodian H, HK a/c 111693XM
	+ 4,000,000	− 4,000,000	

21.3.2   Partial Settlement

Table 21.8 reveals that a partial settlement of 1,500,000 shares was effected on 18th April against a pro-rata cash amount, leaving an open quantity of 2,500,000 shares against a pro-rata cash amount to be settled with the counterparty; the updated securities position is reflected in Table 21.9 and the updated cash position is given in Table 21.10.

Table 21.11 reflects the fact that two partial settlements have been actioned, but still leaving an open balance of securities to be received from, and cash to be paid to the

Table 21.7

Hong Kong Dollars			
Ownership		Location	
Trading book A	− 11,688,500.00	+ 11,688,500.00	Custodian H, HK a/c 111693XM
	− 11,688,500.00	**+ 11,688,500.00**	

Table 21.8

Trade record for trade reference PR30184462: as at 18th April				

		Value date	Settlement date	Quantity	NSV
1	**Trade**	**17th April**		**4,000,000**	**HKD 11,688,500.00**
2	Settlement		18th April	1,500,000	HKD 4,383,187.50
3	Open balance			2,500,000	HKD 7,305,312.50

Table 21.9

TUV Corporation, HKD 1.00 shares			
Ownership		Location	
Trading book A	+ 4,000,000	− 2,500,000	Counterparty PTIF
		− 1,500,000	Custodian H, HK a/c111693XM
	+ 4,000,000	**− 4,000,000**	

Table 21.10

Hong Kong Dollars			
Ownership		Location	
Trading book A	− 11,688,500.00	+ 7,305,312.50	Counterparty PTIF
		+ 4,383,187.50	Custodian H, HK a/c 111693XM
	− 11,688,500.00	**+ 11,688,500.00**	

counterparty. This leaves the updated securities position as in Table 21.12 and the cash position as in Table 21.13.

21.3.3   Securities Only Settlement

Table 21.14 indicates that all the securities have been delivered by the counterparty, but none of the cash has been paid to the counterparty. This is typically the case where FoP settlement has been agreed, and where the STO is not at risk, resulting in the securities position in Table 21.15 and the cash position in Table 21.16.

Table 21.11

		Value date	Settlement date	Quantity	NSV
	Trade record for trade reference PR30184462: as at 19th April				
1	**Trade**	**17th April**		**4,000,000**	**HKD 11,688,500.00**
2a	Settlement		18th April	1,500,000	HKD 4,383,187.50
2b	Settlement		19th April	2,000,000	HKD 5,844,250.00
3	Open balance			500,000	HKD 1,461,062.50

Table 21.12

TUV Corporation, HKD 1.00 shares				
Ownership			Location	
Trading book A	+ 4,000,000	− 500,000	Counterparty PTIF	
		− 3,500,000	Custodian H, HK a/c 111693XM	
	+ 4,000,000	**− 4,000,000**		

Table 21.13

Hong Kong Dollars				
Ownership			Location	
Trading book A	− 11,688,500.00	+ 1,461,062.50	Counterparty PTIF	
		+ 10,227,437.50	Custodian H, HK a/c 111693XM	
	− 11,688,500.00	**+ 11,688,500.00**		

Table 21.14

		Value date	Settlement date	Quantity	NSV
	Trade record for trade reference PR30184462: as at 18th April				
1	**Trade**	**17th April**		**4,000,000**	**HKD 11,688,500.00**
2	Settlement		18th April	4,000,000	0
3	Open balance			0	HKD 11,688,500.00

Table 21.15

TUV Corporation, HKD 1.00 shares			
Ownership		Location	
Trading book A	+ 4,000,000	− 4,000,000	Custodian H, HK a/c 111693XM
	+ 4,000,000	**− 4,000,000**	

Table 21.16

Hong Kong Dollars			
Ownership		Location	
Trading book A	− 11,688,500.00	+ 11,688,500.00	Counterparty PTIF
	− 11,688,500.00	**+ 11,688,500.00**	

21.3.4   Cash Only Settlement

Table 21.17 indicates that all the cash due to the counterparty has been paid, without receipt of the securities. This is a typical representation of the STO having gone on-risk in an FoP settlement situation; this situation would result in the securities position in Table 21.18, with the cash position in Table 21.19.

Table 21.17

		Value date	Settlement date	Quantity	NSV
		Trade record for trade reference PR30184462: as at 18th April			
1	**Trade**	**17th April**		**4,000,000**	**HKD 11,688,500.00**
2	Settlement		18th April	0	HKD 11,688,500.00
3	Open Balance			4,000,000	0

Table 21.18

TUV Corporation, HKD 1.00 shares			
Ownership		Location	
Trading book A	+ 4,000,000	− 4,000,000	Counterparty PTIF
	+ 4,000,000	**− 4,000,000**	

Table 21.19

Hong Kong Dollars			
Ownership		Location	
Trading book A	− 11,688,500.00	+ 11,688,500.00	Custodian H, HK a/c 111693XM
	− 11,688,500.00	**+ 11,688,500.00**	

It is imperative that the trade is updated with the detail of settlement within the STO's books and records immediately upon settlement, as advised by the custodian. This enables the various areas within the STO that are reliant upon such information, to conduct their activities with confidence.

21.4   WHAT TIMELY AND ACCURATE REFLECTION ENABLES

The speedy and accurate updating of the trade record and securities and cash positions internally ensures that the STO has a completely up-to-date picture of all its assets, regardless of their location.

Keeping these records up-to-date enables various reconciliations to be conducted on a daily basis, in order to prove that the STO's internal records agree with the custodian's records. Even where today's reconciliation reveals a discrepancy, the extent of the investigation will be limited to investigation of today's movements, where yesterday's records were agreed previously.

Knowing that internal records agree with the various custodians' records enables the STO to carry out the following with confidence.

- Repo trading: the repo trader needs fully accurate information regarding open and settled trades, and settled securities and cash positions at each custodian. If such information is known to be accurate, the repo trader can execute repo trades with confidence, safe in the knowledge that securities listed on internal reports as available to be used as collateral are truly available at the custodian. The subject of repo is explored in Chapter 23.
- Securities lending and borrowing: in parallel with repo trading, those responsible for the lending and borrowing of securities require completely accurate information to maximise revenues and minimise costs for the STO. This topic is described in Chapter 24.
- Credit risk assessment: the risk management department, when assessing counterparty risk, are able to view the trades listed as open on internal records, confident that the information is factual and correct. In the event of the STO needing to quickly assess its risk with counterparties (for instance, under circumstances such as war breaking out in a country in which some of the STO's counterparties reside), the information held within internal records must be fully up-to-date and accurate.
- Income due to the STO: where a dividend on equity or a coupon payment on a bond is due, and the STO calculates that it is entitled to income, identification of who owes the STO the payment is reliant upon whether a trade was open or not, as at a specified date; therefore, a fully up-to-date and accurate picture of open trades and settled securities positions is essential in ensuring the STO receives its income on the due date. This topic will be explored further in Chapter 26.

21.5   ACHIEVING TIMELY AND ACCURATE REFLECTION

Achieving timely and accurate updating of internal records as a result of trade settlement is a two-stage process:

- obtaining the necessary information from each custodian, and
- updating internal records.

The process of updating internal records initially involves the accurate matching of the settled instruction, as advised by the custodian, to the appropriate trade within the settlement system. To recap, following trade capture, a settlement instruction is generated and matched by the counterparty's instruction, the settlement instruction settles at the custodian and the appropriate trade within the settlement system must be updated with the detail of the quantity of securities delivered or received and the amount of cash paid or received.

21.5.1   Obtaining the Information from Custodians

Immediately after settlement has occurred at the custodian, the exact quantity of securities received or delivered and the amount of cash paid or received must be communicated to the account holder; this is a vital part of the service required of a custodian by its account holders.

The information typically contained on an advice of settlement is given in Table 21.20.

Table 21.20

Detail of settlement instruction issued to the custodian by the STO		Detail of settlement as communicated by the custodian to the STO	
From	WSIL	From	Cust. H, Hong Kong
To	Cust. H, Hong Kong	To	WSIL
Depot account no.	111693XM	Depot account no.	111693XM
Nostro account no.	111693XM	Nostro account no.	111693XM
Trade reference	PR30184462	Instruction reference	PR30184462
Deliver/receive	Receive	Deliver/receive	Received
Settlement basis	DvP	Settlement basis	DvP
Value date	17th April	**Settlement date**	18th April
Quantity	4,000,000	Quantity	4,000,000
Security reference	HK1300848212	Security reference	HK1300848212
Settlement currency	HKD	Settlement currency	HKD
NSV	11,688,500.00	NSV	11,688,500.00
Counterparty depot	110242TP	Counterparty depot	110242TP
Counterparty nostro	110242TP	Counterparty nostro	110242TP
Transmission time	12:16 on 14th April	Transmission time	11:34 on 18th April

The method of communicating this information by the custodian is typically the same method as the STO has used for the transmission of the settlement instruction to the custodian. Where the communication method is electronic (such as *S.W.I.F.T.*), such links are two-way, thereby facilitating communication of settlement instruction statuses (refer to Chapter 18) and the detail of settled trades.

In the case of S.W.I.F.T., the detail of settled trades is communicated by an MT 544–547 message type, whilst both Clearstream Luxembourg and Euroclear transmit via messages based on the MT 544–547 S.W.I.F.T. messages. Where an STO uses a custodian's proprietary system for the communication of settlement instructions, detail of settlement is typically communicated by the same method.

Where there is no electronic link with a custodian and settlement instructions have been communicated by manual means such as tested telex, the custodian is likely to report settled trades by telex.

21.5.2   Updating Internal Records

Once information regarding the detail of settled trades is received from the custodian, the updating of internal records can be achieved either manually or automatically, within the settlement system.

The settlement entries must take account of three components of settlement that are variable.

- The settlement date: may be the same as or later than the value date.
- The quantity of securities: the settled quantity may be less than the trade quantity, where partial settlement has occurred.
- The amount of cash: the settled cash amount may be less than the trade net settlement value (NSV) where partial settlement has occurred. Additionally, if the custodian applies a settlement tolerance, the settled cash amount may be above or below the NSV of the trade, but within the custodian's publicised tolerance (see Section 21.8).

Regardless of the method of updating (whether manual or automatic), it is essential to apply the actual settled details relating to these three components accurately against the trade record, otherwise the settlement system will be holding inaccurate information that is likely to adversely affect the aforementioned activities.

Manual Updating

The receipt of settled trade information from a custodian in the form of, for example, a telex requires the STO to take the settlement instruction reference as supplied by the custodian, locate the appropriate trade within the settlement system, and effect settlement entries to update the trade internally.

By input of the settlement instruction reference number into the settlement system, the appropriate trade detail should appear and be available for updating. Where a trade has already been updated and closed, the system should not allow further settlement updating on that trade (this implies the incorrect trade has been selected for updating). The settlement system should allow the input of the settlement date, the quantity of securities delivered or received and the amount of cash paid or received (whether these are the same or different from the trade details). Within some STOs, validation is applied to the manual updating of settlement, to ensure accuracy.

Automatic Updating

The receipt of settled trade information from a custodian by electronic means (e.g. via S.W.I.F.T.) provides the STO with the opportunity to effect settlement updating automatically, within the settlement system.

The settlement system takes the settlement instruction reference number and attempts to locate a trade record with the same number (and if required as an added safeguard, the same security); where the trade record is found, settlement entries will be effected automatically.

However, where a trade record cannot be found, such update failures must be highlighted as an exception.

Automatic Updating Based on Value Date

Where the rate of successful settlement (i.e. percentage of trades settling on value date) is very high within a specific marketplace, STOs may choose to utilise the capability of some settlement systems to automatically assume full settlement on value date, for the full quantity of securities and for the full cash amount, for all trades due to settle at an individual custodian. This is of particular benefit to the STO where a custodian does not report details of settled instructions in an acceptable timeframe, typically due to time zone differences.

Subsequently, however, if the STO receives the report of settled instructions from the custodian, revealing a settlement failure, it is imperative that the STO reverses the settlement updating (for the appropriate trade) within the settlement system immediately, otherwise the settlement system will again be holding inaccurate information. The act of reversing settlement updating is commonly known as 'unsettling'.

21.6   UPDATE FAILURE

In an automated environment, it is to be expected that a very high percentage of settled trade information will be successfully attached to the appropriate trade. However, settlement instructions issued with reference numbers that do not match with the trade reference may mean that automated updating is not possible.

The generation and transmission to custodians of manually created settlement instructions should form a very low percentage of all settlement instructions, within an efficient and automated operational environment. An example of where the manual creation of an instruction may be necessary is in a situation where, immediately prior to value date, it is realised that a trade has been executed, but not captured. As there may be insufficient time to capture the trade and issue settlement instructions automatically, the instruction may be generated and transmitted manually with a 'dummy' trade reference number. Subsequently, the trade is captured and the transmission of the settlement instruction (from the trade) will need to be suppressed, otherwise duplicate settlement may occur. Under these circumstances, once settlement occurs, the updating of the trade within the settlement system cannot occur automatically, unless the settlement system has a specific mechanism to link the instruction reference number with the trade reference number.

All failures to update the appropriate trade should be highlighted immediately as exceptions, to enable such items to be investigated without delay.

21.7   SETTLEMENT INSTRUCTIONS ISSUED UNDER POWER OF ATTORNEY

In a situation where trades have been executed via an Electronic Communications Network (ECN) or a trading platform, settlement instructions may have been issued by the ECN directly to the STO's custodian, under power of attorney granted by the STO to the ECN.

Consequently, settlement instructions generated by the STO's settlement system would have been suppressed, in order to avoid potential duplication of settlement at the custodian (refer to Chapter 16).

Under such circumstances, the reference number on the settlement instruction will be the ECN's reference. This will not be the same reference number as that typically generated on the trade within the STO's settlement system. Consequently, this will cause attempts to automatically update the trade within the settlement system to fail, unless a prior connection has been made that links the instruction reference with the appropriate trade.

21.8   SETTLEMENT WRITE-OFF

Once settlement of an individual trade has occurred externally and all the securities have been delivered or received and the related cash amount has been paid or received, it is possible to have a small cash amount outstanding.

This can occur where the custodian applies a *settlement tolerance* to the cash values of the seller's and buyer's settlement instructions (such as USD 25.00 or currency equivalent within Euroclear, settling against the seller's cash figure). If, as a result of updating the trade record, zero quantity of securities is outstanding, but a small cash amount remains, the settlement system may facilitate the automatic write-off of the remaining cash amount. Alternatively, such situations will need to be identified by requesting reports from the settlement system, followed by the passing of manually entered write-off accounting entries.

Table 21.21 illustrates a write-off situation. Until the write-off is actioned, the trade within the settlement system will still be regarded as open and therefore outstanding with the counterparty, despite the fact that only a small cash amount remains outstanding. Following write-off, whether automatically or manually, the cash amount concerned is transferred to a write-off account.

Table 21.21

		Value date	Settlement date	Quantity	NSV
	Trade record for trade reference PR30184462: as at 18th April				
1	**Trade**	**17th April**		**4,000,000**	**HKD 11,688,500.00**
2	Settlement		18th April	4,000,000	HKD 11,688,400.00
3	Open balance			0	HKD 100.00
4	Write-off		18th April	0	HKD 100.00
3	Open balance			0	0

Some STOs apply a larger write-off cash amount (e.g. USD 100.00) than the custodian may apply, on the basis that it is not cost-effective for its staff to spend time investigating relatively small differences. However, the decision to have any write-off at all, or the decision as to the size of the write-off, is entirely the STO's.

The write-off of an amount of cash results in zero outstanding cash with the counterparty (as well as zero outstanding quantity of securities); the overall result is that the trade record shows the trade to be fully settled in all respects.

Note that it is normal to write-off only cash amounts, not an outstanding quantity of securities.

21.9   UNSETTLING A SETTLED TRADE INTERNALLY

On occasions, an STO may need to amend or cancel a trade that has been fully settled within the settlement system. Such circumstances arise where, for example, the trade has settled at the custodian with the correct counterparty, but it is realised that the incorrect trading book was applied to the original trade.

The trade will usually first be amended within the trading system, then received by the settlement system in the usual fashion. However, if the trade has been settled within the settlement system, the amendment should be rejected. The rejection of such amendments (and cancellations) is a control mechanism designed to avoid duplicate settlement updating. The solution is to 'unsettle' the original trade within the settlement system, thereafter the trade can be amended, following which the amended trade must be updated with the passing of settlement details (as occurred at the custodian originally).

Note that the settlement instruction resulting from the amendment of the original trade must be suppressed and not transmitted to the custodian, as the reason for the amendment is purely internal to the STO.

21.10 SUMMARY

In order for an STO to remain in full control of its assets at all times, it is vital to reflect trade settlement internally in a timely and accurate manner.

22
Position and Trade Related Operations

Whilst Chapters 10–21 focus primarily on the operational processing of trades, the topics contained within the following six chapters relate to the management of positions, with or without open trades.

For instance, *trading positions* are created as a result of trading, but the settlement statuses of the trades making up the position are usually irrelevant to this particular type of position.

Additionally, a securities position held by a custodian on behalf of the STO may not have altered during the last three years, as a single purchase that created the position may have settled three years ago, and since there has been no further trading activity in the security. However, the position exists (without any open trades) and numerous operational activities must be performed in relation to that position.

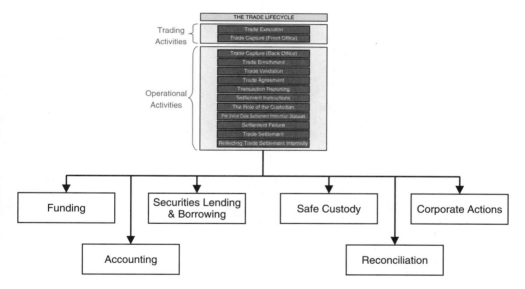

Figure 22.1 Position and trade related operations

Unlike the trade lifecycle that is largely a series of sequential steps, the topics involved in position and trade related operations are typically managed concurrently. The topics covered are represented in Figure 22.1 and are explored within the following six chapters, beginning with the subject of funding and ending with accounting.

23
Funding

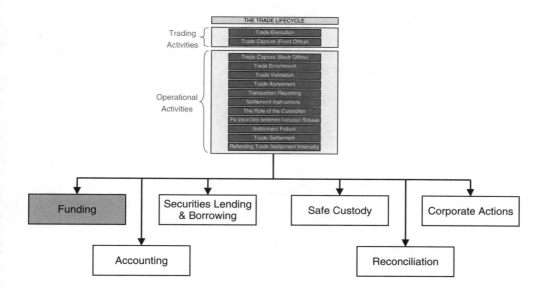

23.1 INTRODUCTION

Following settlement of a purchase of securities on a DvP basis, the STO will be:

* positive of securities, and
* negative of cash (unless a prior credit balance existed)

at the custodian.

The securities typically remain in the STO's account at the custodian until either sold, or repo'd, or lent (the latter will be explored in Chapter 24).

As for a cash overdraft, unless the rate of interest charged by the custodian is reasonable when compared with money market rates, an excessive overdraft cost will have a direct detrimental impact on the STO's P&L. Consequently, STOs typically attempt to minimise the cost of funding their positive securities positions, by borrowing cash from the cheapest possible source.

On occasions, the STO may be positive of cash at the custodian, as a result of one or many sales settling (with a greater cash value than purchases).

Funding is a commonly used term to describe the financing of investments through the borrowing of cash on a secured and/or unsecured basis, and the act of minimising the cost of borrowing cash, and maximising the benefit of lending cash.

The subject of funding is one of the more challenging operational aspects of the securities industry. In order to express the concepts initially, the example of a single purchase of securities and its associated cash will be used to convey the impact on funding, and the choices that STOs have for reducing funding costs.

23.2   FUNDING CHOICES

A typical sequence of events relating to funding is as given in Figure 23.1 (note that this example assumes a starting point of a zero cash balance in the STO's account at the custodian, prior to settlement of the trade). The transmission of the settlement instruction by the STO, the matching of the settlement instruction and the settlement of the STO's purchase at the custodian resulted in the STO having:

- a positive securities position, and
- a negative cash position

at the custodian.

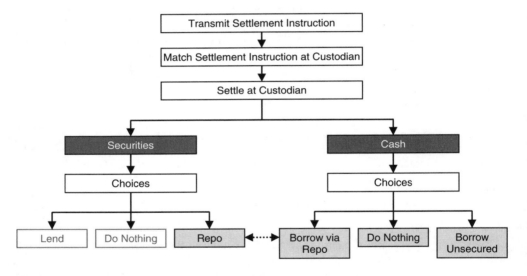

Figure 23.1   Funding choices (purchase by STO)

For completeness, the implications on funding for both securities and cash will be described.

23.2.1   Securities

Following settlement of a purchase, the STO will have a positive securities position at the custodian (assuming no prior trading in the specific security).

Under these circumstances, the STO has a choice of actions relating to the securities.

- Do nothing: should the STO decide not to lend or repo, the securities will remain within the STO's account with the custodian (until such time as the STO issues a further instruction to the custodian).
- Lend the securities: this topic will be explored in Chapter 24.
- Repo the securities: the STO uses the securities as *collateral* to secure the lender of cash (this subject is covered within this chapter).

23.2.2 Cash

Following settlement of a purchase, the STO will have a negative cash position at the custodian (assuming a zero cash balance in the STO's account, prior to settlement of the trade). Under these circumstances, the STO has a choice of action relating to the cash overdraft (although usually STOs aim for a zero balance on their cash accounts at custodians).

- Do nothing: should the STO decide not to cover the overdraft at the custodian, the STO's cash account will remain overdrawn, and attract debit interest on a daily basis, at an interest rate that may be greater than the borrowing rate in the money market.
- Borrow cash unsecured: the STO may decide to borrow cash from a third party such as a bank, where that bank is willing to lend at a lower interest rate (than the custodian will charge the STO).
- Borrow cash via repo: the STO may decide to borrow cash from another STO or an institutional client, by executing a repo transaction. The borrowing of cash by the STO is secured by collateral provided to the cash lender, the collateral normally being the securities that the STO is holding at the custodian. As the cash lender is fully secured (via the receipt of the collateral) and has little or no risk, this is usually the cheapest form of funding for an STO.

The cash choices are explored in the following sections.

23.3   DO NOTHING

Should the STO choose not to borrow cash from another source in order to cover the overdraft at the custodian, the overdraft will continue. Custodians normally charge interest when their account holders are in an overdrawn situation, but from the STO's perspective, the rate of interest charged by the custodian makes this method of funding securities positions typically expensive, when compared with other methods.

Custodians charge interest in the same manner that banks charge interest to the accounts of individuals. The cash interest is typically calculated on overnight balances and derived as follows:

$$\frac{\text{Cash amount} \times \text{Interest rate}\%}{\text{Annual divisor}} \times \text{Number of days}$$

where the annual divisor for each of the world's currencies is calculated on either a 360, 365 or (in a leap year) 366-day basis, and the number of days is normally one, unless the day of the closing balance is a Friday, in which case the interest rate will be applied for the three days of the weekend (Friday–Sunday). There is a similar situation for public holidays, except that the number of days may be four or five.

Note that the calculation of interest on cash is similar to the calculation of bond *accrued interest* (refer to Chapter 8), but should not be confused as the calculations are used for different purposes.

Therefore, in the example of Table 23.1, the two closing balances (on 17th and 18th April) could attract different interest rates (say 5.85% and 5.95% respectively) should the custodian choose to charge it.

Table 23.1

Custodian H, Hong Kong
Statement of *HKD cash account* for World Securities International, London
Account number 111693XM

Entry date	Narrative	Payments	Receipts	Balance
	Balance brought forward from 17th April			−1,120,000.00
18th April	**Instruction reference PR30184462**	**11,688,500.00**		**−12,808,500.00**
	Closing balance as at 18th April			−12,808,500.00

The interest on the closing balance on 17th April would be calculated as follows:

$$\frac{\text{HKD } 1,120,000.00 \times 5.85\%}{365} \times 1 \text{ day} = \text{HKD } 179.51$$

and for the closing balance on 18th April:

$$\frac{\text{HKD } 12,808,500.00 \times 5.95\%}{365} \times 1 \text{ day} = \text{HKD } 2087.96$$

Although the custodian may calculate the interest on the STO's cash overdraft daily, it may debit the cash interest charged to the STO's account periodically (say monthly), rather than daily. Whether there have been any cash movements or not, the custodian is expected to provide the STO with an end-of-day statement of cash balances on a daily basis, to enable the STO to undertake a reconciliation between its records and the custodian's.

In this respect, custodians (just like banks) typically borrow cash in the money markets at a rate of interest, then charge their account holder a higher rate, thereby making a profit on the difference.

Whilst the STO continues to have an overdraft at the custodian, should the STO wish to remove securities from its account with the custodian on an FoP basis, upon receipt of the settlement instruction from the STO, the custodian may reject the instruction on the basis that the overdraft will still be in place but there will be no (or insufficient) securities remaining to secure the overdraft. Conversely, should the custodian choose to act upon the STO's instruction, the custodian will be at risk as there is no guarantee of the STO repaying the overdraft.

If, as a result of the settlement processing at the custodian, the STO's cash account goes into credit (a situation that typically happens only occasionally), dependent upon the currency and the size of the balance, the custodian may pay interest at a rate lower than market rates.

23.4   BORROW (AND LEND) CASH UNSECURED

The STO may choose to borrow cash on an unsecured basis, from a third party, if the cash can be borrowed cheaper than from the custodian.

In order to effect such a borrowing, the STO will need to have set up a prior arrangement with one or many banks, as the STO could borrow the required cash amount from a number of banks. The prior arrangement will be necessary as the STO is unlikely to be successful in borrowing cash just by calling a bank and asking to borrow. The bank will need to assess its risk in lending cash to the particular STO, and should it decide to do so, the bank will place a limit on the amount of cash it is prepared to lend.

The borrower of unsecured cash will normally be charged a higher rate of interest than a borrower of secured cash (e.g. repo), thereby reflecting the cash lender's risk.

Having executed an unsecured borrowing trade, the detail of the trade will need to be recorded within the STO's books and records. The trade will include the following components:

- trade date
- trade time
- operation
- currency
- amount
- counterparty
- start date (opening value date)
- maturity date (closing value date)
- interest rate.

Trade Date

The trade date on an unsecured borrowing or loan is the day the parties to the trade agree to execute the trade.

Trade Time

The exact hour and minute the trade was executed.

Operation

Receipt of cash from the STO's perspective (on the start date) is recorded as a borrowing, whereas payment of cash on the start date is recorded as a loan.

Currency and Cash Amount

The specific currency and amount of cash the STO has borrowed.

Counterparty

The party from whom the STO has borrowed (or to whom the STO has lent) the cash.

Start Date

The intended date of receipt (or payment) of the cash; also known as the opening value date.

Maturity Date

The intended date of repayment to (or by) the counterparty; also known as the closing value date.

Interest Rate

The interest rate is expressed as a percentage, and represents the cost of borrowing cash from the counterparty (or the income receivable from the counterparty when lending cash).

The calculation of interest on the borrowed cash amount is identical to that described in Section 23.3. These actions are represented in Figure 23.2. A trade confirmation is issued by the STO to its counterparty, containing all details of the transaction, including details of the bank to which the STO requires payment to be made.

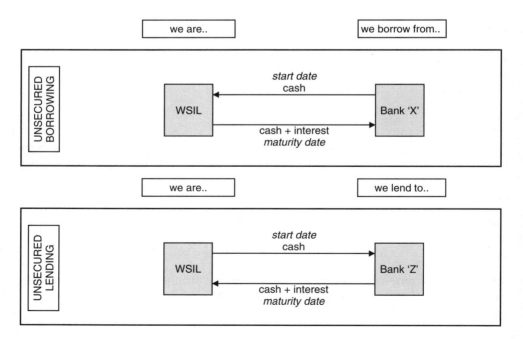

Figure 23.2   Cash transaction types

23.4.1   Settlement Instructions

When borrowing, the STO will require the lender to pay cash to the STO's bank account of its choice:

- the payment could be made directly to the STO's custodian, alternatively
- the STO may require the payment to be made to its main bank account for the specific currency (which may be a different bank from the custodian), requiring that a second payment is then made from the main bank account to the custodian.

In either case, the STO may need to issue a pre-advice of funds to the receiving bank. A pre-advice is an instruction to receive cash, and some custodians may not credit the STO's account with 'good value' if they do not receive a pre-advice by their stated deadline. Pre-advising allows a receiving bank to 'position' its funds while it is still possible to lend or borrow cash in the money market, for the particular value date. For example, if a custodian is aware (by the STO having issued a pre-advice to the custodian) that an STO is arranging for GBP 30 million to be paid to the custodian for value date 'today', the custodian will be able to lend that cash amount in the money market that day, and earn a reasonable rate of interest. Internally, within the custodian's records, the cash amount will be credited to the STO's GBP account that day, thereby reducing or flattening an overdraft. Conversely, if the STO arranges for the GBP 30 million to be paid to the custodian, but fails to issue a pre-advice, dependent upon timing, the custodian may not be aware that the funds are going to be received that day, will not lend the cash in the money market, will not earn interest on the cash, so will not be able to credit the STO's GBP account for value date that day. Typically, in this scenario, the funds will be credited to the STO's account with the custodian the next business day. Clearly, this will be costly to the STO, as not only will the STO be paying interest to the cash lender of the GBP 30 million, but also the STO's overdraft at the custodian will not have been reduced at the earliest time and the custodian will charge overdraft interest accordingly.

When repaying a cash borrowing at maturity, the STO will need to issue a settlement instruction (commonly known as a wire transfer) to either the custodian or its main bank account, to pay the borrowed cash back to the lender, plus interest. The custodian and the main bank will make known to its account holders the deadline by which wire transfers must be received, per currency, per value date. If the deadline is missed, the payment will be delayed and the STO is likely to be penalised by the recipient (i.e. the original cash lender) for loss of interest.

Under the circumstances where the STO has a positive cash position at the custodian (a situation that typically occurs only occasionally), the STO may choose to lend cash, in which case the reverse of the above is necessary. This involves the issuance of a payment instruction to the custodian for payment to the borrower at the start of the borrowing, followed by the issuance of a pre-advice to the STO's receiving bank for the repayment of the funds, plus interest, at maturity.

23.5   BORROW CASH VIA REPO

The following is an overview of what has evolved into a massive supply and demand driven market.

One option for the STO is to cover the overdraft at the custodian by executing a sale and repurchase (commonly known as a repo) transaction. The STO's motivation that results in the execution of a repo trade is typically the need to borrow cash in order to fund a positive securities position (cash-based repo). However, repo can also be used to lend cash and when wishing to borrow or lend securities (securities-based repo).

A cash-based repo is a form of secured (also known as collateralised) cash borrowing, where the STO utilises the securities it holds (or is expecting to receive) at the relevant custodian, to deliver to the cash lender as security for the cash that the STO is borrowing.

In a repo transaction, the securities are effectively sold to the cash lender for the period of the cash loan, with an agreement to repurchase the same (or like) securities at a future date, at which point the borrowed cash will be repaid to the cash lender, plus interest.

Both cash borrower and cash lender benefit from executing repo transactions. The cash borrower benefits because the interest rate charged by the cash lender is generally the lowest of any form of cash borrowing, and the cash lender benefits because he will earn interest on a secured basis where he has little or no risk, and potentially have an asset (the securities) to on-lend. The cash lender could earn interest on an unsecured basis, where the interest rate will be higher than for a repo, but the risk will be that much greater as the loan is not secured.

The following primarily describes a cash-based repo undertaken by an STO that needs to borrow cash to cover a negative cash position at the custodian. Furthermore, the type of repo depicted (of a number of variations which will be described later in this chapter) is a 'classic' repo.

Having executed a cash-based repo, the detail of the transaction will include the following components:

- trading book
- trade date
- trade time
- operation
- currency and cash amount
- collateral
  - security
  - price
  - initial margin
- counterparty
- opening value date
- closing value date
- interest (repo) rate.

Trading Book

Within the STO, repo trades are normally executed by specialist repo traders, whose objective is to minimise the cost of borrowing cash on behalf of all the underlying traders and market makers. Consequently, the trading book for repo trades can be either the underlying trader's trading book, or a central repo trading book.

In a situation within the STO, where two (or more) underlying trading books can trade in the same securities, settle in the same currency, and therefore have an overdraft in the same currency at the same custodian, the repo trader may cover an overdraft at the custodian through the execution of a single repo, effectively on behalf of the two (or more) underlying trading books.

Under these circumstances, the repo trade is likely to be recorded against the central repo trading book, as the cost of the repo is not obviously attributable to a single underlying trading book. This topic will be explored further in Section 23.9.

Conversely, where it is clear that an overdraft at the custodian can be attributed to a single underlying trading book, the repo trade could be recorded directly against that book, rather than the central repo trading book.

STOs normally adopt a policy of either recording all repo trades against the underlying trading book, or against the central repo trading book, but typically not a mixture of both.

Trade Date

The trade date on a repo is the day the parties to the trade agree to execute the trade.

Trade Time

The exact hour and minute that the trade was executed.

Operation

When borrowing cash and delivering collateral to the cash lender, a *repo* has been executed. Conversely, when lending cash and receiving collateral, a *reverse repo* has been executed.

To clarify this, because the nature of the transaction is two-legged, the operation refers to the action on the first leg from the STO's perspective:

- for a repo
  - on the first leg (the opening leg), cash is received by the STO (the cash borrower) and collateral is delivered by the STO to the cash lender
  - on the second leg (the closing leg), cash is repaid by the STO to the cash lender plus interest, and collateral is returned to the STO by the cash lender
- for a reverse repo
  - on the first leg (the opening leg), cash is paid by the STO (the cash lender) and collateral is received by the STO from the cash borrower
  - on the second leg (the closing leg), cash is received by the STO from the cash borrower plus interest, and collateral is returned by the STO to the cash borrower.

These actions are represented in Figure 23.3. Consequently, for a single transaction, the cash borrower regards the transaction as a repo, whereas the cash lender considers the same transaction to be a reverse repo. Note that the above are normally settled on a DvP basis.

Currency and Cash Amount

The specific currency and amount of cash that the STO wishes to borrow is typically the driving force behind a cash-based repo.

Collateral

Collateral is a generic term to describe any asset that is used to secure a borrowing of cash, and may take the form of property, life assurance policy, cash, or in this case securities. In the event that the cash borrower fails to repay the borrowed cash to the lender, the cash lender will sell the collateral in order to raise the cash it is owed. However, this

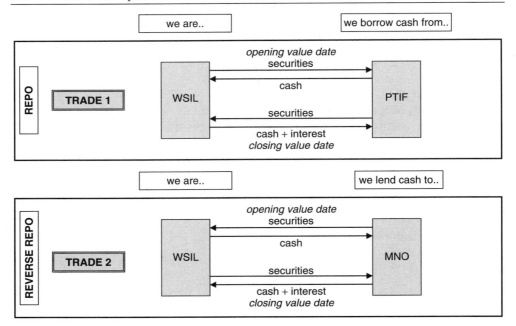

Figure 23.3   Securities and cash transaction types

course of action is very rarely necessary. STOs borrowing cash via repo usually utilise the securities they hold at the custodian as collateral.

The cash lender is likely to require collateral of a certain type and of a certain quality, in an attempt to ensure its value does not fall below a certain level. It is usual for issuer ratings to be used when assessing the quality of securities. These ratings are published by *ratings agencies* such as:

- Moody's Investors Service
- Standard & Poor's

that operate a system of ratings to indicate the ratings agency's opinion of the issuer's ability to repay an individual bond at maturity, according to the bond's characteristics (refer to Section 23.5.10). Table 23.2 indicates typical published ratings classes.

The STO and its repo counterparty will need to agree upon the minimum acceptable collateral rating. It may be possible for the cash borrower to negotiate a lower interest rate, the higher the quality of collateral it is able to deliver. Typically, the collateral used in repo trades is rated Aa, and above.

A single piece of collateral, or multiple pieces (also known as a basket of collateral) may be used in a repo transaction, although the limitations of some settlement systems may restrict some STOs to the use of only single pieces.

Security/Price/Initial Margin. Table 23.3 is an example of a cash-based repo transaction using multiple pieces of collateral. Table 23.3 shows that the STO has agreed to borrow EUR 25 million cash from counterparty PTIF for 10 days (12th–22nd August), at a cost of 4.7% (the interest rate payable).

Table 23.2

Moody's	Description
Aaa	Best quality bonds; extremely strong ability to repay
Aa	High quality bonds; very strong ability to repay
A	Upper medium grade bonds; strong repayment ability
Baa	Medium grade bonds; adequate repayment ability
Ba	Lower medium grade bonds; carry speculative elements; repayment ability uncertain
B	Low grade bonds; degree of vulnerability to non payment
Caa	Poor grade bonds; may be in default; vulnerable to non payment
Ca	Very poor grade bonds; often in default; very high vulnerability to non payment
C	Lowest grade of bonds; extremely poor prospects of ever attaining investment grade rating

Table 23.3

Borrow EUR 25,000,000.00 from PTIF, repo rate 4.7%, trade date 10th August, trade time 09:17, opening value date 12th August, closing value date 22nd August

Collateral			Calculations		
Quantity	Security	Price	Principal (EUR)	Accrued Interest (EUR)	Net Market Value (EUR)
EUR 5m	Bond X	98.75%	4,937,500.00	28,000.00	4,965,500.00
EUR 12.5m	Bond Y	96.25%	12,031,250.00	456,000.00	12,487,250.00
EUR 7.5m	Bond Z	99.45%	7,458,750.00	88,500.00	7,547,250.00
			Total collateral value		**25,000,000.00**

Security: having agreed the trade details with the counterparty, the collateral can be applied by the STO. The collateral must be in line with the minimum quality acceptable to the cash lender, and the STO is able to select from its pool of collateral at the custodian precisely the one or many pieces of collateral, and the quantity of each piece, to provide as collateral. The securities given as collateral are those that the STO holds at the time of repo trade execution, or those it predicts will be held at the custodian by the time of the opening value date. The securities used in repo transactions have historically been debt instruments, due to their cash flow predictability. However, equity repos are gradually being introduced (refer to Section 23.5.10). Clearly, the STO will want to avoid using as collateral any securities already sold and due to be delivered imminently.

In a cash-based repo, the STO selects the securities to be delivered (within the agreed parameters); the collateral used in a cash-based repo is known as 'general collateral' or 'GC'. (If the counterparty to the repo transaction requires specific securities rather than 'general collateral', this changes the motivation for executing the transaction and is referred to as 'specials' trading; refer to Section 23.5.2.)

The cash lender may accept the security used as collateral being denominated in a currency other than the currency of the lent cash; this is commonly known as cross-currency repo.

Price: the price applied to the collateral is the current market price, and (in the case of a bond) accrued interest is calculated to the opening value date. The net market value is the sum of the quantity multiplied by price, plus accrued interest in each case. Note that a price inclusive of accrued interest is known as a *dirty price* or all-in price.

Initial margin: in order to take account of the credit standing of the counterparty, an STO may:

- when executing a repo trade, provide the counterparty with a lesser value of securities, and
- when executing a reverse repo, demand a greater value of securities

than the cash value of the trade. The differential is commonly known as 'initial margin' or 'haircut', and is used where the STO or its counterparty requires an additional level of comfort (over and above the collateral value) when trading with certain counterparties.

Under some circumstances, the security type (equity or debt) and the quality of the security can result in an initial margin being applied. Cross currency repos may also attract margin to account for potential currency volatility.

Consequently, initial margin is not applied to all repo trades.

Counterparty

Those who participate in repos are usually STOs and institutional investors.

Opening Value Date

The opening value date is the intended date of delivery of the collateral versus the borrowed cash; this date is also known as the 'starting leg', the 'open date' or the 'onside'.

Closing Value Date

The intended date of return of cash plus interest versus collateral is known as the closing value date; this date is also known as the 'closing leg', the 'end date' or the 'offside'.

Interest (Repo) Rate

In a cash-based repo, the interest rate payable by the cash borrower is known as the repo rate. In the above example, the calculation of the interest component of the trade is as follows:

$$\frac{\text{EUR } 25{,}000{,}000.00 \times 4.7\%}{360} \times 10 \text{ days} = \text{EUR } 32{,}638.89$$

the interest normally being payable at the close of the transaction, but in some cases interest 'to date' being payable periodically during the life of the repo.

23.5.1   In Credit at the Custodian

If the STO's cash account at the custodian goes into credit as a result of settlement processing, the STO could lend cash via a reverse repo, against receipt of collateral from the cash borrower.

23.5.2   Securities-based Repo

The need to borrow specific securities because they are 'short' is the motivation behind an STO executing a securities-based (reverse) repo. Unlike a cash-based repo, where the individual securities are not specified by either party (only the quality of collateral, as indicated by the rating, is stipulated), a securities-based repo is executed only if the prospective lender has the required securities available for lending.

Under these circumstances, the specific securities are typically exchanged for cash (or other securities), but in this situation, the 'service provider' is the STO's counterparty that supplies the required securities. The STO must expect to pay the counterparty for providing such a service.

However, where the STO provides cash as the collateral for borrowing securities, the STO expects some return on that cash. This situation is overcome by the STO agreeing to receive a lower (than GC) repo rate on its cash, and in some situations where the required securities are in great demand but short supply, the STO may agree to a negative repo rate, resulting in the STO receiving less cash at the close of the repo than was paid at the opening.

23.5.3   Settlement

The settlement of repo trades is essentially the same as for other trades from a risk perspective. Those who undertake repo trades usually wish to avoid the risk of exchanging cash and collateral on a non-simultaneous basis, and so it is normal for repo trades to settle on a DvP basis.

Settlement instructions are generated and transmitted by the STO to the relevant custodian, the custodian attempts to match the instruction with the counterparty's instruction, the custodian applies pre-value date statuses, and settlement occurs on or after value date.

Therefore, in a cash-based repo, the way in which the cash borrower normally receives his cash on the opening leg of the repo is via DvP settlement with the cash lender, as for settlement of the closing leg.

In a minority of cases, where an STO executes a repo with an institutional client, the client may require the STO to hold the collateral in safe custody on the client's behalf. This topic is explored in Chapter 25.

23.5.4   Events During the Life of the Repo

Between the opening and closing value date of a repo, a number of main events (sometimes referred to as subsequent events) can occur. Primarily, these are:

- margin calls
- collateral substitution
- rate changes
- coupon payments.

Margin Calls

Should the value of the collateral rise or fall beyond an agreed level (commonly known as 'variation margin') during the life of the repo, a margin call may be made by whichever party is exposed, in order to bring the value of collateral into line with the cash amount lent or borrowed.

From the day following trade execution, or at any point during the 'life' of the repo transaction, the price of the securities is subject to market fluctuation. Margin calls may be effected when the net market value of the securities surpasses or is less than an agreed level. As soon as prices change, either the STO or its counterparty would be exposed. For example, if the value of the securities increased, the STO would have a greater value of securities with the cash lender than was necessary, and if the value of the securities decreased, the cash lender would be short of collateral and therefore exposed. Margin calls result in an appropriate movement of securities or cash between the two parties.

In order to know whether the STO has an exposure, every day during the life of the repo each piece of collateral is valued for comparison purposes, based on current market prices (and including the current value of accrued interest). The revaluation process is known as *marking to market* (meaning to mark the position to the current market price). The collation of current market prices can be achieved in an automated manner, by the STO subscribing to one or many feeds of prices from *securities data providers*. Note that this is one of a number of uses of current market prices; refer to Section 13.6.2.

Collateral Substitution

As stated previously within this chapter, in a cash-based repo the securities given as collateral by the cash borrower are typically those that, at the time of the repo trade execution, are not required to be delivered because, for example, they have not been sold or lent.

However, the STO's bond or equity trader may decide to sell securities that are, at the time of execution of a principal sale, being used as collateral within a repo transaction. Under these circumstances, the STO will require the security in question to be returned by the cash lender, and substituted by one or many different pieces of collateral of acceptable quality (if agreed at time of trade execution, commonly known as 'right of substitution'). This will typically affect the repo rate.

Rate Changes

The repo rate agreed at the time of trade execution is, in the case of 'open' repos (see Section 23.5.6), subject to change.

Rate changes arise as a result of general daily movements in interest rates, and need to be agreed between the parties to the trade as and when necessary. However, in order to avoid the administrative burden of small rate adjustments on a daily basis, rate changes may be agreed periodically.

In order to calculate the correct value of repo interest payable or receivable on an individual trade, it is necessary to keep a history of rate changes, with their effective date.

Coupon Payments

Coupons that become payable during the life of the repo are due to the legal owner of the securities; legal title changes hands for both classic repo and buy/sell-back trades (see below).

In a classic repo trade, it is usual for the legal agreement (described later in this chapter) to state that the recipient of the coupon payment (the cash lender) is obliged to remit an equal amount to the borrower of cash, on the day of receipt. However, in a buy/sell-back, the cash lender retains the coupon and the cash element of the trade reflects this.

23.5.5 The Closing Leg

At maturity of the repo transaction, the cash lender is repaid the original cash amount lent plus the interest earned (at the repo rate, for the number of days of the loan); the cash borrower receives delivery of its collateral. As for the opening leg, the movement of cash and collateral for the closing leg is usually effected on a DvP basis.

23.5.6 Types of Repo Transaction

Two main types of repo transactions exist, namely:

* classic repo (also known as traditional repo, or simply repo), and
* buy/sell-back.

Note that the type of repo described to this point in this chapter has been a classic repo.

Classic Repo

Classic repos can be traded on a

* term basis: at the time of trade execution the closing value date is agreed, therefore the cash borrowing against delivery of collateral has a fixed time to maturity, and a fixed repo rate for the life of the repo;
* open basis: at the time of trade execution, the parties to the trade agree not to fix the closing value date (yet), and agree to keep the trade open until one of the parties needs to close the trade, at which point a closing value date will be agreed. The repo rate is subject to change during the life of the repo, as interest rates fluctuate.

For both term and open repos, there are two parties to the transaction; this is known as bilateral trading.

Tri-party Repo. Should an STO wish to execute classic repo transactions but, as an example, does not have the internal infrastructure capable of processing multiple pieces of collateral, margin calls and substitution, an option is for the STO to execute classic repos on a tri-party basis. See Section 23.11.

In a tri-party repo, the three parties to the transaction are:

* the cash borrower,
* the cash lender, and
* the tri-party agent.

The tri-party agent acts as a middleman between the cash borrower and lender, ensuring that:

* the securities supplied as collateral by the cash borrower are of the appropriate quality;

- following DvP settlement of the opening leg, the collateral is held in a segregated account by the tri-party agent, for and on behalf of the cash lender, followed by DvP settlement of the closing leg;
- the collateral is revalued on a daily basis and margin calls are made when necessary;
- collateral substitution is effected (often automatically) where the cash borrower requires the return of some or all of the original collateral.

Thereby effecting the administration of the repo, both at the time of trade execution and during the life of the repo.

Those who act as tri-party agents include Bank of New York and the two ICSDs (Clearstream Luxembourg and Euroclear). Where the ICSDs are used as tri-party agents, the collateral given by a cash borrower can be selected:

- by the cash borrower (as per a non-tri-party repo), or
- by the ICSD, via the automatic selection of collateral from the cash borrower's main account at the ICSD.

Buy/Sell-Back

A buy/sell-back is a form of repo whereby securities are sold outright and simultaneously repurchased at a future value date. Typically, a single security is utilised as collateral for the borrowing or loan of cash. Where STOs do not have adequate systems in order to process classic repos, or agreements are not yet in place between the two parties, buy/sell-backs can be used.

In a buy/sell-back, on the opening leg, the security is priced using the current market price plus bond accrued interest to the opening value date. This calculation is identical to that for classic repo.

On the closing leg, the amount of cash interest payable is added to the cash amount borrowed and the total is expressed in the closing (also known as 'forward') price.

The main differences between a buy/sell-back and a classic repo are:

- in a classic repo the repo interest is identifiable as a separate trade component, whereas in a buy/sell-back the interest is integrated into the closing leg price;
- variation margin is applicable to classic repo, but not to buy/sell-back;
- in a classic repo, an amount equivalent to the coupon is paid to the original owner of the collateral, whereas in a buy/sell-back, the coupon received is retained by the cash lender.

23.5.7 Legal Agreement

For classic repo and occasionally for buy/sell-back, trades are typically executed only after the STO and the counterparty have agreed the legal terms for such transactions. Agreements are necessary in order to protect the interests of the parties involved in executing repo transactions. The main agreement used is the TBMA/ISMA agreement.

The terms of such agreements include reference to:

- legal ownership of the securities;
- the circumstances under which margin calls are permitted;

- the party that is entitled to income falling due within the life of the repo;
- in the event of the borrower failing to repay the borrowed cash or return the borrowed securities, entitlement as to the collateral (events of default).

23.5.8   Ownership

On a classic repo and in a buy/sell-back, ownership (rights and title) of the collateral passes to the cash lender for the 'life' of the repo, reverting to the cash borrower as at maturity of the transaction.

23.5.9   Repo Operational Processing Overview

Although repos are executed for different reasons and have fundamentally different components compared with other transaction types, from an operational processing perspective there are many similarities and some differences. For example:

- Static data is required to hold the current rating of the security, to allow automation of collateral selection.
- Trades may be captured within a repo trading system, then fed to the settlement system, or input directly to the settlement system.
- Repo trades require enrichment with accrued interest and custodian details for both the trading company and the counterparty.
- Trade validation should be used in order to trap erroneous information prior to transmission to the outside world.
- Trade confirmations are required to be issued to the counterparty, leading to agreement of all details as soon as possible after trade execution.
- Transaction reporting must be effected in order to inform the regulator of an executed trade, although this is optional in some markets.
- Settlement instructions need to be issued for both the opening and closing legs of the repo, at the appropriate time.
- Unmatched and advisory instructions must be investigated and resolved without delay [these can occur on either (or both) the opening and closing legs].
- A full history of settlement instruction statuses must be maintained (for both legs).
- Settlement instructions are subject to settlement failure at the custodian (for both legs).
- Following settlement at the custodian, the STO's books and records must be updated accordingly (for both legs).

Figure 23.4 is a summarised view of typical actions that occur on a classic repo.

23.5.10   Repo Security Types

Over the many years that repo transactions have been undertaken in the various markets, the normal security type used has been debt, largely due to the predictability of cash flows (i.e. future coupon payment and maturity amounts, and the dates of those payments).

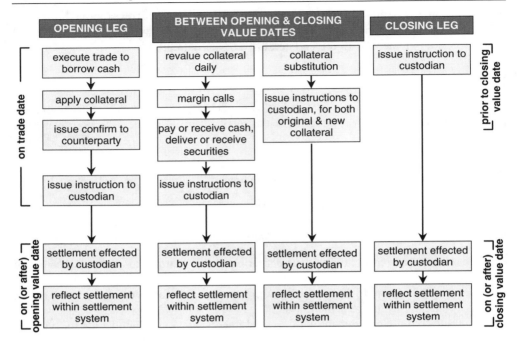

Figure 23.4 Classic repo trade overview

More recently, the holders of equity have been able to use these assets as collateral in repo trades. However, a number of issues require consideration, such as:

- the potential price volatility of equity (and its implications for changes in collateral values);
- the lack of certainty regarding the future value of equity;
- actions to be taken if and when the issuer announces one of the many types of *corporate action* that can affect equity (refer to Chapter 26).

These are in addition to those mentioned previously in this chapter.

23.5.11 Matched-book Repo Trading

As well as undertaking repos for the purposes of funding and borrowing securities, some STOs undertake the independent trading of repos, in order to make profit; this is known as 'matched-book' trading.

Profit is made where, for example, a repo trade with one counterparty is matched by an equal and opposite trade with a different counterparty. Usually, the only differences between the two repo trades are:

- the direction (an STO will execute a repo and a reverse repo)
- the counterparties
- the repo rate

and it is the difference in the repo rates that produces the profit for the STO.

23.6   CURRENCY MOVEMENT DEADLINES

STOs will incur overdraft or credit interest at custodians' rates as a result of settlement processing, unless the STO can take action within a custodian's cash movement deadlines.

23.6.1   Local Custodians and NCSDs

The settlement processing each day at a local custodian or NCSD will result in an STO's cash account having an overdraft, credit or zero balance typically in the local currency.

The timing of the settlement processing may allow sufficient time for the STO to be advised of the new balance, and where in an overdraft or credit balance situation, there may be a window of time prior to the cash movement deadlines in the local money market to pay in cash or pay out cash from the STO's account at the custodian, for value date the same day.

Therefore, providing the STO actively seeks 'today's' cash balance following the settlement processing, it may be possible to minimise funding costs by, in the case of an overdraft, for instance, borrowing cash at a lower interest rate (via secured borrowing) and arranging to pay that cash amount to the STO's account at the custodian, without incurring overdraft interest at the custodian.

As described earlier in this Chapter (Section 23.4) the local custodian or NCSD will have fixed deadlines for account holders to advise the custodian of incoming movements (pre-advising) and outgoing movements (wire transfer) for value date 'today'.

From the perspective of the STO managing its cash account at the custodian and successfully operating within these deadlines, if the STO is located in the same time zone as the custodian, minimising funding costs may be possible. However, it may prove much more of a challenge if the STO is located in a different time zone.

23.6.2   ICSDs

The two *ICSDs*, namely Euroclear and Clearstream Luxembourg, operate cash accounts in numerous currencies on behalf of their participants. At the time of writing, both ICSDs handle at least 25 currencies.

At both ICSDs, the overnight (as opposed to intra-day) settlement processing occurs in the early hours of value date. The results of settlement processing are available at around 05:00 European time on the value date. Participants of the ICSDs are able to obtain post-settlement cash account balances at this time. However, an STO's ability to cover an overdraft or to lend out a credit balance, so as not to incur the ICSDs' interest rates, is dependent upon the currency and geography.

During any one day, banks are open in different parts of the globe at different times, meaning that at 09:00 in Paris it is too late to instruct for movement of Japanese Yen for that same value date, but is not too late to instruct for movement of US Dollars for the same value date.

Along similar lines as for local custodians or NCSDs, ICSDs have prestated deadlines for the movement of all currencies they handle. These deadlines are directly relevant to the deadlines imposed on the ICSDs, by their own network of correspondent banks around the globe. Each correspondent bank (typically one for each currency and located in the main financial centre of the specific country) operates cash accounts for the ICSD, which in turn holds cash accounts for its account holders. When an STO requires cash to be paid out from its account with the ICSD, the STO instructs the ICSD directly. The ICSD then instructs its relevant correspondent bank (according to the currency involved) to make the payment to the recipient's bank. Conversely, when the STO wishes to pay in cash to its account at the ICSD, the relevant correspondent bank of the ICSD must be paid directly, but the STO must also issue a pre-advice to the ICSD to ensure that the STO receives 'good value', meaning that they receive credit on the intended date.

Depending upon the timeliness of the instruction issued to the ICSD, cash will be moved either:

1. on the same day as the receipt of the instruction, or
2. on the next business day following receipt of the instruction, or
3. on the second business day following receipt of the instruction

according to the currency in question.

Those currencies that fall within category 1 are, broadly speaking, the major European currencies (including EUR, GBP, DKK, NOK, SEK, CHF) and all major North and South American currencies (including USD, CAD, MXN, ARS). Cash can be moved in these currencies on the same day as instructed, because the money markets and banks in the relevant countries are still open, or have not yet opened, for 'today'. Note that a selective list of ISO currency codes can be found in Chapter 9.

Category 2 currencies, in general, are currencies where the money markets and banks have closed for 'today'; these are typically eastern currencies, including JPY, HKD, AUD, NZD, IDR, MYR, PHP, SGD and THB. The day that such cash movement becomes effective is the business day following the receipt of the instruction by the ICSD.

Currencies falling within category 3 are all other currencies, such as the ISK and the KWD, where the effective date of the cash movement is two business days after the ICSD receives the instruction.

In summary, if the STO waits for the results of the settlement process at the ICSDs, prior to arranging inbound or outbound cash movements, only for category 1 currencies can the STO avoid incurring overdraft or credit interest on its account at the ICSD. For category 2 currencies, overdraft or credit interest will be incurred for a minimum of one night, whilst a minimum of two nights will be incurred for category 3 currencies.

The only alternative (to incurring overdraft or credit interest on its account at the custodian) is for the STO to project funding requirements in advance, and to act on the projection in anticipation of settlement, so that the receipt into the STO's account at the custodian offsets the overdraft incurred at the custodian as a result of trade settlement, on the same date (see Section 23.7).

23.7   FUNDING PROJECTION

For a currency where the cash movement instruction needs to be issued in advance of a given value date, a projection needs to be undertaken by the STO. Remember that settlement of securities trades on value date is not guaranteed.

The objective is to predict in advance the amount of cash overdraft (or credit balance) that is expected at a custodian on a future date (typically over the next two business days), then to act upon the prediction. If the prediction is accurate, the following should happen: when settlement occurs at the custodian, the resultant debit or credit balance is offset by a corresponding cash movement for the same value date, resulting in a zero cash balance and no debit or credit interest being incurred at the custodian. The incoming cash movement, with a value date coinciding with the expected date of settlement of the trades, would have been instructed one or two days previously, as a result of the funding projection exercise.

To be clear, funding projection is necessary when an overdraft or credit balance occurs at a custodian as a result of settlement, where it is not possible to pay in cash (to cover an overdraft) or pay out cash (to flatten a credit balance) on that same day. At custodians where this situation arises, the alternative to funding projection is to wait for settlement to occur, then pay in or pay out cash as soon as possible, which will typically be either one or two days after settlement has occurred. For those one or two days, overdraft (or credit) interest will be charged at the custodian's rates.

23.7.1 Basic Projection

Basic projection involves calculation of the net cash value that could settle:

- per custodian nostro account
- per currency
- per value date
  - including all trades for the specific value date, plus the cash value of all failed trades and all partially failed trades (i.e. the amount remaining open after partial settlement), as these trades could settle on the next business day.

It is normal for a report to be produced from the settlement system, containing the information listed in Table 23.4. This report is dated three days in advance of the value date; it assumes that all trades will settle on 16th February, and therefore shows that the result will be an overdraft of AUD 4,500,000.00. The STO may choose to act upon this information, and on 13th February arrange to pay in this cash amount to the account, for value date 16th February, having borrowed the cash from an external source such as another STO or a bank, on a secured or unsecured basis.

Table 23.4

Funding projection report dated 13th February, for expected settlements at: Custodian A, Sydney, AUD cash account number 5023598 **Trades value dated 16th February plus current failed trades**			
Trade reference	Transaction type	Outgoing cash	Incoming cash
P005907	Principal buy (fail)	AUD 1,000,000.00	
P006479	Principal buy	AUD 5,000,000.00	
P006485	Principal buy	AUD 7,500,000.00	
P007113	Principal sale		AUD 3,000,000.00
R8001194	Repo onside		AUD 6,000,000.00
		AUD 13,500,000.00	**AUD 9,000,000.00**

The funding projection exercise is usually not an exact science, as in markets other than those where the rate of successful settlement is extremely high (say 95–100%) it may be impossible to project which trades will and will not settle with any degree of certainty. However, if statistics can be gathered from the STO's settlement system concerning the rate of successful settlement, such as:

- the percentage of all past trades that settled successfully on their value date at the custodian, and
- the percentage of all past trades that settled successfully on their value date at the custodian with a specified counterparty

the accuracy of predictions should increase.

A specific funding issue that STOs need to address is a circumstance where, for example, the historic rate of successful settlement at a custodian is 88%, and where the STO has a situation with 10 trades due for settlement in three days' time, the cash value of nine of the trades being of small or average size, with the tenth trade being very large. Table 23.5 shows such an example.

Table 23.5

Funding projection report dated 13th February, for expected settlements at:
Custodian A, Sydney, AUD cash account number 5023598
Trades value dated 16th February plus current failed trades

Trade reference	Transaction type	Outgoing cash	Incoming cash
P005907	Principal buy (fail)	AUD 1,000,000.00	
P006479	Principal buy	AUD 5,000,000.00	
P006485	Principal buy	AUD 7,500,000.00	
P006499	Principal buy	AUD 4,000,000.00	
P006510	Principal buy	AUD 3,500,000.00	
P006511	Principal buy	AUD 1,500,000.00	
P007113	Principal sale		AUD 3,000,000.00
P007119	Principal sale		AUD 2,500,000.00
P007203	Principal sale		AUD 35,000,000.00
R8001194	Repo onside		AUD 6,000,000.00
		AUD 22,500,000.00	**AUD 46,500,000.00**

The predicament for the STO is whether to consider the largest trade (in the example, trade reference P007203) as likely to settle on value date or not; time will tell whether the prediction was correct. If the prediction proves to be correct, the STO's funding cost will be minimised, as little or no cash balance will remain overnight within the STO's account at the custodian. If the prediction proves to be incorrect, the cost to the STO could be large. For example, AUD 50 million for one night at 2% (the difference between the credit rate received and the prevailing market rate) is over AUD 2700.00; if a weekend is involved (Friday–Sunday inclusive), the amount would be over AUD 8000.00. *Reminder:* this is on one currency only; an STO could be in a similar situation in a number of other currencies, in parallel. Ultimately, the STO can only attempt to predict accurately, by use of experienced operations staff and by use of statistics of past settlement success and failure, by market and by counterparty.

Particular care must be taken when public holidays are approaching, as to leave a cash balance earning interest at anything other than market rates over a holiday that, for example, includes Friday and the following Monday will result in five nights of potentially high overdraft interest (or of low credit interest) being incurred by the STO.

To provide an idea of scale, the daily funding requirements of a large STO can be several billion (in USD terms), typically made up of balances in numerous currencies.

23.8   COLLATERAL MANAGEMENT AT CUSTODIANS

STOs that are active in the use of their collateral must ensure that sufficient collateral remains in their account at each custodian, to enable settlement of everyday purchases to occur (refer to Chapter 20).

In a situation where an STO has ample collateral at a custodian, if large amounts of collateral are removed from the account (for example, to secure the borrowing of cash through repo trades), this may leave a dangerously low level of remaining collateral in the STO's account at the custodian. Under such circumstances, some of the STO's purchases may not settle due to insufficient collateral in its account.

Some STOs focus on collateral management at custodians by running reports of the projected collateral position from the settlement system, to ensure that maximum use of collateral is made (e.g. to enable the borrowing of cash at the cheapest rates), but also to ensure sufficient collateral remains at custodians.

23.9   INTERNAL FUNDING ALLOCATION

In a situation where an STO has a single trading book per currency, the rightful 'owner' of funding costs is not difficult to identify. Regardless of the method of funding used (whether the cash balance has been left at the custodian, whether cash has been borrowed unsecured, or whether cash has been borrowed via repo), the funding costs can be attributed to that one trading book. This enables funding costs to be offset against trading P&L calculations, thereby producing reasonably accurate P&L at trading book level.

However, in a situation where two or more trading books have settled securities positions at the same custodian and in the same currency, the identification of the rightful owner of funding costs can become much more of a challenge.

The allocation of funding costs may be relatively straightforward if the combined settled securities positions of the two trading books are funded at the same rate of interest via, for example, a single, unsecured cash borrowing.

Under the following type of circumstance, funding costs are more difficult to allocate. An STO's trading book A has a settled bond position at the custodian of USD 15 million, at a cost of USD 15 million (so as to make the explanation of the concept simple), and trading book B has USD 6 million bonds at a cost of USD 6 million, with all the bonds held within the same account at the custodian. The STO will be charged at a rate of, say, 7% by the custodian, if the overdraft of USD 21 million is continued. The repo trader borrows USD 12 million via a classic repo executed with another STO, at a rate of 5.1%, and the remaining USD 9 million is funded via an unsecured borrowing at a rate of 6.2%.

A number of views could be taken regarding how to allocate funding costs (remember though, that funding has a negative impact on traders' P&L, so individual traders are likely to contend any method that results in more than minimum cost). For example:

• trader A is likely to take the view that all USD 12 million borrowed via a repo should be allocated against his book, on the basis that he had more than this entire amount at the custodian, so why should the benefit be shared? If this occurs, out of trader A's total position of USD 15 million, USD 12 million will be charged at a rate of 5.1%, the remaining USD 3 million will be charged at 6.2%;

- trader B is just as likely to take a similar stance, so that his entire USD 6 million settled position is charged to him at the lowest rate, namely 5.1%. He is very likely to be unwilling to accept the entire USD 6 million being charged at the highest rate, namely 6.2%. He may be happier with the first USD 3 million being charged at 5.1%, the second being charged at 6.2%;
- the management may take the view that under such circumstances, the STO as a whole has benefited from reduced funding costs (compared with the cost of borrowing at the custodian), so both traders should be charged at a blended rate (in this case 5.5714%), being the weighted average rate taking into account all methods of funding adopted for a given currency.

It is generally accepted that there is no one correct way of allocating funding costs internally, and the method of allocation within an individual STO is typically the decision of its trading management.

23.10　UPDATING INTERNAL BOOKS AND RECORDS

Where the STO takes funding related action, whether:

- only cash is involved (as in an unsecured borrowing or loan), or
- where securities are involved (as in a repo)

there is a need to update internal records for the purpose of reflecting action taken in the outside world.

Having borrowed cash on an unsecured basis, for example, the STO will need to record:

- the details of the transaction;
- that cash has been received into the STO's bank account on the start date;
- that cash is due to be repaid to the specific lender on the maturity date, plus interest;
- that cash plus interest has been repaid on the maturity date.

Having executed a classic repo where, for example, cash has been borrowed against securities as collateral, the STO will need to record:

- the details of the transaction;
- that cash has been received from, and collateral delivered to, the counterparty on the opening value date;
- that the cash borrowed is due to be repaid, plus interest, versus receipt of the outstanding collateral, on the closing value date;
- in the event of a margin call, the receipt or payment of cash, or the receipt or delivery of securities;
- in the event of collateral substitution, the movements of the returned security and the replacement security (or securities);
- that cash plus interest has been repaid, and that the outstanding collateral has been returned.

Unless such records are kept:

- the STO will have a false view of the situation, potentially affecting the actions of the repo trader and those responsible for securities lending and borrowing (refer to the following chapter);
- the STO will not be able to reconcile its bank accounts or its securities account with the custodian;
- the credit risk of the STO's assets (whether cash or securities) being held outside of its control will not be assessed;
- corporate actions calculations may be adversely affected (refer to Chapter 26).

In general, the STO will not be in control of its assets.

23.11   AUTOMATION

The amount of administration involved with the full processing of repos should not be underestimated. An STO that is active in the execution of repo trades will need to:

- apply collateral to each newly executed trade,
- mark to market each piece of collateral on all 'live' repos every day,
- process margin calls, and
- manage collateral substitution.

Unless an STO has adequate systems, the repo traders are likely to be prevented from executing as many repo trades as are necessary to minimise the STO's funding costs, otherwise the settlement department would soon be unable to cope.

Additionally, it is imperative that a complete record of all components of repo trades is kept within the STO's books and records, including details of each piece of collateral, all margin calls, collateral substitutions, etc.

23.12   SUMMARY

For STOs wishing to minimise the cost of holding positive securities positions, focusing on funding is of paramount importance. Much cash can be saved by predicting cash balances in advance (where necessary), and operating within the cash movement deadlines set by the various custodians.

In addition, rather than allowing securities holdings to remain idle by leaving them in the account at the custodian, maximising their use (as used in repo trades, for example) increases income and reduces costs for the STO.

24
Securities Lending and Borrowing

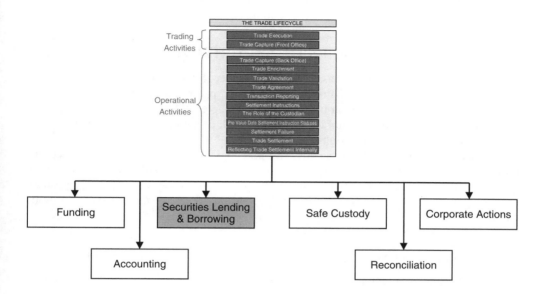

24.1 INTRODUCTION

Investors who own securities can enhance the return on their investment by lending securities to those who wish to borrow.

Various investors have different outlooks on the subject of securities lending:

- some investors choose to lend their entire inventory of securities,
- some investors choose to lend their securities selectively, and
- other investors choose not to lend their securities at all.

For those who choose to lend their securities, the motivation is to increase the return on their investment.

Conversely, those who need to deliver securities (typically as a result of selling), but have none or an insufficient quantity of securities, may choose to borrow the necessary securities. Borrowing enables the delivery to be completed, in turn enabling the seller to receive the sale proceeds at the earliest opportunity. Refer to Section 19.4.

Where the value date of a sale has been reached, but the sale proceeds have not yet been received, the seller is losing cash. The primary motivation behind securities borrowing, therefore, is to enable timely receipt of sale proceeds. Incoming funds can then, for example:

- reduce the overall cash borrowing requirement, or
- be lent in the money market.

In addition, the continued failure of the seller to deliver securities to the buyer may cause the buyer to invoke buy-in procedures, when the buyer is in urgent need of the securities. *Buy-in* can be avoided, however, if the seller is able to borrow the securities and deliver them to the buyer. Consequently, another motivating factor behind securities borrowing is for the seller to deliver securities to the buyer, in order for the seller to avoid the cost of the buy-in. The subject of buy-in is covered within Section 19.7.

24.2   PRINCIPLES OF SECURITIES LENDING

Legal title to the lent securities passes from the lender to the borrower for the period of the loan. However, all the lender's rights are protected regarding events such as *dividends* on equity or *coupon* payments on bonds (refer to Chapter 26).

Some owners of securities avoid lending some or all of their securities, as under certain circumstances they lose voting rights.

In order to secure the lender against the potential non-return of the lent asset, the borrower typically provides *collateral* to the lender in the form of either securities or cash.

The lender of securities receives income from the borrower periodically (typically monthly), in order to avoid the administrative burden of paying the fee on a per-trade basis.

24.3   PRINCIPLES OF SECURITIES BORROWING

There are two main situations where securities borrowing can be of benefit to the seller:

• where the STO has bought and sold, and
• where the STO has sold short.

24.3.1   STO has Bought and Sold

For instance, suppose an STO (WSIL) has bought and sold, on exactly the same terms for both the purchase and the sale, but with different counterparties, with details as in Table 24.1. The securities due from PTIF may not be delivered to the STO on 8th January, the value date. Such circumstances present the STO with an opportunity to make an operational profit (where from a trading perspective, zero profit has been made) by borrowing the securities in order to complete the delivery of the sale and maximise the use of the resultant cash, without having paid for the purchase.

To explain: at the earliest opportunity after the securities due from PTIF have failed to be delivered on value date, if the STO seeks to borrow the necessary securities (from a third party) and is successful, the borrowed securities can then be delivered to the buyer (SFMS) on a DvP basis, resulting in the sale proceeds being received by the STO. The incoming cash can then be offset against an existing cash overdraft, resulting in a benefit of, say, 6.5%. If the cost of borrowing the securities was, say, 3.5%, the STO enjoys a 3% benefit, on the basis that the STO has not paid for the purchase, but has received the

Table 24.1

	The purchase	The sale
Trading book	Book A	Book A
Trade date	5th January	5th January
Trade time	08:38	08:46
Value date	8th January	8th January
Operation	Buy	Sell
Quantity	NZD 40,000,000.00	NZD 40,000,000.00
Security	NZ Govt. 7.75% bond 1st December 2015	NZ Govt. 7.75% bond 1st December 2015
Price	99.125%	99.125%
Counterparty	PTIF	SFMS
Principal	NZD 39,650,000.00	NZD 39,650,000.00
Accrued days	37	37
Accrued interest	NZD 318,611.11	NZD 318,611.11
NSV	**NZD 39,968,611.11**	**NZD 39,968,611.11**

sale proceeds, albeit at a cost of 3.5%. Had the STO decided not to borrow the securities, no benefit would be gained.

This situation can continue until PTIF delivers the securities to the STO, at which point the STO must pay the purchase cost. The incoming securities from PTIF can then be used by the STO to deliver to the third party, from whom the securities were borrowed, at which point the particular borrowing arrangement will cease.

It should be noted that under these particular circumstances (where the STO has bought and sold), it is highly unlikely that the STO can predict in advance the settlement failure of the STO's purchase. Consequently, the STO is unlikely to borrow securities in advance, instead it is a case of acting as quickly as possible to effect a borrowing, after having been informed of *settlement failure* by the custodian. However, if an STO participates in an automated lending and borrowing programme operated by a custodian, the STO's failed purchase can be detected and a borrowing effected immediately in order to settle the sale (refer to Section 24.4).

Under the same trading circumstances as described above, should the STO decide not to borrow the securities, only when the purchase settled would the sale settle, giving the STO no possibility of an opportunity gain.

In summary, for failed sales, borrowing securities in order to maximise the use of incoming cash is a wise financial exercise provided that the cost of borrowing is less than the benefit derived from receiving the cash from the buyer.

24.3.2 STO has Sold Short

Short selling is a term that is used to describe an investor having adopted a negative trading strategy, resulting in a negative trading position, where securities have been sold before being purchased. Those taking negative trading positions do so in the hope that prices will fall and the securities can be bought back at a profit.

If an STO has sold short, the only way that settlement of the sale will occur without borrowing the securities is to wait until the securities are purchased. The receipt of the securities from the purchase will be used to deliver to the counterparty to which the STO sold. The implications of this are that the sale proceeds will not be in the possession of the STO at the earliest opportunity, thereby failing to maximise the use of the receivable funds.

Conversely, where an STO does wish to maximise the use of the receivable funds, because short selling enables identification of securities borrowing opportunities prior to the value date of the sale, borrowing can be arranged in advance of the value date, for delivery by the securities lender to the STO on the value date, followed immediately by onward delivery to the buying counterparty on value date on a DvP basis. The financial result of this from the STO's perspective is that the difference between the cost of borrowing and the benefit derived from reducing an existing overdraft is an operational profit made by the STO. This situation can continue until either:

• the STO buys the securities—the receipt of the securities by the STO from this purchase will then be used to return the borrowed securities to the securities lender;
• the securities lender requests the return of the borrowed securities from the STO—should this situation arise, the STO is likely to attempt to borrow the securities from a different lender and, if successful, use those securities to deliver to the first securities lender.

24.4   METHODS OF LENDING AND BORROWING SECURITIES

Two main methods exist to effect the lending and borrowing of securities:

• direct lender to borrower contact;
• automated lending and borrowing via custodians.

24.4.1   Direct Lender to Borrower Contact

Many STOs employ specialists in the subject of securities lending and borrowing (typically known as the SL&B desk), whose role is to identify opportunities to lend and/or borrow securities, in order to maximise income and minimise costs for the STO.

Having identified an opportunity, the challenge is to find a counterparty who wishes to effect a loan or borrowing on the terms required by the STO (Figure 24.1).

Identifying Opportunities

The identification of a lending or borrowing opportunity is normally achieved by running reports from the STO's settlement system, that predict the movements of securities and their resultant balances over the coming days.

Note that the source of this information can be any record-keeping method, providing it contains:

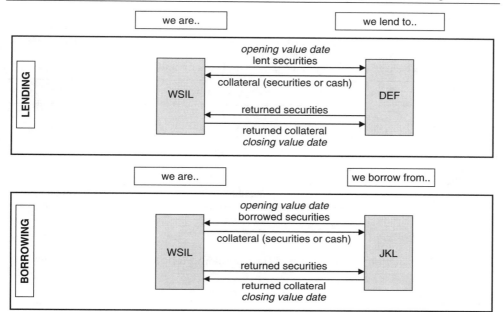

Figure 24.1   Securities lending and borrowing direct with counterparties

- current settled securities positions at custodians
- all trades, for all relevant transaction types for future value dates, and
- all current failed trades.

The STO's settlement system should certainly contain this information, but some STOs utilise specialist securities lending and borrowing systems that will need to be updated with new, amended and cancelled trades, plus current failed trades; the latter typically being available only within the settlement system.

Such information is required to be presented along the lines of Table 24.2, thereby enabling the SL&B desk to attempt to lend and/or borrow securities accordingly.

Contacting Counterparties

Having identified an opportunity to lend or borrow securities, the STO's SL&B desk would normally telephone its contacts within the counterparties most likely to be interested in lending the specific securities the STO wishes to borrow, or borrowing the specific securities the STO wishes to lend. When the STO's requirements meet with a counterparty's requirements, a loan or borrowing of securities will be executed, following negotiation.

For example, the STO's SL&B desk identify from the securities projection report (Table 24.2) that EUR 8,500,000.00 Kingdom of Spain (fictitious) bonds are a candidate for lending, on the basis that the bond trader (the owner of the position within the STO) expects to hold the position for at least two weeks.

The STO's SL&B desk execute a trade with a counterparty (borrower 'B'), who wishes to borrow the bonds.

Table 24.2

Securities projection report dated 13th February, for expected settlements at: Custodian D, Madrid
Securities account number 771324 *Kingdom of Spain 6.75% bonds 15th August 2022*
Current balance plus trades value dated 16th February plus current failed trades

Trade reference	Transaction type	Outgoing securities	Incoming securities
	Current balance		2,000,000.00
P012 898	Principal sale (fail)	10,000,000.00	
P014 033	Principal buy		15,000,000.00
P014 178	Principal sale	7,500,000.00	
P014 226	Principal sale	3,000,000.00	
R8133 295	Reverse repo onside		12,000,000.00
		20,500,000.00	**29,000,000.00**

Recording Trade Details

As a result of executing the trade, the STO records the following trade components:

- trading book
- trade date
- trade time
- operation
- quantity of securities lent/borrowed
- security lent/borrowed
- price of security lent/borrowed
- collateral
  - security
  - price
  - initial margin
- counterparty
- opening value date
- closing value date
- fee.

Many securities lending and borrowing trade components have the same or similar meanings as for repos. In order to avoid repeating the explanation in full, the reader is asked to refer to Section 23.5 for a fuller explanation of those components marked**.

- Trading book: trades may be recorded against the underlying trader's trading book, or to a central securities lending and borrowing book**.
- Trade date: the date the lender and borrower agree to execute the trade.
- Trade time: the exact hour and minute the trade was executed.
- Operation: either lend securities or borrow securities.
- Quantity of securities lent/borrowed: the number of shares or bonds lent or borrowed.
- Security lent/borrowed: the identifier of the specific security that is the purpose of and motivation behind the transaction.
- Price of security lent/borrowed: the price applied to the lent or borrowed security is the current market price, to which, in the case of a bond, the value of accrued interest must be added (calculated to the opening value date) to derive the net market value.

- Collateral: the collateral supplied by the securities borrower can be in the form of cash. Collateral in the form of securities is subject to the same criteria as for repos, namely
  - a minimum quality that is acceptable to the securities lender**
  - assessment of collateral quality by use of ratings supplied by ratings agencies**
  - a single piece of collateral or multiple pieces may be used**
  - the collateral will be general collateral, unspecified by the securities lender**
  - in order to calculate its net market value, the current price plus accrued interest (if relevant) must be calculated
  - margin is necessary to apply a cushion against collateral value increases or decreases**.
- Counterparty: those who participate in securities lending and borrowing are STOs, agents for investors and institutional investors.
- Opening value date: the intended date of delivery of both the lent or borrowed securities, and the collateral**.
- Closing value date: the intended date of return of the lent or borrowed security, and the collateral. Securities lending and borrowing trades can be effected on a term basis (with a fixed closing date), or an open basis (where the closing value date is agreed during the life of the loan or borrowing)**.
- Fee: in the case of a securities loan, the fee due from the borrower and in the case of a securities borrowing, the fee payable to the lender. The fee is usually expressed as a percentage of the full market value of the security lent or borrowed. The size of the fee payable by the securities borrower is dependent upon the availability of the security. As for any commodity, the lender of a freely available security can command a mediocre fee, whereas a security that is scarce is very likely to require the borrower to pay a high fee.

The trade is captured within the STO's securities lending and borrowing system (if the STO uses one), but in any case must be captured within the settlement system.

The characteristics of securities lending and borrowing trades executed direct with counterparties are similar to repos and, as such, some aspects require similar treatment in an operational sense. Therefore, after trade capture within the settlement system, the following steps are applied.

- Static data is required to hold the current rating of the security, to allow automation of collateral selection.
- Trades may be captured within a specific securities lending and borrowing system, then fed to the settlement system, or input directly to the settlement system.
- Trades require enrichment with accrued interest (where relevant) and custodian details for both the trading company and the counterparty.
- Trade validation should be used in order to trap erroneous information prior to transmission to the outside world.
- Trade confirmations are required to be issued to the counterparty, leading to agreement of all details as soon as possible after trade execution.
- Transaction reporting may be necessary (dependent upon the market) in order to inform the regulator of an executed trade.
- Settlement instructions need to be issued for both the opening and closing legs of the loan or borrow.
- Unmatched and advisory instructions must be investigated and resolved without delay [these can occur on either (or both) the opening and closing legs].

- A full history of settlement instruction statuses must be maintained (for both legs).
- Any settlement failure (on either leg) must be investigated.
- Following settlement at the custodian, the STO's books and records must be updated accordingly (for both legs).

Settlement

The settlement of securities borrowing and lending trades is effected on either a DvP basis (preferred), or on an FoP basis.

Typically, custodians cannot process the movement of securities versus securities (i.e. the lent securities versus the collateral), therefore requiring that the lent securities are delivered to the borrower, and the collateral is delivered to the lender independently, on an FoP basis. However, where STOs wish to avoid the inherent risk in delivering securities on an FoP basis, the following practice is usually adopted: the lent security is delivered by the securities lender to the borrower against its net market value on a DvP basis, with the collateral being delivered in the opposite direction against the same cash value.

By adopting this method of settlement, the borrower receives his borrowed securities, the lender receives his collateral, and the net cash effect is zero for both the lender and borrower. These actions occur on both the opening and closing value dates.

Events During the Life of the Loan

Should the market value of the collateral fall below or rise above an agreed margin, margin calls may be made by the exposed party, either lender or borrower (as for repos).

Following delivery of the lent securities versus the collateral, the collateral can be substituted providing the agreement between the lender and the borrower permits it.

Closing Leg

At closure of the trade, the lent securities are returned to the securities lender and the collateral is returned to the borrower, either on an FoP or DvP basis.

The fee owed by the borrower to the securities lender is not usually paid at closing date, instead all the fees for a given period are aggregated and paid periodically, for instance monthly.

Legal Agreement

Securities lending and borrowing trades are normally executed only after the signing of a legal agreement between the two parties, otherwise the lender and borrower may have little legal backing in the event that their lent securities or the collateral are not returned by the counterparty. Standard agreements exist as the basis for a signed agreement between the two parties.

The content of such a legal agreement covers areas such as:

- collateral
- collateral substitution
- margin requirements
- corporate actions

- return of securities
- events of default (e.g. failure to return securities).

Securities Lending versus Repo

As mentioned within Section 23.5, repo can be used as an alternative medium for the lending and borrowing of specific securities, against collateral in the form of cash or other securities.

24.4.2 Automated Lending and Borrowing via Custodians

Large custodians, in particular global custodians, NCSDs and ICSDs typically maintain very large aggregate securities holdings for their account holders. For some securities, the NCSD or ICSD is very likely to hold a sizable percentage of an entire issue.

   Under such circumstances, the account holders can benefit if the custodian, NCSD or ICSD offer a securities lending and borrowing service. In essence, such a service can operate along the lines of Figure 24.2. Successful lenders effectively lend their securities to one or many borrowers, via an agent, the NCSD or ICSD whose role is to match the needs of lenders and borrowers whilst preserving their anonymity.

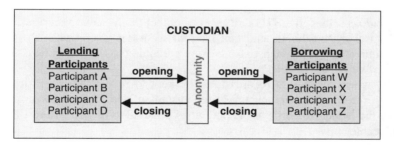

Figure 24.2   Securities lending and borrowing via custodians

Lenders

Those account holders (e.g. STOs and institutional investors) that have a positive holding of securities within their account at the custodian, NCSD or ICSD may elect to:

- lend all securities, or a category of securities (e.g. Spanish equities, New Zealand Government bonds), automatically;
- lend specific securities upon request
- not participate in the lending service.

Note that there can be no guarantee of being able to lend as, for example, there may be no borrowers of a particular security at a time when an account holder has securities available for lending.

Borrowers

Those account holders that wish to take advantage of borrowing securities can elect to:

- borrow all required securities, or a category of securities, automatically;
- borrow upon request.

Some account holders may choose not to participate in the borrowing service.

Borrowing on an automatic basis means that any time the account holder has matching instructions to deliver securities from the account, the value date has been reached, and the full quantity of securities is not available for delivery, there will be an attempt to borrow the necessary quantity. The account holder may have some, but not all, of the required quantity, in which case the custodian, NCSD or ICSD may be successful in obtaining the remaining amount. However, attempts to borrow may not be successful due, for example, to a lack of lenders in a specific security.

The custodian, NCSD or ICSD attempts to match the needs of account holders wishing to lend their securities with those who wish to borrow. The result of successful lending and borrowing (including income/cost) will be advised to the account holder:

- those who have lent will be made aware of the quantity of the individual security lent;
- those who have borrowed will be made aware of the quantity of the individual security borrowed, and in addition, as a result of borrowing, one or many sales will have been settled (securities will have been delivered to, and cash received from, the counterparty).

24.5   UPDATING INTERNAL BOOKS AND RECORDS

Whether an STO is a lender or a borrower of securities, there is a need to update internal records for the purpose of reflecting reality in the outside world.

Having lent securities, the STO will need to reflect the fact that securities have left its main account at the custodian, and that the lent securities are owed to the STO by the borrower. Equivalent records must also be kept pertaining to the incoming collateral from the borrower, where applicable.

Similarly, when borrowing, records must be kept to reflect that securities have been received into the STO's main account at the custodian, and that the borrowed securities are owed to the lender. Records of the outgoing collateral to the lender must also be kept, where applicable.

Unless such records are kept:

- the STO will have a false view of the situation, potentially affecting the actions of the repo trader and the SL&B desk;
- the STO will not be able to reconcile its securities account with the NCSD or ICSD;
- the credit risk of the lender's assets being held outside the lender's control will not be assessed;
- corporate actions calculations may be adversely affected.

In general, the STO will not be in control of its assets.

24.6   SUMMARY

For sales that cannot settle due to a lack of securities, STOs can maximise their income by borrowing securities (providing the costs of borrowing do not outweigh the benefit).

The combined effect of using securities as collateral in repo transactions, as well as the lending of securities, results in reduced costs and increased income for the STO. Rather than sitting inactive within the STO's account at the custodian, the securities are being made to work to the benefit of the STO.

The lending and borrowing of securities improves liquidity (the ease with which securities can be traded) and enhances settlement efficiency within a marketplace.

Safe Custody

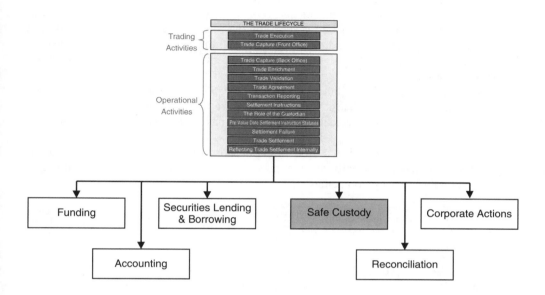

25.1 INTRODUCTION

Some STOs provide a service to their institutional clients, whereby securities (and some-times cash) owned by the client are held and managed by the STO.

Most commonly, this arrangement comes about when the STO sells securities to an institutional client who does not have an external custodian for the securities in question. Under such circumstances, the STO may offer to hold the securities (and cash) on the client's behalf.

The STO offering a safe custody service to its clients is, in a number of respects, acting in a similar capacity as the specialist custodian organisations used by the STO, but usually on a much smaller scale. As far as the safe custody client is concerned, the STO is the custodian of their securities (and cash), and therefore the STO must have the necessary infrastructure in place to provide such a service successfully.

Some STOs do not offer a safe custody service. This may prevent execution of trades by institutional clients with such STOs, as the client may be prepared to trade only if the STO is able to hold the securities purchased by the client, in safe custody.

Other STOs provide a limited safe custody service, designed to cater for institutional clients who will trade only if the STO holds the securities on the client's behalf. Offering such a service ensures that the STO does not lose the relationship with the client. From the STO's perspective, offering a safe custody service of this nature means catering for occasional trades with a limited number of institutional clients. In terms of the number of securities movements, this type of service may necessitate the processing of up to 50 movements per day. STOs offering such a service typically do not market or promote the service, as they may not want their safe custody business to expand, due to a lack of infrastructure to provide a fully comprehensive service.

Finally, some STOs choose to offer a wide range of safe custody services to their institutional clients, normally requiring the STO to have a significant infrastructure in place, including a dedicated custody system for the management of securities and cash owned by many (potentially hundreds) of clients. Within some STOs, the safe custody function may be set up as a different division or legal entity for confidentiality, regulatory and service reasons.

Securities owned by clients but managed by the STO must be held in segregated accounts at the STO's custodians. These accounts are therefore in the name and under the control of the STO, and typically the custodian has no knowledge of the beneficial owner's identity.

Note: as well as the specialists custodian organisations mentioned above, provision of safe custody services is normally an integral part of the service provided to individual and institutional clients by companies such as:

- stockbrokers
- retail brokers
- internet brokers.

Many of the services provided by such organisations are similar to those described within this chapter; that is, services offered by STOs to their institutional clients.

The topic of safe custody is an extensive subject in its own right; the following should be regarded as an overview of the topic.

25.2   BASIC SAFE CUSTODY SERVICES

At a fundamental level, an STO may provide safe custody services:

- for securities only, or
- for securities and cash.

The custody of a client's securities typically involves the:

- safekeeping of securities positions,
- receipt and delivery of securities,
- updating of holdings as a result of *corporate actions*,
- valuation of securities holdings, and
- provision of statements of securities holdings.

The operation of clients' cash accounts involves the:

- safekeeping of cash in one or many currencies,
- receipt and payment of cash,

- updating of cash accounts as a result of corporate actions,
- application of debit and credit interest, and
- provision of statements of cash balances.

Such services may be subject to fees charged by the STO to the custody clients.
More advanced safe custody services are described later in this chapter.

25.3   SAFE CUSTODY LEGAL AGREEMENTS

The legal arrangements regarding the STO holding securities (and cash) in safe custody on the client's behalf are typically detailed within a legal agreement, for the protection of both the client and the STO.
Such agreements typically cover:

- legal ownership of securities and cash held by the STO;
- the requirement to hold the securities and/or cash in segregated accounts from the STO's own holdings;
- the frequency and method of transmission of securities and/or cash statements;
- the collection of income (and other corporate actions) falling due on the securities;
- the charging of interest on cash balances;
- the method of transmission of settlement instructions from the client, relating to the delivery of securities and payments of cash.

25.4   SAFEKEEPING CLIENTS' SECURITIES AND CASH

When an STO holds securities on behalf of a safe custody client, the client entrusts the STO to take adequate measures to safeguard its assets.
The normal situation when an STO executes a purchase of securities for its own account is that, following the transmission of a settlement instruction by the STO, the custodian effects the exchange of securities and cash on the STO's behalf, and the STO expects a high quality safekeeping service from the custodian thereafter. When an STO operates a safe custody service, that situation is effectively reversed, as it is the safe custody client who expects the STO to take care of its assets and to action the movements of securities and/or cash instructed by the client.
With regard to the safekeeping of clients' cash (commonly known as 'client money'), in order for the client's cash to remain properly safeguarded whilst in the STO's control, a number of regulations apply. Such regulations include the segregation of client cash from the STO's cash.
Some STOs are unable to offer a cash service to their clients as, in order to provide the necessary service required by its clients, the STO would need to operate like a bank, with:

- one or many cash accounts per client,
- cash accounts in various currencies,
- the maintenance of cash balances,
- calculation of interest on cash balances, and
- the ability to produce periodic statements of balances and movements.

Some STOs do not have the necessary infrastructure to provide this type of service.

25.5   SAFE CUSTODY HOLDINGS AT EXTERNAL CUSTODIANS

The securities and cash owned by an STO's clients must be kept segregated from the STO's own assets, externally at the STO's custodian. This is law in many countries and is designed to clearly separate the assets of the STO and those of its clients, so that in the event of liquidation of the STO, the assets belonging to its clients are not considered part of the STO's assets.

For this reason, an STO will normally maintain one account (referred to within this book as the main account) at each custodian, in which its own positions are held. For its safe custody clients' holdings, one or more safe custody accounts are typically used at each custodian, although an STO may decide to set up numerous safe custody accounts at each custodian, to suit its own methods of handling its clients' assets.

25.5.1   Taxation and Safe Custody Accounts

The following relates to the need for STOs to maintain at least two safe custody accounts, at certain custodians.

Most payments of income (i.e. *dividends* on equity and *coupon* on bond holdings) are subject to *withholding tax* deducted by the issuer, according to the laws within the country of residence of the issuer. For example, the standard rate of withholding tax deducted when paying a dividend by an issuer resident in country A may be 15%.

However, many countries have *double-taxation agreements* (also known as *treaties*) with other countries. Such treaties may allow an investor who is resident in a treaty country to have a lower rate of withholding tax deducted, compared with the standard rate that is applicable for residents of countries having no treaty with the paying country.

Therefore, in order for an STO to have the correct rate of withholding tax deducted (according to the residency status of its clients), the STO is likely to set up two safe custody accounts at its custodian in country A, and at its custodians in all other countries where treaties have been made. This arrangement is illustrated in Figure 25.1.

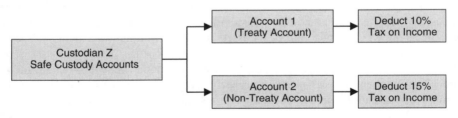

Figure 25.1   Safe custody: taxation and safe custody accounts at external custodians

The STO must then ensure that securities are moved into and out of the relevant safe custody account, according to the residency status of the safe custody client who owns the securities. The consequence of these actions is that income is paid by the custodian to the STO's safe custody accounts, following deduction of the applicable rate of withholding tax, according to the owner's residency status. A third safe custody account may be used to cater for holdings that are exempt from withholding tax (e.g. for local residents).

The subject of withholding tax on income is explored further in Chapter 26.

25.6   SAFE CUSTODY BOOKS AND RECORDS

An STO operating a safe custody service must ensure that its internal record-keeping is up-to-date, and takes account of client (ownership) positions and the custodian (location) positions reflecting where the securities are held.

Figure 25.2 represents a typical set of safe custody records for a specific security where (under the heading of 'Ownership') the holdings relating to each safe custody client are listed, whereas (under the heading of 'Location') the specific custodians who hold the securities are listed. In this case, the total of the clients' securities is held within two safe custody accounts at the same custodian.

DEF Corporation Shares			
Ownership		Location	
Client L	+2000	−5000	Custodian Z Custody A/c 1
Client M	+3000	−1500	Custodian Z Custody A/c 2
Client N	+1500		
	+6500	−6500	

Figure 25.2   Safe custody: books and records

In parallel with the STO's own securities positions, it is imperative that the total of the ownership (client) positions is equal to the sum of the location (custodian) positions. Refer to Chapter 27 for further detail.

Whenever securities are received into or delivered from the STO's safe custody accounts at the external custodian, it is essential that the STO's safe custody books and records are updated accordingly. If this is done in a timely manner, the STO will be maintaining an up-to-date record of the reality in the outside world, in turn allowing successful daily reconciliation with the external custodians. The various reasons for the receipt into and delivery of securities from the STO's safe custody accounts at the custodian are given in Section 25.10.

A further reason for maintaining up-to-date books and records is that entitlement to any corporate actions that fall due on the securities will be accurate, both in terms of the clients' holdings and the effect of the action at the STO's external custodian.

25.7   UPDATING HOLDINGS AS A RESULT OF CORPORATE ACTIONS

As part of the service provided by STOs to their safe custody clients, payments of income and benefits accruing from other corporate actions (refer to Chapter 26) must be passed on to the entitled clients at the agreed time. For example, dividends on equity are paid by the issuer as at a specified date, and the individual safe custody clients will require to be credited by the STO on (or very shortly after) the payment date. The handling of such circumstances will be detailed within the safe custody agreement between the STO and the client.

The various types of corporate action result in benefits or costs, additional or fewer securities, receipt or payment of cash; some corporate actions require a decision to be made by the securities owner. Whatever the type of corporate action, the STO's safe custody client expects the STO to look after its interests, and to take the necessary steps to provide such a service. The typical handling of the result of corporate actions is described in Section 25.10.

A large safe custody operation within an STO may have hundreds of clients, many of whom may be holding the same security. Should a corporate action occur on that security, the STO would have a major operational exercise to effect the necessary action manually on behalf of all its safe custody clients holding the security in question. Under such circumstances, automation of corporate actions processing allows the necessary actions to be effected in a timely manner for all the STO's safe custody clients.

25.8   VALUING CLIENTS' SECURITIES HOLDINGS

Part of the service offered by STOs may include the valuation of their safe custody clients' securities. Where a client purchases securities, the client would be able to track the progress of his investment if the STO provides the current market price and its revised value on a periodic basis.

The updating of clients' security positions with current prices may be performed manually or automatically. If the STO decides to automate this task, current security prices are available from *securities data providers,* also known as data vendors; refer to Section 9.9.

[This is yet another use of current market prices, uses mentioned within various chapters being:

- comparison with trade prices (Chapter 13);
- marking-to-market (Chapter 28);
- valuation of collateral (Chapter 23);
- valuation of collateral (Chapter 24)].

25.9   STATEMENTS OF SECURITIES AND CASH BALANCES

As part of the service provided by the STO to its safe custody clients, the STO will produce statements of securities holdings and cash account statements, on a periodic basis. However, institutional clients who trade actively may demand such statements on a daily basis, in order to verify the balances held by the STO.

The method of communicating such statements can include paper, fax and S.W.I.F.T.

25.10   SAFE CUSTODY MOVEMENT TYPES

Movements of securities and cash for safe custody clients can occur as a result of a number of different circumstances, including (from the safe custody client's perspective):

- trading with the STO that provides the safe custody service,
- trading with other STOs,
- transfer of securities from or to another STO,

- corporate actions with a securities impact,
- cash receipts and payments,
- cash transfers between the client's accounts, and
- corporate actions with a cash impact.

These movements are explained below.

25.10.1   Trading with the STO that Provides the Safe Custody Service

When the STO processes a trade (in the manner described in earlier chapters), any trade that has been executed with a safe custody client should be identified automatically through the static data held for the client.

In the case where the STO has sold securities to the client, the STO's trading book position will be reduced (as usual), and the client's trading position must be increased within the STO's safe custody books and records. Figure 25.3 depicts this example.

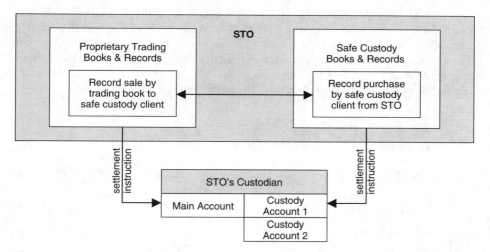

Figure 25.3   Safe custody movement types: trading with the STO that provides the safe custody service

The securities held by the STO at its custodian must be removed from the STO's main account and transferred into the appropriate safe custody account at the custodian. In order to effect this movement of securities, two *settlement instructions* may need issuing by the STO:

- one instructing the removal of securities from the main account, and
- the other instructing the receipt of securities into the appropriate safe custody account

on an *FoP* basis, as at the value date of the trade. Where the client sells securities to the STO that provides the safe custody service, the reverse of the above is necessary.

Note: the STO is the account holder of both the main account and the safe custody account at the custodian; therefore, the STO has the power to transfer securities to or from both accounts. Under the circumstances described for this trade, some custodians require one instruction to be issued to deliver the securities (from the main account in the above example) and a separate instruction for the receipt of securities (into the safe custody account); the instructions must match prior to settlement. Other custodians allow the issuance of a single instruction (commonly referred to as an Own Account Transfer), which does not require matching.

As for the cash payable by the safe custody client and receivable by the STO, the method of payment depends upon whether the STO provides a securities only, or a securities and cash safe custody service. In a securities only safe custody service, the client will need to instruct its bank to pay the STO's bank on value date. The STO will need to issue a pre-advice to its bank, to ensure it receives good value for the cash receipt. In a securities and cash safe custody service, the client's cash account will be debited and a payment made to the STO's bank.

25.10.2   Trading with Other STOs

The safe custody client typically is not tied to trading only with the STO that provides the safe custody service, and therefore has the freedom to trade with other STOs.

Where the STO holds securities on behalf of a safe custody client, and the client then sells the securities to another STO ('party Q'), the client must issue an instruction to the STO, requesting delivery of the securities to the custodian of party Q. However, the STO must first verify the origin of the instruction, prior to carrying out the instruction (refer to Section 25.11). The steps involved are illustrated in Figure 25.4.

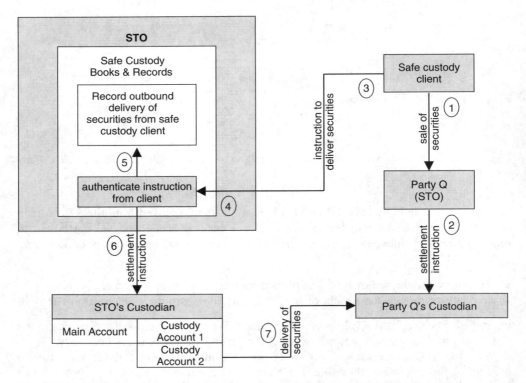

Figure 25.4   Safe custody movement types: safe custody client trading with other STOs

Step 1: the STO's safe custody client sells securities (currently held by the STO) to another STO (party Q). (Party Q will not receive delivery of the securities it has purchased unless the client instructs the STO to deliver its securities to party Q's custodian.)

Step 2: party Q instructs its custodian to receive securities from the client's custodian (the STO's custodian).

Step 3: the safe custody client issues an instruction to the STO to remove securities from its account and deliver to party Q's custodian, on a specified date (the value date of the client's sale to party Q.)

Step 4: upon receipt of the client's instruction, the STO must authenticate the instruction, to ensure that the true owner of the securities has issued it.

Step 5: the STO must update its safe custody books and records (ownership position) with the pending outgoing delivery of the client's securities.

Step 6: the STO issues a settlement instruction to its custodian, requesting the withdrawal of securities from the relevant safe custody account, and delivery to party Q's custodian.

Step 7: following matching of the two custodians' settlement instructions, delivery of the securities is effected.

The STO's safe custody books and records (location position) must be updated following delivery of securities by its custodian, to reflect the fact that the securities are no longer within the STO's possession.

In addition, when the client buys securities from another STO (for example party Q), the client may request party Q to deliver the securities to the safe custody STO. Again, the client must advise the safe custody STO to receive the securities, and add the securities to their existing holdings. Occasionally, the selling STO may deliver securities on an FoP basis to the safe custody STO's account, without the safe custody client having informed the safe custody STO to expect delivery. This is a dangerous situation, as unless the owner of the securities is identified quickly, the securities may remain within the STO's custodian's account, unallocated to any owner.

The STO must update its custody books and records as a result of the receipt or delivery of securities, at both ownership and location level.

25.10.3 Transfer of Securities from or to Another STO

An institutional investor may be holding its securities and/or cash at one STO, when it decides to become a safe custody client of another STO. This typically occurs when the investor feels that by moving their assets to another STO, the service they receive will be better, or service charges will be less, or a combination of both. This action is commonly referred to as a 'custody transfer'. Where an STO is acting in a custodian capacity, it can therefore receive or deliver securities resulting from such transfers.

Under such circumstances, the transfer of all the client's securities is usually effected by the issuance of settlement instructions requesting the underlying custodians to deliver and receive securities on an FoP basis, on an agreed date. The example of an incoming custody transfer is illustrated in Figure 25.5.

Step 1: the safe custody client instructs its existing custodian to deliver all its securities to the STO, on an FoP basis, on a specified date.

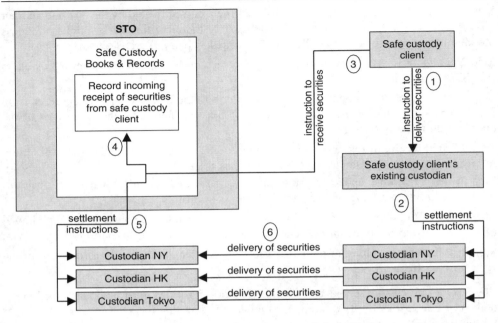

Figure 25.5 Safe custody movement types: incoming custody transfer from another custodian

Step 2: the client's existing custodian issues settlement instructions to all of its underlying custodians where the client's securities are held, instructing them to deliver on an FoP basis, on a specified date, to the equivalent custodians of the STO.

Step 3: the safe custody client informs the STO that it has arranged to transfer all its securities to the STO, on a specified date.

Step 4: the STO must update its safe custody books and records (ownership position) with the pending incoming deliveries of the client's securities.

Step 5: the STO issues settlement instructions to the relevant custodians for all securities being received on behalf of its new safe custody client.

Step 6: following matching of the relevant custodian's settlement instructions, delivery of the securities is effected.

The STO's safe custody books and records (location position) must be updated following receipt of securities by its custodians, to reflect the fact that the securities are now within the STO's possession.

25.10.4   Corporate Actions with a Securities Impact

Some corporate actions result in the owner of the securities:

- gaining an additional quantity of existing securities,
- needing to exchange the original security for a new security, or
- losing the original security as it no longer exists.

Under such circumstances, the STO must update its custody books and records, for both ownership and location, at the appropriate time.

Figure 25.6 illustrates the result of corporate actions on two separate securities owned by safe custody clients and held by the STO at different custodians. The reasons for such changes in holdings are described in Chapter 26.

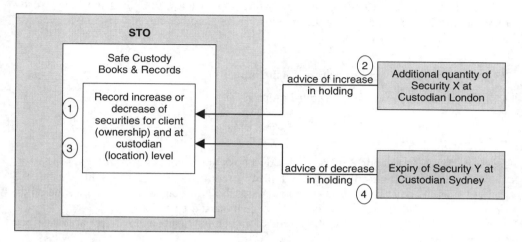

Figure 25.6   Safe custody movement types: corporate actions with a securities impact

Step 1: the STO should update its clients' (ownership) positions within its safe custody books and records as at the effective date of the corporate action. In this case, the safe custody client is entitled to additional securities from its original holding in security X, as a result of the corporate action.

Step 2: the custodian at which security X is held advises that the STO's safe custody account(s) has been increased by the additional quantity.

Step 3: for its holding in security Y, the safe custody client will lose the holding as the security has expired, and the STO must update all its clients' (ownership) positions accordingly, as at the effective date.

Step 4: the custodian at which security Y is held advises that the holding has been decreased as a result of the expiry.

The STO's safe custody books and records (location position) must be updated following receipt of the advices from the custodians, to keep the STO's custody records in line with the outside world.

The subject of corporate actions is explored within the following chapter.

25.10.5   Cash Receipts and Payments

If the STO provides a cash account service to its safe custody clients, where the client may have credit or debit cash balances, the client may decide to pay cash into or out of its cash account at any time. In this respect, the cash accounts of safe custody clients are like any normal bank account.

Where the STO receives a request to debit a client's cash account and pay funds elsewhere, the STO will first need to satisfy itself that the request has originated from the client.

25.10.6   Cash Transfers Between the Client's Accounts

Where the safe custody client owns two or more cash accounts in the same currency, the client may require funds to be transferred from one account to another.

If the STO provides cash accounts in different currencies, the client may request the debit of cash in one currency and the credit of cash in another currency, thereby involving a foreign exchange transaction.

25.10.7   Corporate Actions with a Cash Impact

Many types of corporate action result in either:

- a cash cost to the owner of securities, or
- a receipt of cash

requiring the STO to update its safe custody books and records accordingly.

The result of such corporate actions typically requires the STO to credit or debit the entitled safe custody clients as at the due date of the payment, whilst receiving the credit or incurring the debit of cash on its cash accounts at the custodian.

As for Section 25.10.4 above, the reasons for such payments and receipts are described in Chapter 26.

25.11   AUTHENTICATING INSTRUCTIONS RECEIVED FROM CLIENTS

For trades the STO executes for its own account, the STO issues settlement instructions to its custodian. Upon receipt of an instruction, it is the custodian's responsibility to ensure that the instruction has been sent by the account holder (or the account holder's agent to whom the account holder has given *power of attorney*). Failure to verify that an authorised party has issued the instruction could result in the fraudulent removal of securities or cash from the account holder's account.

When an STO provides a safe custody service, the STO is in a position of needing to substantiate the origin of settlement instructions received from its clients, for the protection of the client and itself.

For clients of the STO who issue settlement instructions electronically, such as via *S.W.I.F.T.* which has inbuilt security protocols, the STO is on safe ground to act upon such instructions.

If clients issue instructions by other methods, such as fax, telex or mail, without use of a secure coding method such as tested telex (refer to Section 16.5), the STO may need to contact the client to confirm the client has in fact issued the instruction before the STO acts on the instruction.

25.12   ADVANCED SAFE CUSTODY SERVICES

Should the STO choose to offer more advanced services than the basic services listed earlier in this chapter, such services are likely to relate to the management of clients' collateral.

This may include the lending of clients' securities, for which a prior agreement will need to be in place, and for which the client will receive a fee. The STO may decide to borrow a client's securities in order to settle a sale by the STO, or the STO can become an agent where another STO wishes to borrow securities.

Another service that may be provided by the STO is clients' borrowing of cash from the STO on a secured (also known as collateralised) basis. The amount of cash that the STO is prepared to lend will be directly related to the market value of a client's securities, less an adequate margin to take account of fluctuation in the market value of the securities. The STO may also impose a credit limit, beyond which the STO would not be prepared to lend.

25.13   SERVICE CHARGES

The STO will incur costs imposed by its various custodians, for holding its safe custody clients' securities at the custodians. These costs are normally based on the number or market value of holdings, and the number of movements within a given period.

STOs normally wish to charge each of their safe custody clients with, at a minimum, the pro-rata costs incurred by the STO. Other STOs charge their clients based on a multiplier relevant to the costs incurred by the STO, for example 1.5 times, or double.

25.13.1   Charges Based on Holdings

If the safe custody client is an owner of bearer securities, the custodian that holds the securities may pay insurance premiums in case of loss. In the case of registered securities, the custodian's costs are typically much smaller. Under both circumstances, the custodian's costs will be charged to the STO.

25.13.2   Charges Based on Movements

If an STO's safe custody client requests the incoming or outgoing movements of securities, such as:

- the result of trading with other STOs, and the
- transfer of securities from or to another STO

(Section 25.10), the administrative costs of handling such movements may be charged to the client. Settlement instructions issued by the STO to effect the necessary movements will be charged by the underlying custodian, and so these costs are typically passed-on to the client. Note that where the STO's safe custody client trades with the STO, typically the STO will not charge the client for the transfer to or from safe custody.

Additionally, the cost of processing corporate actions may be charged to the client, and the administrative costs of handling cash payments and receipts may also be passed to the client.

25.14   SUMMARY

The majority of issues relating to operation of an STO's proprietary business apply to the management of clients' assets held in safe custody, except the latter is typically on a much smaller scale in terms of the volume of daily movements. Consequently, many of the controls and risk mitigation measures described in earlier chapters apply equally in the case of safe custody.

Safe custody has been treated by many STOs as a secondary business (to the management of its proprietary business), exemplified through highly manual practices and procedures. As a result, safe custody can prove to be a high-risk area to the STO in its own right, if the necessary level of attention is not applied.

Particular attention should be given by the STO to:

- the authentication of instructions supposedly issued by safe custody clients;
- the issuance of FoP settlement instructions to custodians (as in a safe custody environment, FoP instructions typically form a large percentage of movements);
- the accurate and timely upkeep of safe custody books and records;
- the reconciliation of clients' assets held within books and records, versus the balances held at custodians.

This is in order to remain in control and to mitigate the risks involved.

26
Corporate Actions

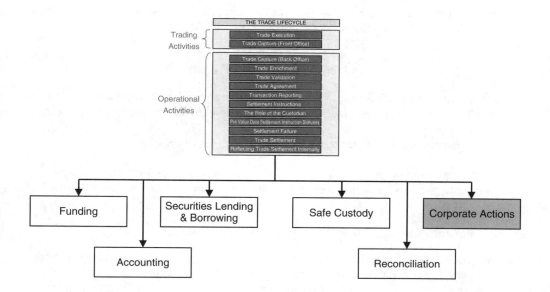

26.1 INTRODUCTION

If and when the *issuer* of an existing security distributes benefits to shareholders or bondholders, or chooses to change the security's structure, such events are commonly known as *corporate actions*.

Because corporate actions are events that occur on a security, they are relevant to all holders of the security, including STOs holding proprietary trading positions, and safe custody clients with positions managed by STOs.

The STO's main objective as far as any corporate action is concerned is to ensure that all benefits due to it and to its safe custody clients are collected in full and at the earliest available time, and that the result of changes to the structure of a security are reflected correctly within the STO's proprietary and safe custody books and records.

Because the nature of corporate actions differs, this chapter is split into three main sections: *Benefits, Reorganisations* and *Multifaceted Actions*, followed by a general section (applicable to all three) and summary.

All corporate action events can be classified as either mandatory or voluntary, where:

- participation by the owner in mandatory events is compulsory, but the owner may or may not be given an option to select its form, and
- participation by the owner in voluntary events is initiated by the owner.

Due to the fact that a number of terms used within this chapter have been explained earlier in the book, it is recommended that this chapter is read after having read the prior chapters.

Note: the subject of corporate actions is a substantial topic in its own right. The following is designed to provide an overview of the topic only; the corporate actions listed within this chapter are representative examples of corporate actions, and do not constitute an exhaustive list of such events.

26.2 BENEFITS

Those corporate actions that result in the holder of the security receiving additional securities and/or cash (whilst retaining the original holding) will be referred to as *benefits* within this book.

Benefits payable by the issuer to the holders of the security are either:

- known at the time of issue of the security (and are therefore predictable), or are
- announced by the issuer during the 'life' of the issue (and are therefore not predictable).

26.2.1   Benefits Known at the Time of Issue of the Security

Benefits known at the time of issue of the security (hereafter referred to as predictable benefit events) are included in the characteristics of those securities that are publicised when the security is first issued. As there are normally no specific events relating to equities that are known in advance, such benefits primarily relate to coupon payments on bonds. The example of coupon payments will be described below.

Note: it may help the reader's understanding of the benefits if Chapter 7 is read before, or in conjunction with, the following.

Coupon Payments

Fixed Rate (Straight) Bonds. The most common form of predictable benefits are coupon payments. When a bond issue is first brought to the marketplace, the rate of interest (commonly referred to as the *coupon rate*) and the dates that interest or coupon is payable (commonly referred to as *coupon payment dates*) are clearly stated by the issuer, within the issue prospectus (Table 26.1). Each of the coupon payments is considered as an individual benefit event.

26.2.2   Benefits Announced by the Issuer During the 'Life' of the Security

The majority of benefits falling within the category of announced by the issuer during the 'life' of the security (hereafter referred to as announced benefit events) result from decisions made by the issuer's board of directors. Such decisions by the issuer can be made at any time and in general are not predictable. Such benefits primarily relate to equities, and include:

Table 26.1

Characteristics of coupon payments	
Predictable or announced?	Coupon payments on straight bonds are predictable, as the date of each payment is stated in the prospectus of the issue
Issuer's objective?	To pay interest on the borrowing of cash from the bondholders, at a predetermined rate and time
How expressed?	The interest rate is expressed as a percentage of the bond face (nominal) value
Benefit to holder?	Bondholders receive predictable cash amounts at predetermined dates
Mandatory or voluntary event?	These are mandatory events, where bondholders typically have no choice as to the form of payment
Effect on security holding?	There is no effect on the security holding as a result of a coupon payment
Effect on trading?	There is no direct change to the value of the existing bonds as a result of a coupon payment

- dividends, and
- bonus issues.

Dividends

The payment of a dividend results from a decision by the directors of a company to distribute earnings to shareholders. The most common form of dividend is one that is paid in the issue currency, where the beneficiary has no choice as to its form (e.g. cash or securities). However, some dividends are given in the form of securities, whilst for other dividends the beneficiary may be given the option to select its form (for example, the currency in which the payment is made, or securities). Note that dividends paid in the form of securities are known as *stock dividends* or scrip dividends (Table 26.2).

The normal frequency of dividend payments made by issuers varies around the globe; Table 26.3 lists the conventions in a selection of countries at the time of writing.

Bonus Issues

A bonus issue is an issue of additional shares given free of cost to the existing shareholders, in proportion to their existing holding, from the issuer's capital reserves.

Rather than pay a cash dividend, the company's capital reserves are increased and new shares are issued to represent the increase. As this benefit is made from the issuer's capital reserves, it is not normally liable to taxation (see Section 26.2.4; Table 26.4).

The effect on trading can be illustrated through an example. If an STO is the owner of 100 shares that have a current price of GBP 60.00, following the receipt of 50 bonus shares, the share price will fall to GBP 40.00; the cash value pre and post the bonus issue remains at GBP 6000.00.

Note: ratios of new shares to existing shares are quoted differently in various parts of the globe. For example, an existing holding of 100 shares and the addition of 50 bonus shares, totalling 150 shares (post-bonus), would be quoted as:

Table 26.2

	Characteristics of dividends
Predictable or announced?	Dividends are announced by the issuer, following a decision by the board of directors
Issuer's objective?	To reward the shareholders for their investment participation by way of distributing profits
How expressed?	Cash dividends are normally expressed as a cash amount per share; stock dividends are typically expressed as a ratio relating to the cash value of the dividend
Benefit to holder?	The shareholder receives a cash payment or additional securities
Mandatory or voluntary event?	The benefit is mandatory, with an owner option under some circumstances to elect the payment currency or the securities in lieu of cash
Effect on security holding?	There is no impact on security holdings for cash dividends, but the shareholding will increase following a stock dividend
Effect on trading?	At the entitlement date, the share price will decrease to take account of trading without the benefit

Table 26.3

Country	Normal number of payments per year	Country	Normal number of payments per year
Australia	Two	India	One
Brazil	Various	Japan	Two
Canada	Four	Korea	One
Denmark	One	New Zealand	Two
France	One	Taiwan	One
Germany	One	UK	Two
Hong Kong	Two	USA	Four

Table 26.4

	Characteristics of bonus issues
Predictable or announced?	Bonus issues are announced by the issuer, following a decision by the board of directors
Issuer's objective?	To distribute new shares to shareholders following an increase to its capital reserves
How expressed?	Bonus issues are typically expressed as a ratio of new shares versus existing shares (see note)
Benefit to holder?	The shareholder receives additional shares to the original holding, at no cost
Mandatory or voluntary event?	The issuer decides to provide the benefit on each share issued, and is mandatory with no owner option
Effect on security holding?	Existing shareholdings will need to be increased, at the relevant ratio
Effect on trading?	The price per share in the marketplace will be reduced to take account of the increased number of shares in issue

- a '3 for 2' (result of 3 with a starting point of 2) bonus issue in the USA, which emphasises the resultant position after the bonus, and
- a '1 for 2' (additional 1 for every 2 original shares) bonus issue in the UK, which emphasises the number of additional shares

requiring the STO to take care when calculating entitlement to bonus issues.

Floating Rate Notes

As far as FRNs are concerned, even though when the notes are issued the frequency of coupon payments is known (e.g. semi-annually or quarterly), the actual coupon rate payable is not known until immediately prior to each coupon period. Therefore, the coupon payments on FRNs are regarded as benefits announced by the issuer during the 'life' of the issue.

26.2.3 Benefits Management Overview

The process of an STO successfully receiving benefits due to it and/or its safe custody clients involves a series of steps as illustrated in Figure 26.1.

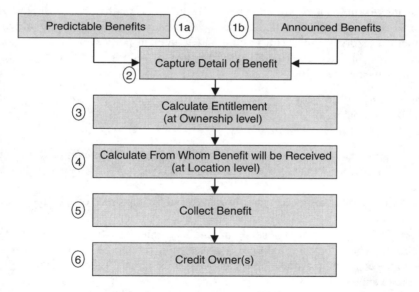

Figure 26.1 Corporate actions: overview of benefits management

Steps 1a and 1b: the details of both predictable and announced benefit events must be gathered, whether from internal or external sources.

Step 2: once the gathered details are believed to be accurate, the details must be captured either manually or within a corporate actions processing system.

Step 3: if the STO (or its custody clients) has a trading position in the security as at the *entitlement date*, the benefit due to the owners will be calculated.

Step 4: having calculated that there is an entitled position, the STO must assess from whom the entitlement will be received. This is normally the custodian, the issuer (in the case of registered securities) or the counterparty from whom purchases have been made (or a combination of these), according to the settlement status of trades. This is explained later in this chapter.

Step 5: as at the payment date of the benefit event, the STO will receive (or collect) the benefit from those that owe the benefit to the STO.

Step 6: having collected the benefit, the STO must distribute the benefit to owners. Note that some STOs operate by distributing benefits to owners on payment date (regardless of whether the credit has been received externally, or not).

The following describes these steps in greater depth.

Gathering and Capturing the Detail of Benefit Events

Before the STO is able to calculate entitlement, it must first become aware of such events and then capture the detail, either manually or within a specific corporate actions processing system. The method of being made aware of such events is dependent upon whether the benefit event is predictable or announced.

Predictable Events. The capture of a benefit event that is predictable is usually extracted from the STO's repository of static data, as the necessary information should already exist within the STO's organisation (for trading and settlement purposes).

As mentioned in Chapter 9, the STO's repository of security static data may originate from various means, namely:

- the *prospectus* of the issue,
- the STO's custodian, or
- by feed from *securities data providers*.

Whichever method is used, it is essential that the information is completely accurate if the STO is to ensure it (and its safe custody clients) receive the benefits due on their securities.

Table 26.5 describes the necessary information to be captured for a coupon payment.

Announced Events. In order to ensure that the STO (and its safe custody clients) receive all benefits to which they are entitled, it is essential for the STO to make itself aware of all announced benefit events. This can be a considerably greater challenge than for predictable events.

Where the STO invests in well-known securities within mature marketplaces, the announcement by an issuer of a benefit falling due is likely to be well publicised, and thus the STO becomes aware of the announced benefit.

Conversely, where an STO invests in less well-known securities in an immature marketplace, located in a different financial centre or even the other side of the world, it may be much more of a challenge for the STO to become aware of announced events.

Some STOs rely upon their custodian to supply the necessary detail of a benefit event. However, others wish to receive independent notification by subscribing directly to a

Table 26.5

Component	Coupon payments
Original security	✓
Entitlement date	✓
Record date	✓
Payment date	✓
Coupon rate	✓
Currency of payment	✓

corporate actions provider, the same or similar organisations that provide securities static data. Those STOs that choose to subscribe are provided with the details of individual corporate actions electronically by companies such as Valorinform and Xcitek. Those who are prepared to pay for a corporate actions feed may choose to subscribe to more than one service and then compare the data for consistency (this is known as data cleansing) before accepting the data for entitlement calculation and associated processing.

For each of the announced events listed earlier in this chapter, Table 26.6 describes the necessary information to be captured.

Table 26.6

Component	Cash dividends	Stock dividends	Bonus issues
Original security	✓	✓	✓
Entitlement date	✓	✓	✓
Record date	✓	✓	✓
Payment date	✓	✓	✓
Cash rate per share receivable	✓		
Security rate per share receivable		✓	
Ratio (of existing to new shares)			✓
Currency of payment	✓		
New security receivable		✓	✓

Typical information requiring capture for a cash dividend, for example, is given in Table 26.7, and each of the dates will be explained in the coming sections within this chapter.

Table 26.7

Component	Example cash dividend
Original security	British Airways ordinary shares
Entitlement date	Ex-dividend date: 15th May
Record date	19th May
Payment date	5th June
Cash rate per share receivable	GBP 0.20
Currency of payment	GBP

Calculation of Beneficiary (Owner) Entitlement

For all of the following benefit events:

- coupon payments
- dividends
- bonus issues

there are rules to determine the party that is entitled to the benefit. Entitlement to the benefit falls to whoever is the owner of the securities at the *entitlement date*. This is a generic term, in the case of coupon payments the entitlement date is known as the *record date* and in the case of benefits on equity the *ex-date*. The entitlement date is usually set by the market (not the issuer), so that trades executed immediately prior to the entitlement date allow just sufficient time for settlement on value date to occur, resulting in the buyer receiving the benefit directly. However, in the event of settlement failure, the buyer will need to claim the benefit from the seller.

For benefit events where an ex-date applies, the period immediately prior to the ex-date is known as the *cum period* (meaning with the benefit) and the period from and including the ex-date forward is known as the *ex period* (meaning without the benefit).

Entitlement to Coupon Payments. As described above, the coupon payment date on fixed rate bonds is predictable, as is the record date which is normally a fixed number of days (commonly one business day) prior to the coupon payment date. In general, entitlement is determined by the value date of trades in relation to the record date (although different practices exist in different markets). It is recommended that the 'Accrued Interest' section of Chapter 8 be read prior to or in conjunction with the following.

When buying an interest bearing bond, the buyer compensates the seller for the proportion of coupon earned since the previous coupon payment date. In turn, that buyer will be compensated by either:

- selling the bond and receiving compensation from the (new) buyer, or
- retaining the bond beyond the entitlement date for the next coupon payment and receiving compensation from the issuer on the coupon payment date.

Figure 26.2 illustrates the principles of how to calculate entitlement to a coupon payment.

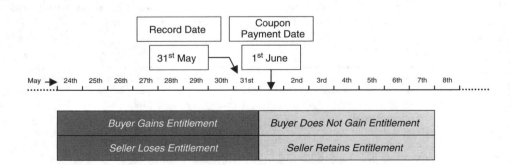

Figure 26.2   Corporate actions: calculation of beneficiary entitlement (coupon payments)

In essence, during the period immediately prior to the coupon payment date:

- the purchaser of a trade with a value date on or prior to the record date will be entitled to the coupon payment, and
- the seller of a trade with a value date on or prior to the record date will lose entitlement to the coupon payment.

During the period immediately following the coupon payment date:

- the purchaser of a trade with a value date after the record date will not gain entitlement (to the coupon payment that is being made), and
- the seller of a trade with a value date after the record date will retain entitlement.

For example, using the dates within Figure 26.2, if an STO buys USD 1 million bonds on (trade date) 25th May, for value date 28th May (T+3) from counterparty G, the STO will have needed to pay the seller the cash value of 357 days of accrued interest. From the seller's perspective, he has received compensation (via the 357 days paid by the STO), so cannot also expect to receive the coupon payment of (in this case) a full year of 360 days. However, from the buying STO's perspective, it has paid out 357 days to the seller, and therefore does expect to receive the coupon payment for the full year, providing the STO does not sell with a value date on or prior to the record date.

Assuming that the STO executes no more trades on or before the record date, on 31st May the STO's books and records will show the situation in Figure 26.3.

XOX AG 8.25% Bonds 1st June 2020 As at 31st May			
Ownership		Location	
Trading Book A	+1,000,000	−1,000,000	Custodian X Main Account
	+1,000,000	−1,000,000	

Figure 26.3 Corporate actions: books and records

Having previously captured the detail of this particular coupon payment, the STO needs to assess whether it (or its safe custody clients) is entitled to the coupon payment, by viewing its books and records as at the record date. The STO is therefore entitled to the coupon for the entire coupon period (in this case one year) on USD 1 million bonds, which at a rate of 8.25% equates to USD 82,500.00. The next task is to determine from whom the benefit will be received.

Providing the STO continues to own the bonds, it will be entitled to future coupon payments. The above example looked at entitlement relating to trades executed immediately prior to the coupon payment date within a particular year; however, should the STO maintain its holding of USD 1 million bonds beyond the record date of the following coupon payment (due 12 months later), the STO will be entitled to that particular coupon payment.

Entitlement to Dividends. The ex-dividend date is decided by the local stock exchange over which the security is normally traded. In general, entitlement is determined by the trade date of trades in relation to the ex-dividend date (although different conventions exist in different markets). Figure 26.4 illustrates the principles of how to calculate entitlement on a cash dividend (based on a T+5 settlement cycle).

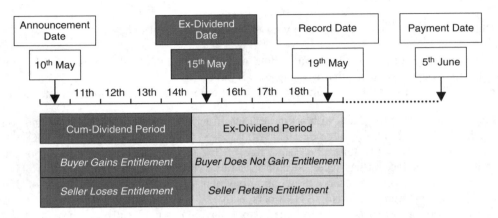

Figure 26.4   Corporate actions: calculation of beneficiary entitlement (cash dividends)

In essence, during the *cum-dividend period* (the period immediately prior to the ex-dividend date):

- the purchaser of a trade with a trade date prior to the ex-dividend date will be entitled to the dividend, and
- the seller of a trade with a trade date prior to the ex-dividend date will lose entitlement to the dividend.

During the *ex-dividend period* (the period that begins with the ex-dividend date):

- the purchaser of a trade with a trade date on or after the ex-dividend date will not gain entitlement, and
- the seller of a trade with a trade date on or after the ex-dividend date will retain entitlement.

For example, using the dates within Figure 26.4, if an STO buys 10,000 shares on (trade date) 13th May, for value date 18th May (T+5) from counterparty T, the STO will have bought the shares cum-dividend, and therefore be entitled to the dividend.

If, on 14th May, the STO sells 6000 shares to counterparty V, the STO will have sold cum-dividend and will not be entitled to the dividend on the number of shares sold.

Assuming that the STO executes no more trades before the ex-dividend date, on 15th May the STO's books and records will show the situation in Figure 26.5.

Having previously captured the detail of this particular cash dividend, the STO needs to assess whether it (or its safe custody clients) is entitled to the dividend, by viewing its books and records as at the ex-dividend date. Figure 26.5 shows that the STO is entitled to the dividend on 4000 shares, which at a rate of GBP 0.20 per share equates to GBP 800.00. The next task is to determine from whom the benefit will be received.

British Airways Ordinary Shares			
As at 15th May			
Ownership		Location	
Trading Book A	+4000	−10,000	Counterparty T
		+6000	Counterparty V
	+4000	−4000	

Figure 26.5   Corporate actions: books and records

However it is important to note that in some markets, entitlement can be reversed by specifically buying or selling during the cum-dividend period on an ex-dividend basis, and similarly during the ex-dividend period on a cum-dividend basis. This is known as 'special-ex' and 'special-cum' trading respectively.

Providing the STO continues to own the shares, it will be entitled to future dividend payments. The above example looked at entitlement relating to trades executed immediately prior to the ex-dividend date for British Airways' May dividend; however, should the STO maintain its holding of 4000 shares beyond the ex-dividend date of the following dividend paid by British Airways (expected to be the November dividend), the STO will be entitled to that particular dividend payment as the STO will have effectively purchased the shares cum-dividend, more than six months previously.

The accurate calculation of beneficiary entitlement by the STO is completely reliant upon the timely and accurate recording of new, amended and cancelled trades. Where the STO records trades as and when executed and has a low error rate, the resultant calculation of entitlement will prove to be as accurate as the books and records are accurate. However, trying to calculate entitlement under the circumstances where trades are recorded late, and with a high error rate, not only increases the workload for those responsible for corporate actions, but increases the risk that entitlement is not calculated accurately, and ultimately that the STO (and its safe custody clients) do not receive benefits to which they are entitled.

Calculating from whom Benefits will be Received

The STO, having established that it (and/or its safe custody clients) is entitled to the benefit due on a security, then needs to determine from whom the benefit will be received. Again, it is the STO's books and records that provide the answer. The 'location' side of books and records will tell the STO from whom benefit is receivable, but only providing that the books and records are completely up-to-date, and the reflection of trade settlement internally has been effected exactly as and when it occurred in the outside world.

Registered Securities. Payment of benefits by the issuer of registered securities is made on the payment date to all holders registered as at the close of business on the *record date* (also known as *books-closing date*).

In the past, prior to the common use of book-entry clearing systems, benefits payable on registered securities (refer to Chapter 6) would typically have been paid directly to the registered holders of the securities as at the record date. The registered holder may or may not have been entitled to the benefit. For example, where an STO purchased securities cum-dividend (and was therefore entitled to the benefit), in order to receive the benefit directly from the issuer, the securities would:

- first have to be delivered to the STO,
- then be sent for registration to the registrar, and
- then the registrar would need to update the register (with the name and address of the new holder)

all by the close of business on the record date. On the payment date of the benefit, the issuer would remit the benefit payments to all those on the register as at the close of business on the record date. If the STO's purchase was not registered in time, the issuer would remit the benefit payment to the seller (as the issuer would not have been aware of the sale). In order for the buying STO to receive its entitled benefit, the STO would need to issue some form of claim to the seller that the benefit they had received should be paid to the STO.

Similar concepts apply in the present day. Registered securities can be settled within book-entry clearing systems, and registration occurs electronically where the registrar of a security is effectively a member of the book-entry clearing system. Under these circumstances, in order for an entitled buyer of securities to receive his benefit without having to claim it from the seller, the buyer is dependent upon receipt of the securities to his account within the book-entry clearing system, followed by the electronic updating of the register prior to the close of business on the record date. As in the past, payment is made to those holders registered as at close of business on record date.

Bearer Securities. Payment of coupon by the issuer of bearer securities is made on the payment date, to those who present the relevant coupons (originally attached to the bond certificate; refer to Chapter 6) to the issuer's appointed *coupon paying agent*.

In parallel with registered securities, an entitled buyer will receive his benefit without having to claim it from the seller, providing the security is delivered to the buyer (or his custodian) on or prior to the record date. The buyer would then detach the relevant coupon from the bond certificate and present the coupon to the coupon paying agent, who will firstly verify the authenticity of the coupon before paying the interest amount on the *coupon payment date*. The holder of a bond who fails to present the coupons by the coupon payment date will suffer a delay in receiving his benefit.

The majority of STOs use local custodians, NCSDs or ICSDs as custodians in order to hold their securities and to receive and deliver securities that have been purchased or sold. One custodian is likely to hold the securities on behalf of numerous account holders, and part of the service that custodians provide to their account holders is:

- the cutting of coupons,
- the presentation of coupons to the coupon paying agent,
- the collection of the benefit, and
- the distribution of the benefit to the appropriate holders.

For example, a custodian may be holding a total of USD 95 million face value of bonds, from which it cuts the relevant coupon, the latter being presented to the coupon paying agent. Typically, this occurs just prior to the coupon payment date, to ensure that the payment of the benefit is not delayed. The custodian will need to distribute the coupon payment on USD 95 million bonds, in proportion to the holdings of its account holders. This is achieved by the custodian adopting a record date method, where all holders of the security as at close of business on the record date will be credited with the coupon amount proportional to their record date holding. In the case of Clearstream Luxembourg and Euroclear, the record date is usually one day prior to the coupon payment date.

Therefore, providing the STO's books and records are up-to-date and accurate, the information held on the 'location' side of the books and records will tell the STO from whom the benefit is receivable. For instance, if the entire quantity of entitled securities was held within the STO's account at the custodian on or before the record date, this would tell the STO to expect the benefit to be received from the custodian (without needing to claim from a selling counterparty). Alternatively, if as at the record date the delivery of securities relating to the STO's purchase had not occurred, this shows that the benefit is due from the seller.

Note that for both registered and bearer securities, when selling securities that are not delivered to the buyer prior to the close-of-business on record date, the STO will receive a benefit payment to which it is not entitled.

Benefit Collection. Having calculated from whom a benefit will be received, the payment of benefit due from the custodian will be credited to the STO's account at the custodian:

- (usually) on the benefit payment date for the securities held within the STO's account by the close-of-business on record date, or
- on or after the benefit payment date for the securities failing to be received within the STO's account at the custodian by close-of-business on the record date, following the issuance of a claim (where necessary) to the seller.

Note that at some custodians, payments of benefit received by the seller but due to the buyer can be recognised and may be automatically adjusted (this is commonly known as benefit compensation) by incorporating the cash benefit due to the buyer into the settlement value of the underlying open trade. When settlement of the trade occurs, the buyer pays the original net settlement value less the value of the benefit. However, entitled holders should remain alert as in some markets it is normal practice for sellers not to pay benefits to the entitled buyer, unless a claim is received.

Whenever the STO receives income (e.g. cash dividends and coupon payments), the credit of cash at the custodian will need to be taken into account when maximising the return on credit cash balances and minimising interest on overdrafts (refer to Chapter 23).

Crediting Owners

Within the STO's books and records, the STO may adopt a policy of crediting the owner (whether the STO's trading book or its safe custody client(s)) either:

- on the benefit payment date, regardless of whether the STO has received credit externally (this is commonly known as *contractual settlement* of benefits), or
- only after receipt of cash externally (*actual settlement of benefits*).

Table 26.8

Entries passed on benefit payment date			
Debit		Credit	
Dividend receivable account	CAD 1000.00	CAD 1000.00	Trading book A

If the STO adopts the former policy, having credited the owner on benefit payment date by the passing of the entries in Table 26.8, the cash due to be received externally must be monitored to ensure it is received. This is typically achieved through the monitoring of the cash balance on the dividend receivable account or dividend control account until the cash is received externally at the custodian and the entries in Table 26.9 are passed, at which point all necessary entries have been completed, leaving zero balance on the dividend receivable account.

Table 26.9

Entries passed once cash is received externally			
Debit		Credit	
Custodian X nostro account	CAD 1000.00	CAD 1000.00	Dividend receivable account

If the STO's policy is to credit owners only after the receipt of cash externally, all four entries in Table 26.8 and 29.9 will usually still be passed, but this will occur on the same date (the date the cash is received).

In the case of safe custody clients who have been credited with benefits, the STO may issue some form of advice to the clients, as part of the service provided by the STO.

Where the STO does not maintain cash accounts for safe custody clients (refer to Chapter 25), cash benefits payable to clients will need to be paid to the clients' bank account externally.

26.2.4   Tax on Benefits

Note: the following should be regarded as an overview as tax on benefits is another intricate subject in its own right.

The receipt of income by a beneficiary is usually subject to two different taxes, namely:

- withholding tax, and
- holder's residency income tax.

Withholding Tax

Legislation in many countries demands that withholding tax is deducted at a standard rate, from income paid by companies (that are domiciled in that country) to non-residents of that country.

However, under some circumstances, non-residents of certain countries may be liable for tax at a reduced rate. This occurs when a *double-taxation agreement* (also known as a *treaty*) exists between the country of the issuer and the country of the beneficiary.

Rates of withholding tax vary from country to country, and may vary between income on debt and equity within a country. The concepts are illustrated in Figure 26.6, revealing that:

Country of Issuer	Issue Type	Country of Residence of Investor			
		Canada	Japan	UK	USA
Country A	Equity	15%	20%	15%	20%
	Bond	10%	20%	10%	20%
Country B	Equity	15%	15%	10%	10%
	Bond	20%	20%	20%	20%
Country C	Equity	30%	30%	30%	30%
	Bond	30%	30%	30%	30%

Key: Double-tax agreement   No double-tax agreement

Figure 26.6 Corporate actions: example withholding tax at standard and treaty rates

- a resident of Canada who invests in the equity of an issuer domiciled in country A is liable for withholding tax at the reduced rate of 15% due to the treaty between country A and Canada, whereas a resident of the USA investing in the same security is liable for withholding tax at the standard rate of 20%, as there is no treaty in place between country A and the USA;
- a resident of Japan investing in a country B bond is liable for tax at the non-treaty rate of 20%, as there are no treaties relating to bonds issued in country B;
- all non-residents of country C will be taxed at 30% on income from equity and bond investments, as there are no treaties in place.

(Note that withholding tax rates on bonds issued by a country may differ according to, for example, the issuer being a government or a company, whilst some securities (e.g. Eurobonds) are not subject to withholding tax).

In a situation where the STO operates a safe custody service, its clients may be resident in various countries. When income is due on the clients' holdings, the STO would usually want to credit individual clients with the benefit, after deduction of the applicable rate of withholding tax, according to each client's residency status.

In order to ensure the correct rate of withholding tax is deducted for each client, the STO typically sets up two safe custody accounts at each custodian, where all securities owned by residents of treaty countries would be held within one account, and within the other account all securities owned by residents of non-treaty countries would be held. Note that a third account may be used to cater for holdings that are exempt from withholding tax (e.g. for local residents).

The consequence of the STO setting up the two safe custody accounts at the custodian is that, when income is paid, the STO's safe custody accounts will be credited after deduction of the appropriate rate of withholding tax, which in turn enables the STO to credit the owners after deduction of the correct rate of withholding tax. These actions avoid any discrepancy arising between the withholding tax rate at which the client is liable, and the tax deducted when the STO is credited at the custodian.

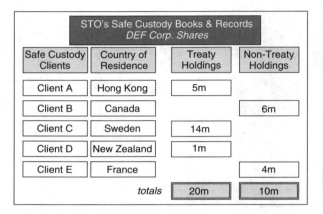

Figure 26.7   Corporate actions: ensuring correct withholding tax is deducted

Figure 26.7 illustrates (using fictitious treaty/non-treaty information):

- the STO's books and records showing
  - the individual client
  - the residency status of each client
  - the custodian account within which each client's holding should be held, and
- the holding at the custodian showing
  - the actual holding within each of the STO's accounts

which reveals that the STO's ownership records reconcile with the holdings within the STO's accounts at the custodian.

Where safe custody clients' securities are moved into or out of the STO's custodian accounts, procedurally the STO must ensure that the appropriate safe custody account at the custodian is credited or debited, according to the client's residency status.

Where a country has no treaties with other countries, the STO would set up a single account only, as all investors would be liable for withholding tax at the same rate, regardless of their residency.

Where an investor is liable for tax at a treaty rate but has been taxed at a non-treaty rate, the investor is normally able to reclaim the overpaid withholding tax from the tax authorities within the issuer's country of residence. Some STOs provide a service to their clients of administering such reclaims on the clients' behalf.

Holder's Residency Income Tax

In addition to withholding tax that may have been deducted from income paid by issuers to non-residents, the tax authorities within the owner's country of residence may impose income tax on the owner. Generically, this tax will be referred to as Holder's Residency Income Tax (HRIT) within this book.

Although tax regimes differ from country to country, the HRIT payable by owners will be either:

- deducted at the full income tax rate, in addition to the withholding tax already deducted, or
- deducted at the difference between the HRIT rate and the withholding tax rate, where the withholding tax can be offset against the HRIT.

HRIT at the Full Income Tax Rate. Where the tax laws within an owner's country of residence demand that the full rate of HRIT is deducted in addition to the withholding tax already deducted, it is normal for the HRIT rate to be applied to the gross value of the income.

For example, where the owner of 500 shares is entitled to a dividend of AUD 0.20 per share, the gross dividend receivable will be AUD 100.00. Withholding tax (at say 15%) and HRIT (at the full rate of, say, 25%) would result in a net dividend of AUD 60.00 (Table 26.10).

Table 26.10

	AUD
Gross dividend (quantity of shares × rate per share)	100.00
Deduct withholding tax at 15%	−15.00
Net income after withholding tax	85.00
Deduct HRIT at full rate of 25%	−25.00
Net dividend after all taxes	**60.00**

HRIT Offset by Withholding Tax. The tax authorities within the owner's country of residence may permit the compensation or offsetting of the withholding tax deducted against the HRIT. Under these circumstances, where withholding tax has been deducted at, for example, 15% and the full rate of HRIT is 25%, the owner will have HRIT of just 10% deducted. Therefore, using the same tax rates as above, an owner who is resident in such a country would receive a net dividend of AUD 75.00 (Table 26.11).

Table 26.11

	AUD
Gross dividend (quantity of shares × rate per share)	100.00
Deduct withholding tax at 15%	−15.00
Net income after withholding tax	85.00
Deduct HRIT at 10% (offset rate of 15%)	−10.00
Net dividend after all taxes	**75.00**

The STO that collects the income on behalf of the owner (for example, where the STO operates a safe custody service) may be required to deduct HRIT from its clients who are resident in the same country as the STO. Where the STO deducts HRIT from such clients, the STO will be required to remit the tax amount to the tax authorities periodically.

If the HRIT has not been deducted by the STO, the owner is likely to be required by law to declare the income to his tax authority, which will require payment of the tax.

26.3   REORGANISATIONS

Those corporate actions that result in the holder of the security having their holding altered will be referred to as *reorganisations* within this book.

Such reorganisations include:

- stock/share splits,
- bond final redemptions, and
- takeovers.

Comparable characteristics of reorganisations to those of benefits are:

- the method of capture is the same;
- the effective date on a reorganisation is equivalent to the entitlement date on a benefit;
- the method of collection will differ according to the type of reorganisation and procedures for claiming in given markets.

26.3.1   Stock/Share Splits

A stock/share split is the reduction in capital value (or par value) of an equity security versus a proportional increase in the quantity of shares held.

When the market price of a share reaches a certain level, for example USD 100.00, opinion within the securities marketplace states that the shares become less attractive to potential investors, in particular to individual investors. If the board of directors feel strongly that they wish to maintain or increase the number of individual investors, in order to encourage individual investors to buy the shares, they may decide to undergo a split. The increase in shares from the split will result in a reduced share price in the market (Table 26.12).

Table 26.12

Characteristics of stock/share splits	
Predictable or announced?	Stock/share splits are announced by the issuer, following a decision by the board of directors
Issuer's objective?	To make its shares more widely available by increasing the number of shares in issue and impacting the market price
How expressed?	Stock/share splits are normally expressed as a ratio of new shares to existing shares
Benefit to holder?	A larger pool of potential buyers exists as a result of the split, making the shares easier to sell
Mandatory or voluntary event?	The issuer decides to effect the split to all shares in issue, and is mandatory with no owner's option
Effect on security holding?	The existing security is cancelled and replaced by a new security of a greater quantity than the original
Effect on trading?	The share price will fall in proportion to the ratio of new versus existing shares

The effect on the share price is explained in the following example. If a shareholder in company X has a holding of 200 shares, and the security is trading at a price of HKD 120.00 (market value HKD 24,000.00), a stock/share split of two new shares to replace one existing share would result in the shareholder having its existing holding of:

>200   Company X
>Common stock of HKD 1.00 par value

cancelled and replaced by a holding of:

>400   Company X
>Common stock of HKD 0.50 par value

Post the stock/share split, the share price would be approximately half the original price (HKD 60.00), and the market value of the holder's shares would still be HKD 24,000.00.

26.3.2   Bond Final Redemptions

When a bond issue is first brought to the marketplace, the date of capital repayment (also known as the maturity date or final redemption date) is clearly stated by the issuer, within the issue prospectus (Table 26.13).

Table 26.13

Characteristics of bond final redemptions	
Predictable or announced?	Bond redemptions (on non-callable bonds) are predictable, as the date of redemption is stated in the prospectus of the issue
Issuer's objective?	To repay capital borrowed from the bondholders, at a predetermined price and date
How expressed?	The redemption price is expressed as a percentage of the bond face (nominal) value
Benefit to holder?	Bondholders receive predictable cash amounts at a predetermined date
Mandatory or voluntary event?	These are mandatory events, where bondholders typically have no choice as to the form of payment
Effect on security holding?	Following the final maturity date, the bonds cease to exist and therefore must be removed from the STO's books and records
Effect on trading?	As the bond no longer exists after the final maturity date, the bond can no longer be traded

In parallel with the collection of coupon payments, the owner of a maturing bond receives his cash by presenting the bond to the issuer (or its agent), on or shortly before the maturity date. Failure to present the bond on time will result in the payment of cash by the issuer being delayed, thereby causing a delay in the owner receiving his cash.

Because STOs typically use custodians to hold their securities, part of the service usually provided by custodians is the presentation of the bond to the issuer (or its agent), the collection of redemption proceeds from the issuer and the crediting of owners.

26.3.3 Takeovers

In general terms, a takeover is the attempt to purchase by one company (the bidder) all or part of the issued share capital of another company (the target).

Many different situations arise concerning takeovers, including:

- friendly takeovers, where the management of the target company support the actions of the bidder, and
- hostile takeovers, where the bidding company attempts to replace the management of the target company which may take measures to counter the bidder's offer.

A takeover normally involves three stages from the shareholder's perspective (Table 26.14).

Table 26.14

Characteristics of takeovers	
Predictable or announced?	Takeovers are announced by the bidder, following a decision by its board of directors
Bidder's objective?	To gain a majority (also known as controlling) or full interest in the target company
How expressed?	An amount of cash or quantity of securities per share is offered to the shareholders of the target company
Benefit to holder?	Shareholders in the target company receive assets of a greater value than the market value of the target shares
Mandatory or voluntary event?	Prior to the offer close date it is voluntary to accept. Post the close date it is a mandatory acquisition (where a full takeover)
Effect on security holding?	Where the offer was accepted by the shareholders, their holding in the target company ceases to exist
Effect on trading?	During the period of the takeover, the price of the target company's shares may rise

1. Initially voluntary, the shareholder may elect to accept the offer, or not. The offer can be accepted at any time between the offer opening and closing dates.
2. Where the offer is for all of the issued share capital, once acceptance (by the shareholders) approaches 100%, any shareholders who have not accepted are known as dissenting shareholders and their shares become compulsorily acquired.
3. Distribution of the offer proceeds to shareholders whose shares have been acquired. Note that the offer proceeds can be in the form of cash or securities (either in the bidder's shares or in another security of the bidder's choice).

26.4 MULTIFACETED ACTIONS

Multifaceted actions are corporate actions that consist of multiple stages involving combinations of events referred to previously within this chapter, which may include benefits, reorganisations and subscriptions. A subscription relates to the effective purchase of a security (normally direct from the issuer) in exchange for a security the subscriber already owns.

Whilst there are other examples of multifaceted actions (and issuers frequently bring into being creative ideas as to restructuring), *rights issues* are a prime example.

26.4.1   Rights Issues

If a company decides to raise further capital, one option it has is to offer additional shares to the existing shareholders (in proportion to their existing shareholding), at a discount on the current market price, through a rights issue.

There are three main stages in the lifecycle of a rights issue (Table 26.15).

1. The distribution of the rights entitlement by the issuer to the shareholders (a mandatory benefit).
2. The subscription to the offer of new securities by the shareholders (a subscription).
3. The expiry of non-subscribed rights (a mandatory reorganisation).

Table 26.15

	Characteristics of rights issues
Predictable or announced?	Rights issues are announced by the issuer, following a decision by the board of directors
Issuer's objective?	To raise additional capital in order to expand its business, whilst avoiding shareholders diluting their investment
How expressed?	Rights issues are typically expressed as a ratio of new shares versus existing shares (refer to 'Bonus Issues' above)
Benefit to holder?	The shareholder is given the right to subscribe to the new shares at a discount on the market price
Mandatory or voluntary event?	The issuer offers the right to all its shareholders, but the decision to purchase is the shareholder's own
Effect on security holding?	Where the new shares have been purchased, existing shareholdings will need to be increased, at the relevant ratio
Effect on trading?	The price per share in the marketplace will be reduced to take account of the increased number of shares in issue

Gathering and Capturing the Detail of Rights Issues

The detail of all three stages of a rights issue (listed above) are declared by the issuer as a single announcement, including:

- the entitlement ratio,
- the subscription price, and
- the expiry date.

Distribution of Rights Entitlement by the Issuer to the Shareholders

The first step in the rights issue lifecycle is the allotment of entitlement to additional shares, to shareholders on the company's register (electronic or otherwise), as at a record date. As for equity related benefits mentioned earlier in this chapter, those who receive the rights entitlement (because they appear on the register as at close-of-business on the record date) are not necessarily entitled to the benefit. Consequently, calculation of beneficiary (owner) entitlement is effected, the entitlement date being the *ex-rights date*.

The form in which an entitled owner of shares receives his 'rights' is by an allotment letter or subscription warrant. Such documents have a finite life, as the issuer imposes a deadline by which owners wishing to subscribe to the offer must make their payment.

Some types of rights issue (known as renounceable or tradable) allow the rights to be sold in the marketplace, thereby transferring the opportunity to purchase additional shares from the issuer. Other types of rights issues are non-renounceable or non-tradable.

For tradable rights issues, the rights have a value (separate from the underlying shares), because rights provide the owner with a means of gaining shares at a discount. Therefore, prior to the subscription deadline, a market exists for the rights, which may be bought and sold. A buyer of rights acquires the subscription opportunity.

For non-tradable rights, the subscription opportunity remains with the original rights owner.

Subscription to the Offer of New Securities by the Shareholders

All owners of the rights (whether the original allottee or a buyer of the rights) will need to decide whether to subscribe to the offer, or not. This decision is likely to be based upon the owner's view of the future share price of the underlying shares.

For example, if the price of the underlying shares is substantially higher than the rights offer price immediately prior to the subscription deadline, and the rights owner believes that the underlying share price will continue to increase, the rights owner may well decide to subscribe to the rights on the basis that the underlying shares can be gained at a substantial discount.

However, if the underlying share price immediately prior to the subscription deadline is around the same price as the rights offer price, the rights owner may decide not to subscribe if it is felt that no financial advantage can be gained (refer to next section).

Rights owners who choose to subscribe to the offer are required to remit their payment, along with the allotment letter or subscription warrant, to an agent appointed by the issuer, by the stated deadline.

Subscribers to the offer will become the owners of shares in the issuer's underlying equity, and will therefore appear on the issuer's register of holders. Subscribers will receive either:

* share certificates, or
* an update to their book-entry holding

(whichever is applicable in the particular market), typically within weeks following the subscription deadline.

Expiry of Non-subscribed Rights

Where a rights owner chooses not to subscribe to the rights, the rights will have expired as at the subscription deadline and have no value thereafter.

26.5   GENERAL (RELEVANT TO ALL CORPORATE ACTIONS)

26.5.1   Timing of Passing Internal Entries

In order for the STO's books and records to remain accurate, the timing of the passing of entries resulting from corporate actions is all-important.

There are two main actions that must be considered. The passing of securities and cash entries within internal books and records:

* relevant to the equivalent entries within the STO's trading system, and
* relevant to the equivalent entries at the custodian.

Relevant to the STO's Trading System

Whenever a trading book is the owner of a position that is affected by a corporate action, whether the action results in:

* increased quantity of securities (e.g. bonus issue),
* reduced or zeroised quantity of securities (e.g. bond final redemption),
* addition of new securities (e.g. takeover),
* increased cash (e.g. cash dividend), or
* decreased cash (e.g. rights subscription)

the trader's records within the trading system will need to be updated to ensure the trader trades from the revised position following the corporate action, but equally the settlement system will need to be updated with the same information.

Unless both sets of records are updated at the same time, the reconciliation of trading positions between the trading and settlement systems (refer to Chapter 27) will reveal a discrepancy between the securities positions within the two systems. In addition, the P&L on cash will differ.

Relevant to the Custodian's Records

In parallel with the updating of the trader's records above, when the STO's custodian passes entries resulting from corporate actions (as per the list above), unless the equivalent entries within the STO's settlement system are passed at the same time, the reconciliation of securities and/or cash between the custodian's records and the settlement system will reveal a discrepancy.

26.5.2   Risks Associated with Safe Custody Services

STOs providing a safe custody service will need to receive instructions from their clients regarding optional and voluntary events, for example in the case of a rights issue, whether to subscribe or not.

Unless a formal arrangement exists between the STO and its clients allowing the STO to make discretionary judgements, the STO may be at risk if it decides to act on behalf of a safe custody client in good faith, without having received formal instructions from the client.

For instance, in the case of a rights issue where the STO has decided to subscribe to the rights on the client's behalf, should the share price fall after the subscription deadline, the subscription decision will look less attractive. Under these circumstances, the client may decide not to reimburse the subscription cost to the STO, on the basis that it was not their decision.

Because of such risks, it is essential that the STO has thorough and well-structured operational procedures in place for optional and voluntary events for safe custody clients. These procedures are likely to include:

- deadlines for decisions from safe custody clients, in order to meet the deadline imposed by the issuer, and
- clearly stated default actions, in the event that the safe custody client does not respond by the deadline

if the STO wishes to minimise such risks.

26.6 SUMMARY

In parallel with the settlement of securities trades, for which the STO needs to remain in complete control, the processing and management of corporate actions should also be fully controlled by the STO.

For the STO's own positions and for its safe custody clients' positions (if a safe custody service is offered by the STO), corporate actions will have the following results:

- an increase or decrease in securities, and
- the receipt or payment of cash

over which the STO should have complete control. Additionally, optional or voluntary corporate actions requiring a decision by the STO (or its clients) should be fully controlled.

Controlling corporate actions means the STO:

- being aware of each corporate action that may affect a position or outstanding trades;
- understanding the nature of each corporate action;
- operating within the necessary deadlines;
- knowing the cost or benefit of each corporate action;
- ensuring receipt of entitled assets at the appropriate time;
- ensuring costs are charged at the appropriate time.

Failure to adequately control corporate actions may result in entitled assets due to the STO and its clients not being received.

27

Reconciliation

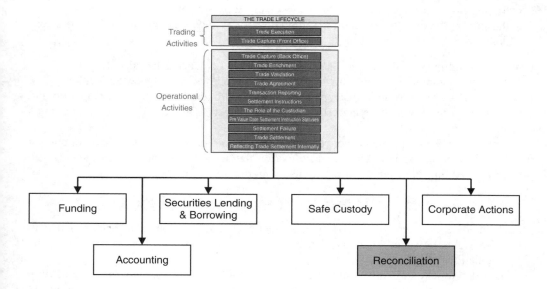

27.1 INTRODUCTION

The process of proving that an STO's books and records are accurate is commonly known as reconciliation. From any perspective, reconciling positions and trades within internal books and records with the outside world is paramount in ensuring that the STO remains in control of its assets and liabilities.

In the first chapter of this book, it was stated that a company remaining in control of its goods and cash is fundamental to successful and efficient operation of its business through maintaining up-to-date internal records of:

- trades
- trading positions
- open trades
- settled trades
- settled positions

thereby enabling the prediction of future goods and cash flows, which in the case of an STO in turn enables:

- funding costs to be minimised through efficient funding projection, repo and securities borrowing activity, and
- income to be maximised through the efficient lending of securities.

An efficient STO actively seeks proof that its books and records are accurate, by comparing each component of its securities positions and cash balances with the outside world on a daily basis, as well as ensuring that its books and records reconcile internally.

An STO's complete picture of an individual security can be summarised by comparing its:

- trading position (also known as the 'ownership' position) with
- the sum of the open trades and the settled position (collectively known as the 'location' position)

which should prove that the STO's books and records balance internally.

Through reconciliation, internal records will be shown to balance and either agree with the outside world, or a discrepancy will be highlighted requiring investigation and resolution. After having corrected such items, all aspects of the STO's books and records should agree.

Unless an STO keeps the task of reconciliation up-to-date, the necessary level of control will be lost, resulting in a detrimental effect on the activities of the various areas within the STO, leading to a reduction in efficiency and increased costs.

27.2 OVERVIEW OF RECONCILIATION

Each major component of an STO's securities and cash position must be reconciled in its own right; however, there is also a logical relationship that connects each of the reconciliations together.

In order to explain the components that must be reconciled, and the connectivity between them, reconciliation topics will be viewed from the perspective of a newly formed STO that owns no securities positions, and that buys securities for the first time. For the moment, the focus of reconciliation will be on the quantity of securities, and cash reconciliation will be described separately. Each diagram in this chapter is intended to represent the view within the settlement system, and the 'callouts' indicate how each component should be reconciled.

27.2.1 Trade Date

The trader responsible for trading book A buys 1000 EFG Corporation common stock at a price of USD 46.00 per share from counterparty C, and captures the trade within the trading system; the trade is automatically fed to the settlement system. The following is based upon a T+3 value date for ease of understanding.

A DvP settlement instruction is issued by the STO to custodian T, and the custodian applies a status of 'matched'.

The positions held within the STO's books and records (the settlement system) at the close of business on the trade date are as shown in Figure 27.1.

Ownership

Whatever the trader has purchased must be shown as being owned as at the trade date (regardless of whether the securities have been delivered at the custodian). Similarly, when securities are sold, the resultant position must be shown on trade date. This position (the 'trading position') must reconcile with the trader's view of his position in this security. For

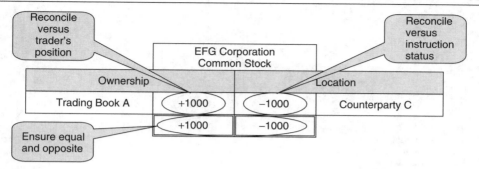

Figure 27.1   Reconciliation overview: on trade date

the purposes of this particular reconciliation, the 'outside world' as far as the settlement system is concerned is the trading system, as that is the source of the information.

Location

The trade must be shown as open with the counterparty, until such time as settlement occurs. The proof that this trade is outstanding with the counterparty is evidenced through the settlement instruction status, which is 'matched' (indicating that the counterparty agrees the trade detail, and that it has a future value date and is therefore not yet settled).

Internal Integrity

Within internal books and records the total ownership position, per individual security, must be equal and opposite to the total location position, as every entry must have a contra effect. In the case of this individual security, the positive ownership position forced a negative location position; this is a necessary feature of double-entry bookkeeping and is explained below.

   In its internal books and records, when the STO has a positive securities trading position (the total of purchases being greater in quantity than the total of sales) it is normal to represent this position with a positive (+) sign; in order to maintain the discipline that *double-entry bookkeeping* provides, the STO is forced to treat the opposite side (the open trade with the counterparty) with a negative (−) sign. This should be interpreted as securities due from the counterparty. The signing convention that the STO chooses (i.e. whether to show a positive trading position as a positive or negative sign) is the STO's choice, but having decided, it must be able to interpret the information correctly, for example, whether securities are due from or to be delivered to a counterparty.

27.2.2   Trade Date+1 and Trade Date+2

On the two days that follow the trade date, the settlement instruction status remains as 'matched' at the custodian (Figure 27.2).

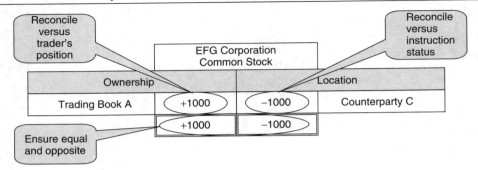

Figure 27.2   Reconciliation overview: trade date+1 and trade date+2

Ownership

No further purchases or sales of this security have been received by the settlement system since the trade date of the first trade, therefore the trading system's position should not have changed; however, this should be proved through reconciliation.

Location

As settlement has still not occurred, the trade must continue to be shown as open with the counterparty, and this should be substantiated via the settlement instruction status.

Internal Integrity

As there have been no changes to the ownership and location positions within the settlement system, there should be no change in the ownership position equalling the location position; however, this should still be checked and confirmed.

27.2.3   Value Date (and Settlement Date)

On the value date of the trade, custodian T advises the STO that the trade has settled. 1000 EFG Corporation shares have been received against payment of USD 46,000.00; the settlement system has been updated to reflect settlement (Figure 27.3).

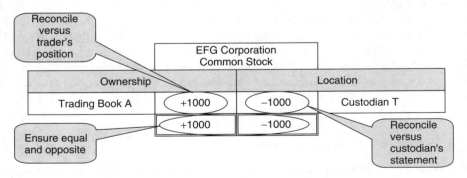

Figure 27.3   Reconciliation overview: value date (and settlement date)

Ownership

No further purchases or sales of this security have been received by the settlement system since trade date of the first trade, so the position within the trading system should not have changed; again this should be proved through reconciliation.

Location

Upon receipt of notification of settlement from the custodian, the relevant trade must be updated within internal books and records with the quantity of securities settled (as described in Chapter 21). This must result in the trade showing as settled (no longer open) with the counterparty, and the custodian position as having been updated. This must be reconciled with the statement of securities holdings issued by the custodian.

Internal Integrity

The reflection of settlement against the trade with the counterparty causes an equal and opposite entry against the custodian (resulting in a zero balance against the counterparty); as both counterparty and custodian are considered to be on the location side, the net effect should be zero. Again, the total ownership position must be equal and opposite to the total location position, but must be proved. Note that the position at the custodian is represented within the settlement system as a negative position; this should be interpreted as securities held at the custodian. The act of settlement at the custodian, and the reflection of settlement internally within the STO's records, does not impact the ownership position.

27.2.4 Continued Holding of the Security

Should the trader continue to hold this security position for, say, many months, the situation as represented in Figure 27.3 should not change, and reconciliation of the settlement system's:

- ownership position (versus the trader's view of his position),
- location position (versus the custodian's statement of holdings), and
- internal integrity

should continue to be carried out on a daily basis, to ensure this remains the case.

27.2.5 Selling the Entire Security Holding

Months after the trader purchased the security, he sells (as trading book A) the 1000 EFG Corporation common stock at a price of USD 48.50, to counterparty H. Following trade capture within the settlement system, on trade date the internal books and records would appear as in Figure 27.4.

Ownership

The resultant trade dated position following the sale is now zero, and this requires reconciling with the trading system's position.

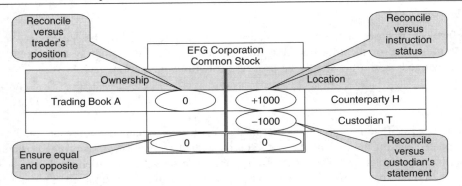

Figure 27.4   Reconciliation overview: on trade date of sale

Location

The sale must be shown as outstanding with the counterparty, until such time that settlement occurs; the proof that the trade is outstanding with the counterparty is achieved via the settlement instruction status.

In addition, the securities held by the custodian (from the purchase many months before) will remain in place until settlement occurs; the holding must be proved via reconciliation with the custodian's statement of holdings.

Internal Integrity

At all times, the total ownership position must equal the sum of the location positions, but this still needs to be proven on a frequent (preferably daily) basis. Note that the open sale to the counterparty is represented by a positive sign, meaning that securities are due to be delivered to the counterparty, whilst the holding at the custodian continues to be represented by a negative sign, and should be interpreted as securities held at the custodian.

27.2.6   Selling Part of the Security Holding

If, instead of selling all 1000 shares, the trader sold 600 to counterparty G, following trade capture within the settlement system, on trade date the internal books and records would appear as in Figure 27.5.

Ownership

The resultant trade dated position following the sale of 600 shares is now a positive position of 400, which should be reconciled with the trading system's position.

Location

The sale of 600 shares must be shown as outstanding with the counterparty, until settlement occurs. In addition, the securities held by the custodian (from the purchase many months before) will remain in place until settlement of the sale occurs. The outstanding trade and the settled position must be verified via the settlement instruction status and the custodian's statement of holdings, respectively.

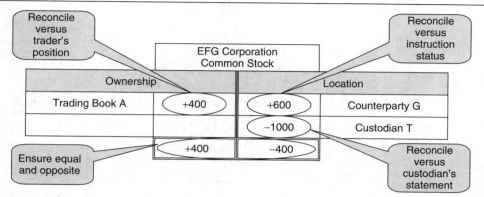

Figure 27.5 Reconciliation overview: on trade date of sale (of 600 shares)

Internal Integrity

At all times, the total ownership position must equal the sum of the location position, but again this must be proven.

A pattern should now be evident, where sales and purchases, and deliveries and receipts of securities cause logical positive and negative (*double-entry bookkeeping*) entries within internal books and records; the result of these entries should reconcile with the information in the outside world.

27.3 RECONCILIATION TERMINOLOGY

The various actions in relation to reconciliations mentioned above, namely:

- reconcile versus trader's position
- reconcile versus instruction status
- reconcile versus custodian's statement
- ensure equal and opposite

will be referred to from this point forward as:

- trading position reconciliation
- open trades reconciliation
- custodian (depot) position reconciliation
- settlement system integrity reconciliation

respectively.

Figure 27.6 reflects this terminology, whilst illustrating a more complicated situation than those described previously, where:

- two trading books own positions,
- two trades are open with different counterparties, and
- a settled securities position exists at the custodian

with each component needing to be reconciled, including settlement system integrity.

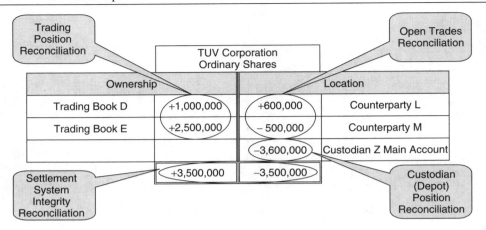

Figure 27.6   Reconciliation overview (with outstanding trades)

27.4   TYPES OF RECONCILIATION

Many of the main securities reconciliations to be conducted from an operational perspective were referred to earlier in this chapter; the following expands on those reconciliations and explores each of the securities reconciliations in more detail.

The expanded list of reconciliations is represented in Figure 27.7, entitled:

1. trade-by-trade reconciliation,
2. trading position reconciliation,

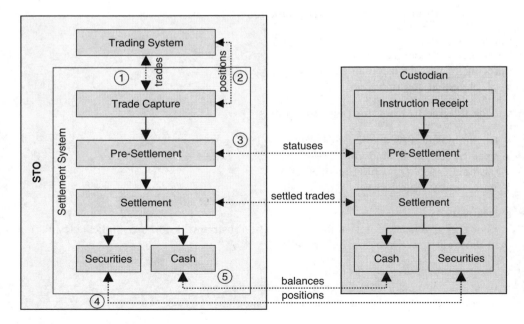

Figure 27.7   Types of reconciliation

3. open trades reconciliation,
4. custodian (depot) position reconciliation,
5. custodian (nostro) position reconciliation, and
6. settlement system integrity reconciliation (not shown in the figure).

27.4.1 Trade-by-Trade Reconciliation

The purpose of this automated reconciliation is to prove that all trades captured by the traders are successfully captured within the settlement system; not conducting this reconciliation can result in failure to process individual trades. The possibility of trades failing to arrive within the settlement system is real, particularly when taking into account daily trading volumes of an average sized STO can be upwards of 5000 trades.

This is a simple but essential control, as without it, trades that are missing from the settlement system may take days to come to light. This control will become imperative as settlement cycles shrink, as an STO's failure to process a trade that has a T+1 value date immediately after trade execution is likely to cause settlement failure at the custodian and the STO to incur associated costs.

This reconciliation is typically performed by the trading system seeking acknowledgement of receipt from the settlement system, of each trade sent, or by the settlement system detecting missing (non-consecutive) trading system trade reference numbers. Failure of the trading system to receive an acknowledgement within a specified time of sending (say, 15 minutes) should result in appropriate rectifying action.

Any trade detected as not being received by the settlement system should be re-sent by the trading system as a matter of urgency; however, before taking such action the STO must be certain that the settlement system has not received the trade, in order to avoid duplication.

This reconciliation should be conducted not just for principal trades, but for all transaction types, in order to ensure the settlement system has received all trades; this may therefore necessitate such reconciliation between the settlement system and multiple trading systems.

27.4.2 Trading Position Reconciliation

This reconciliation is designed to prove that the trade dated securities positions (by security within trading book) calculated by the trading system agree with the equivalent positions calculated by the settlement system. Failure to conduct this reconciliation can result, for example, in trades being executed from the incorrect trading position, where the trading system is found to be incorrect.

The reconciliation is achieved by comparing three pieces of information:

- trading book
- individual security (within trading book)
- trading position (by security within trading book)

as in Table 27.1. Note that all positions agree, with the exception of those marked with an asterisk.

Discrepancies can arise where trades have not been successfully received by the settlement system, and where trade amendments and cancellations have been effected within one system (e.g. the settlement system) but not the other (e.g. the trading system).

Table 27.1

	Trading system	
Book	**Security**	**Position**
Book A	Colgate-Palmolive common stock	+28,000,000
Book A	IBM Corporation common stock	+1,600,000
Book B	IBM Corporation common stock	+14,800,000
Book B	News Corporation ordinary shares	−6,000,000
Book C	Singapore Airlines shares	+8,750,000
Book D	US Treasury 6.25% 1st February 2020	+32,000,000
Book D	City of Oslo 7.0% 15th November 2018	−10,000,000
Book E	World Bank 7.5% 1st December 2018	+4,000,000*
Book E	World Bank 6.75% 15th May 2022	+12,250,000
↕	↕	↕

	Settlement system	
Book	**Security**	**Position**
Book A	Colgate-Palmolive common stock	+28,000,000
Book A	IBM Corporation common stock	+1,600,000
Book B	IBM Corporation common stock	+14,800,000
Book B	News Corporation ordinary shares	−6,000,000
Book C	Singapore Airlines shares	+8,750,000
Book D	US Treasury 6.25% 1st February 2020	+32,000,000
Book D	City of Oslo 7.0% 15th November 2018	−10,000,000
Book E	World Bank 7.5% 1st December 2018	+5,000,000*
Book E	World Bank 6.75% 15th May 2022	+12,250,000

It is important that this reconciliation should not be conducted in place of the trade-by-trade reconciliation described above, as in a situation where a purchase and sale of the same quantity (of the same security) has been executed, captured within the trading system, but not within the settlement system, the trading position reconciliation between the trading and settlement system will agree; however, the missing trades will not have been identified. To be certain of being in a fully reconciled condition, both the trade-by-trade reconciliation and the trading position reconciliation should be performed.

27.4.3   Open Trades Reconciliation

The objective in conducting this reconciliation is to prove that open (i.e. not yet settled) trades held within internal books and records are in reality open at the relevant custodian, or generally have the same status as the equivalent settlement instruction at the custodian.

Discrepancies can arise where settled trades, as advised by a custodian, have failed to be updated within the settlement system due to, for example:

- manually generated settlement instructions, or
- settlement instructions generated on the STO's behalf by an ECN; refer to Chapter 21 for further detail.

Furthermore, at each custodian, there should be no settlement instructions for which no trade can be found internally. Any such instructions could indicate, for example, that the settlement instruction was issued manually, but that the trade has not been recorded internally; if this is the case, the trader's trading position may be incorrect or it may indicate an attempted fraud.

In addition to the basic reconciliation, the following situations should be sought, within internal books and records:

- no past value dated trades exist that are shown as fully or partially open, and
- no future value dated trades

are without an open status at the relevant custodian.

Trade Agreement

The act of gaining agreement of the trade details with the counterparty (refer to Chapter 14) is a type of reconciliation. Although it achieves its objective of an STO knowing that the details of a trade are agreed immediately after trade capture, it does not provide a means of the STO proving that a trade is either open or settled, on or after the value date.

27.4.4   Custodian (Depot) Position Reconciliation

The aim of this reconciliation is to prove that settled securities positions (by depot account, within custodian) held within internal books and records agree with the equivalent positions as advised by each custodian. This is another fundamental control, as without it the STO cannot know whether the securities it believes are held by the custodian are in fact present.

Table 27.2 is an example of the settlement system having reconciled positions with the custodian, with the exception of the discrepancy marked with an asterisk. The STO will of course have securities holdings (sometimes in the same security) at numerous custodians, each of which is likely to hold one main account, plus one or many safe custody accounts, all of which require reconciling.

Table 27.2

Settlement system: Custodian X main account		Statement from custodian X: STO's main account	
Security	Position	Security	Position
Colgate-Palmolive common stock	−25,000,000	Colgate-Palmolive common stock	+25,000,000
IBM Corporation common stock	−16,400,000	IBM Corporation common stock	+16,400,000
Ford Corporation common stock	−1,200,000	Ford Corporation common stock	+1,200,000
Xerox Corporation common stock	−9,000,000*	Xerox Corporation common stock	+4,000,000*

In addition to confirming that positions between internal books and records and the custodians' records agree, any balances shown as being:

- held within internal records, but not at the custodian, or
- held by the custodian, but not held within internal books and records

should be investigated immediately, as failing to do so may disguise for example:

- an error made by the STO when transmitting settlement instructions;
- a failure to update settled trades within the settlement system;
- the unexpected receipt of securities within the STO's account at the custodian, for instance as a result of a corporate action;
- the unauthorised removal of securities from the STO's account at the custodian.

Once a discrepancy is identified, individual movements will need to be compared in order to reveal the cause of the discrepancy.

This reconciliation should be conducted for all securities positions, within all securities accounts at all the STO's custodians.

27.4.5   Settlement System Integrity Reconciliation

This reconciliation is intended to prove that the settlement system remains in balance; that is, the total of the securities owned is equal to the sum of the location position. This is achievable providing that double-entry bookkeeping methods are employed when passing any entry within internal books and records.

For instance, the integrity of the settlement system will be upheld if the internal books and records appear as in Table 27.3, where the total ownership and location positions are equal and opposite.

Table 27.3

Inter-American Development Bank 4.8% bonds 1st October 2025			
Ownership		Location	
Trading book A	+ 1,000,000	+ 600,000	Counterparty L
Trading book B	+ 2,500,000	− 500,000	Counterparty M
		− 3,600,000	Custodian X main account
	+ 3,500,000	**− 3,500,000**	

Table 27.4 shows an example of the system being out of balance. If the double-entry accounting principle is practiced by the STO for all securities and cash entries, theoretically the system cannot go out of balance. However, it is recommended that this

Table 27.4

Province of British Columbia 5.2% bonds 1ˢᵗ July 2020			
Ownership		Location	
Trading book C	+ 4,000,000	+ 1,000,000	Counterparty F
Trading book D	– 1,000,000	– 22,000,000	Custodian X main account
Trading book E	+ 15,000,000		
	+ 18,000,000	**– 21,000,000**	

reconciliation is performed frequently (preferably daily) in order to prove that the system is in balance.

27.4.6 Safe Custody Reconciliation

Where an STO holds its clients' securities positions in safe custody, it is of fundamental importance for the STO to reconcile every aspect of the securities position. A typical safe custody securities position is represented in Figure 27.8, where the sum of the clients' holdings is normally held in either one or two accounts (segregated from the account containing the STO's own positions) at the custodian. (Refer to Chapter 25 for further details.)

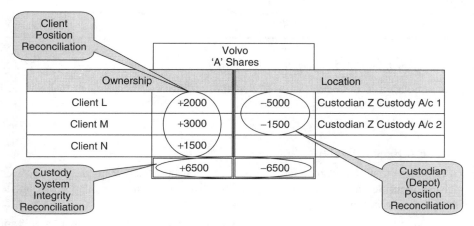

Figure 27.8   Reconciliation overview: safe custody

Client Position Reconciliation

This reconciliation is comparable to the trading position reconciliation, in that the objective is to gain agreement with clients as to their securities holding, regardless of settlement status. However, the client position reconciliation is more difficult to achieve, as the agreement of each client's holdings needs to involve the client checking and agreeing, or alerting the STO if a discrepancy is identified.

The method of communication of securities positions has historically occurred through the STO issuing a periodic statement of holdings to the client, but this is not necessarily conducive to frequent reconciliation and tight controls. If an STO's safe custody clients can access their securities positions via the Internet, for example, agreement of positions or identification of discrepancies will become more efficient.

Custodian (Depot) Position Reconciliation (for Safe Custody Holdings)

This reconciliation is designed to reconcile the STO's safe custody clients' positions held internally versus the (one or more) safe custody accounts at the custodian, and is in parallel with the reconciliation of the STO's own positions described earlier in this chapter.

Such a reconciliation typically shows the results in Table 27.5.

Table 27.5

STO's custody system: Custodian Z safe custody account no. 1		Statement from custodian Z: Safe custody account no. 1	
Security	Position	Security	Position
Volvo 'A' shares	−5000	Volvo 'A' shares	+5000
STO's custody system: Custodian Z safe custody account no. 2		Statement from custodian Z: Safe custody account no. 2	
Security	Position	Security	Position
Volvo 'A' shares	−1500	Volvo 'A' shares	+1500

Custody System Integrity Reconciliation

This reconciliation is intended to prove that the custody system remains in balance, by comparing the total of securities owned by safe custody clients with the total of the location position.

27.4.7 Cash Reconciliations

All of the above-mentioned reconciliations have been described from the perspective of reconciling securities positions and open trades. However, cash must also be reconciled, and the following is a list of such reconciliations.

- *Trade-by-trade reconciliation*: the main purpose of the trade-by-trade reconciliation mentioned above is to ensure that the full population of trades have been received into the settlement system; therefore, this particular reconciliation is not specific to cash. However, where a trading system calculates the NSV of trades, some STOs require a comparison of the settlement system calculated NSV with that of the trading system (where possible), in order to ensure that the correct figure is applied to the trade.
- *Open trades reconciliation*: the status of open trades received from custodians includes (in the case of DvP instructions) the matching of cash values on each instruction, therefore no additional reconciliation of open trades for cash purposes is necessary.
- *Custodian (nostro) position reconciliation*: this reconciliation is specific to cash, and is the cash equivalent of the custodian (depot) position reconciliation; its purpose is to prove that the cash balances (by currency, by nostro account, within custodian)

held within internal books and records agree with the equivalent balances held at each custodian. This is an elementary control to ensure that the cash balances the STO believes should be present at the custodian are in fact present.

- *Settlement system to corporate ledger reconciliation*: where the settlement system feeds information to the STO's corporate ledger (refer to Chapter 28), it is usual to reconcile certain information such as the following, from a cash perspective:
  - ○ open trades with counterparties
  - ○ balances at custodians
  - ○ profit and loss

in order to prove that the same information is held in both systems.

27.4.8   Other Reconciliations

Other reconciliations that are important to conduct on a daily basis are listed below.

Inter-company Reconciliations

Where an STO executes trades with other offices within its group of companies (which can be a substantial number of daily trades for some STOs), it is very important to conduct reconciliation of the details of such trades, and any securities and cash balances an overseas office may hold on the STO's behalf.

It can prove costly to believe that because the counterparty is internal to the STO's group, there is no need to reconcile and that no losses can be incurred.

Inter-account Reconciliations

Some STOs use 'wash' accounts in order to allocate an amount (either securities or cash) into a number of smaller amounts, or vice versa. The wash account is the intermediary account over which the two sets of entries are passed. As there is a possibility that the account does not clear to zero, such accounts should be reconciled daily.

27.5   METHODS OF RECONCILIATION

Each of the reconciliations described above can be categorised into either a:

- non-cumulative reconciliation—the trade-by-trade reconciliation, the open trades reconciliation and the settlement and custody system integrity reconciliation are 'snapshot' type reconciliations, where the reconciliation does not involve an opening and closing balance;
- cumulative reconciliation—the trading position reconciliation, the custodian (depot) position reconciliation and the custodian (nostro) position reconciliation are cumulative type reconciliations, involving opening balances, movements and closing balances.

For cumulative reconciliations, the information required to perform reconciliation is a statement of positions from:

- the STO's settlement system, and
- the external system; for the trading position reconciliation this will be the trading system, and for the custodian depot and nostro position reconciliations this will be the custodian.

Once the statements are available, the following steps are then taken:

1. conduct comparison of statement information
2. identify items that agree
3. identify discrepancies (both internal and external)
4. investigate discrepancies
5. rectify discrepancies.

Two methods of conducting the comparison are typically practiced.

27.5.1   Opening/Movements/Closing Method

This method involves the comparison of:

- today's opening balance,
- today's individual movements, and
- today's closing balance

in each of the accounts being reconciled, and if all agree, the position is fully reconciled.

If any aspect disagrees, there will be a need to go back one level, for instance, if today's opening balances disagree, it will be necessary to first ensure that the previous day's closing balances were reconciled.

If today's opening balances agree, but the movements disagree, there will be a need to analyse, and then rectify the individual entries causing the discrepancy. This method is very comprehensive and is strongly recommended.

27.5.2   Closing Only Method

The alternative approach is to begin the reconciliation by comparing today's closing balances; should the comparison reveal a difference, the discrepancy should be investigated by firstly comparing the previous day's closing balances.

If yesterday's balances agree, the cause of the discrepancy must lie within the movements, in which case a one-by-one comparison of movements must be made until the cause is revealed, following which rectifying entries must be made.

This method is not as thorough as the opening/movements/closing method, as it is possible to agree closing balances where the movements do not agree; this can occur when there are compensating movements of the same value. However, this method is certainly far better than not attempting to reconcile at all!

27.6   FREQUENCY OF RECONCILIATION

Regardless of the scale of trading activity within an STO, each of the above-mentioned reconciliations should ideally be performed on a daily basis.

To perform reconciliation less frequently than daily will mean that the STO cannot prove it is in control of its assets. If the last time an STO reconciled was two days ago, the STO cannot be certain that its books and records are factual as at 'today', if 'yesterday' new trades were executed by the traders, and securities and cash movements were effected at the custodian.

In an extreme case, securities could have been removed from the STO's account in error or by design; the STO surely has a responsibility to itself to trap such errors or attempts at fraud, at the earliest opportunity. Discovering that securities or cash have been fraudulently removed from an STO's account 'today' is a great deal better than realising it, say, four weeks after the event.

With the best of intentions, mistakes can be made within operational areas, which frequent reconciliation can detect at the earliest opportunity. Rectifying action can then be taken without delay, thereby limiting the risk of loss and the knock-on effect of unreconciled trades and positions.

For example, conducting the custodian (depot) position reconciliation on a daily basis can prove very beneficial in detecting errors. STOs typically operate at least two accounts at each of their custodians; usually a main account in which the STO's own securities are held and one or more safe custody accounts within which their clients' securities are held. On a daily basis, an STO may issue settlement instructions to its custodian to transfer securities on a free of payment basis between the STO's accounts. Even with tight controls in place, manually created settlement instructions can contain errors, such as the incorrect recipient account number, resulting in the delivery of securities going astray (particularly when using settlement instructions that do not require matching) and outside of the STO's control.

If (in this case) the custodian (depot) position reconciliation is conducted daily, such errors should be highlighted immediately, and corrective action can be taken without delay. Conversely, failure to identify such a discrepancy in a timely manner may mean that when it is identified, and an investigation conducted, there would be no guarantee of the securities being available for immediate return to the STO.

27.7   EXTERNAL MOVEMENTS AFFECTING POSITIONS

The STO's books and records must take account of all types of securities and cash movements, not just the exchange of securities and cash when buying and selling, repoing, or lending or borrowing securities and cash.

The following must be reflected within internal books and records at the appropriate time in order to have a completely accurate reflection of reality in the outside world, and for the comparison of positions to agree:

- securities added or deducted at custodians, for example
  - maturing bonds deducted
  - rights issues added
  - converted bonds deducted
  - equity (result of conversion) added

- cash paid or received at custodians, for example
  - dividends and coupon payments received
  - bond maturity proceeds received
  - overdraft interest paid or credit interest received
  - custody fees paid.

Should such items not be reflected at the appropriate time, a discrepancy will be caused.

27.8   MANUAL VERSUS AUTOMATED RECONCILIATION

Historically, reconciliations were conducted by STOs on a manual basis; the issues with this approach are that it:

- is prone to human error,
- is time-consuming, and
- typically results in investigation and rectification of discrepancies not being undertaken in good time.

Some STOs overcome these issues by automating the reconciliation process; specialist reconciliation software products have been developed to make comparisons of the detail contained within files of information from two (or more) sources.

An example of where such software can be used is in the trading positions reconciliation, where a file of the positions held within the settlement system would be compared automatically with a file of the positions held within the trading system, with the result that matching items and discrepancies are revealed in a fraction of the time it would take to perform the same reconciliation manually.

A real benefit that the STO can derive from automated reconciliation is the identification of discrepancies within minutes rather than hours (if conducted manually). This allows the investigation of discrepancies to begin within minutes, and rectifying action to occur much earlier than is the case when a manual reconciliation method is employed. Another benefit of automation is the reduction in the impact of increased trading volumes on the reconciliation process.

27.9   INDEPENDENCE OF THE RECONCILIATION FUNCTION

In some STOs, it is considered that sufficient control over assets is exercised providing those who are responsible for operational processing (for instance, the generation of settlement instructions) are not involved with the various reconciliation tasks; this is known as segregation of duties.

An STO that does not practice segregation of duties takes a risk that those conducting reconciliation may, for example, be a party to and may hide discrepancies resulting from unauthorised activity.

27.10   BENEFITS DERIVED FROM RECONCILIATION

The knowledge that the STO's internal records are complete and accurate enables:

- equity and bond traders to execute new trades knowing that their trading positions are complete,
- repo traders to execute new trades based on reconciled information such as trading positions, securities positions at custodians, and outstanding trades with counterparties,
- the securities lending and borrowing desk to lend securities that are truly present at the custodian, and to borrow securities where a shortfall at the custodian is predicted,
- credit risk personnel to view open trades with counterparties, knowing they are looking at factual information,
- operations management to focus on settlement of truly open trades,

- the accounting department to calculate accurate profit and loss, and
- corporate action personnel to calculate entitlement to dividend and coupon payments precisely

through the information held within the settlement system.

27.11 SUMMARY

Without doubt, reconciliation plays a major role in an STO controlling its business and therefore close monitoring of the number and value of discrepancies is vital. However, giving focus to such discrepancies requires good management information.

Despite the growing level of automation within the securities industry, errors will continue to be made, as will attempts to defraud. In view of the size of positions taken by STOs and the monetary value of even an average sized trade conducted within the industry, STOs take a huge risk if they do not give the required level of focus to completion of all essential reconciliations, on a daily basis.

28
Accounting

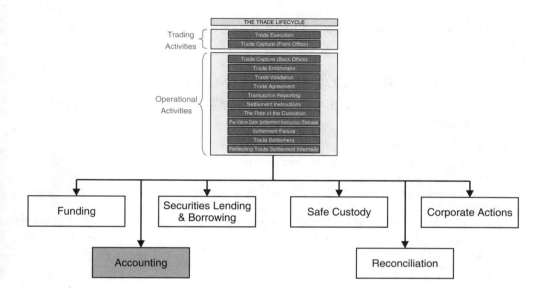

28.1 INTRODUCTION

The need to maintain a record of all monetary transactions is applicable to all companies including STOs, as it is a requirement of the regulatory authorities.

The term accounting is generally synonymous with a structured approach towards the recording of monetary transactions. The following are typical characteristics of the accounting function within an STO:

- the accounting function is usually performed by qualified accountants who reside within the accounting department (also known as finance department or financial control)
- the accounting department is usually responsible for maintaining the ledgers (the books containing accounts) of the company's entire business, including:
  - trading activity
  - employee salaries (payroll)
  - the cost of office furniture
  - premises heating and lighting costs
  - the cost of computer equipment

  and which will be recorded within the company's corporate (or general) ledger
- accounting for trading and settlement is usually processed within a trading ledger, which feeds and forms part of the corporate ledger

- accounting information generated by the STO is used for control (reconciliation and internal audit), management decision making (P&L analysis) and regulatory (stock exchange and company law) reasons.

It is recommended that this chapter is read after having read the prior chapters, as a number of terms are used that have been explained earlier in the book. The subject of accounting is a very large topic in its own right; this chapter will therefore cover only the typical core accounting functions relating to an STO's securities trading, settlement and positions.

28.2   GENERIC ACCOUNTING PRINCIPLES

Certain basic principles and practices are common in the accounting of any organisation's business, including:

- double-entry bookkeeping
  - ○ every entry recorded within a corporate ledger is effected using a minimum of two equal but opposite (debit versus credit) entries—this is known as *double-entry bookkeeping*, and is designed to provide control through offsetting entries
- journal entry
  - ○ a set of balancing debit and credit entries which are used to update the account balances, and which may comprise various combinations of debit and credit entries (Table 28.1)

Table 28.1

Number of entries	
Debit	Credit
One	One
One	Many
Many	Many
Many	One

- balance sheet—a set of accounts which relate to the assets and liabilities of the business
  - ○ asset: something which is owned by or owed to the business (e.g. investments)
  - ○ liability: something that is owed by the business (e.g. long-term borrowing)

  and which is a 'snapshot' of the company's financial position at a particular point in time
- profit & loss (P&L)—the revenue (income) and expense (cost) accounts are referred to as P&L accounts. A collection of particular income and expense headings is known as the P&L report
- accruals—a fundamental accounting concept is that revenue and costs are recognised as they are earned or incurred, not as money is received or paid. For example, interest

on holdings of fixed rate bonds will be accrued for on a daily basis, even though interest is not received until the next coupon payment date
- accounting basis—the method used to prepare a set of accounts. For example, preparing accounts on a trade date accrual accounting basis means that all bookings will occur on the trade date and all accrued income and expense will also be recorded on that date. Conversely, a value date accrual accounting basis means that all bookings and accruals occur on the value date
- revenue recognition—a generally applied principle that all losses are accounted for at the earliest opportunity, whereas revenues are only accounted for when they are reasonably certain. This notion ties in with the prudence principle of accounting which states that caution should be used when recognising profits, but losses should be recognised immediately.

28.3   ACCOUNTING FOR SECURITIES TRADES AND POSITIONS

In order to convey how securities trades and resultant positions are accounted for, the accounting implications of a principal trade from its trade date through to settlement and beyond will be explored.

Firstly, each of the components of a trade will be viewed from an accounting perspective, the components being:

- trading book
- trade date
- trade time
- value date
- operation
- quantity
- security
- price
- counterparty
- principal
- accrued days
- accrued interest
- net settlement value (NSV)

of which, some may have accounting implications, while others may not.

Trading Book

A trading book represents the holdings of investment assets by the STO and therefore only holds the value of the 'asset'. An entry (also known as 'posting') to the trading book indicates ownership and risk on the part of the STO from which future benefit to the business will hopefully be derived. Each time a principal trade (whether a buy or a sell) is executed, the cost or proceeds are recorded by way of accounting entries against the trading book that performed the trade, on the trade date.

The cash amounts recorded to the trading book usually do not include accrued interest (in the case of a bond) or amounts such as stamp duty (in the case of an equity), as these amounts are accounted for separately.

- accrued interest does not form part of the posting to the trading book as, in an accounting sense, it is not considered to be part of the value of the trading assets, but is a payment for unearned income;
- stamp duty does not form part of the posting to the trading book as the relevant amount is usually not a cost to the STO, but is collected by the STO on behalf of the tax authorities.

Therefore, in both cases, these are accounted for separately.

Trade Date

This date is the date that an STO executes a trade with a counterparty, and it is on this date that accounting entries are usually passed.

Trade Time

The time at which the trade was executed; this has no impact on accounting.

Value Date

The date that cash is expected to be paid to or received from the counterparty, in exchange for securities; accounting entries are typically recorded on value date.

Operation

Indicates whether securities have been bought or sold. This determines how accounting entries are recorded (for example, a purchase will be debited to a trading book, whereas a sale would be credited to the trading book).

Quantity

The quantity of securities purchased or sold is a component in determining cash values.

Security

The specific security being purchased or sold. Accounting entries will be passed against this security within the trading book.

Price

The price at which a security is bought or sold is used to determine the cost of purchases and the proceeds of sales.

Counterparty

The specific counterparty the STO has purchased securities from or sold securities to. Accounting entries will be passed against this counterparty.

Principal

The principal is the gross cash value of a trade and, in the case of a bond, excludes accrued interest.

Accrued Days

The number of accrued days on a trade determines the cash value of accrued interest payable (on a purchase) or receivable (on a sale).

Accrued Interest

The value of accrued interest is paid to the seller when the STO buys, and is received from the buyer when the STO sells.

Net Settlement Value

The NSV represents the full cash amount due to be paid to the counterparty when the STO purchases securities, or the full cash amount receivable from the counterparty on a sale.

28.4   ACCOUNTING ENTRY LIFECYCLE (1)

In order to convey typical accounting entries passed by an STO as a result of executing trades, a purchase will be explored, followed by a partial sale of the same security.

Although the example used is a bond, the accounting entries depicted could be used for other security types, such as equity (excluding the accrued interest component). The details of the trade are given in Table 28.2.

It should be assumed that this is the first trade the STO has executed in this particular security, within the individual trading book. Settlement occurs on value date 7th February against the full NSV at the STO's custodian T.

Table 28.2

Basic trade details	
Trading book	Book A
Trade date	4th February
Trade time	09:16
Value date	7th February
Operation	Buy
Quantity	USD 25,000,000.00
Security	XOX AG 8.25% 1st June 2020
Price	99.125%
Counterparty	Counterparty M

Cash values		
Principal		USD 24,781,250.00
Accrued days	246	
Accrued interest		USD 1,409,375.00
NSV		USD 26,190,625.00

28.4.1 On Trade Date

On trade date (4th February), three entries are passed (Table 28.3):

- the principal of the purchase is recorded as a debit to the trading book account as the STO becomes the owner of the securities on trade date;
- the value of accrued interest is recorded as a debit to the accrued interest receivable account, to represent the interest element within the NSV that is owing on that security. The accrued interest amount is recorded in a separate account to track the interest accrual independently, by segregating it from the principal element of the asset;
- the NSV of the trade is recorded as a credit against the counterparty account, to reflect the fact that the STO owes the cash to the counterparty (to be paid on value date), inclusive of accrued interest

Table 28.3

Entries passed on trade date (4th February)			
Debit		Credit	
Trading book A	USD 24,781,250.00	USD 26,190,625.00	Counterparty M
Accrued interest receivable	USD 1,409,375.00		
	USD 26,190,625.00	**USD 26,190,625.00**	

28.4.2 Evening of Trade Date

On the evening of trade date (4th February), the following action is effected against the trading position created by the purchase of securities on the same day (Table 28.4).

Marking to Market and Unrealised P&L

When an STO has a positive or negative trading position, it is standard practice to revalue the position to the current market price (commonly known as *marking-to-market*), regardless of whether settlement has occurred or not. Conceptually, the purpose of marking to market is to compare the current value of a trading position against the original (or previous day's) value, in order to determine whether a theoretical profit or loss would be made if the securities were sold (in the case of a positive position), or purchased (in the case of a negative position) immediately. The topic of marking to market is explored in more detail later in this chapter.

Table 28.4

Entries passed on evening of trade date (4th February)			
Debit		Credit	
Trading book A	USD 31,250.00	USD 31,250.00	Unrealised profit/loss
	USD 31,250.00	**USD 31,250.00**	

At the close of business on this day, the market price was 99.25%, an increase of 0.125% compared with the purchase price; when the increase is multiplied by the quantity of bonds (USD 25 million), a theoretical profit of USD 31,250.00 is made. As the profit is theoretical (the bonds have not actually been sold, only revalued) this is known as *unrealised profit*; had the price fallen, an *unrealised loss* would be made. The topic of unrealised P&L is covered in more detail later in this chapter.

Only when a positive trading position is sold in full or in part (or a negative trading position is purchased in full or in part) can a *realised profit or loss* be made; realised P&L is described later in this chapter.

28.4.3   Evening of Trade Date+1

On the evening of trade date+1 (5th February), the action below is again effected against the trading position created by the purchase of securities on the previous day (Table 28.5).

Marking to Market and Unrealised P&L

The market price of the bond as at close of business on this day was 99.10%, a fall of 0.15% on yesterday's closing price; the cash value of 0.15% on USD 25 million bonds is USD 37,500.00. Accounting entries are passed in order to reflect the difference in market value between yesterday's and today's closing prices. The trading book will be credited to reflect the reduction in value, and the unrealised P&L account will be debited to reflect the loss.

Table 28.5

Entries passed on evening of trade date+1 (5th February)			
Debit		Credit	
Unrealised profit/loss	USD 37,500.00	USD 37,500.00	Trading book A
	USD 37,500.00	**USD 37,500.00**	

28.4.4   Evening of Trade Date+2

On the evening of trade date+2 (6th February), the following action is again effected against the trading position created by the purchase of securities two days previously (Table 28.6).

Table 28.6

Entries passed on evening of trade date+2 (6th February)			
Debit		Credit	
Unrealised profit/loss	USD 50,000.00	USD 50,000.00	Trading book A
	USD 50,000.00	**USD 50,000.00**	

Marking to Market and Unrealised P&L

The closing price on this day was 98.90%, a fall of 0.20% on the previous day's closing price. Accounting entries to the value of USD 50,000.00 (0.20% on USD 25 million bonds) are passed in order to reflect the difference in market value between yesterday's and today's closing prices. The trading book will be credited to reflect the reduction in value, and the unrealised P&L account will be debited to reflect the loss.

28.4.5 On Value Date

On value date (7th February), the trade settles and the custodian advises the STO that the full NSV has been paid to the counterparty. The payment of cash from the STO's account is reflected on the custodian's statement of account which is sent to the STO.

As a result of receiving the notification of settlement from the custodian, the STO reflects settlement of the trade by passing accounting entries to update its records. The custodian account is credited whilst the counterparty account is debited (Table 28.7).

Table 28.7

Entries passed on value date (and settlement date) (7th February)			
Debit		Credit	
Counterparty M	USD 26,190,625.00	USD 26,190,625.00	Custodian T USD account
	USD 26,190,625.00	**USD 26,190,625.00**	

The results of these entries are that the STO's records show:
- no outstanding cash is owed to counterparty M for this particular trade, and
- the STO has an overdraft at custodian T.

28.4.6 Evening of Value Date

On the evening of value date (7th February), the action below is again effected against the trading position created by the purchase of securities on 4th February (Table 28.8).

Table 28.8

Entries passed on evening of value date (7th February)			
Debit		Credit	
Trading book A	USD 100,000.00	USD 100,000.00	Unrealised profit/loss
	USD 100,000.00	**USD 100,000.00**	

Marking to Market and Unrealised P&L

The closing price on this day increased by 0.40% to 99.30% (from the previous day's closing price). Accounting entries to the value of USD 100,000.00 are passed in order to reflect the difference in market value. The trading book will be debited to reflect the increased value, and the unrealised P&L account will be credited to reflect the profit.

Accruing for Accrued Interest

Where the STO has a positive trading position, each day that passes without the bond being sold will result in the receipt of accrued interest income for that day, at a future point in time. The income will be received by the STO either through the issuer's payment of the next coupon, or (should the STO sell the bond) the buyer paying the accrued income as part of his purchase cost. Where the STO has a negative trading position, each day that passes without the STO buying will result in the eventual payment of accrued interest income.

At the time of holding a bond, the rate of interest (also known as the *coupon rate*) due to the owner is predictable; this applies to both fixed rate bonds and *FRNs*. Therefore, providing the STO does not sell, the STO will be entitled to the coupon on a day-to-day basis. Normal practice for STOs is to accrue for this future income (or payment in the case of a negative trading position) on a day-to-day basis by passing accounting entries to an accrued interest account. In the case of a positive trading position, the accrued interest will be shown as receivable (i.e. due to be received at a future point in time) versus coupon interest income, and in the case of a negative trading position, will be shown as payable versus coupon interest expense. This is reflected in Figure 28.1, which shows the period from the purchase value date to the coupon payment date as part of the overall coupon period (in this case a 12-month period). Figure 28.2 represents the days from the purchase value date to the coupon payment date in more detail. The number of days of accrued interest increases day-by-day, beginning with the close of business on the value date; for each day the bond is held, accounting entries will be passed to reflect the additional income due (represented by the shaded area at the top of each column).

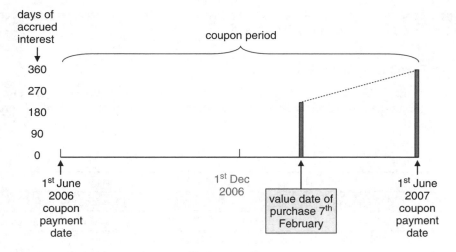

Figure 28.1   Accounting: accruing for accrued interest

In the particular case of the STO's purchase, one day's accrued interest on USD 25 million of the bond paying 8.25% coupon amounts to USD 5729.17 (using the 30/360 accrued interest calculation convention).

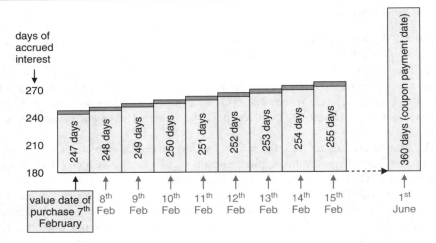

Figure 28.2   Accounting: accrued interest

Table 28.9

Entries passed on evening of value date (7th February)			
Debit		Credit	
Accrued interest receivable	USD 5,729.17	USD 5,729.17	Coupon interest income
	USD 5,729.17	**USD 5,729.17**	

The credit entry in Table 28.9 reflects the fact that the STO can recognise the accrued interest earned to date, as profit.

28.4.7   Evening of Value Date+1

On the evening of value date+1 (8th February), the following action is again effected against the trading position created by the purchase of securities on 4th February (Table 28.10).

Table 28.10

Entries passed on evening of value date+1 (8th February)			
Debit		Credit	
Accrued interest receivable	USD 5,729.17	USD 5,729.17	Coupon interest income
	USD 5,729.17	**USD 5,729.17**	

Marking to Market and Unrealised P&L

The market price remains at 99.30%, requiring no entries to be passed this day as no further unrealised profit or loss has been made.

Accruing for Accrued Interest

As the bond has not been sold, a further day of accrued interest is earned and accounted for (Table 28.10). *The trade example continues after the following summary section.*

28.4.8 Summary of Entries

All the entries passed between 4th and 8th February over the various accounts are listed below:

Trading Book A's USD Account (Table 28.11)

The accounting entries result in an overall balance of debit USD 24,825,000.00. This figure should equate to the current value of the bonds, without accrued interest; therefore, USD 25 million bonds at the latest market price of 99.30% amounts to USD 24,825,000.00. This shows that the accounting entries represent the purchase cost plus revaluation (based on market price) on a daily basis.

Table 28.11

Trading book A—USD account				
Entry date	Narrative	Debit	Credit	Balance
	Balance brought forward from 3rd February			*0*
4th February	Principal value of purchase of 25m	24,781,250.00		24,781,250.00dr
4th February	Unrealised profit on 25m	31,250.00		24,812,500.00dr
5th February	Unrealised loss on 25m		37,500.00	24,775,000.00dr
6th February	Unrealised loss on 25m		50,000.00	24,725,000.00dr
7th February	Unrealised profit on 25m	100,000.00		24,825,000.00dr

Unrealised P&L USD Account (Table 28.12)

The unrealised P&L account reveals that as at 7th February, an unrealised profit is being made. This can be verified by multiplying USD 25 million bonds by the difference between

Table 28.12

Unrealised P&L—USD account				
Entry date	Narrative	Debit	Credit	Balance
	Balance brought forward from 3rd February			*0*
4th February	Unrealised profit on 25m		31,250.00	31,250.00cr
5th February	Unrealised loss on 25m	37,500.00		6,250.00dr
6th February	Unrealised loss on 25m	50,000.00		56,250.00dr
7th February	Unrealised profit on 25m		100,000.00	43,750.00cr

the purchase price and the current (market) price (purchase price 99.125%, less price at close of business 7th February of 99.30%). The price differential is an increase of 0.175%, and when multiplied by the quantity of bonds equates to a profit (unrealised) of USD 43,750.00.

Counterparty M's USD Account (Table 28.13)

Following full settlement of the trade on 7th February, counterparty M's account reveals a zero cash balance, therefore showing that no outstanding cash is due to counterparty M. Had partial settlement occurred, or if the trade had settled with a small cash difference (without automated write-off; refer to Chapter 20), the remaining cash balance would appear on this account until further entries were passed.

Table 28.13

Counterparty M—USD account				
Entry date	Narrative	Debit	Credit	Balance
	Balance brought forward from 3rd February			*0*
4th February	Cost of purchase of 25m		26,190,625.00	26,190,625.00cr
7th February	Settlement of purchase of 25m	26,190,625.00		*0*

Custodian T's USD Account (Table 28.14)

The cash paid to the counterparty by the custodian has incurred an overdraft at the custodian; the credit balance shows that the amount is owed to the custodian. In other words, viewing this credit balance in the STO's accounting records must be interpreted to mean that the account is overdrawn at the custodian.

Table 28.14

Custodian T—USD account				
Entry date	Narrative	Debit	Credit	Balance
	Balance brought forward from 3rd February			*0*
7th February	Settlement of purchase of 25m		26,190,625.00	26,190,625.00cr

Accrued Interest Receivable USD Account (Table 28.15)

This account reflects the fact that the STO 'purchased' accrued interest from counterparty M on trade date 4th February, for value date 7th February.

On 7th February, the accrual of one day's accrued interest earned on USD 25 million bonds is reflected.

Table 28.15

Accrued interest receivable—USD account				
Entry date	Narrative	Debit	Credit	Balance
	Balance brought forward from 3rd February			0
4th February	Purchase of 25m (+246 days)	1,409,375.00		1,409,375.00dr
7th February	Accrued interest for 1 day on 25m	5,729.17		1,415,104.17dr
8th February	Accrued interest for 1 day on 25m	5,729.17		1,420,833.34dr

The balance on this account allows the STO to identify the total amount of accrued interest due from the issuer.

Coupon Interest Income USD Account (Table 28.16)

The balance on this account allows the STO to identify the total accrued interest recognised as revenue. The amount recognised as revenue is the difference between the accrued interest purchased on trade date and the accrued interest receivable to date.

Table 28.16

Coupon interest income—USD account				
Entry date	Narrative	Debit	Credit	Balance
	Balance brought forward from 6th February			0
7th February	Accrued interest for 1 day on 25m		5,729.17	5,729.17cr
8th February	Accrued interest for 1 day on 25m		5,729.17	11,458.34cr

28.5 ACCOUNTING ENTRY LIFECYCLE (2)

Continuing with the accounting entry lifecycle, the STO sells part of its holding of USD 25 million bonds. The details of this trade are given in Table 28.17. This is the second trade the STO has executed in this particular security and trading book. Settlement occurs on value date 12th February against the full NSV, at the same custodian as settled the purchase (custodian T).

28.5.1 On Trade Date

The trade date (9th February) accounting entries will be similar to those for the earlier purchase, however, the following should be noted (Table 28.18):

- the trading book is credited with the quantity of bonds multiplied by price (USD 4,960,000.00), the accrued interest account is credited with the value of accrued interest receivable, and the counterparty account is debited for the full NSV;

Table 28.17

Basic trade details	
Trading book	Book A
Trade date	9th February
Trade time	11:58
Value date	12th February
Operation	Sell
Quantity	USD 5,000,000.00
Security	XOX AG 8.25% 1st June 2020
Price	99.20%
Counterparty	Counterparty D

Cash values		
Principal		USD 4,960,000.00
Accrued days	251	
Accrued interest		USD 287,604.17
NSV		USD 5,247,604.17

- the number of days of accrued interest has increased since the purchase;
- the calculation of realised P&L can now be performed on the quantity sold (see below);
- the calculation of unrealised P&L will continue to be performed each evening, but on the post-sale trading position of USD 20 million bonds;
- upon settlement of the trade, counterparty D will be credited (leaving zero cash balance outstanding) and custodian T will be debited.

Table 28.18

Entries passed on trade date (9th February)			
Debit		Credit	
Counterparty D	USD 5,247,604.17	USD 4,960,000.00	Trading book A
		USD 287,604.17	Accrued interest receivable
	USD 5,247,604.17	**USD 5,247,604.17**	

Figure 28.3 provides an overview of the P&L calculation stages for the above-mentioned trades and positions.

Realised P&L

As USD 5 million bonds have been sold, realised P&L can be calculated. However, realised P&L can only be calculated on the quantity of bonds sold, as the purchase and sale prices for USD 5 million bonds are now known. Calculation of unrealised P&L will need to continue for the remaining positive trading position of USD 20 million bonds (until all or part are sold). The USD 5 million bonds were purchased at a price of 99.125% and sold at 99.20%, a difference of 0.075%; when multiplied by the quantity of bonds, a profit of USD 3750.00 is revealed.

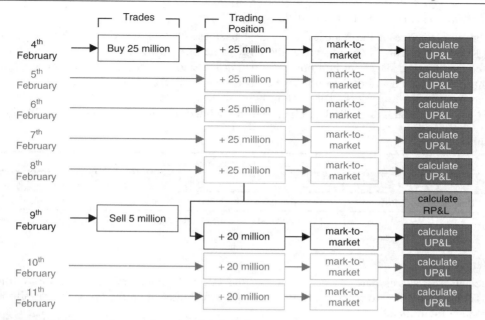

Figure 28.3   Accounting: profit and loss calculation stages

The entry in Table 28.19 is passed in order to reverse the unrealised profit to date (on the 5 million bonds sold), as the unrealised profit has been superceded by the realised profit. The unrealised profit amount is the difference between the purchase price (99.125%) and the last market price applied to the position (99.30% applied on the evening of 8th February); the difference of 0.175% on USD 5 million bonds is USD 8750.00.

The entry in Table 28.20 reflects the realised profit:

Table 28.19

Entries passed on trade date (9th February)			
Debit		Credit	
Unrealised profit/loss	USD 8,750.00	USD 8,750.00	Trading book A
	USD 8,750.00	**USD 8,750.00**	

Table 28.20

Entries passed on trade date (9th February)			
Debit		Credit	
Trading book A	USD 3,750.00	USD 3,750.00	Realised profit/loss
	USD 3,750.00	**USD 3,750.00**	

Marking to Market and Unrealised P&L

The market price of the bond as at close of business on this day was 99.15%, a fall of 0.15% on yesterday's closing price; the cash value of 0.15% on USD 20 million bonds (reduced from USD 25 million bonds following the sale) is USD 30,000.00. Accounting entries are passed in order to reflect the difference in market value between yesterday's and today's closing prices. The trading book will be credited to reflect the reduction in value, and the unrealised P&L account will be debited to reflect the loss (Table 28.21).

Table 28.21

Entries passed on evening of 9th February			
Debit		Credit	
Unrealised profit/loss	USD 30,000.00	USD 30,000.00	Trading book A
	USD 30,000.00	**USD 30,000.00**	

Accruing for Accrued Interest

Because, as at this date, the value date of the sale (12th February) is in the future, the STO is still entitled to receive a further day of accrued interest on the full USD 25 million bonds (Table 28.22).

Table 28.22

Entries passed on evening of 9th February			
Debit		Credit	
Accrued interest receivable	USD 5,729.17	USD 5,729.17	Coupon interest income
	USD 5,729.17	**USD 5,729.17**	

28.5.2   Summary of Entries

All the entries passed between 4th and 9th February over the various accounts are listed in Table 28.23. Note that entries summarised previously are in grey text.

Trading Book A's USD Account (Table 28.23)

The accounting entries result in an overall balance of debit USD 19,830,000.00. This figure should equate to the current value of the remaining bonds, without accrued interest; therefore, USD 20 million bonds at the latest market price of 99.15% amounts to USD 19,830,000.00. This shows that the accounting entries represent the purchase cost plus revaluation (based on market price) on a daily basis.

Realised P&L USD Account (Table 28.24)

The realised P&L account shows that as at 9th February, a realised profit has been made, resulting from the sale of USD 5 million bonds on 9th February.

Unrealised P&L USD Account (Table 28.25)

The unrealised P&L account reveals that as at 9th February, an unrealised profit is being made; this can be verified by multiplying USD 20 million bonds by the difference between

Table 28.23

	Trading book A—USD account			
Entry date	Narrative	Debit	Credit	Balance
	Balance brought forward from 3rd February			*0*
4th February	Principal value of purchase of 25m	24,781,250.00		24,781,250.00dr
4th February	Unrealised profit on 25m	31,250.00		24,812,500.00dr
5th February	Unrealised loss on 25m		37,500.00	24,775,000.00dr
6th February	Unrealised loss on 25m		50,000.00	24,725,000.00dr
7th February	Unrealised profit on 25m	100,000.00		24,825,000.00dr
9th February	Principal value of sale of 5m		4,960,000.00	19,865,000.00dr
9th February	Reverse unrealised profit on 5m		8,750.00	19,856,250.00dr
9th February	Realised profit on 5m	3,750.00		19,860,000.00dr
9th February	Unrealised loss on 20m		30,000.00	19,830,000.00dr

Table 28.24

	Realised P&L—USD account			
Entry date	Narrative	Debit	Credit	Balance
	Balance brought forward from 8th February			*0*
9th February	Realised profit on 5m		3,750.00	3,750.00cr

Table 28.25

	Unrealised P&L—USD account			
Entry date	Narrative	Debit	Credit	Balance
	Balance brought forward from 3rd February			*0*
4th February	Unrealised profit on 25m		31,250.00	31,250.00cr
5th February	Unrealised loss on 25m	37,500.00		6,250.00dr
6th February	Unrealised loss on 25m	50,000.00		56,250.00dr
7th February	Unrealised profit on 25m		100,000.00	43,750.00cr
9th February	Reverse unrealised profit on 5m	8,750.00		35,000.00cr
9th February	Unrealised loss on 20m	30,000.00		5,000.00cr

the purchase price and the current (market) price (purchase price 99.125%, less price at close of business 9th February of 99.15%). The price differential is an increase of 0.025%, and when multiplied by the quantity of bonds equates to a profit (unrealised) of USD 5000.00.

Counterparty D's USD Account (Table 28.26)

Counterparty D's account shows that counterparty D owes cash to the STO, as the value date of the sale is in the future (12th February).

Table 28.26

Counterparty D—USD account				
Entry date	Narrative	Debit	Credit	Balance
	Balance brought forward from 8th February			0
9th February	Proceeds of sale of 5m	5,247,604.17		5,247,604.17dr

Custodian T's USD Account (Table 28.27)

The balance since settlement of the purchase has not changed, as the value date of the sale is in the future (12th February).

Table 28.27

Custodian T—USD account				
Entry date	Narrative	Debit	Credit	Balance
	Balance brought forward from 3rd February			0
7th February	Settlement of purchase of 25m		26,190,625.00	26,190,625.00cr

Accrued Interest Receivable USD Account (Table 28.28)

This balance reflects the total amount of accrued interest for which the STO will be compensated at a future date.

Coupon Interest Income USD Account (Table 28.29)

The balance on this account allows the STO to identify the total accrued interest recognised as revenue, to date.

28.6 MARKING TO MARKET

As mentioned previously within this chapter, the purpose of marking to market is to determine unrealised P&L by comparing the current market value of a trading position against:

Table 28.28

Accrued interest receivable—USD account				
Entry date	Narrative	Debit	Credit	Balance
	Balance brought forward from 3rd February			*0*
4th February	Purchase of 25m (+ 246 days)	1,409,375.00		1,409,375.00dr
7th February	Accrued interest for 1 day on 25m	5,729.17		1,415,104.17dr
8th February	Accrued interest for 1 day on 25m	5,729.17		1,420,833.34dr
9th February	Sale of 5m (+ 251 days)		287,604.17	1,133,229.17dr
9th February	Accrued interest for 1 day on 25m	5,729.17		1,138,958.34dr

Table 28.29

Coupon interest income—USD account				
Entry date	Narrative	Debit	Credit	Balance
	Balance brought forward from 6th February			*0*
7th February	Accrued interest for 1 day on 25m		5,729.17	5,729.17cr
8th February	Accrued interest for 1 day on 25m		5,729.17	11,458.34cr
9th February	Accrued interest for 1 day on 25m		5,729.17	17,187.51cr

- (in the case of a positive trading position) the cost price of the purchased security, or against the previous day's value of the security, in order to determine whether a theoretical profit or loss would be made if the securities were sold now;
- (in the case of a negative trading position) the sale price of the sold security, or against the previous day's value of the security, in order to determine whether a theoretical profit or loss would be made if the securities were purchased now.

Two main steps are involved in marking to market on a daily basis, namely:

- the gathering of market prices, and
- the updating of books and records.

28.6.1   Gathering Market Prices

The market price should be gathered from an independent source, in order for the STO to revalue its positions on a conservative and cautious basis, so as not to overstate potential profit, or to understate potential losses.

The current market price of securities can be received automatically from *securities data providers*, should the STO choose to subscribe to such a service. Alternatively, security prices can be found through the publication of prices (on computer screens) by market makers, to which the STO may subscribe.

The STO will need to decide whether to mark to market using the bid and offer prices (refer to the section entitled 'Market Makers' in Chapter 2), or the mid-price which is the average of the bid and offer prices.

If the STO decides to use bid and offer prices:

• when in a positive trading position, the STO should apply the *bid price* in the market. This price enables calculation of the potential P&L if the securities were sold at that point in time;
• when in a negative trading position, the STO should apply the *offer price* in the market. This price enables calculation of the potential P&L if the securities were purchased at that point in time.

28.6.2   Updating Books and Records

By whatever mechanism current market prices are gathered, those securities that have trading positions (whether positive or negative) will need to be updated within the STO's books and records, in order to calculate unrealised P&L.

Where a feed of prices is taken from a securities data provider, the relevant position is typically updated automatically; where prices are not received automatically, the position is typically updated manually.

28.7   P&L CALCULATION CONVENTIONS

In order to calculate P&L, both realised and unrealised, it is necessary to know the price at which a positive trading position was acquired and the price of any subsequent sales of that position.

In a situation where a positive trading position is the result of a single purchase against one or many sales (as in the example trades used earlier in this chapter), there is no choice as to the purchase price of the trading position. The trading position of USD 25 million bonds was acquired through a single purchase at 99.125%, on 4th February, and the price of the single sale of USD 5 million bonds was 99.20%. This resulted in a realised profit of USD 3750.00 (USD 5 million bonds at a profit of 0.075%).

This particular calculation of realised profit is uncomplicated, as there is a single purchase to be compared with the sale. In a situation where the STO has multiple purchases of differing quantities of the same security, at different prices, such as in Table 28.30, there is a choice as to what the STO considers its purchase cost price to be. For example, as stated in the table, the STO has a positive trading position of 18,500 shares, acquired from numerous purchases at different prices. If, on 12th October, the STO sells 2500 shares at a price of HKD 5.30 per share, in order for the STO to calculate realised P&L, it must first decide the cost price of its purchase.

Table 28.30

Purchase date	Quantity	Price (HKD)
6th August	3000	5.275
20th August	1000	5.250
15th September	8500	5.310
17th September	750	5.295
2nd October	5250	5.305
Total 18,500		**Average price 5.299 054**

In order to calculate the purchase cost price, STOs typically use one of the following conventions:

- weighted average cost (WAC),
- first-in, first-out (FIFO), and
- last-in, first-out (LIFO)

which, according to the convention used, reveals a different profit or loss amount, as shown in Table 28.31. Whichever method is chosen, it is important to remain consistent and not switch between methods, otherwise meaningless P&L figures will be produced.

Table 28.31

Quantity of shares	Convention	Cost price (HKD)	Cost value (HKD)	Sale proceeds (HKD)	Profit (HKD)
2500	WAC	5.299054	13,247.64	13,250.00	Profit 2.36
2500	FIFO	5.275	13,187.50	13,250.00	Profit 62.50
2500	LIFO	5.305	13,262.50	13,250.00	Loss 12.50

28.7.1 Weighted Average Cost

Using WAC, the same cost price would be used consistently to calculate P&L for all sales (providing there were no further purchases at prices that caused the average price to change).

28.7.2 First-In, First-Out

Using FIFO, sales are compared with purchase cost in the chronological sequence in which the security was purchased. Consequently, as all 2500 shares sold were a lesser quantity than the first purchase (3000 shares), the cost price would be the purchase price of the 3000 shares, namely HKD 5.275.

However, had the sale been of 5000 shares (instead of 2500 shares), under the FIFO method the following would have been used to calculate cost price:

- all 3000 shares at HKD 5.275 per share purchased 6th August,
- all 1000 shares at HKD 5.250 per share purchased 20th August, and
- 1000 (out of 8500) shares at HKD 5.310 per share purchased 15th September.

28.7.3   Last-In, First-Out

LIFO is the reverse of FIFO, where sales are compared with purchase cost in the reverse chronological sequence in which the security was purchased. Therefore under LIFO, as all 2500 shares sold were a lesser quantity than the last purchase (5250 shares), the cost price would be the purchase price of the 5250 shares, namely HKD 5.305 per share.

Had the sale been of 15,000 shares (instead of 2500 shares), under the LIFO method the following would have been used to calculate cost price:

- all 5250 shares at HKD 5.305 per share purchased 2nd October,
- all 750 shares at HKD 5.295 per share purchased 17th September,
- all 8500 shares at HKD 5.310 per share purchased 15th September, and
- 500 (out of 1000 shares) at HKD 5.250 per share purchased 20th August.

28.8   REALISED P&L

Realised profit or loss is actual P&L that arises as a result of:

- a sale of securities from a positive (long) trading position, where the securities were sold at a price other than that at which the securities were purchased, and
- a purchase of securities into a negative (short) trading position, where the securities were purchased at a price other than that at which they were sold.

28.8.1   Selling from a Positive Trading Position

In the example trades and trading positions earlier in this chapter, following the purchase on 4th February, the STO had a positive trading position of USD 25 million bonds; the price paid for these bonds was 99.125%. The STO sold the 5 million bonds on 9th February at a price of 99.20%.

Following the sale, it is possible to calculate profit or loss as both the purchase and sale prices are known; however, P&L can be calculated only on the quantity of securities sold. It is not possible to calculate realised P&L on the unsold trading position, until sold. Furthermore, the purchase cost must take account of the P&L calculation convention used by the STO, whether WAC, FIFO or LIFO.

Realised P&L is calculated as follows:

$$\text{Quantity of securities sold} \times (\text{Sale Price} - \text{Purchase price})$$

and in the above example the figures are:

$$5,000,000 \times (99.20\% - 99.125\% = 0.075\%) = \text{USD } 3750.00 \text{ profit}$$

28.8.2   Buying from a Negative Trading Position

Where an STO has a negative trading position, only when securities are purchased can realised P&L be calculated, as prior to that point in time, any P&L calculation could only be unrealised P&L.

Furthermore, the sale price must take account of the P&L calculation convention used by the STO, whether WAC, FIFO or LIFO.

28.9   UNREALISED P&L

Unrealised profit or loss is theoretical (also known as 'paper') P&L that arises as a result of:

- holding a positive trading position, where the securities have been revalued in order to determine whether a profit or loss would be made if the securities were sold;
- holding a negative trading position, where the securities have been revalued in order to determine whether a profit or loss would be made if the securities were purchased.

The calculation of unrealised P&L must take account of the P&L calculation convention used by the STO, whether WAC, FIFO or LIFO.

Unrealised P&L is usually calculated at the close of business every evening.

Note that STOs have a choice as to how to perform unrealised P&L postings, both to calculate and effect postings:

- on an incremental basis, where the profit or loss for 'today' is calculated in relation to the previous day's closing market value (this is the method employed in the example trades quoted earlier in this chapter), or
- on a reverse and re-post basis, where the previous day's unrealised P&L postings are reversed and replaced by a full mark to market on the original book value of the position.

28.10   AUTOMATION OF ACCOUNTING ENTRIES

Certain aspects of accounting, such as:

- accounts postings on trade date, value date and settlement date (according to defined posting rules for each transaction type), and
- the calculation of realised and unrealised P&L

can typically be automated within settlement systems.

28.11   SUMMARY

The STO must account for all events that have a monetary impact, and ensure that all entries passed are effected using the balancing double-entry bookkeeping method.

29

Objectives and Initiatives

The prior chapters in this book are intended to set the scene for the fundamental oper-ational aspects of the industry. The intention of this chapter is for the reader to be made aware of the objectives and initiatives currently shaping the industry's operational characteristics.

The topics within this chapter are approached with the focus on two main areas of operational activity, namely:

• trade processing and
• corporate actions.

Whilst the objectives and initiatives of both have common elements, the lifecycles of each and the application of initiatives to each will have differing impacts and emphasis.

29.1 TRADE PROCESSING RELATED OBJECTIVES

29.1.1 Introduction

At the start of the 21st century, in an operational sense, the securities industry recognises the need for continued evolution, in order to address the objectives of:

• minimising risk,
• minimising operational cost,
• servicing clients,
• managing increasing trading volumes, and
• maximising internal efficiency.

Minimising Risk

Different types of risk exist as a result of trading and holding securities positions; not all of these risks are settlement or operations related. Examples of non-settlement risks are market risk (the risk that the value of a security falls due to market forces) and issuer risk (the risk that the issuer goes into liquidation and the securities become worthless, or freezes obligations, for example).

Another type of risk is *counterparty risk*, the risk that the counterparty to one or many transactions will fail to fulfil its contractual obligation (to settle the open trade(s)). Counterparty risk begins the moment a trade is executed and ends with full settlement of the trade. If an STO executes, for example, 5000 trades per day on a T+3 settlement cycle, approximately 15,000 trades would fall into this category of risk (plus any settlement failures from prior value dates).

Therefore, the greater the number of open trades at any one time, the greater the scale of risk of counterparties defaulting on their obligations. In order to mitigate this risk, those within the securities industry who buy and sell securities are searching for ways to reduce the numbers of trades that are open at any one point in time, especially with the same counterparty.

Minimising Operational Cost

As competition between those who provide services to investors (specifically STOs and agents for investors) becomes greater, the profit margins made by such organisations are likely to become tighter. If the trading area makes increasingly lower profit per trade, the pressure on the operational areas will grow to keep costs to an absolute minimum. Consequently, costs will need to be contained within such organisations, in the communication links to and from the outside world, and in the operational methods employed by those who provide services to STOs and agents for investors (primarily custodians).

Servicing Clients

In the years to come, institutional and individual investors are very likely to demand the highest level of service from STOs and those organisations that act as agents for investors, in terms of, for example:

- access to global securities markets, as investors identify opportunities to invest in new and *emerging markets* around the globe;
- the timeliness of response to the placement of orders to buy or sell securities;
- the accuracy of trade execution details transmitted to the investor (for example, the calculation of the net settlement value of trades);
- the media by which such information is conveyed (for example, the transmission of trade confirmations via the Internet).

The impact of reduced settlement cycles (such as T+1 and T+0) will affect all those who buy and sell securities, including institutional investors. As with all market participants, these organisations will be subject to the new deadlines for, as an example, the issuance of settlement instructions to their custodians, and they will therefore demand the highest level of accuracy and urgency from those who execute *orders* on their behalf.

Managing Increasing Trading Volumes

Studies of future trading volume in global securities markets have resulted in predictions of continued growth on a global basis.

Due to the trend towards financial planning for retirement falling to the individual rather than to employers or governments, allied with the ageing of the world's population, it is predicted that investment in securities by individuals will increase. This is likely to reveal itself through the direct trading by individuals in specific securities through the likes of retail brokers and stockbrokers, and in the investment in (for example) mutual funds by individuals that will lead to trading by the mutual fund via brokers and STOs.

Additionally, the advent of the Internet has made the process of investing in securities by individual investors easier than ever before, whether in domestic or overseas securities.

A further reason for increasing volumes is the likelihood of 24-hour trading.

It is therefore essential that the securities industry seeks the optimum method of operation and becomes, as far as possible, insensitive to trading volume without loss of control.

Maximising Internal Efficiency

It will become increasingly important to become very efficient internally, in an operational sense. Efficient organisations will seek to employ seamless methods of operation:

- prior to execution of trades; for example, the timely and accurate setting up of *static data*,
- throughout the trade lifecycle, from order receipt and trade execution to the reflection of trade settlement internally, and
- in position related activities (outside the trade lifecycle),

with the minimum of cost, but with maximum control.

The implementation and continued use of such operational efficiency should result in the automated processing of a very high percentage of trades, and the need to closely manage only those trades that, for example, may be sensitive in terms of client service, and trades that give rise to risk.

The consequences of failing to operate efficiently are likely to be revealed through poor service to clients, exceptional numbers of settlement failures and a failure to maintain proper control over the business (e.g. failure to reconcile positions) and increased costs to the organisation.

Ultimate operational efficiency will also result in the processing of new business (e.g. trading in new markets or in new transaction types) being absorbed seamlessly.

Prior to focusing on the initiatives that pursue the objectives above, it is necessary to appreciate the background against which the objectives are set.

29.1.2 Historically

Up to and including the 1970s, securities trading was primarily focused on domestic securities, as very few organisations within the securities industry had the capability of trading and settling on a cross border basis. Doing so entails:

- understanding the nature of the overseas securities from a trading perspective;
- having the internal infrastructure to record multicurrency positions;
- having settlement and custody arrangements with either a custodian in the settlement location, or with a *global custodian*;
- the ability to transmit settlement instructions in a safe and secure manner, to all overseas custodians;
- the ability to pay or receive funds in foreign currencies;
- the set-up of incoming communication channels, from the custodian (regarding pre-settlement statuses and details of trade settlement);
- ensuring that income due on overseas holdings is received in a timely fashion.

During the 1980s, securities trading and settlement began to expand beyond purely domestic trading and into overseas markets, where *cross-border settlement* became an everyday reality for some market participants. However, the complete infrastructure required

Table 29.1

Operational area	Situation
Static data	Static data within the settlement system was updated manually, with the trading system static data being updated from a different source (with the possibility of discrepancies between trading and settlement systems). Internal ownership of static data was unclear
Trade capture—front office	Trades in some security types were captured into trading systems, while others needed to be recorded manually
Trade capture—back office	Automatic trade capture within the settlement system for those trades entered into trading systems, and manual capture for all other trades
Trade agreement	Early trade agreement (ensuring the counterparty agreed the detail of the trade immediately after trade execution) was possible, but was dependent upon the practices in the markets in which the STO traded
Settlement instructions	The various custodians used by an STO had no standard method by which settlement instructions could be transmitted, as some custodians required their account holders to use S.W.I.F.T. while others required use of their proprietary systems, telex or fax. Furthermore, the various custodians required different information to be given within settlement instructions
Pre-value date settlement instruction statuses	Some custodians would be capable of providing pre-settlement statuses in an automated fashion, while others could only communicate such statuses by telex, fax or telephone
Settlement failure	Settlement success (settling trades on value date) and failure rates differed dramatically between the various markets
Trade settlement	Some markets had a high incidence of physical settlement, while others operated on a mainly book-entry basis
Reflecting trade settlement internally	Advices of trade settlement (issued by the various custodians) would range from highly automated to telex, fax or telephone, with some advices being issued immediately after trade settlement, and others taking days to be received by the STO
Reconciliation	Statements of securities holdings and cash balances issued by the various custodians differed in terms of their transmission media and timing

to achieve cross-border settlement in an efficient, risk-free and controlled manner was not in place to an adequate extent, and operational processing was usually a series of ill-connected steps, typified by large amounts of manual processing. Some STOs set up regional offices in many of the world's financial centres, in order to trade and conduct operational activities locally, as this was considered by some to be the most effective method of handling the business.

At the time, settlement cycles in many markets were typically much less aggressive than the T+1 and T+0 objectives being discussed at the time of writing, leaving many days in which to input settlement instructions and resolve discrepancies prior to value date.

During the 1990s, it became normal practice for many organisations within the securities industry to trade in overseas securities (as well as domestic securities) on a daily basis, necessitating cross-border settlement. However, internally within some STOs, restrictions needed to be placed on traders wishing to expand their trading volumes, or on the types of securities in which they traded, as operationally, there was an unsatisfactory level of infrastructure. Although many STOs invested in new trading systems to aid the traders in their volume and efficiency of executing trades, it was also usual to find a reluctance to invest in the back office systems and infrastructure required to keep pace with the ever-increasing volumes and types of trades emanating from the front office.

The situation that resulted within an STO was typically as listed in Table 29.1. From the perspective of the STO's various custodians, their practices and procedures had evolved in order to suit the needs of their account holders, who were originally local to the custodian. In general terms, there had been little or no reason for custodians in various locations to operate in the same or similar fashion. Only with the advent of cross-border trading did the need become much more apparent (from the perspective of the STOs) for standardised treatment by custodians.

This lack of standardisation resulted in a relatively low percentage of trades processed on an STP basis, and the cost of processing differed according to the security type and location of settlement.

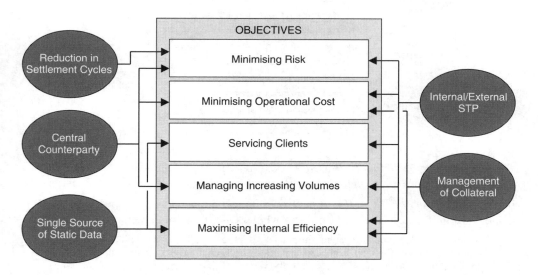

Figure 29.1   Objectives and initiatives: trade processing

Figure 29.1 illustrates the initiatives that are underway (at the time of writing) in pursuit of the above-mentioned objectives. As can be seen, at times the objectives themselves may have a relationship with each other.

The terms describing the initiatives within Figure 29.1 should be familiar to the reader, with the exception of 'Central Counterparty'; such entities reduce risk and costs for their members, and are described within Section 29.2.3.

29.2 INITIATIVES IN PURSUIT OF TRADE PROCESSING OBJECTIVES

At the time of writing, the main industry-wide initiatives that are underway are the:

- reduction in settlement cycles
- straight-through processing of trades
- increased use of central counterparties
- use of static data from a single source
- active management of collateral.

Clearly very few, if any, of the initiatives described below can be achieved without the direct involvement of Information Technology (IT). A major reason for writing this book is the need for IT personnel to attain an adequate level of understanding of the necessary steps in the securities operational environment, so that they (along with those who have the detailed business knowledge and the long-term business vision) can contribute to change quickly and effectively, and have an awareness of the impact of such changes.

29.2.1 Reduction in Settlement Cycles

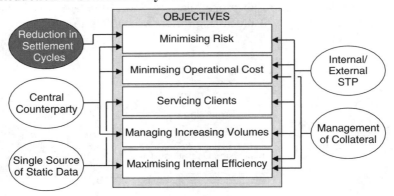

The term 'trading participants' is used in order to indicate that these changes will affect all those who trade securities, including institutional investors, agents for investors and STOs.

In 1989, the *Group of Thirty* (G30) published its recommendations for clearance and settlement within the securities industry as a whole. One of the nine recommendations was:

> 'A "Rolling Settlement" system should be adopted by all markets. Final settlement should occur on T+3 by 1992. As an interim target, final settlement should occur on T+5 by 1990 at the latest, save only where it hinders the achievement of T+3 by 1992.'

This recommended reduction in settlement cycles was (and still is) seen as a means of reducing the number of open trades at any point in time, thereby reducing the risk of counterparties defaulting on their contractual obligation (to settle executed trades). As mentioned at the beginning of this chapter, in a T+3 environment, an STO that executes an average of 5000 trades per day would have up to 15,000 trades open at any one moment in time, as value date had not yet arrived. This is represented in Figure 29.2. As at the viewpoint on Thursday morning, trades dealt from and including Monday of the same week would all be open and still to be settled with counterparties.

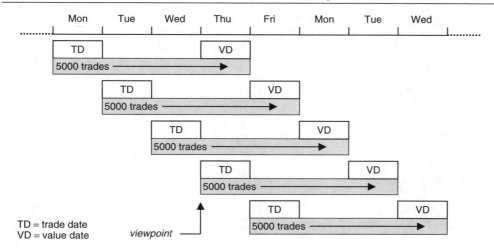

Figure 29.2 Reduction in settlement cycles: open trades in a T+3 environment

However, in a T+1 environment, the same STO executing the same number of trades would have only 5000 trades open, excluding settlement failures. See Figure 29.3. As at the viewpoint on Thursday morning, only trades executed on the previous day would be open.

Since the G30 recommendation, substantial progress has been made in reducing settlement cycles in many markets around the globe. At the time of writing, many government bond markets settle on a T+1 basis, and many equity markets settle either on T+2 or T+3.

The ultimate aim is for same-day settlement (T+0).

Implications of T+1 and T+0

The window of time available for the processing of transactions and the actioning of discrepancies will reduce. For example, moving from T+3 to T+1 is likely to cause a

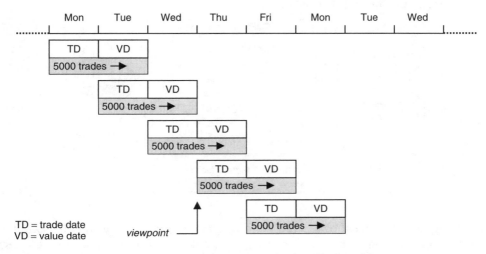

Figure 29.3 Reduction in settlement cycles: open trades in a T+1 environment

much greater impact than moving from T+5 to T+3, as the available window to process and, where necessary, correct discrepancies will reduce to hours rather than days.

All industry participants will be impacted by reduced settlement cycles, including:

- institutional investors
  - mutual fund managers
  - pension funds
  - insurance companies
  - hedge funds
  - charities
- agents for investors
  - clearing banks
  - brokers
  - stockbrokers
  - retail brokers
- STOs
- custodians
  - local custodians
  - global custodians
  - sub-custodians
  - NCSDs
  - ICSDs
- registrars
- stock exchanges
- market regulators
- legislative bodies
- banking authorities.

It is generally accepted that for the industry (as a whole) to operate successfully within a T+1 environment, it will be necessary for Straight Through Processing to be adopted.

29.2.2 Straight Through Processing

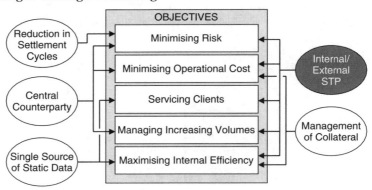

In order to reap the benefit of reduced risk, each trading participant within the securities industry will need to invest time and resources in order to meet the shrinking settlement deadlines.

The introduction of T+1 and T+0 will mean that all trading participants will need to have their internal procedures working and proven, if they are to survive in such an environment. The entire pre-settlement trade lifecycle, from order capture through trade execution, capture, validation, agreement and transaction reporting, will need to be completed within deadlines that are considerably more aggressive than T+3. Some organisations may view such changes as an opportunity to gain an advantage over their competitors.

Achieving such changes will require trading participants to analyse their existing internal procedures, so as to identify the optimum method of operation through all the steps, from order capture to transaction reporting.

Rather than focusing on efficiencies within a single department, threads of business affecting all the points in the trade lifecycle should be identified and collaborative efforts made to identify the optimal method for the entire process, spanning multiple departments if necessary.

If the organisation (rather than individual departments) can agree a vision early on in the analysis process, the component parts can be tackled as part of the vision; by taking this approach, individual pockets of effort will not be wasted.

Additionally, when conducting the analysis, trading participants should not only look at improvements to their existing business, but also take into account the organisation's plans for the future. In the case of STOs, these plans may include areas such as levels of service to clients, the markets in which trading may be effected and projected trading volumes.

The result of this analysis is likely to show the need for internal STP (within the organisation). The necessary milestones to achieve internal STP are likely to contain the following elements.

- Static data—accurate security and counterparty data should be updated to the relevant internal systems (e.g. order management, front office trading and settlement systems) from a single source, at the same time. This action is intended to ensure that information passed from one system (e.g. an order management system) is successfully received into the destination system (e.g. a trading system), avoiding duplicate input, conflicting data between systems and the need for on-the-spot updating within the recipient system, and thereby also avoiding delays in processing.
- Order capture—the passing of order details electronically from the point of origin to the point of trade execution, via a series of interfaces, where necessary. Only at the point of origin should manual input occur. For example, institutional clients could input their orders to an order management system that is viewable instantly by the receiving STO's salesperson, and automatically forwarded for execution to the relevant (external) exchange, or to the (internal) trader or market maker.
- Trade capture (front office)—where the STO's trader or market maker has executed trades originated by orders received, for example from institutional clients, both the order management system and the front office trading system should be updated immediately upon trade execution. The updating of the order (with the details of trade execution) into the order management system should trigger execution messages to the STO's salesperson and to the institutional client, and should also trigger the closure of the order. Where a trade has not been originated from an order (e.g. the STO's trader executes a trade directly with another STO), the trader should input the details to the trading system immediately. Where a trade has been executed by an ECN, the details

of the trade should be fed to the STO's trading system immediately. In all cases, the trade within the front office system will need to be sent to the back office settlement system immediately, for operational processing.

- Settlement processing (back office)—this will contain a number of essential elements (as described within the trade lifecycle chapters), including those listed in Table 29.2.

Table 29.2

Trade capture	As the static data within the settlement system should be the same as in the trading system, the trade should be received successfully within the settlement system
Trade enrichment	All relevant information (e.g. attachment of the relevant cash values of stamp duty or accrued interest) should be defaulted automatically, provided that all necessary information has been set up when originally setting up the security or counterparty
Trade validation	All trades that meet the business rules (e.g. FoP settlement, large cash value, trade with a specific counterparty) should be automatically held (STP should be prevented) and forwarded to the desktop of the appropriate user, for validation. Following validation, the trade should continue processing. All other trades should be processed on an STP basis
Trade agreement	All trades that have passed validation should be routed to the appropriate electronic trade matching mechanism automatically, without delay. All trades with a status other than matched should be treated as exceptions automatically
Transaction reporting	All relevant trades should be forwarded to the appropriate regulator automatically, within the specified deadline
Settlement instructions	All settlement instructions that are necessary to send to custodians (may not be necessary for trades executed via ECNs) should be generated and transmitted automatically (inclusive of message encryption), without delay
Pre-value date settlement instruction statuses	All statuses applied to settlement instructions by custodians should update the relevant trade within the settlement system automatically. All instructions with a status other than matched should be treated as exceptions automatically
Settlement failure	All instructions with a failed (on or after value date) status should be treated as exceptions automatically
Reflecting trade settlement internally	All instructions that have fully or partially settled at custodians should update the relevant trade within the settlement system automatically. All failures to update the settlement system should be treated as exceptions automatically

Internal STP and Management by Exception

At the time of writing, STP is an objective that many participants within the securities industry as a whole are attempting to meet. However, the interpretation of exactly how STP is adopted can differ between organisations.

In essence, if STP operates as required by most organisations, trades will be processed seamlessly, without requiring information to be added or repaired. STP is not, however, a panacea or magic potion. The processing of trades on an STP basis could itself be regarded as risky if there is insufficient control over trades that create risk for the organisation (albeit on a minority of trades).

An essential part of the analysis effort, therefore, is to identify such circumstances that give rise to risk. It is likely that trades with specific attributes will be required to be reviewed by relevant personnel, prior to transmission to the outside world. For example:

- trades that are due to settle on an FoP basis,
- trades with a large cash value, and
- trades that are with a specified counterparty

should be prevented from being processed on an STP basis.

Such trades should be treated as exceptions to the STP rule, where automatic detection of such trades occurs according to rules set up within the settlement system. Where such exceptions are detected, the trade should be forwarded to the desktop of the appropriate personnel, according to the business rule that has been met; following investigation, the trade will either be released to the settlement system for continued processing, amended or cancelled. Exceptions will need to be prioritised and escalation procedures adopted in order to ensure timely actions. These actions will need to occur very quickly in order not to miss deadlines in a T+1 or T+0 environment.

In summary, fast, efficient and well-controlled operational processing should result, providing:

- for trades that do not meet the risk criteria (represented by the business rules), STP occurs, and
- for trades that do meet the risk criteria, STP is prevented, and management by exception is activated.

Such methods of processing can only occur, however, where software with the appropriate capabilities exists, or is developed.

A recent refinement to management by exception is a tool that prompts operations and other staff to perform actions at designated points throughout the trade (or corporate action) lifecycle, in order to prevent exceptions. This is known as *workflow,* and can be viewed as the evolution of basic management by exception. An example workflow is used within Section 29.3.

External STP

In order for the securities industry as a whole to become as efficient as many of its participants would wish, STP must be fully operative outside the trading community, as well as internally within each trading participant.

Full STP can only be achieved with the cooperation of the trading participant's counterparty and the counterparty's custodian, whether the counterparty is an STO or an institutional investor.

In general terms the steps that can be taken outside the trading community to facilitate STP include standardised:

- security and counterparty reference data;
- trade agreement methods between counterparties;
- trade confirmation formats and transmission media;
- settlement instruction messages;
- pre-value date settlement instruction statuses issued by custodians;
- settlement failure statuses issued by custodians;
- advices of trade settlement issued by custodians;
- format and frequency of securities and cash statements issued by custodians;
- within each marketplace where physical certificates are used (regardless of the extent to which they are used), full dematerialisation of securities should occur to allow book entry to become the only means of transferring ownership of securities.

At the time of writing, two initiatives are underway designed to transform trade processing specifically in relation to STOs and brokers trading with institutional clients. The passing of information between such parties to a trade has historically been very slow and error prone, and not conducive to successful operational processing in a T+1 or T+0 environment. The two initiatives are by:

- Omgeo (a joint venture between Thomson Financial and the Depository Trust & Clearing Corporation, DTCC), and
- the GSTPA (Global Straight-Through Processing Association).

In each case trade details and settlement information per trade, relating to the:

- the institutional client,
- both seller's and buyer's custodians, and
- STO or broker

will be brought together at the earliest point in the trade lifecycle, with the intention of gaining agreement to the trade details and the matching of settlement instructions automatically, via STP.

29.2.3 Central Counterparty

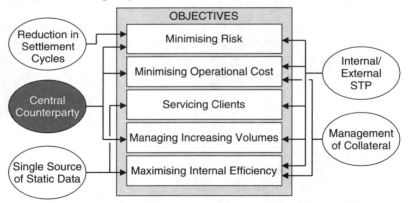

For many years, the trading community has sought means of reducing risk and cost associated with their trading activity. The adoption of central counterparties (CCPs) is regarded as a major step in achieving those aims.

In essence, CCPs:

- Reduce risk for their members by becoming the counterparty to trades, and
- Reduce costs for their members through the netting of settlement movements.

CCPs are responsible for *clearing*, the practice (post trade execution and pre-settlement) of defining net settlement obligation and assigning responsibility for undertaking net settlement. Settlement of the obligation occurs at the relevant CSD following the clearing process at the CCP.

Central Counterparty Concepts

Reduction in Risk. Historically, when a trade is executed between seller and buyer, until settlement occurs both the seller and the buyer perceive they have a risk that their counterparty will fail to honour their contractual obligation to settle the trade; this is known as *counterparty risk*.

In markets where CCP is practiced, the responsibility for the settlement obligation of trades is adopted by the CCP; the seller's counterparty becomes the CCP, as does the buyer's counterparty. The CCP effectively substitutes itself as the counterparty to both seller and buyer; one contractual obligation (seller to buyer) is replaced by two contractual obligations (seller to CCP, buyer to CCP). By the use of a CCP model within a marketplace, both the seller's and the buyer's exposure (risk) is with the CCP and both are therefore shielded from default by one another.

Dependent upon the circumstances in a specific marketplace, risk is transferred to the CCP in one of two ways:

- substitution of the settlement contract between the seller and buyer (as described above), this is known as *novation*;
- at the point of trade execution (normally via an automated, order-driven exchange), the seller is not always informed of the buyer's identity (or vice versa), and the CCP becomes counterparty to both seller and buyer immediately.

Reduction in Costs. Historically, trades between counterparties have been settled on a trade-for-trade (gross) basis. Therefore each of the five trades listed in Table 29.3 (taken from the perspective of one trading participant, ABC) would have been settled individually.

Table 29.3

Trade number	Operation	Quantity of shares	NSV (HKD)	Security	Counterparty
1	Buy	+5000	−25,000.00	HSBC shares	QRS
2	Buy	+7500	−36,000.00	HSBC shares	XYZ
3	Buy	+4000	−20,500.00	HSBC shares	EFG
4	Sell	−6000	+31,000.00	HSBC shares	LMN
5	Sell	−2000	+10,500.00	HSBC shares	QRS
		+8500	**−40,000.00**		

This is still true today, unless:

- automatic netting of multiple trades in a single security is practiced by a CCP within a marketplace, in which case a single net receipt of 8500 shares against payment of

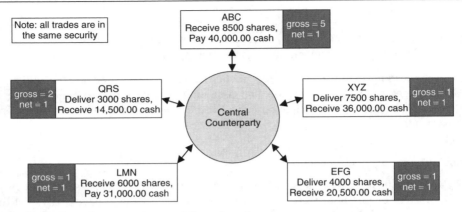

Figure 29.4　Central counterparty: multilateral netting

40,000.00 cash would have occurred at the CSD, resulting in the effective settlement of all five trades. This is known as *multilateral netting*. An example of multilateral netting via a CCP is illustrated in Figure 29.4. Taking account of all trades listed in Table 29.3, from the perspective of both buyer and seller, multilateral netting at the CCP would result in five net movements (one for each party involved in the transactions), whereas on a gross basis 10 movements would have been required (one for the buyer and one for the seller for each trade). Party ABC has gained the greatest advantage from a cost reduction and settlement efficiency perspective, as one net movement has replaced five settlements on a gross basis;

- in markets where automatic netting is not practiced, where trading between two parties had resulted in two or more trades in the same security being due to settle, in order to derive the benefit of netting, the parties would need to specifically agree to net the relevant trades, resulting in a single movement of securities and a single movement of cash in order to effectively settle the original trades. This is known as *bilateral netting*. In the above example, of all five trades, only the trades between ABC and counterparty QRS (trades 1 and 5) are candidates for such netting (as all other trades are with different counterparties). Had agreement to net been made with counterparty QRS, a single movement of 3000 shares against 14,500.00 cash would be made, resulting in the effective settlement of trades 1 and 5. The three remaining trades would need to be settled on a trade-for-trade basis.

Whilst both bilateral and multilateral netting reduce the cost of settlement as only one settlement occurs rather than one settlement for each of the original trades, bilateral netting cannot provide the (maximum) benefits of multilateral netting with a CCP.

Because the CCP is counterparty to trades executed by its members, it is able to identify net securities and cash obligations (clearing); the settlement of these obligations then occurs at the CSD. Consequently, the greater the number of trades executed by a trading participant that are netted via the CCP, the greater the saving of settlement costs.

Due to multilateral netting, the number of settlements (net movements of securities and net movements of cash) can be a very low percentage in relation to the number of underlying trades that are effectively settled by the net movements. For instance, the Depository Trust & Clearing Corporation (DTCC) in the USA, has published the statistics

Table 29.4

Number of transactions processed	18.1 million
Value of transactions processed	USD 722.0 billion
Values settled after netting	USD 21.7 billion
Netting factor	97%

Source: Depository Trust & Clearing Corporation.

in Table 29.4, relating to trades processed on 4th April 2000. This shows that, after netting, the number of trade obligations requiring actual cash movements was reduced by 97%. Further benefits of CCP are:

- simplified settlement—beside the main benefits of reduced risk and reduced costs for trading participants, the process of settlement is more simplified through the CCP model, due to the netting procedure;
- anonymity—for those trading participants who wish to remain anonymous, under the circumstances where neither the seller nor the buyer are aware of one another's identity at the time of trade execution, CCP upholds anonymity;
- simplified risk management—trading participants do not need to assess the creditworthiness of their counterparties for settlement purposes, as the CCP will carry the risk. The CCP uses standard risk management techniques to ensure it is always fully collateralised against member obligations.

Note that as settlement cycles reduce, the risk reduction benefits of CCP diminish, as the number of open trades in a T+1 environment (compared with, say, T+3) should be considerably fewer.

CCPs in Current Operation. CCPs are in use in a number of locations around the globe, for instance:

- Australia   CHESS for equities
- Brazil   Brazilian Clearing & Depository Corporation (CBLC) for Brazilian equities, corporate and government bond issues
- Canada   Canadian Depository for Securities (CDS) for Canadian equities
- Hong Kong   Hong Kong Securities Clearing Co. Ltd (HKSCC) for Hong Kong equities
- Japan   Tokyo Stock Exchange (TSE) for Japanese Government bond issues and equities
- Singapore   Central Depository Pte. Ltd. (CDP) for Singapore equities
- UK   London Clearing House (LCH) for UK equities and bonds
- USA   Government Securities Clearing Corporation (GSCC) is a CCP for US Government bond issues. National Securities Clearing Corporation (NSCC) is a CCP for US equities.

Note that CCP services are only offered to those organisations that can fulfill the membership requirements. Such requirements may include the size (capital) of the company and its membership of relevant exchanges/markets.

The Trading Participants' Perspective. From the viewpoint of an individual STO that trades within many marketplaces, it is likely to trade in some markets where CCP is not practiced, in which case the STO will record trades as being with the original counterparty, and in other markets where CCP is practiced, trades should be recorded as being with the CCP.

In marketplaces where CCP and netting is practiced, at any one time the STO may have a number of trades in a single security that are due to settle on a given value date; this may include a number of purchases and sales. Upon receipt of notification from the CSD that settlement has occurred on a net basis, the STO will need to update all underlying trades immediately, if its books and records are to be accurate, up-to-date and in a position to enable successful reconciliation.

Summary. The driving force behind the introduction within more marketplaces, and the use by all trading participants of CCPs, is the reduction in risk and the monetary saving associated with net trade settlement.

At the time of writing, CCPs are operative in a number of individual marketplaces around the globe, and discussion is ongoing regarding the introduction of CCP:

- within more domestic marketplaces,
- regionally, through cooperation between a number of domestic CCPs, and ultimately
- globally, where a number of regional CCPs may join forces.

Rather than implementing CCPs to meet solely local needs, participants within the industry would benefit from the development of fewer and larger CCPs (through merger or otherwise), that also have the ability to net between themselves.

29.2.4   Single Source of Static Data

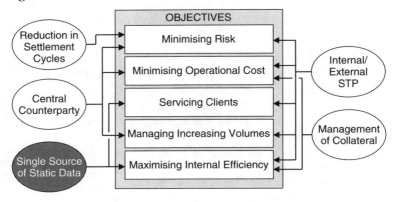

The importance of accurate static data that is set up in a timely fashion cannot be over-emphasised. A trading participant's ability to:

- provide a high quality service to its clients, and
- meet the necessary deadlines, particularly in a T+1 or T+0 environment

will be extremely difficult (if not impossible) to achieve, without such data being available (refer to Chapter 9).

From a trading participant's perspective, the source of security static data can include custodians, *securities data providers* and stock exchanges. Unfortunately, the detail of an individual security can differ between different sources. Therefore the dilemma for trading participants is to either accept a single source of data and use that information in its processing (and trust that it is correct), or to accept two or more sources that, upon receipt, require comparison (often referred to as data cleansing).

Furthermore, despite the fact that ISIN (International Securities Identification Number) codes are intended for use around the globe, in some countries the local coding system continues to be used. This prevents the holding of only the ISIN for a particular security within the static data of organisations that trade in such securities, additionally forcing the holding of the local identifier.

ISINs are usually allocated to new securities by National Numbering Agencies (NNAs) in the country of issue of the security. The Association of National Numbering Agencies (ANNA) is an organisation made up of NNAs from around the globe, and its objectives include adherence to the ISIN standard by NNAs and promoting the use of ISINs globally.

This lack of consistent and accurate data is an aspect of the securities industry that leaves a great deal of scope for improvement. These improvements will need to be in place in advance of T+1 and T+0 if high quality services are to be provided to clients and if deadlines are not to be missed.

Many STOs suffer from a common static data problem. For historically valid reasons, security and counterparty data from different sources has been used to set up the static data within various systems internally. Such systems may include:

* order management,
* equity, bond and repo trading,
* settlement,
* corporate actions,
* reconciliation, and
* risk management.

The use of different static data across connecting systems (e.g. trading to settlement systems) can be the major cause of trades not handled on an STP basis.

At the time of writing, an initiative is underway to standardise the components of securities data originating from various sources. The Market Data Definition Language (MDDL) is being developed to provide a single data record of each security, thereby reducing the STOs (and other trading participants) efforts in developing and maintaining complex systems needed to transform different formats of information from multiple sources into a common standard.

A further important point is the cooperation of STOs and institutional investors in ensuring that current counterparty related data is exchanged enabling, for example, trade matching messages and settlement instructions to be transmitted at the earliest time after trade execution.

29.2.5 Management of Collateral

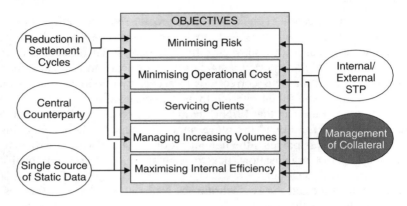

Historically, many organisations that have taken positive trading positions in securities have not necessarily looked to gain maximum use of the securities they own.

When, for example, an STO has a positive trading position and the STO's custodian is holding the securities, the securities can be used for the benefit of the STO in a number of ways (Table 29.5). The maximum benefit could be gained if (only) sufficient collateral for each purpose were made available at the relevant time, without leaving a significant excess in one location.

One specific issue is that securities being held by one custodian on behalf of an STO may be well in excess of collateral requirements at that particular custodian, whilst the same STO may have a shortfall of collateral at a different custodian. Such a shortfall may well prevent settlement of securities from occurring at that custodian. This situation is highlighted in Figure 29.5.

The use by custodian B of collateral owned by the STO, but which is excess to requirements and held in custodian A (without the transfer of securities between the custodians), will clearly require cooperation between the custodians. It is possible that the CCP initiative will provide the root of such collateral realignment on behalf of the owner of securities, through the linking of two or more CCPs and the use of cross guarantees.

Table 29.5

Use of securities	Benefit to securities owner
As collateral to allow the settlement of trades at a custodian	Allows cash to be drawn against the value of the collateral (up to a credit limit)
As collateral in a repo transaction	Allows cash to be borrowed on a secured basis, thereby cheaper than on an unsecured basis
As the lent security in a securities lending transaction	Income in the form of a fee will be received from the borrower

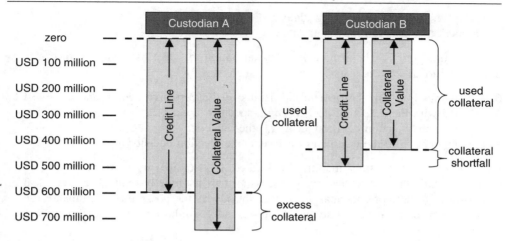

Figure 29.5   Management of collateral

Those who need to borrow cash in order to fund a positive trading position may give thought to executing repo or secured borrowing transactions; this will reduce the trading participant's cost of borrowing cash.

Owners of securities and in particular long-term owners may wish to consider lending their securities. This will make the market more liquid (settlement is more likely to occur on time as more securities will be available for delivery) and provide increased return on the owner's investment. In 1989, the *Group of Thirty* made this recommendation:

> 'Securities lending and borrowing should be encouraged as a method of expediting the settlement of securities transactions. Existing regulatory and taxation barriers that inhibit the practice of lending securities should be removed by 1990.'

The owners of the collateral are placing increasing emphasis on maximising the utilisation of assets against their contractual obligations. In general terms, the proactive use of collateral to its fullest extent will prove to be a major contributory factor in the operational efficiency of trading participants.

29.3   CORPORATE ACTIONS RELATED OBJECTIVES

29.3.1   Introduction

Corporate actions processing is an operational activity that has historically been managed with very little automation.

The processing of most types of corporate action essentially involves a series of sequential steps. For example, the processing of a cash dividend where the owner is not given an option to select the form of the benefit is likely to require the following processing steps:

1. capture of dividend details (e.g. ex-dividend date, record date, payment date and rate per share);
2. calculation of entitlement as at ex-dividend date;
3. calculation of location position as at record date;

4. receipt of payment on payment date;

5. payment to owners on payment date.

For corporate actions where the owner has an option to select its form, a series of integrated additional steps is usually necessary, such as:

6. communicating with the owners the details of the corporate action, and a request to respond with their election decision by a specified date;

7. gathering the election decisions from all the owners;

8. communicating to the custodian (or issuer) the election decision.

Particularly in organisations that provide safe custody services where there may be many owners of individual securities, such processing has historically required a great deal of manpower. Furthermore, manual processing introduces the possibility of human error.

The management of corporate actions has broadly similar objectives as for trade processing.

Minimising Risk

Risk becomes apparent where, for example:

- an STO fails to identify that a corporate action is due on its own holdings and/or on its clients' holdings, and may be required to recompense its client from its own funds;
- securities or cash due (from a custodian or from a claim issued to a counterparty) on a corporate action have not been received as at the due date. If the STO has paid its client on the due date, the STO will be exposed;
- an owner has not been given the opportunity to select the form of a corporate action (where relevant), and the STO holding the position makes the election decision, which may prove to be against the wishes of the owner. This may result in the STO needing to comply with the client's wishes and correct the result, potentially at a cost to the STO.

Furthermore, the manual nature of corporate actions processing in itself introduces a risk due to shortfalls of manpower.

Minimising Operational Cost

As many organisations process corporate actions fully or partially manually, the manpower cost to the organisation is often out of proportion to the relatively low cash value of most corporate actions, particularly when compared with the cost of processing trades, relevant to their cash value.

Servicing Clients

Where an STO holds securities in safe custody on behalf of its clients, the clients will expect a level of service relating to corporate actions due on their positions, such as:

- receiving a pre-advice advising that a corporate action has been announced and stating the benefit due, providing the position is not sold prior to the entitlement date;
- receiving notification of a corporate action where the owner may select its form, well in advance of the deadline date for the decision;
- the automatic payment of corporate action cash proceeds to the owner's external bank account.

Managing Increasing Volumes

The projected increase in trading volumes (described earlier in this chapter) may result in an increase in the number of securities positions held by individual and institutional investors, across a broader range of securities than has been the case historically.

For individual STOs, if this situation results in an increase in the quantity of corporate actions and the number of clients (in a safe custody situation) who are entitled to the corporate action, this combination will result in the need for increased processing capability.

Furthermore, volumes of collateral related trades (such as repo and securities lending and borrowing) are likely to increase as greater numbers of investors become aware that returns can be enhanced by undertaking such trades.

Maximising Internal Efficiency

The increasing number of corporate actions caused by increasing ownership in a wider range of securities will require greater efficiency in the processing of corporate actions, with the minimum of resources, but with maximum control.

Failure to operate in an efficient manner (for instance, minimising manual tasks) may result in individual corporate actions being overlooked and clients being serviced in an inadequate manner and possibly looking for recompense for the error made.

Figure 29.6 illustrates the initiatives that are underway (at the time of writing) in pursuit of the above-mentioned objectives.

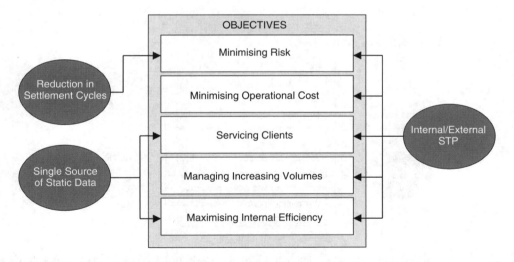

Figure 29.6   Objectives and initiatives: corporate actions

29.4   INITIATIVES IN PURSUIT OF CORPORATE ACTIONS OBJECTIVES

At the time of writing, the main industry-wide initiatives that are underway are the:

- reduction in settlement cycles,
- straight through processing of corporate actions, and
- use of static data from a single source.

29.4.1   Reduction in Settlement Cycles

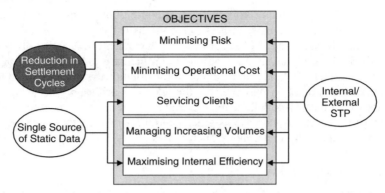

A beneficial side effect of the global trend towards reducing settlement cycles is that, for example, in a T+1 environment compared with T+3, there should be substantially fewer corporate action claims needing to be issued to sellers.

Because settlement is more likely to occur prior to record date of a corporate action, there is a greater likelihood that buyers will receive deliveries of securities and be on record as at the close of business on the record date, thereby receiving the benefit directly.

29.4.2   Single Source of Static Data

In parallel with the issue of securities static data for trade processing, information regarding announced corporate actions is typically available from a number of sources, such as custodians, corporate actions data vendors and stock exchanges.

As the data may be inaccurate or inconsistent, the predicament for trading participants is whether to accept a single source of corporate action data, or to accept two or more sources that require comparison.

Again, the lack of accuracy and consistency of data is an area that needs to be improved greatly. However, it is anticipated that the MDDL initiative (described earlier in this chapter) will focus on corporate actions data and result in information from various sources being transformed into a common standard.

29.4.3   Straight Through Processing

In parallel with the requirement to process trades on an STP basis, at the time of writing there is also a great deal of scope for the processing of corporate actions to be handled on an STP basis.

Internal

The steps that can be taken internally to facilitate STP include:

- standardised corporate action event data;
- standardised corporate action advice formats and transmission media;
- static data relating to standing client elections (for example, in an optional stock and cash dividend, always electing for stock);
- giving safe custody clients the ability to record their election decisions directly into the STO's records (for example, via the Internet).

However, automation should minimise human involvement and only allow such intervention where management of high-risk and/or complex events is necessary.

Some may adopt the approach to automation by addressing the most straightforward corporate actions first, followed by further refinements to ultimately include the more challenging of corporate action types.

External

The ability to process corporate action information on an STP basis externally to trading participants will require:

- the standardisation in the communication of corporate action details from the point of origin to trading participants;
- the standardisation in the communication of election decisions from trading participants to custodians and issuers (in order to overcome the common use of proprietary links, fax and telex).

When allied to internal STP capability, these will greatly assist in addressing many of the corporate actions related objectives.

29.5   WORKFLOW

Earlier in this chapter the topic of workflow was introduced. Although workflow is relevant to both trade processing and corporate actions, the latter will be used as a vehicle to illustrate the topic.

The nature of corporate actions processing (a series of sequential steps, with typically a time lag between each step) calls for automation that allows:

- identification of each step, according to the type of corporate action;
- tracking the progress of each step;
- issuing alerts if the status of a step is unsatisfactory at predefined points in time;
- issuing escalation alerts.

The term that is given to such automation is workflow, which can be viewed as the evolution of basic management by exception. Its primary use is as a reminder of events or decisions that must occur by a specified deadline, allowing proactive and well-controlled corporate actions management. Figure 29.7 represents the (example only) milestones set as part of a workflow for a cash dividend with a currency option.

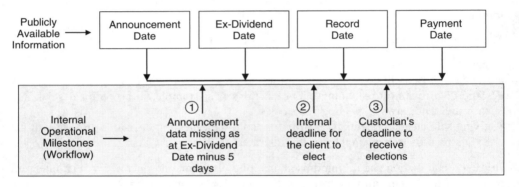

Figure 29.7   Objectives and initiatives: corporate actions example workflow

Step 1: if any part of the standard components of a cash dividend with currency option are missing five days prior to the ex-dividend date (for example, missing the rate per share), the workflow mechanism detects and highlights this to the relevant operations personnel.

Step 2: as at the deadline set internally for the election by owners as to their currency preference (for example, three days prior to the custodian's deadline), any entitlements without an associated election will be highlighted to the appropriate staff.

Step 3: as at the deadline set by the custodian to be informed of currency preferences, a failure to detect the necessary communication (for example, a S.W.I.F.T. message) to the custodian will be highlighted to the relevant personnel.

Providing sufficient analysis is undertaken to identify all the essential steps in the management of:

- corporate action events, and
- the trade lifecycle

the use of workflow is likely to be a major step in achieving the required level of automation, whilst retaining maximum control.

29.6   OUTSOURCING

Increasing trade processing costs, increasing trade volumes, the need to support new types of securities and to minimise operational risk is causing the management of some STOs to consider passing the responsibility for settlement, or for various aspects of operations, to companies that specialise in handling the operational processing on behalf of a number of companies. This is commonly known as *outsourcing*.

Those organisations that offer settlement outsourcing services include global custodians (refer to Chapter 17) and the larger investment banks that operate on a global basis. Such outsourcing service providers can achieve economies of scale by processing the business of many organisations within an existing and established infrastructure; such economies of scale can be passed on to clients (the STO).

With regard to settlement outsourcing, two methods exist:

- the outsourcing service provider operates their client's business over the service provider's own custodian accounts;
- the outsourcing service provider operates their client's business over the client's custodian accounts.

Furthermore, the outsourcing of the IT infrastructure within an STO can result in the IT systems being managed by an organisation on behalf of the STO, where the settlement and operational responsibilities remain within the STO. Such arrangements may appeal to certain STOs as the responsibility for growing the IT infrastructure in order to cater for increasing trade volumes and changes within the marketplace lies with the outsourcing service provider, with the cost to the STO typically based upon a fixed charge for each trade processed.

29.7   SUMMARY

The current and impending changes within the securities industry (as described within this chapter) mean that STOs need to be capable of adapting their working practices and systems, preferably in advance of such changes, if they are to succeed in tomorrow's environment.

Glossary of Terms

This glossary contains many of the terms mentioned within the book, but additionally contains frequently used terms not used within the book, but which may be of use to the reader. Words and phrases in *italics* within the description of terms indicate that an associated glossary item exists.

Account Settlement	The practice of applying a predefined *value date* to all trades executed within a predefined period of days. The alternative is *rolling settlement*.
Accrued Interest	On interest bearing bonds, the accumulated interest since the most recent *coupon payment date* and payable at the next coupon payment date.
Advisory	A communication received by a securities trading organisation advising the details of a trade that a counterparty believes it has executed with the *STO*, for which the STO has not issued a matching message (e.g. a *settlement instruction*)
Agency Trading	Effecting the purchase or the sale of securities (on behalf of clients) in the capacity of an agent.
Agent for Investors	An organisation that acts as an intermediary between its client and a market participant with whom the agent trades. Agents usually do not hold securities positions on their own behalf. See *Proprietary Trading*.
American Depository Receipts	Documents that represent shares held in overseas companies and which enable U.S. investors to invest in such securities in a tax-efficient manner. ADRs are traded in their own right at a US Dollar price. See *Global Depository Receipts*.
Bearer Security	A *security* having no facility for the issuer to record the owner of the security, and where proof of ownership is physical possession of the security *certificate*; historically, mainly *bonds* rather than *equities* were issued in bearer form. See *Registered Security*.
Benefit	An amount of cash or a quantity of securities payable by an issuer to *share* or *bond* holders as a reward for or return on their investment.

Bid Price	The price at which an *STO* is prepared to buy a security. See *Mid Price* and *Offer Price*.
Bilateral Netting	The single movement of *securities* and/or cash in order to settle two or more *open trades* in the same security, between two parties. See *Multilateral Netting*.
Board Lot	A standard trading quantity (such as 100 or 500 shares) for a given *security*; trading is usually conducted in multiples of the board lot. The cost of trading in board lots is typically cheaper than for trading in non-board lot quantities. Also known as Round Lot. See *Odd Lot*.
Bond	A type of *security* that represents a loan of cash by an investor to a government, government agency, *supranational organisation* or company, for which the investor usually receives a fixed rate of interest periodically during the term of the loan, and receives repayment of capital at maturity of the bond, usually years later.
Bondholder	The owner of bonds.
Bonus Issue	The grant of additional *shares* by an issuer to its *shareholders*, free of cost to the shareholders, typically at a fixed ratio of additional shares to original shares.
Book Entry	A method by which securities holdings are maintained and the *settlement* of trades is effected. The exchange of *securities* and cash involves no physical movement of securities, as both the seller and buyer use the same *CSD*. Under such circumstances, settlement results in a transfer of securities and cash between seller and buyer, within the CSD's books.
Books and Records	The official record of an organisation's trading activity, *securities* positions and cash positions.
Books Closing Date	The date at which the *shareholders* on an issuer's register are identified for the purpose of distributing *corporate action* benefits, such as *dividends* or *bonus issues*. Also known as *record date*.
Borrower	An entity that issues bonds as a means of raising cash is said to be the borrower of cash. Also known as the *issuer*.
Bridge	The term used for the electronic link between the two *ICSD*s (*Euroclear* and *Clearstream Luxembourg*), over which settlement of trades is effected.
Broker	An organisation that executes trades on behalf of its clients (rather than on its own behalf), by finding buyers where clients wish to sell and finding sellers where clients wish to buy *securities*. Brokers normally charge *commission* to clients for providing this service.

Broker/Dealer	An organisation that is licensed to trade, on an individual trade basis, either as an *agent for investors* (on its client's behalf), or on a *proprietary trading* basis (on its own behalf).
Buy-In	A formal procedure for a buyer to bring about the closure of an *open trade* that has passed its *value date*, by forcing the seller (via a Buy-In Agent) to deliver the securities owing, with associated costs being borne by the seller. Such procedures must be conducted under the rules of the exchange/market over which the trade has been executed. See *Sell-Out*.
Capital Adequacy	Regulatory requirement for *securities trading organisations* and other financial institutions to have sufficient capital (funds) available to meet their obligations.
Cash Dividend	The payment to *shareholders* by an issuer of income in the form of cash; whilst such payments are not guaranteed, many large companies pay cash dividends at regular intervals.
CCASS	Central Clearing & Settlement System; the normal place of settlement for *equities* traded in Hong Kong.
CDS	Canadian Depository for Securities; the normal place of settlement for *equities* traded in Canada.
Central Counterparty	An organisation that is counterparty to both buyer and seller, and which practices *clearing*, resulting in the identification of net settlement movements.
Central Securities Depository	The ultimate storage location of *securities* within a financial centre, in which the record of ownership is typically maintained electronically (by *book-entry*); usually, the ultimate place of *settlement*. A type of *custodian* organisation.
Certificate	Document of ownership in a *security*; certificates have historically been issued in *registered* or *bearer* form. In many financial centres today, certificates are not issued and proof of ownership is held electronically within *book-entry* systems.
CHESS	Clearing House Electronic Subregister System; the normal place of *settlement* for equities traded in Australia. CHESS effects settlement for its account holders on a *book-entry* basis.
Chinese Wall	The separation of parts of a financial institution that may have a conflict of interest in relation to the servicing of clients; the figurative 'wall' is intended to preclude the passing of sensitive information between such areas.

Clearing	The practice (post trade execution and pre-settlement), of defining settlement obligation and assigning responsibility for effecting settlement.
Clearstream Banking Luxembourg	One of the two *International Central Securities Depositories* (ICSDs) offering custody and settlement services to its participants; the other ICSD is *Euroclear*.
Client Money	Cash owned by clients and held by *Securities Trading Organisations* or other companies offering financial services; regulatory requirements demand the segregation of such monies due to clients, so that it is separately identifiable from the cash owned by the company.
Collateral	Assets (either cash or securities) pledged by a borrower to a lender as a guarantee against non-return of the borrowed asset or other financial obligation. Should the borrower fail to repay/re-deliver the borrowed asset, the lender may utilise the collateral in order to recover the value of its loan. Both cash and securities (of acceptable quality) are used as collateral.
Collateral Substitution	In a *repo* or a *securities lending and borrowing* trade, the exchange of a *security* (currently being used as collateral) for one or many securities in replacement.
Commission	Amount charged by an *agent for investors* or *broker* to its client, for execution of a purchase or sale of securities on the client's behalf.
Common Stock	The standard description of *shares* issued by companies in the USA. See *Ordinary Shares*.
Contractual Settlement	The crediting or debiting of *securities* and/or cash to reflect settlement on *value date*, regardless of when the exchange of securities and cash actually occurs.
Contractual Settlement Date	The intended date of exchange of *securities* and cash between buyer and seller. Another term for *value date*.
Corporate Action	The distribution (by an *issuer*) of benefits to existing *shareholders* or *bondholders*, or a change to the structure of an existing security.
Corporate Actions Provider	An organisation that supplies information to subscribers regarding the detail of *corporate actions* as and when announced, typically on an electronic basis.
Counterparty	The opposing entity with which a *securities trading organisation* executes a *securities* transaction.
Counterparty Risk	The risk that the *counterparty* to a trade will fail to honour its contractual obligation to pay cash or deliver *securities*.

Coupon	On interest bearing bonds, *bond certificates* are issued with coupons attached; each coupon represents interest due on one specified *coupon payment date*. In order to receive interest on the bond, the coupon must be detached and presented to the *coupon paying agent*.
Coupon Paying Agent	An organisation appointed by an *issuer* to collect *coupons* from the *bondholders*, verify the validity of the coupons and make coupon payments to the bondholders on behalf of the issuer.
Coupon Payment Date	The scheduled date of a coupon payment.
Coupon Period	The period of time between each payment of interest on a bond.
Coupon Rate	The rate of interest payable by the bond *issuer* to the *bondholders*.
CREST	The normal place of *settlement* for UK and Irish equities and other securities; CREST effects settlement for its members on a *book-entry* basis.
Cross-Border Settlement	The exchange of securities and cash that occurs between one country's *CSD* and another country's CSD, or between a country's domestic CSD and an ICSD. See *Domestic Settlement*.
Cross-Border Trading	The agreement to buy or sell *securities*, where the parties to the trade are located in different countries.
CSD	Abbreviated form of *central securities depository*.
Cum-Dividend	Execution of a trade on a cum-dividend basis entitles the buyer to the *dividend* whilst the seller loses entitlement.
Cusip	Committee on Uniform Securities Identification Procedures; an organisation that provides standardised and unique reference numbers (Cusip numbers) for individual *securities* traded in the United States and Canada, enabling unambiguous identification of the issue being traded and delivered. See *ISIN*.
Custodian	An organisation that specialises in holding *securities* and (usually) cash and effecting movements of securities and cash on behalf of its account holders.
Debt	The issuance of *bonds* signifies that the issuer is in debt to the investors; a 'debt issue' is synonymous with the term 'bond issue'.
Default	Failure by a bond *issuer* to make payments of interest and/or repayments of capital at the scheduled time, or failure by a *counterparty* to meet its contractual obligation.
Deferred Delivery Date	The earliest date that settlement can occur on a new issue of *securities*; also known as *primary value date*.

Delivery versus Payment	The simultaneous, final, irrevocable and risk-free exchange of *securities* and cash between seller and buyer (or their custodians). Commonly known as *DvP*.
Dematerialised	*Securities* holdings represented only by electronic records; settlement of sales and purchases are effected via *book entry*.
Depot	An organisation that holds *securities* and effects *settlement* of trades on behalf of its account holder; also known as *custodian*.
Depot Account	The specific account held by a *depot* or *custodian* in which *securities* are held.
Deregulation	The removal or relaxation of government controls pertaining to operation of *securities* markets.
Dirty Price	The price of a bond inclusive of *accrued interest*, as opposed to 'clean' price (without accrued interest). Also known as 'all-in' price.
Disaster Recovery	The partial or complete duplication of a live trading and operational environment, to enable the continuation of business in the event of a disaster, such as fire or flood.
Dividend	The distribution of earnings by a company to its *shareholders*, whether in the form of cash or *securities*.
Domestic Settlement	The exchange of securities and cash in the *central securities depository* of the security's home country/market. See *Cross Border Settlement*.
Double-Entry Bookkeeping	A basic accounting principle whereby each accounting entry is offset by a contra (debit or credit) entry.
Double Taxation Agreement	An arrangement between two countries, whereby residents of one country that invest in *securities* issued by *issuers* within the other country, will have *withholding tax* deducted at a lower rate than the standard rate payable by investors. Also known as a treaty.
DTC	Depository Trust Company; the normal place of *settlement* of *equities*, corporate and municipal bonds traded in the USA. DTC effects settlement for its account holders on a *book-entry* basis.
DvP	Abbreviated form of *Delivery versus Payment*.
Electronic Communications Networks	A generic term to describe software systems that match sellers and buyers of securities electronically, but which have not achieved exchange status. Following trade execution, some ECNs issue *settlement instructions* on behalf of one or both of the parties, under *power of attorney*.
Emerging Markets	A collective term that refers to recently established *equity* and *bond* markets in former communist or newly developing countries.

Entitlement	The right of ownership relating to certain types of *corporate action*.
Entitlement date	A generic term to describe the date used to determine whether seller or buyer is entitled to a *corporate action*. See *Ex-Date*.
Equity	An alternative description for the term *shares*; an 'equity issue' is synonymous with the term 'share issue'.
Eurobond	A type of *bond* that is usually sold to investors outside the country relating to the currency of issue.
Euroclear	Located in Brussels, one of the two *International Central Securities Depositories* (ICSDs) offering *safe custody* and *settlement* services to its participants; the other ICSD is *Clearstream Banking Luxembourg*.
Ex-Date	The date used to determine whether seller or buyer has *entitlement* to certain types of *corporate action* on (primarily) equity *securities*.
Ex-Dividend	Execution of a trade on an ex-dividend basis entitles the seller to the *dividend* whilst the buyer does not gain *entitlement*.
Exchange-traded	Trades executed over a registered stock exchange are said to be 'exchange traded'. An alternative is *OTC Trading*.
Execution	The agreement to undertake a specific securities trade on specified terms, between two parties (whether buying or selling, lending or borrowing, etc.).
Exercise	The process of converting a security to an associated (or underlying) security. See *Warrant*.
Floating Rate Note	A form of *bond* where the *issuer* may change the rate of interest payable on predetermined dates (typically *coupon payment dates*), as opposed to the majority of bonds that have a fixed rate of interest throughout their lives.
FoP	Abbreviated form of *Free of Payment*.
'Four Eyes' Principle	The practice of having work verified by another person prior to acting on the information.
Free of Payment	The separate (non-simultaneous) exchange of *securities* and cash between seller and buyer (or their *custodians*). Commonly referred to as *FoP*.
FRN	Abbreviated form of *Floating Rate Note*.
Fund Manager	An organisation that usually operates a range of funds in which end investors place their cash; the fund manager decides how to invest the cash in order to maximise the return on investment or to maximise regular income, in accordance with the objective of each fund operated by the fund manager. Also known as mutual fund.

Funding	The financing of investments through the borrowing of cash on a secured and/or unsecured basis.
Fungible Certificates	Documents representing ownership of *securities* which are interchangeable with each other and where no specific *certificates* are assigned to any one of the owners, i.e. 'co-mingled identical securities'; the record of ownership is usually held electronically. See *Non-Fungible Certificates*.
Gilts	An abbreviation for 'gilt-edged' securities; these are *debt* securities issued by the UK Government.
Global Custodian	An organisation that offers a broad range of services to its clients, including the holding of *securities* and other financial instruments, the holding of cash in various currencies, the *settlement* of trades and the collection of *corporate actions*. Global custodians typically operate a network of sub-custodians that hold such assets on its behalf.
Global Depository Receipts	Documents that represent *shares* held in overseas companies and which enable investors located in a different country to invest in such *securities*. See *American Depository Receipts*.
Grey Market Trading	Buying and selling *securities* that are in course of being brought to the marketplace, when it is still possible that the *issue* may be withdrawn and not come to fruition.
Group of Thirty	An international body that focuses on worldwide economic and financial issues. Also known as 'G30'.
GSTPA	Global Straight Through Processing Association; an organisation that promotes the efficient, electronic flow of trade and settlement information on *trade date*.
Hedge Fund	An organisation that invests its clients' funds, but which is subject to fewer restrictions than other funds (such as *mutual funds*); typically, hedge funds indulge in speculative investments, including but not limited to *securities*. Such speculation may earn hedge fund investors large profits, at the risk of large losses.
Hedging	Investing in *securities* (or other financial instruments) as a safeguard against loss in the event of adverse price movements in other investments.
ICSD	Abbreviated form of *International Central Securities Depository*.
Immobilised	Securities holdings maintained electronically, where certificates of ownership are held in secure storage and where delivery of physical certificates is not permitted. Settlement of sales and purchases is effected by *book entry*.

Indeval	The normal place of *settlement* for *bonds* and *equities* traded in Mexico.
Initial Public Offering	A method of bringing a new *equity issue* to the *securities* marketplace; commonly known as IPO. See *Offer for Sale*.
Insider Trading	A criminal offence where an individual trades in *shares,* or passes information to others, based upon non-public, price-sensitive knowledge.
Institutional Investors	A generic term given to end-investors that are organisations, as opposed to individuals; such investors include *fund managers*, *hedge funds*, insurance companies and *pension funds*.
Interest Claim	A request by a seller to the buyer for reimbursement of lost cash interest, where the seller was able to deliver securities (on or after the *value date*) but the buyer was unable to pay/settle.
International Central Securities Depository	A *central securities depository* that holds domestic and international *securities* and which usually facilitates *settlement* of trades in numerous currencies. Euroclear (Brussels) and Clearstream Banking (Luxembourg) are two recognised ICSDs.
Investor	An individual or institution that has purchased and owns *securities*.
IPO	Abbreviated form of *Initial Public Offering*.
ISIN	International Securities Identification Number; a uniform global standard providing unique reference numbers (ISIN numbers) for individual securities, enabling unambiguous identification of the issue being traded and delivered. See *Cusip*.
ISMA	International Securities Market Association; a self regulatory organisation and trade association (headquartered in Zurich) that makes rules and recommendations governing trading and *settlement* in the international *securities* markets, including *Eurobonds*. ISMAs members are located around the globe.
ISO	The International Organisation for Standardisation promotes the development of consistency around the globe relating to goods and services within many industries.
ISO 15022	A standard for the transmission of electronic messages between participants in the securities industry.
ISO Currency Codes	A set of internationally recognised three-digit codes representing each of the world's currencies; a selective list of such codes can be found in Chapter nine, Static Data.

Issue	An individual *security*.
Issuer	The originating entity that issues *securities* to the marketplace in order to raise cash; such entities include companies, sovereign entities, governments, government agencies and *supranational organisations*.
JASDEC	Japan Securities Depository Center; the normal place of *settlement* for *equities* traded in Japan.
KSD	Korea Securities Depository; the normal place of *settlement* for *bonds* and *equities* traded in Korea.
Lead Manager	An organisation appointed by the *issuer* of a *security*, that is responsible for the launch and distribution of the security to investors and for ensuring that the issuer receives the cash it wishes to raise.
Local Custodian	An organisation that specializes in holding *securities* and (usually) cash and effecting movements of securities and cash on behalf of its account holders, and which is typically a member of the *central securities depository* in the financial centre in which it is located.
Long First Coupon	A term given to the first payment of interest after a *bond* has been issued, specifically where the elapsed time between issuance of the bond and the first *coupon payment date* is greater than the normal *coupon period* for that bond. See *Short First Coupon*.
Margin Call	Additional *collateral* requested by a lender to avoid being under-collateralised. In the event that collateral (used to secure the borrowing of cash or *securities*) loses its value due to a reduction in its market price, additional collateral (margin) may need to be delivered to the lender. Margin calls can also be made by the collateral provider (where the market price of the collateral increases), in order to avoid over-collateralising.
Mark to Market	Revaluation of a *securities* position with the current market price; this is used, for example, when calculating *unrealised profit & loss* and when calculating the current value of *collateral*.
Market	An environment within which *securities* are traded, for example the US Treasury bond market, the Hong Kong equity market.
Market Maker	A *securities trading organisation* that publicises the price at which it is prepared to buy and sell specific *securities*. Also known as specialists on some stock exchanges.

Matched Settlement Instruction	See *Settlement Instruction*. Following receipt of a settlement instruction, the custodian compares the details with the counterparty's settlement instruction details and, if they agree (within certain predefined tolerances), reports them as 'matched'.
Maturity Date	The intended date of repayment of borrowed cash. Specifically, the date of capital repayment by a bond *issuer* to investors, and the date of repayment of cash borrowed via (for example), an unsecured cash borrowing trade.
Mid Price	The average of the bid (to buy) and offer (to sell) prices. See *Bid Price* and *Offer Price*.
Money Market	The marketplace in which cash is lent and borrowed over varying periods of time. Some *securities* are regarded as Money Market Instruments, including Certificates of Deposit, Commercial Paper, Medium Term Notes and *Floating Rate Notes* with less than five years to maturity.
Moody's Investors Service	An issuer ratings agency that analyses and publishes its view of an issuer's ability to repay debt. See *Ratings Agencies*.
Multilateral Netting	The single movement of securities and/or cash in order to settle *open trades* in the same security, between many parties. See *Bilateral Netting*.
Mutual Fund	See *Fund Manager*.
NCSD/National CSD	A *central securities depository* that holds domestic *securities* and which typically facilitates *settlement* of trades in the domestic currency on a *book entry* basis.
NECIGEF	The normal place of *settlement* for *bonds* and *equities* traded in the Netherlands.
Net Settlement Value	The final cash amount payable on a purchase and receivable on a sale of securities.
Nominee Name	The name into which securities will be registered, where purchased securities are to be held in *safe custody* (for example by an *STO*), on behalf of the beneficial owner.
Non-Fungible Certificates	Documents representing ownership of *securities* that are assigned to specific owners, rather than to a pool of owners. See *Fungible Certificates*.
Nostro	A term used within the securities industry to describe third parties (e.g. correspondent banks) that hold and settle cash over accounts operated on behalf of an *STO*.
Nostro Account	The specific account held by a nostro in which cash is held on behalf of the account holder.

Novation	The replacement of one obligor with another; for example, the substitution of an individual counterparty with a *central counterparty*.
NSV	Abbreviated form of *Net Settlement Value*.
Odd Lot	Where a standard trading quantity of *shares* for a given *security* exists (known as a board lot), trading in a quantity other than the board lot is commonly known as an odd lot. The cost of trading in odd lots is typically greater than for trading in board lots. See *Board Lot*.
Offer for Sale	A method by which a company brings its *shares* to the marketplace and the buying public apply for such shares. See *Initial Public Offering*.
Offer Price	The price at which an *STO* is prepared to sell a security. See *Bid Price* and *Mid Price*.
Open Trade	A trade for which *settlement* has not yet occurred, whether *value date* is in the future or in the past.
Order	A request (issued by an investor to a *securities trading organisation* or to an *agent for investors*) to buy or to sell *securities*, typically at a specified price or at the current market price.
Ordinary Shares	The standard description of *shares* issued by companies in various parts of the globe, including Australia, India and the UK. See *Common Stock*.
OTC Trading	Trading conducted 'over-the-counter' via a method (e.g. telephone) other than via a registered stock exchange. See *Exchange-traded*.
P&L	Abbreviated form of profit and loss.
Par Value	The face value of an *equity security*.
Partial Settlement	The exchange of a quantity of *securities* and a proportionate amount of cash that are less than the full quantity and cash value of the trade.
Pension Funds	Organisations that invest pension contributions in securities, in order to maximise future pension payments. A type of *institutional investor*.
Physical Delivery	The actual movement of *securities certificates* for the purposes of *settlement*, outside a *central securities depository* or other *custodian*. Typically a rare occurrence today, as in many financial centres settlement is usually effected by *book entry*.
Placing	The issue of new or additional *shares* directly to a targeted group of investors (typically *institutional investors*); an alternative to the offering of shares for sale to the general public. Also known as Private Placement. See *Initial Public Offering* and *Offer for Sale*.

Power of Attorney	Authority given by the owner or operator of a *depot* or *nostro* account to a third party to issue instructions to receive or deliver securities or to pay or receive cash over that account.
Preference Shares	A type of *share* that entitles the holder to a different amount of dividend (in relation to the *ordinary shares* or *common stock*) and, should liquidation of the company occur, the return of the *shareholder's* capital as a priority over ordinary shares.
Primary Market	A generic term to describe the issuance of and trading in *securities* that are in course of being brought to the marketplace. See *Secondary Market*.
Primary Value Date	The earliest date that *settlement* can occur on a new issue of *securities*; also known as *deferred delivery date*.
Privatisation	The process of denationalising a state-owned industry, to become a privately owned and operated company; upon privatisation, *shares* are typically offered to the general public, often resulting in a broad base of individual *shareholders*.
Proprietary Trading	Buying, selling and holding *securities* for an organisation's own account, not acting as an *agent for investors*. See *Securities Trading Organisation*.
Prospectus	A document that details the terms and conditions applicable to the issuance of a new *security*.
Ratings Agencies	Organisations that analyse and publish their view of an *issuer's* ability to repay debt. Such views (typically expressed as an alphanumeric rating) are used in the assessment of risk associated with buying and selling *bonds*, and in the use of bonds as *collateral*. See *Moody's Investors Service* and *Standard & Poor's*.
Realignment	The transfer (by a seller) of securities from one *CSD* to another, thereby enabling settlement of a sale within the same CSD as the buyer. The alternative is *Cross Border Settlement*.
Realised Profit & Loss	Actual profit or loss following sales and purchases of securities. See *Unrealised Profit & Loss*.
Record Date	*Equities*: the date at which the *shareholders* on an *issuer's* register are identified for the purpose of distributing *corporate action* benefits, such as *dividends* or *bonus issues*. Also known as *books closing date*. *Bonds*: the date at which a custodian identifies its account holders to whom *coupon payments* and redemption monies will be made.
Redemption	The repayment of capital by an *issuer* to a *bondholder*.

Register	The list of holders of a registered *security*, maintained by an *issuer* or a *registrar* acting on the issuer's behalf; this allows direct communication (for example, payments of income) by the issuer with the owners of the security.
Registered Security	A *security* where the *issuer* (or a registrar acting on the issuer's behalf) maintains a record of owners of the security; this usually requires that when securities are sold, the seller's name is replaced by the buyer's name on the register. Typically, *equities* rather than *bonds* are issued in registered form. See *Bearer Security*.
Registrar	An organisation appointed by an *issuer* of a *registered security* to maintain the register of holders of that security. Also known as transfer agent.
Registration	The act of updating the *issuer's* register of owners (of a *registered security*) in order to reflect transfer of ownership.
Regulator	An entity that is responsible for the monitoring and control of activities within a securities marketplace, to ensure compliance with rules and regulations.
Regulatory Reporting	The mandatory provision of information (to a regulator) by a *securities trading organisation* regarding its trading activity, securities positions and resultant risks.
Rematerialised	*Securities* holdings that were previously represented electronically and in *dematerialised* form, but which have been replaced by *certificates* of ownership.
Reorganisation	A term normally applied to the restructuring of a company's issued share capital, for example a share split.
Repo	A trade in which *securities* are sold for delivery on one date and simultaneously repurchased for delivery on a later date. Repo trades are used as a mechanism to borrow and lend cash on a secured basis, and to borrow and lend specific securities, against the receipt of cash. See *Reverse Repo*.
Retail Broker	An organisation that specialises in trading on behalf of private individuals, as opposed to *institutional investors*.
Reverse Repo	See *Repo*. A repo in which *securities* are initially received from the counterparty (against payment of cash), and which will require to be returned to the counterparty at closure of the transaction.
Rights Issue	An offer by an *issuer* (that wishes to raise further capital) to the existing *shareholders* to purchase additional *shares* in proportion to their existing shareholding; in order to entice the shareholders to take up the offer, the price of the rights is typically offered at a discount to the current market price of the existing shares.

Rolling Settlement	Trades executed with a *value date* of a fixed number of days forward from their *trade date*, so that trades executed on a new trading day will have a value date one business day later than trades executed the previous day. The alternative is *account settlement*.
Safe Custody	The holding of *securities* (and in some cases cash) in safekeeping on behalf of the owner of the assets, and the provision of associated services, such as the collection of income payable to the owner.
Salesman	An employee of a *securities trading organisation* that is the liaison point between *institutional investors* and the STO.
Secondary Market	A generic term to describe the marketplace where existing *securities* are traded (as opposed to those securities that are in course of being brought to the marketplace, within the *primary market*).
Securities	Financial instruments that may be purchased and sold, the most common forms of which are *equities* and *bonds*.
Securities Borrowing	In the event that *securities* sold cannot be delivered to the buyer, the practice of borrowing securities from a *shareholder* or *bondholder* at a cost, in order to complete delivery of securities owed to the buyer, thereby enabling the seller to receive the sale proceeds at the earliest opportunity.
Securities Data Providers	Organisations that supply detailed information concerning individual *securities*, usually electronically, to those that subscribe to the service; also known as 'data vendors'.
Securities Lending	The practice of a *share* or *bond* holder loaning its *securities* to a borrower for a fee, in order to enhance the lender's return on its investment.
Securities Trading Organisation (STO)	An organisation that practices *proprietary trading*, involving the buying, selling and holding of *securities* for its own account; the meaning as used within this book excludes the trading activities of *Agents for Investors*, as those organisations typically purchase, sell and hold securities for the account of their clients, and not for themselves. However, the vast majority of post-trading activities are common to both STOs and Agents for Investors.
Sell-Out	A formal procedure for a seller to bring about the closure of an *open trade* that has passed its *value date*, by forcing the buyer (via a Sell-Out Agent) to pay for the securities owing, with associated costs being borne by the buyer. Such procedures must be conducted under the rules of the exchange/market over which the trade has been executed. See *Buy-In*.

Settled Position	The quantity of *securities* held in the account of an account holder, at a *custodian*; differences in the settled position and *trading position* are usually due to one or many *open trades*.
Settlement	The act of buyer and seller (or their *custodians*) exchanging *securities* and cash in order to fulfil their contractual obligation.
Settlement Cycle	The standard or default period of time between *trade date* and *value date* of trades, within each marketplace. See *Account Settlement* and *Rolling Settlement*.
Settlement Date	The date the actual exchange of *securities* and cash has been effected; this date is known only after settlement has occurred. (Note that in some countries 'settlement date' is used to mean the intended date of delivery of securities and cash). See *Value Date*.
Settlement Failure	Trades where securities and cash have not been exchanged on *value date* (the *contractual settlement date*).
Settlement Instruction	A message issued by an account holder to its *custodian* that requests the custodian to deliver or receive *securities* and/or receive or pay cash on a specified date (the *value date* of the trade).
Settlement Netting	Instead of settling each open trade independently, the *settlement* of two or more trades effected by the single delivery (or receipt) of the remaining quantity of *securities* and the single receipt (or payment) of the remaining amount of cash.
Settlement Status	The condition of a *settlement instruction* reported by a custodian to its account holder; typical statuses are unmatched with counterparty, matched with counterparty, settled and failed.
Settlement Tolerance	A predefined cash limit (set by a *custodian*), within which differing cash amounts on seller's and buyer's *settlement instructions* are deemed to match; such tolerances avoid small cash differences from preventing *settlement* occurring.
Settlement Write-Off	The clearance of a small cash balance on an individual trade (within internal *books and records*), leaving no cash amount due to or from the *counterparty*
Share	That which represents *equity* ownership in a company.
Shareholder	The owner of *shares* in a company.
Short First Coupon	A term given to the first payment of interest after a *bond* has been issued, specifically where the elapsed time between issue of the *bond* and the first *coupon payment date* is less than the normal *coupon period* for that bond. See *Long First Coupon*.

SICOVAM	The normal place of *settlement* for *bonds* and *equities* traded in France. Following a merger with Euroclear in January 2001, Sicovam was renamed Euroclear France.
SIS	SegaIntersettle AG; the normal place of *settlement* for *bonds* and *equities* traded in Switzerland.
Special Cum	Specifically agreed terms whereby a trade dealt during the 'ex' period is treated as having been traded on a 'cum' basis, resulting in the buyer gaining entitlement, and the seller losing entitlement to the benefit.
Special Ex	Specifically agreed terms whereby a trade dealt during the 'cum' period is treated as having been traded on an 'ex' basis, resulting in the seller rather than the buyer being entitled to the benefit.
Standard & Poor's	An *issuer* ratings agency that analyses and publishes its view of an issuer's ability to repay debt. See *Ratings Agencies*.
Static Data	A store of information pertaining to, for example trading companies, *counterparties*, *securities* and currencies which is used in the processing of trades, position management and *corporate actions*.
Static Data Defaulting	The automatic attachment of appropriate information to basic trade details, according to predefined rules.
STO	Abbreviated form of *Securities Trading Organisation*.
Stock Dividend	A *dividend* paid by an *issuer* to its shareholders in the form of *securities*; also known as scrip dividend.
Stock Exchange	A recognised body through which securities can be issued and subsequently bought and sold by investors. Members of the exchange are bound by the rules and regulations set by the exchange.
Stock Record	A system of *double-entry bookkeeping* that accounts on the one side for the ownership of securities (e.g. *trading positions*) and on the other side for their location (e.g. at the *custodian* or with the counterparty awaiting settlement).
STP	Abbreviated form of *Straight Through Processing*.
Straight Through Processing	An objective of *securities trading organisations*, suppliers of communications software, *custodians*, etc. to manage the entire trade lifecycle in an automated and seamless manner, without the need for review or repair. The benefit of straight through processing is reduced costs and the ability to process high volumes of trades in a secure and risk-free manner.
Supranational Organisations	Entities formed by two or more central governments for the purpose of promoting economic development. Such entities include the International Bank for Reconstruction and Development (World Bank).

S.W.I.F.T.	The Society for Worldwide Interbank Financial Telecommunications; a worldwide organisation providing secure message transmission between parties that subscribe to S.W.I.F.T. Message types include *trade confirmation*, *settlement instructions*, *securities* and cash statements and *corporate actions*.
Syndicate	A group of *securities trading organisations* that together *underwrites* and allots to investors a new *security*.
Takeover	An attempt to purchase by one company, all or part of the issued share capital of another company.
Trade	An agreement to exchange specific securities (for cash or for another asset) on specified terms, between two parties (whether buying or selling, lending or borrowing, etc.).
Trade Agreement	The act of one party gaining agreement to the details of a *trade* with its *counterparty*, whether by electronic or manual means.
Trade Confirmation	A communication of the details of a *trade* from one party to its *counterparty*; various media are used for the communication method. A means of achieving *trade agreement*.
Trade Date	The date the parties to a *trade* agree to trade; the date of *trade execution*.
Trade Execution	The agreement to undertake a specific securities trade on specified terms, between two parties (whether buying or selling, lending or borrowing, etc.).
Trade Matching	The process of comparing a seller's and a buyer's *trade* details electronically, shortly after *trade execution*. A means of achieving *trade agreement*.
Trade Time	The hour and minute (within a *trade date*) that *trade execution* occurred.
Trader	An individual who buys and sells securities for the account of the *securities trading organisation* that employs the trader; one or more traders are typically responsible for the operation of a *trading book*.
Trading Book	A subdivision of a trading department within a *securities trading organisation* in which trading in a specific grouping of *securities* (for example) is conducted and kept separate from the business of other trading books.
Trading Position	A positive or negative trade-dated *securities* holding.
Treaty	See *Double Taxation Agreement*.
Underwriting	The act of guaranteeing to an *issuer* of *securities* that the issuer will receive the funds it wishes to raise, at the specified time; one or many underwriters will buy any unsold portion of the new issue.

Unmatched Settlement Instruction	A *settlement instruction* issued to a *custodian* to deliver or receive *securities* (typically versus payment or receipt of cash) that has no direct (and opposite) equivalent issued by the *counterparty* to the trade.
Unrealised Profit & Loss	Theoretical profit or loss on a positive or negative *securities trading position* following revaluation of the position. See *Realised Profit & Loss*.
Unsecured Cash Borrowing	The borrowing of cash without supplying *security* (also known as *collateral*) to the cash lender; the rate of interest payable by the borrower is usually higher than for secured borrowings, to reflect the lender's risk.
Value Date	The intended date of exchange of *securities* and cash between buyer and seller. Also known as *contractual settlement date*. (Note that in some countries, the term Settlement Date is used to mean the intended date of exchange of securities and cash).
VPC	Vardepapperscentralen; the normal place of *settlement* for *bonds* and *equities* traded in Sweden.
Warrant	A type of *security* entitling (but not obliging) the holder to subscribe to another security in proportion to the number of warrants held, at a fixed price, at or before a prespecified date; beyond that date, subscription is no longer possible and the warrant expires.
Withholding Tax	Tax deducted in the issuer's country of residence, on income paid by *issuers* to investors, whether on *equities* or *bonds*. Investors resident in certain countries may be subject to a lower rate of withholding tax, if the issuer's country and the investor's country have a *double taxation agreement* (or *treaty*) in place.
Zero Coupon Bond	*Debt securities* that do not pay interest, but which are issued at a deep discount and redeemed at their full face value on the bond maturity date.

Recommended Reading

An Introduction to Western Financial Markets; *Stephen Valdez*
An Introduction to Equity Markets; *David Dasey*
An introduction to Repo Markets; *Moorad Choudhry*
Mastering Repo Markets; *Robert Steiner*
Treasury Management; *Robert Hudson*
Dictionary of Finance and Banking; *Oxford Paperbacks*
Dictionary of Finance and Investment Terms; *Barron's Financial Guides*
Dictionary of Financial and Securities Terms; *Securities Institute.*

Index